The Training and Experience of a Quaker Relief Worker

January 1946 – March 1948

THE TRAINING AND EXPERIENCE OF A QUAKER RELIEF WORKER

January 1946 – March 1948

Hugh W. Maw

Produced in association with

www.wordsbydesign.co.uk

ISBN: 978-1-909075-24-5

British Library Cataloguing in Publication Data
A catalogue record for this book is available from the British Library

All photos by H.W.M. except for those by Manfred Durnick as noted in the text

To my wife Daphne,

With my love and thanks
on our Golden Wedding,
28th July 1999

From Hugh

1949

Contents

Foreword

In January 1996 I was invited, along with other veteran relief workers from the American Friends Service Committee and the Friends Relief Service, to the opening of the 'Stille Helfer' Exhibition of Quaker Relief Work, at the Berlin Historical Museum. I was also invited back to Berlin to make contact once more with the Berlin Ecumenical Council, and in the following year was guest of honour at the 50th anniversary celebrations of the 'Karolinger Youth House'. During conversations and discussions it became apparent that my German friends had little or no knowledge of what the so-called 'victors' were going through in post-war Britain. And after reading my German Journals they asked me about the run up to the training I had received before my period of service.

So, for the record, and with the encouragement of friends and family, I have added to this volume the amended diary which I kept during the training course. I have adopted a different style and approach, and am greatly indebted to Mike Oke of *Bound Biographies* for his help and professional guidance. This has enabled me to include in this edition many more photographs, a few maps and some extracts from letters to illustrate the text of the Journals.

The book has been transcribed from the diaries I wrote at the time, often in note form. There has not been time to eliminate all errors and mistakes, for which I apologise.

I dedicate this book to my wife and family, and to many of the people listed in the indexes, from whom I have learned and gained so much more than I was able to give.

> A German refugee told me of the rickets and TB he'd witnessed among the children of Berlin in 1919 and 1939. If more people had come to feed them like the British Quakers, he said, Hitler would probably never have come to power and the horrors never happened.
>
> Rabbi Lionel Blue,
> BBC Thought for the Day,
> 12.11. 2007

SECTION I

THE SIX MONTHS TRAINING OF A QUAKER RELIEF WORKER

JANUARY 1946 – JUNE 1946

Chapter 1

In January 1996, exactly 50 years after I was trained as a Quaker Relief Worker, during a visit to Berlin with a group of Friends Relief Service and American Friends Service Committee veteran relief workers invited to the 'Stille Helfer' Exhibition, Tim Evens handed me a copy of the following: The Qualifications Of A Good Relief Worker. Tim was a member of the Goslar Team in Germany and had been trained at the Mount Waltham Relief Training course two years before me. He had noted down these qualifications from a lecture by Major Sandford Carter, who had done relief work in North Africa. They were:

1) Good health and the ability to rough it for long periods.
2) Ability to work as a member of a team.
3) Ability to report administratively on technical matters.
4) Languages.
5) Perseverance in the face of obstacles.
6) Poise in the midst of confusion.
7) Political savoir-faire.
8) A specialist qualification (stores handling, medicine, etc.).

There followed a discussion between us as to how far we thought we had measured up to these standards.

Having completed my German Journals, this conversation then led me to return to the diary I had kept from January 1946 until the time I was posted to Berlin in June 1946, during my own training and the letters I wrote to my parents in India and to Daphne, my future wife. Just how well were these qualifications or qualities achieved, caught or taught, and just how much of a nuisance was I as an individualist? These questions and the ex-FRS and FAU gatherings encouraged me at least to try and write down my side of the story and from my own personal point of view.

Several people, having read my German Journals, had asked me what had led up to my 2½ years of service with the (FRS). In the same way, family and friends have also asked, "What did you do in the War?"

During the first winter of the War, while I was beginning my second year aged 19at Bristol University, 'Uncle' Jack Hoyland, my early boyhood hero, at Woodbrooke College, in one of his famous post cards, asked me if I would be willing to join any of his short courses in practical relief work during my vacations. This came at a time when I was agonising about the position I would take on receiving my National Service Call-up papers. My two older brothers, Allen and Stafford, had already made up their minds. I was sharing a room at Wills Hall with John Tonkin, an engineering student with whom I had become a firm friend. He had come from a military background and was destined for a military career and I, from a Quaker family, hoped to teach.

Jack's rough and ready, and immediate response to any appeal for help, was digging – digging not for victory, but for Peace. This great giant of a man, with his booming voice, infectious laugh and enormous energy, inspired anyone at any time to roll up their sleeves and get down to it, whatever 'it' might be and made it all seem worth while and fun.

When Birmingham, particularly Northfield and part of the Woodlands hospital opposite Dame Elizabeth Cadbury's Manor House and the Manor Farm, where the Friends Ambulance Unit (FAU) was training, received some of the first bombs, a few of us went up to the hospital with Jack and started to dig huge holes in the bare earth and waste ground to provide air raid shelters for children and staff.

The Woodlands hospital was well-known to me because, not only was my sister, Gill, trained there as a nurse, but my father had spent a year there on his back, with operations on an osteo-arthritic hip. This injury was probably due to a football accident when playing with some of the lads at the Hoshangabad School in India and not from his extensive pilgrimages on foot to the source of the Ganges[1], though the privations he endured on these trips aggravated the condition and caused great pain. The family frequently visited father; and Stafford, training to be a Doctor himself, was friendly with one of the nurses at the hospital.

Undoubtedly, this 'down to earth' practical work, inspired by Jack's leadership and enthusiasm, sparked off something in me. And when my call-up papers arrived through the post and I registered as a Conscientious Objector (CO), Jack was the first to send supportive postcards and provide testimonials whenever needed.

Almost as soon as the war, both VE and VJ (Victory over Japan) day were over in mid-August 1945, I wrote a letter to Friends House, applying to join the FRS. Before my application could be considered, I had to give two months' notice to *Cadbury*s, though in fact I gave a full term's notice, terminating my teaching post at the Bourneville Day Continuation School and as a Youth Leader in the factory Youth Club.

I was thoroughly enjoying the work and, in my free time, not only the sport – cricket and hockey for the Bourneville 1st XI, but also Opera and Drama Society productions in the Social Clubs of the factory.

However, I was also under considerable and continuous pressure and stress at work from the long hours and physical exhaustion from the lack of normal teacher's holidays. In the summer 'industrial fortnight' holiday, "Eddie" (Arnold Edmundson, my senior colleague) and I had to run the firm's annual Youth Summer Camp at Teignmouth.

---

[1] See *Pilgrims in Hindu Holy Land.* Edited by Gill Conacher and Marjorie Sykes.

My resignation after such a short time (9 months) was accepted with complete understanding, sympathy and support by Jack Herbert, Charles Gillett and Cyril Harrison. They explained that *Cadburys* had undertakings to reinstate former employees now being demobbed and who were applying for their old jobs back, including my post. So, I began to work out my term's notice.

Meanwhile, Eustace Gillett, the Personnel Secretary at Friends House, acknowledged my application and enclosed a set of "Notes for the Guidance of those wishing to undertake relief work." The notes indicated that there were immediate openings for suitable people with administration, office, or warehouse experience; for staff for old peoples' hostels, and skilled men for the auxiliary Works and Equipment and Transport service in this country.

I did not seem to qualify in any of these areas and the only experience I had had of work with FRS in this country, which could be regarded as a valuable qualification for work abroad, was two summer vacations, working as a general assistant handyman/gardener at the FRS hostel, *Tyn-y-cae* near Brecon. There, with two other non-Quaker COs, we were helping to care for the wives and children of Austrian Jewish refugees, whose husbands were interned in one of the camps, probably as far away as Southampton or the Isle of Man, and were classed as 'Enemy Aliens'.

This had been an amazing experience and interlude for me after my tribunal and had extraordinary consequences, some of which are mentioned in my Berlin Journal and elsewhere.

The initial response though was disappointing, but at least I knew that my name had been added to a Register of new workers, from which 'selected applicants would be called for interview as fresh openings occurred'. However, it was also emphasised that, though a large number of people were already enrolled, consideration would readily be given to the addition of a few more provided that they were:

1) especially interested in working with Friends rather than another relief organisation,
2) they had good language or technical qualifications,
3) they were thoroughly fit,
4) they could remain overseas for at least 12 months, and
5) they were between 25-50 years of age, though exceptions might be made in certain cases.

This was encouraging. I was really only interested in joining the FRS; I had recently started taking German lessons at *Tyn-y-cae*, but only had Higher School Certificate French. I was thoroughly fit from my work at *Cadburys*, and could remain overseas for at least 12 months, probably longer. I had also just had my 25th birthday and would be amongst the youngest it seemed. There was also a reminder that it must be clearly understood that no undertaking could be given to those on the register that they would be sent abroad.

The notes went on to outline the scheme of training: "Normally, members of FRS provisionally selected for overseas service attend an 8-10 week course held at the FRS Training Centre. The course is also open to those on the register who are free to attend either at their own expense or with the aid of a bursary." Fortunately, I was in the position of being able to pay, having accumulated some savings from a generous salary given me by *Cadburys* for the past nine months

It was also pointed out that, as far as allowances were concerned, members of the FRS worked on a voluntary basis, receiving their keep; a leave grant and, in this country, 14/-(shillings) a week to cover clothing and pocket money. Overseas allowances were adjusted to suit local conditions.

With regard to Insurance, the notes continued: "Work with FRS is not recognised as insurable employment, nor is it covered by any pension scheme. Members of FRS undertake work at home or abroad entirely at their own risk." Though I had taken out a small life insurance endowment (with profits) policy with the *Friends Provident*, I was not worried about keeping up the premiums and was prepared to take the risks. FRS was prepared to pay the Health and Pensions contributions "of those eligible to be voluntary contributors and, where necessary, would meet medical and dental expenses, and consider making some contribution towards premiums on insurance policies." So I considered myself fortunate and I had no dependants.

Reading through these notes, I began to wonder how my change of work might affect my Tribunal conditions as a CO in relation to the Ministry of Labour. FRS had notes on these matters too. "Release: The Ministry of Labour is at present unwilling to consider releasing for relief work, men under 30 or in essential work, and women born in and after 1918 (except nurses), unless they are registered as Conscientious Objectors with suitable conditions." So this appeared no obstacle since at my Tribunal, I had been given unconditional exemption from Military Service, and was expected to finish my professional training as a teacher, which, in the end, I had.

The final note on "Offers for Service", encouraged me to apply on the printed form, but warned me that its completion implied no commitment on either side. Suitable applicants would normally be invited to meet a member of the Personnel Department and I should provide some indication of convenient dates for this preliminary interview in London 7-12 days ahead.

It was quickly arranged and, after a brief but thorough interview, I was verbally accepted for both training by the FRS and for overseas work. I was overjoyed and so were my parents on my return to Birmingham, with whom I was living at the time in one of the Missionary Guest House flats in Selly Oak, while they were preparing to return to India.

Then, suddenly, disaster struck. Unfortunately, while playing rugby for the Old Leightonians against the School, under the weight of two hefty forwards, both my knees collapsed and a cartilage became displaced. I ended up in the Woodlands Hospital, Northfield, over Christmas 1945.

Having worked my notice at *Cadburys* and said my fond farewells there, I found myself in a considerable predicament and rendered totally disabled and physically unfit.

Just before going into hospital, I received from William H. Noble in the FRS Office in Friends House, particulars of their Overseas Training course X for potential relief workers, a synopsis of the course and a yard-long book list. I was invited to be considered for selection on this course, though it also warned that I might be asked to attend a further interview in London and a further medical by the FRS doctor before final selection was made.

The cost of this course, it was explained, including full board residence and tuition was £20. "FRS is anxious not to spend more of its relief funds on training than is absolutely necessary," and I was asked whether I was in a position to cover the whole or part of the cost – which fortunately I was.

"Membership of the FRS" was then outlined: "Trainees are admitted to the course as provisional members and will become full members after a trial period provided they have shown themselves to possess the qualities and abilities necessary for relief work. At the end of the course they will form part of the overseas reserve from which workers can be chosen as openings for service occur. They must be prepared for considerable delays before leaving the country, but the time will be usefully spent in gaining experience in the home field and in further training."

Standard Maintenance Allowance. "Trainees are entitled to claim standard maintenance allowance (14 shillings per week) from the beginning of the course."

Synopsis of the course. courses of lectures will be given on:

1) Christian and Quaker Fundamentals.
2) The Historical and Political background of Contemporary Europe.
3) Relief Work
    a) Medical Aspects
    b) Psychological and Spiritual aspects
    c) Practical work
    d) Organisations engaged in Relief Work
    e) Quaker experience in Relief Work
4) The Relief Worker
    a) Qualifications

b) Experience

5) Languages

Book List.

I still have the 'short' book list. This is a shortened sample.

1) Quakerism: 3 books (which fortunately I had read)
3 booklets (un-read). (Total price of the latter 3/-)

2) Relief a) Medical – 6 books (2 of which I bought for 4/6d)
b) Nutrition and Food (5 books. I bought one for 5/-)
c) Displaced Persons (DPs) 4 Books.
d) Historical and General (8 books and booklets – I bought 3 for £1.0s.6d)
e) European and Background (12 books).

I gave up on this list, having already spent two weeks' allowance and hoped to borrow others. But there was now precious little time left for any preliminary and background reading.

Eagerly, I filled in the application form for selection for course X at once, even though I was about to be hospitalised. The starting date was a month ahead and I was not feeling unwell – only injured. The second interview was waived and the medical by the FRS doctor postponed.

Fortunately, the operation on my offending knee was completed well before Christmas Day, which was lucky because, on Christmas Day itself, most of the nurses and doctors seemed to be the worse for drink. I was able to enjoy the celebrations after recovering from an extremely painful operation with the whole leg in heavy plaster. Others in the ward were less fortunate and there was little sleep. The patients were very friendly as were all the staff – mostly footballers and accident patients, short and long term, and with a zany sense of humour in common adversity. The *Mirror* and the *Pink Un* were the most popular newspapers and there were headphones to listen to the wireless. There were plenty of visitors and 'get well' cards. The physiotherapists began their work very soon and I was subject to abject torture and bullying by mine, who, if I complained or shouted out, only increased the electric current on the infernal black box to make bigger muscular contractions. Beyond the banter, the sexy innuendoes and the wolf whistles at certain nurses, there was pathos behind the eyes of some of the men. They were not sick, but many were in pain. Anxiety showed – about family, job and future, and yet there was, somehow, a special atmosphere in that ward, a tender consideration for the new arrival, tinged with curiosity and compassion, and rejoicing for the one who was being discharged.

I was out of hospital in time for the New Year of 1946. Early in January, William Noble, the Personnel Secretary, sent me the outline of the Overseas Training course X for which I had been duly selected, I was thankful to say.

"The course will be held at 'Woodstock' for the 9 weeks from January 21st – March 23rd." So I had a very short time to get completely, or as nearly fit and mobile again as I could, get my things together and my affairs settled up. Directions were given on how to find Woodstock, 7 Elsworthy Road, NW3, where trainees would be living. It was expected that, between us, we would be responsible for all the household work except cooking. The weekday programme and timetable was outlined:

07.30	Breakfast
08.00	House duties
09.10	Devotional
09.30	Language Classes
10.45	Lecture
12.15	Physical Training
13.15	Lunch
14.15	Language and Reading Period, or visit
16.30	Tea
17.00	Lecture
19.00	Supper
20.00	Informal talk or discussion on 2 nights/week.

On Saturdays, formal activities will end at noon and Sundays will normally be free, apart from household jobs.

Language instruction will be given in small groups, arranged according to the needs and the proficiency of the trainees, though the main emphasis will be placed on a really effective working knowledge of German. And we were assured of a Relief Work Library at Woodstock.

A list of things to bring with us was also provided. It included:

"Identity Card, Ration Book, Driving Licence (if any), bed linen, towels, a minimum amount of clothing and toilet requirements, including shirt or blouse, shorts, gym shoes for PT and old clothes for rough work. A limited stock of bed linen will be available for those who cannot bring their own. It is also useful to bring, if possessed, a rucksack, a torch, and English and foreign dictionaries.

Inoculations will be commenced early in the course, so that they can be completed before members disperse.

The Transport Officer will test and grade all trainees who have had driving experience and it will help if trainees will advise Personnel Office immediately of details of their own knowledge and experience." I had none, but, for the last 10 years, had used a wide variety of bicycles and never learnt to drive.

"The Staff for this course will be the following resident members, together with many external lecturers and tutors:

Louisa Roberts – Warden
John Saunders – Assistant Warden
Betty Baker – Languages

Course Members List

Alice Eden
Mary Elwell
Edith Fyleman
Maurice Ginat
Kathleen Gough (Berlin)
Marjorie McEwan
Hugh Maw (Berlin)
Constance Madgen
Kjell Nahnfeldt (Solingen)
Josephine Noble (France)
Mary Partridge
John Pettigrew (Cologne)
Phyllis Reith (S. France)
Alice Scares
Morna Smith (Dortmund)
Alice and Walter Southwell
Mabel (Biddy) Weiss (Hanover)
Barbara Whitaker (South France)

After my operation, when I had to learn to walk again, I returned to the Woodlands almost daily for outpatient treatment, physiotherapy and a programme of exercises in the gym. Here, my ballet training helped enormously and I made rapid progress, though I admit, from time to time, I suffered some depression, feeling I should never get there. But my diary records that, by Saturday January 19th, I had begun to run and jump again and feel the thrill of movement returning. I said my goodbyes to the rest of the hospital ward and set about packing my things and checking the lists.

My cousin, Marjorie Gregory, came over for the day and, together, we went down by train to my sister-in-law, Nahia Maw and Allen in Bristol, to see my first niece, Leila. Allen had been demobbed and was having a job interview with *Cadena* again. It was foggy and cold and we were delayed returning.

Chapter 2

On Sunday January 20th, I went to Selly Oak Meeting with my parents for the last time. Friends there, including Winifred Littleboy, Charles Garland, Chief Probation Officer for Birmingham, and Leonard Broomfield and others gave me their warm good wishes, promised me their support and to keep in touch. In saying goodbye to my parents after the usual Sunday lunch of a roast lamb joint at the Guest House Flats, there was one thing I wished I could take with me. That was my mother's wonderful ability to laugh at herself and not take things or herself too seriously. But there were other things too – my father's patience, humility and courage, as they too prepared themselves for continued service in India for Friends.

With a lump in my throat, a rucksack, battered case and holdall, I took a taxi to New Street Station. The train was packed and already thick with tobacco smoke. Outside it was a glorious sunny day. As I stared out of the window, everything was covered with frost. Though I kept a lookout for lambs, none were to be seen, even on the Chilterns, or perhaps I wasn't concentrating. This was, for me, the start of a whole new chapter. I was under concern and felt called. My Meeting had listened and tested my concern and now I was on the way.

From Euston, it was only a short bus ride north and I soon found Woodstock. A warm welcome awaited me from Louisa Roberts, the Warden, and Dorothy Smith. A good, hot meal was about to start and I began to meet my fellow course members, none of whose names I had recognised, except the Southwells.

The silent Grace before the meal seemed to be prolonged, but we soon started to chatter and find connections. Having dumped my things, I had already noticed the smell of paint and the spartan furniture in what was a large old house, but it was warm. At the end of the meal, we were collectively welcomed and the first of the announcements was that there was a fuel shortage and only enough coal and coke for just a few more days. However, we were told that conditions here were much better than at Mount Waltham, where the previous course had been held, so we were lucky.

In a circle that first evening, in turn we introduced ourselves and outlined briefly our life histories and journeys up to that point. It proved absorbingly interesting and, tired as we all were, it took us well on towards midnight. We seemed to be mostly teachers or youth workers and soon found we had many links and contacts in common. There was a sense of laughter and fun as we began to reveal more of ourselves to each other. Some of the men living there were not course members, but had been getting the place ready for us and did the cooking. Anyway, for the next six months, Woodstock was to be our home and base and would be what we made it.

One of my birthday presents had been a *Parker* fountain pen. I have always loved writing and receiving letters and already was in the habit of writing a diary. Since I had been given one for Christmas, I started it at once. I have kept my lecturer notebook also and many of the books and manuals, which we used and found invaluable.

I soon found myself about the youngest member on the course and with the least knowledge of German. It was bitterly cold and my greatest, initial difficulty was my stiff knee and getting the leg exercised frequently enough. However, there were two staircases and 61 steps from the small men's dormitory I was to share with three or four others in the basement (which had once been the billiard room), to the bathroom and the toilets. So this was useful and the regular exercise helped to keep me warm. I suffered from cold extremities and chilblains, so I was glad to be put on 'boiler duty' straightaway and onto a very *ad hoc* entertainments committee. Things were moving fast.

A few days later, a Swedish CO joined the group. Kjell Nahnfeldt – a delightful man who charmed us all at once by his beautiful extemporary fiddle playing. Soon, we were welded into a very happy and united group and made friendships, many of which have lasted over 50 years. Some of us were nervous about getting back to the higher education conditions of the school room, but what was so refreshing was the easy transition from almost riotous fun to a real depth of silent worship that the group was able to make so quickly. We felt 'gathered' in the truly Quaker sense. The daily if morning devotional meeting was a source of continual inspiration to us all, as was the silence before and after each meal, and became truly sacramental.

As we got down to work, there was much humming and singing in evidence. My first household duty, shared with others, was oiling the bare wood, hall and landing floors, and polishing them afterwards. If I found myself humming Keble's hymn: "New every morning is the love our wakening and uprising prove; through sleep and darkness brought, restored to life, and power and thought." I would then skip to the line: "The trivial round, the common task, would furnish all we ought to ask" – and for the life of me, I could not remember the rest of the words, until someone else joined in and supplied them. Keble had been one of the leaders with Newman and Pusey of the Oxford Movement. The daily programme began to feel almost monastic.

Hampstead Friends Meeting was the nearest on Sundays and I was soon invited to the home of Corder and Gwen Catchpool for lunch. Gwen was Daphne's aunt and Daphne was at Sidcot with their youngest daughter, Annette. Weekends, from after lunch on the Saturday at Woodstock, often seemed rather deserted, but we also had plenty of visitors. But it was the

Catchpools, particularly, who reinforced my longing to get to Germany and to Berlin.

There was one event that I must record which occurred on January 28th 1946. In the kitchen, the wireless was almost permanently on. On the news that morning, it was announced that the first post-war bananas were arriving in Britain. Fruit, especially soft fruit, was in very short supply. As I was on 'washing up' duties, followed by scrubbing the front stairs, I was able to tell the good news to the others, that we would soon be able to slip up on banana skins again.

The following day, after a considerable gale in the night, I was up early at 6.15 am to prepare breakfast. Kjell joined me and was able to announce at breakfast that a Norwegian, Trygvie Lie, had been chosen as the first Secretary General of the United Nations. We clapped and cheered. This was followed by a timely lecture on the new United Nations Organisation (UNO) by Roger Soltau, well-known Quaker historian at the London School of Economics, who had been at the University of Beirut for 18 years. The UN Assembly was about to meet at the Central Hall, Westminster. The delegates of 51 nations were to be welcomed by King George VIth and addressed by the Prime Minister, Mr Atlee, and the Archbishop of Canterbury would say a prayer.

"Do you realise what a historic event this is?" Roger asked us.

Constantly in the News broadcasts, we were reminded also of the Nuremberg War Trials. Of particular interest to some of us was the trial of Rudolph Hess, Hitler's Deputy, who parachuted into Scotland on May 10th 1941 – on a peace mission, he maintained.

I soon became friendly with John Pettigrew. It turned out that we were both unofficially engaged – John to Jane and myself to Daphne. So we were both frequently writing letters and awaiting the first post each morning. John, three years older than myself, was also a PE teacher at Taunton School and had a Biology degree. We soon discovered that we were about the only two birthright Friends on the course. Together, we decided to take the PE classes each morning, on alternate days.

Louisa Roberts, the Warden, was an exceptionally approachable person and John Saunders was an experienced FRS veteran, who had served in Greece. He was joined by Ron Thacker, who was able, initially, to give us a broad outline of FRS work overseas. Edgar Dunstan came early on in the course to give members a thorough grounding in the fundamentals of Quakerism.

I began my regular house duties as the boiler man and was faced immediately with a severe and uncertain coal shortage. Fortunately, the weather was mild and I, with others, kept ourselves warm by oiling and polishing what had been a rather grand front hall and landing floor.

At break times almost every day, we soon got used to, and enjoyed, a slice of bread of uncertain colour, with peanut butter and/or *Marmite.* I had to frequently return to damp down the boiler and only draw it up in the evening for baths. Sometimes it was a job to keep it going.

Quite early on, for we all had voracious appetites, there was an introductory lecture by a Miss Abrahams of the United Nations Relief and Rehabilitation Association (UNRRA) on 'Nutrition' and we were invited to read the listed handbooks for 'homework'. She was followed by W.D. Hogarth, the First Secretary of the newly-formed Council of British Societies for Relief Abroad (COBSRA), who correlated the work of the 23 Voluntary Societies, contributing 1,600 voluntary relief workers now overseas, and he gave us some statistics. The FRS contribution was 150 workers, of whom 60 were in Germany, 35 in France, 24 in Greece, 16 in Holland, 2 in Palestine and one in Africa. Six were soon to be sent to Poland and five to Austria, including Ken Francis. It was possible that a few AFSE relief workers would be seconded to work overseas as well.

One morning soon after this, we all went off to Friends House, Euston Road, where Stephen Thorne, the Recording Clerk, received us and gave the group a talk on 'Quaker Organisation' and the work of the various sections and committees. We also had a chance to browse in the Friends Book Shop. In return, we invited Friends House Staff to an evening party, entertainment and supper at Woodstock, which I was asked to MC. We had learned a number of 'Rounds', singing in different languages, so this was a good opportunity of practising them.

As soon as the beds in our dormitory had been pushed to one side at the following weekend, I took a PE class. As we were assorted shapes and sizes, the exercises became a combination of PT and Modern European Dance and Ballet. Most people again seemed to vanish for the rest of the weekend. I was able to walk a few blocks away to visit Marianne Beisinger, a Jewish Modern Dance and PE teacher I knew well from Loughborough College Summer School days.

I had to put in a great deal of extra study on my German, as I was about the weakest in the group and only French words would come. I enjoyed long talks with Kjell, whose English was only fair, until after midnight and we tested each other's vocabulary. We were both helped by Magda Kelber's excellent German language classes and her illustrated newly published text books. But we had visitors as well, including my brother, Stafford, in uniform, and his wife, Sheila, also a doctor.

By the end of January, I was on cook's washing-up duties, which were heavy. It was sometimes hard work to get the residue of burnt food off the well-used ancient pans and it was invariably a race to get through in time for any talks or lectures. One such was by Edith Pye, a veteran and widely experienced relief worker of both World Wars. Ruth Fry's book, *A Quaker*

Adventure,[1] contained many of her letters from the Maternity Unit in Reims and the move to Chalons in 1918. She had taken linen and relief supplies to Vienna in 1921 for hospitals and orphanages during the threat of famine, and the feeding of some 64,000 infants. She had what has been described as 'a genius for detailed organisation' and experience of infant welfare.[2] In 1934, with Hilda Clarke, she returned to Vienna a second time, by then in a state of civil war, and was given permission by Chancellor Dollfuss to organise relief again. In January 1939, these two intrepid women, with Dr. Audrey Russel, were in Perpignon at the break-up of Republican Spain, helping the thousands of refugees and wounded soldiers streaming over the mountain passes to the refugee camps in Southern France. It was about this work that she gave us such an absorbing account. She was still actively going to and fro between England and France, and told us of a fascinating venture for land settlement and an experimental school for young Germans, *La Coumb*, in a derelict farm in the Pyrenees after the Second World War[3]. "*La Coumb* became one of the most unusual and productive educational experiments of our time," wrote Ormerod Greenwood. "In its free community of adults and children, all share the domestic and agricultural work, including a fruit farm and, in the winter, go off on skiing trips. The persuasive influence of music has been fostered by visits from celebrated artists attending the Prades Festivals, so long directed by Pablo Casals; they have included Yehudi Menuhin, Paul Tortelier, Wilhelm Kempff and Kare Engels." How I would have loved to work in a place like that.

It was quite hard to come down to earth after this, but it was followed by a quite different topic from Dr. Eleanor Sawdon, whom I knew from Selly Oak Meeting with her parents and who was with the FAU in China. Her subject was the treatment of Scabies and Lice and inoculations! We soon knew what to look out for amongst the refugees and the Displaced Persons' camps. She had us all itching by the end and reaching for bug rakes.

On top of it all, there was a talk from Philip Zealey, who was our guest at supper that evening. He gave us a harrowing account of work of the FRS team in Holland. Philip was on leave before being transferred to lead a team in Poland.

During an unexpected bit of free time, I walked over to Wentworth House to see where Keats and Fanny Braun lived, but it was closed. However, the museum and library were open next door and proved exceptionally interesting.

---

[1] *Victories without Violence.*

[2] O.G. p231.

[3] Ibid. p265.

A lecture next morning by Graham Hughes on Practical Plumbing and Household Repair Work proved timely and very useful. Several leaks, dripping taps and the old lead pipes were giving trouble, and dodgy drains were needing attention, along with extra lagging on pipes and tanks, against winter freeze-ups.

I was up next day at 6.15, to prepare the breakfast. The boiler was out and, so it seemed, was any solid fuel. However, we did have gas to boil the huge black kettles.

In a rather cold house, Roger Soltau came to give us a second talk on the work of the League of Nations and Geneva and our Quaker interests there. This included an enlightening survey of the historical and political background of Europe since the First World War and the mistakes the Allies had made since then.

My notebook then appears to be full of details on mass feeding, catering and recipes, quantities and calorific values; the use of milk and egg powders, tinned foods and food poisoning, from a Mrs Bickersgill, who was introduced to us as being in charge of LCC School feeding programmes. This proved very useful information for what might follow.

Soon after this, I went over to Friends House to ask about my Superannuation contributions, amongst other personnel matters. I was told that they could not be kept up because the Government refused to recognise relief work as war service. So that was that.

Back at Woodstock, Robert Rossborough gave us more up-to-date reports from field workers and Michael Lee, whilst on leave, as leader of the Cologne team, dropped in to give us a detailed account of the problems and difficulties of his team's situation. In Cologne, it seemed there were complex relationship tangles between the military authorities and the German civil administration – what he referred to as 'the Herrenvolk and Army set-up'. His advice (which was to prove so useful in Berlin) was, "Get to know the chain of command and authority of both administrations. Get to know the officers in person. You may do things officially if you inform the responsible people unofficially. If we do this or that, you won't mind not knowing about it unofficially, will you? Off the record!"

On the Friday evening of February 1st, after work, we gave a house-warming party to members of the other Hostels and FRS members and I was again asked to be the MC. With Kjell on the lute and violin, we gave them songs and games. John Pettigrew and I put on mimes and Mabel (Biddy) Weiss and Phyllis Reith did a sketch with great hilarity. We soon realised that there was a lot of talent in our group. Norman the cook and helpers put on a remarkable spread for 100 people and we finished with country-dancing, led by John and Kjell. We did not finally get to bed till after one o'clock.

The following day, we rose pretty late and casually. Some of us are 'owls' and others 'larks' we discovered. Everyone was tired and it was raining, which was in danger of turning to sleet. Those of us remaining for the weekend each started the task of working out the calories in our normal diet, and the food values exercise we had been set. I had been invited out to tea with the Braithwaites in Golders Green on the Sunday and met their charming little daughter, Anna. Millior Braithwaite's mother, Mrs Barlow, was there – still the same lovely old lady, with her benign and charming smile.

Back to Monday morning, I was on 'vegetables' again and cook's washing-up rota. Spud peelings and all edible waste was to be kept for collection for pig food. The wireless was on as usual and the news was grim. From Moscow, it was reported that the USSR said it had found 190,000 bodies of Russian, Polish, French and British prisoners in Silesia – unbelievable! What more would be discovered?

Horace Pointing gave us a humorous and very stimulating talk on Quakerism, in his own very quiet and inimitable way and it led to a good discussion. There were one or two of Horace's inspirational sentences I shall always treasure:

"The spiritual life is its own reward."
"Nothing that is given up is of any value. All is gain."

"We must be as ready not to do something we want to do, as to do it. The motives must be clear. The grace to know must be acquired in practice. Man can raise himself up on his dead selves by his own efforts and self-discipline. Life is an art and every advance is creative living."

This was followed by another lecture from Dr Eleanor Sawdon, on setting up emergency field hospital units and equipment; the treatment of accidents and First Aid, etc. We began to practise on each other, which caused considerable amusement and clearly we needed much more.

There were some new arrivals and so the German class expanded, ably led by Betty Baker, who was always prepared to give me extra help to catch up on the others. And then we received our first Typhoid and Tetanus injections. One person nearly fainted. By the evening, my arm was very painful.

Maude Rowntree came to supper and I got into conversation with Hedwig Lion, who, knowing of my friendship with Vera Brittain, told me that Vera's great friend, Winifred Holtby, had been a pupil of hers and that she had "shed sunshine wherever she went at school." Winifred Holtby's *South Riding* was an enormous success, though it never left the impression on me that Vera Brittain's *Testament of Youth* did. Hedwig reminded me that Vera Brittain, way back in 1942, had pleaded for famine relief in Europe, and again in 1943 along with Charles Raven, Donald Soper, Alex Wood and the frail Quaker Labour MP, Alfred Salter, on the conditions in Greece. But it was not until December 1945, while I was in hospital and reading 'Peace News', much to the curiosity and amusement of the other patients, that I learned of the launch of the 'Save

Europe Now' movement to send food to central Europe. It had had the backing of a letter in *The Times* signed by Bishop George Bell of Chichester and other International Fellowship of Reconciliation (IFOR) members such as Percy Bartlett, Gilbert Murray, Bertrand Russell and Eleanor Rathbone. However, it was the Jewish Publisher, Victor Gollancz, who was the spearhead of the movement to save the life of the German people.

"Was I a member of the IFOR and in touch with Victor Gollancz?" she asked.

One of the most moving talks we had was from Beth Clarkson of the Holland FRS team, which was called off to work in the Bergen Belsen concentration camp as soon as the British Army had liberated it just before the end of the war. Her brief was to instruct us about relief work in Displaced Persons' and Refugee camps; the chain of command and administration, numbers and nationalities, welfare, food supplies, feeding schemes, mass cooking, distribution of medical supplies, materials and clothing, setting up classes and hobbies (occupational therapy) rehabilitation, provision for different religions and faiths, sanitation, hygiene and health matters, water supplies and washing facilities, laundry and latrines, drainage and refuse disposal. "In short," she said, "nit-picking and unblocking drains!"

Under the heading 'Miscellaneous', Beth included clothing, bedding, accommodation, schools and occupations, heating and fuel, office administration, records and reporting, tracing relatives and, finally, she underlined, the value of making recommendations to the authorities first, before the Press, and accurate reporting.

"We can't do everything, however much compassion we may feel, but surely we can find something to do and do it to the best of our ability. You will find the energy."

We were left gasping and breathless. Some of us were still suffering from the effects of the inoculations, but this really hit us and was most overwhelming. I, for one, wondered what on earth I had taken on. We looked each other in the eye and blinked. The inference was clear: One is shocked by nothing in war and the aftermath of war – only surprised. You do not lose your cool, just get on with something that needs to be done and, if possible after a pause for two deep breaths and trust in 'that which is good' and 'that of God' in everyone, yes everyone, regardless…

Until now, I had neglected reading some of the recommended text books on our lists, especially the rather dull looking "Official Copy" of the 1934 edition of the *Army Manual of Hygiene & Sanitation* (reprinted with amendments 1940), which had a First World War look about it, particularly the diagrams. I was now stimulated to do so. If this was the kind of relief work with which I might be faced, this text book (half-a-crown from HMSO) had the basic practical answers and needed to be taken with me.

Another book was *Nutrition and Relief Work, A Handbook for the guidance of Relief Workers*, published by COBSRA in 1945, which would also prove invaluable. The third was *Malnutrition, a history of Quaker Work in Austria 1919-1924, and Spain 1936-39*, by Norah Curtis and Cyril Gilbey.

All this information arrived at an auspicious moment when the press and media were underlining a world shortage of food and forecasting a return to rationing on a near-wartime basis. The wheat content of our bread was to be reduced. Butter, margarine and cooking fat rations were to be cut from 8 to 7ozs weekly. Rice was no longer to be imported. The biggest single factor, the wireless said, was the need to feed 30 million Germans for whom famine loomed after their agricultural industry had been destroyed. The Government was also telling us that we must save coal and that there was one week's supply left for Londoners.

One afternoon, we all went off to the *Bedford* Institute to see the set-up there for baling clothes for Europe, and it was there that I first met Reg Rowntree on the job. With him, we learned how to do this really tough work ourselves by joining in, for they were always short of workers. Between us that afternoon, we made up ten massive bales and, by the end of the shift, we were exhausted, but promised to return.

It was Kjell's birthday party that evening and we had guests to supper, who included Myrtle Wright[1] and another member of the Greece team, who had just flown back from Rome. So there was a lot to ask and talk about.

Robert Rossborough, the FRS Secretary, outlined for us the Committee structure behind the organisation. There were 3 committees: Ways and Means, Finance and Overseas, of which Edith Pye was Chairman and Charles Carter Acting Chairman. This latter committee also had four sub committees under Roger Wilson, which included Information (Secretary Leonard Elliot), Personnel Overseas (Secretary Amy Lewis) and Finance and Services (Reg Rowntree). It was explained what each person and committee dealt with. It also outlined and made clear what was expected of Team Leaders and their relationships to Friends House; how to make reports and to whom letters and enquiries were to be addressed.

At the weekend, again there were few of us left at Woodstock, so Kjell and I had opportunities of getting to know each other at a deeper level. He told me of his home life in Northern Sweden close to the Norwegian border and how he had been to school until he was 14. He had been a timid, lonely boy, fond of nature and the forests and would not harm a fly. To him, I related some of my early childhood days in India and early schooling in England, where, being small, I was sometimes subjected to bullying. Kjell had been afraid to read books and, except for skiing, was little interested in sport. From the ages of 10 to 14, he had had to work as a paperboy and he left school with a distaste for

[1] See her magnificent Norwegian Diary, 1940-45.

life and suffered from depression – probably due to the wartime occupation of Norway and the cruel stories he had heard, and the threats of military service ahead. He learned hairdressing, but found it a meaningless occupation. At Woodstock, he was much in demand for haircuts from all of us.

Kjell then tried Physical Education for teaching, without success, and turned to music instead. He was beginning to find happiness, when, in 1936, he was first called up for military service. This he found meaningless and banal. In 1940, he was called up again and his Company was placed near the Norwegian border, in case of trouble with the Germans. However, a comradeship sprang up between the members of forces across the border, which he missed, after the unconditional capitulation and the appalling destruction and atrocities committed by the Nazis. As soon as he got out of the Army, Kjell had already decided to offer himself for relief and reconstruction work, having by this time, become a convinced Pacifist, but did not know how to set about it.

"God has a certain meaning for each of us, Hugh," he said, "and a plan for our lives. It is our business to find out what it is. We are being led – and here I am."

Following a talk on refugees in Britain by Ada Jordan, Assistant Secretary of the Friends section of Bloomsbury House that deals with refugees, other than those of the Jewish faith, we all paid a visit to Bloomsbury House and were shown some of the organisation and workings of the Search Bureau. I was invited to pick out the name of a refugee I knew and see for myself if it was recorded. I discovered, through the record cards, that Elizabeth Wexler, who had given me my first German lessons at *Tyn-y-cae* near Brecon – the Quaker refugee hostel I had worked in – had changed her name to Elizabeth Warren. It also gave the address of where she had settled. I hoped to take it up.

That same evening, we were introduced to William R. Hughes and this proved a momentous occasion for us all. William's service and experience in Germany between the two World Wars was well-known among Quakers at least, along with the work of Corder and Gwen Catchpool in Berlin, and their relationships with the Nazis. He was a veteran worker of the First World War internment camps and paid many visits to German concentration camps between 1933-35, such as Dachau, Lichtenburg and Sachsenhausen, on behalf of Emergency Committee. He also visited the families of political victims of persecution or non-Aryans (persons of partly Jewish blood, but not usually of Jewish faith.)[1]

William Hughes was also the first British civilian allowed to 'wander' in Germany after the Great War and to resume his contacts. He later adopted the Quaker grey uniform, as did all the other visiting FRS officials and staff. With great patience and quiet good humour, he answered our many questions and

---

[1] Ormerod Greenwood *Quaker Encounters Vol.1* pp261-3.

told us of his hopes for the future, promising to support any of us who evidently might be posted out there.

Just before the next weekend began, we had a lecture on casework, which I found very helpful. This was supplemented with a showing of FRS films: "The Hard Road Back" – the work of 'Secours Quaker' in France, and another on AFSC work with children in Europe and 'Quäker Speisung'.

By this time, we were feeling rather like sponges full of water from so much listening and absorption of information, on what I call 'ficts and faggers'. So it was a relief suddenly to have a practical session on toy-making, with loads of paper and paste – any recyclable stuff or scrap and waste materials that could be found. It started like a game, for we were sent out in all directions to search for things. This exercise, which had started here, was to stand us in good stead later on.

Those of us left at Woodstock on this particular weekend were able to attend the morning session of the United Nations at Central Hall, Westminster. By a very narrow margin, Mr Paul Spaak, a Belgian, had been elected, only after a skirmish when Russia and her satellites had been outvoted, as the first U.N. President. To me, he looked extraordinarily like Winston Churchill at a distance, and an impressive figure. We had read in the press that Mr Atlee had said in his inaugural speech: "It is for the people of the world to make their choice between life and death. Our aim is the negation of war and the creation of social justice and security." We had said 'Amen' to that.

I was particularly interested to get into this session and compare it with the Quaker League of Nations Summer School in Geneva, which I had attended in 1937 from Leighton Park, at the Palais des Nations. Atlee had commented also that the outlook for the world was brighter now than when the League of Nations was formed without the presence of the United States and Russia. Now, with them both involved, he said the world was more united. But many people were already wondering if the euphoria was premature.

On the platform, I could not identify Trygvie Lie. The speeches in French, English and Russian were being skilfully translated by interpreters, but even so, I found it difficult to follow. There was so much movement and shuffling with reams of paperwork. The session was mainly taken up with a condemnation of General Franco's Spain and, from the tone of what was going on, I found it disturbing.

It was with some relief that John and I left and joined the crowds wending their way to the Cup tie football match between Chelsea and Aston Villa. John and I were supporters of the opposing sides and, to my delight, a very exciting match ended in a win for Aston Villa 1-0. It was another example for me of the electric atmosphere that can be generated by a vast crowd – in this case, 65,000 – and behaviour that can so easily degenerate by the excessive consumption of beer and bottle smashing.

We were almost out of coal again for the boiler, so John and I went over to Haddo House to fetch a lorry-load of firewood for Woodstock, which had become available. As soon as this was stored, we took the Underground to the Mile End Road Co-operative Society to be measured up for our FRS Quaker grey uniforms, which were made, we learned, in Manchester. This caused us some excitement because it seemed to indicate that we might be chosen for Europe, for the uniforms were of considerable weight. We were already aware of the dissension in the Society about the wearing of uniforms and, personally, I was never keen on the khaki uniforms of the FAU, but.... Waring is my middle name!

We were back in time for another, invaluable practical toy-making course with Nellie Rossman, this time making papier-mâché puppets, raffia dolls, etc., which was fun.

I had already read the remarkable book, *In the Margins of Chaos* by Francesca Wilson, when the author, a Friend, came herself and gave us a personal account of her work in the DP camps in American-occupied South Germany, with UNRRA. The complexity of the refugee problem and the amazing amount of movement and displacement of some 7 million DPs, unwanted by the Germans, astonished us.

That same evening, we were joined by a number of Germans and women about to return to Germany for Magda Kelber's party, where only German was to be spoken. Kjell and I were asked to accompany the folk songs on our violins, since we had no piano – only an old black 'squeeze-box'. Clearly some of the women were so overcome and choked with emotion, they could not sing. But they soon cheered up with the silly games, choruses and general hilarity and we all thoroughly enjoyed the evening.

I was learning to type on a heavy, old typewriter and bashing, with two fingers, letters to Daphne, whose parents, Kenneth and Phyllis Southall, were moving from Oxford to Cotteridge in Birmingham, while she was doing her Higher School Certificate at Sidcot School.

My father was an expert typist and working on a book he hoped to publish on his Pilgrimages to the Source of the Ganges. He had just acquired the latest *Remington* portable typewriter to take back with him to India. I practised on my letters to my parents as well and picked up speed fairly rapidly. The typewriter was in great demand, as there were good typists amongst us. They wanted to type up and collect all their lecture notes, for copies of which we had to rely on carbon paper, which was in short supply.

Two such lectures were by Dr Stevenson on Infectious Diseases and Dr Marsh on the Organisation and Work of UNRRA, with whom we were bound to be associated overseas. Precisely at this moment, the news was telling us about an 'Electronic Brain' capable of doing in seconds calculations, which could take a human Mathematician many hours, now operating at the

University of Pennsylvania. Fine, but the idea, we read, had originated to 'assist gunnery in war'! The shape of things to come?

Anyway, I had no time to copy out neatly all the valuable notes on every appalling infectious disease we were likely to come across; recognising the symptoms, some of the early treatments and incubation periods, before we had an equally interesting talk, packed with facts from Dr Audrey Russell (Ellis) – the child welfare and nutrition expert, formerly Medical Officer for the British Quaker Unit of the International Commission for the Assistance of Child Refugees in Spain, with Edith Pye and Francesca Wilson. She had just returned from Germany (under COBSRA) after making a survey of children's needs.

With her deep psychological insight and experience, Dr Russell was able to make us feel as if we were already out there and she described vividly the physical and mental state of the shattered German population, attempting to exist and revive their devastated social welfare services. At all times, she emphasised that it was not our job to take over and show them how or what we did in Britain, but to work alongside, befriend, listen and support, make mini-surveys, report, build confidence and quickly hand over.

Berlin was a particularly difficult situation because of the four-power administration and military Government over the four different sectors, when compared with the four separate Zones and domination by the Americans. Audrey was able to describe in detail the set-up in the British Zone and the evolution towards a Control Commission for Germany (CCG). She described also the shattered state of the German civil administration and their internal affairs. The people at the head, whom she had met, were elderly but sound; the lower ranks and administrators were exhausted. Our main task would be to get the Non-Governmental Organisations (NGOs), voluntary agencies and Church Welfare organisations reactivated, and harness the workers, using university students wherever possible. In general, our task would be to act impartially, in a liaison capacity, between the local administration on the ground and the Military Government officials, under the protection of the British Red Cross. We would find that the 'Quäker Speisung' after the First World War had not been forgotten, was trusted and many doors would be opened for us.

Audrey also provided us with charts, nutritional survey and sampling methods and questionnaires to conduct, in order to find out what was happening and what the particular needs were in different situations. She emphasised particularly the importance of Infant Mortality surveys, listing the child welfare clinics and those attending; the recording of heights and weights and getting the feeding centres going again as a top priority. Most of the FRS Units had Red Cross medical supplies to administer and so her charts on running emergency clinics and handling epidemics seemed extremely useful.

The course had been together for a month now and we were working as a team already. There was a willingness to tackle anything, and a spirit of joy and fun prevailed, though we were aware too that we were being unobtrusively observed and assessed for qualities of leadership and personality.

At this point in the course, I took a weekend of leave and caught the afternoon train back to Birmingham. With Mum and Dad at the Guest House flat I had a quiet evening playing cards as of old. Dad was packed and ready and, on the following morning, we went into town to see him off to India. Our feelings were rather sad and gloomy – like the weather, but, on Sunday, it was a mild and sunny spring-like day. After the Meeting, I copied out what my father called, "mother's Pearls of Wisdom", a special gift she had and which was worth recording for posterity. father had noticed during the first few months of their marriage that his wife possessed a peculiar gift of combining portions of proverbs, mixed metaphors and sundry malapropisms in such a way as to produce results sometimes even more striking than the originals. Allied to this was the ability to coin new words, and the test of their purity is that they sound so sensible that they often pass unnoticed by the ordinary individual and excite no comment. He wrote them down as delivered and the family contributed to the collection also, because the remarkable thing was, that, once one's ears were opened to the possibility, it was surprising to discover how often such gems and treasures may be found.

My father's comment was that this very special gift seemed to occur more frequently in women, though men are no mean contributors. I can still hear Jack Hoyland's resounding laugh as they were recounted to him and mother was the first to join in with: "Well, what's wrong with that?"

When I asked her how she did it, her reply was that they always came to her quite naturally and without thinking!

These gems hardly come under the *Reader's Digest* categories of 'Laughter the Best Medicine', 'Life's Like That', or 'Points to Ponder', which we all enjoyed, but they certainly caused much laughter, endless amusement to all and even lowered the tension sometimes when the family felt vulnerable or fragmented. So perhaps they deserve a little higher category than 'Towards More Picturesque Speech', endearing as they are.

Gems of Mum

1) The trouble with John is that he has too many fiddles in the fire!
2) Now you've gone and given the cat away!
3) It's enough to take the heart out of a stone!
4) That young man's name in the paper has suddenly burst into flame!
5) It's killing Peter to save Paul.
6) There's too many cooks in the broth already, get out!

7) Go on, give it to him from the elbow.
8) The Smiths kept empty house in Bristol you know?
9) He was absolutely enhanced with Blackpool.
10) He'll get on if he knows how to pull the ropes.
11) He's falling between two straws.
12) They never go hot nails and dead nuts on all sorts of cranks.
13) Do you know, at that concert she never had a stitch of music in front of her.
14) I left absolutely no loophole unturned.
15) Were you hoping for that last sausage up your sleeve dear?
16) Yes, I can see he's a bit of a blind goose chase!
17) (Bread shortage) I think we shall just skim through by the skin of our teeth.
18) He's gone and dug a deep trench and filled it with bric-a-brac, would you believe?
19) Do you know, the other day I found a pound note by mistake?
20) (After unexpected Sunday visitors had stayed all day) Well, that's nipped the Evening Service on the head.
21) Oh, it's second-hand nature to me now, but I'm no great snakes at it yet.
22) There's another couple in the same shoes.
23) She always was inclined to butter him up with cups of tea.
24) I must say, the fish from that shop is very toss and go.
25) The frontispage from the magazine is exceptionally dull.
26) I caught him red hot at it.
27) She's gone and left me to swim in my own juice.
28) I'm utterly at my beams' end!
29) I didn't feel I could take up the cudgeons for her.
30) In that talk there was absolutely nothing I could button on to.
31) (For a crossword puzzle) Let's see, the stage beyond dotage – which would be 'adage' wouldn't it?
32) Those mosquitoes were round me like bees round a honey pot.
33) They (the Biglands) wouldn't take any hokey-poky.
34) Dropped like hot bricks.
35) Too old and hulky looking to last out for cricket much longer.
36) They never got a ha'penny dime out of it.
37) You simply tread on tender hooks the whole time.
38) I knew there was some stick in his mind.
39) She soon realised she had gone a peg too far.
40) That flattened his sails!
41) There's a disparagement between the rates.
42) I'm as hungry as two hoots.
43) My hair was nearly blown out of its sockets.

44) He was as happy as two pins.
45) (Yellow, after a course of Atebrin) She went the colour of a guinea fowl.
46) I suppose she's hanging on to him like a man to a drowning straw.
47) It does take the bite off the edge of your holiday.
48) I just couldn't subside on bread and butter and cocoa.
49) That has rather taken the pith off it.
50) I'll tell you afterwards in cameo.
51) Their tails might be turned on their own selves.
52) I saw them myself with my own naked eyes.
53) They kept up a continuous jabble.
54) A regular cavalcade of coke comes down that chute.
55) That fire looks rather negligée.

The weekend was over too soon, but not before I had taken mother for a walk on the Lickey Hills, along the same paths by the golf course I had shared with Daphne. We were still far too early for the primroses and blue bells that mother adored. I had to catch my train back and say farewell to her for what was to be a long period. On the way back, I just had time to drop off the tram and nip back in to the Woodlands Hospital to see some of the patients still left in the ward and some of the nurses who had been so kind to me.

At New Street station, I linked up with two others, but the train was already so crowded we had to stand for the whole three-hour journey. The passengers looked tired and rather drab ('negligée', as mother might say). Tobacco smoke drifted along the corridor and made me cough, as my eyes began to smart.

Back at the hostel, the weather turned wild and, though I got soaked, I managed to find a packet of soap flakes in the Swiss Cottage shops for some clothes washing. At the same time, I managed to find some wire to continue making flowers and toys, and to finish off some of the puppets for putting on show.

Having already studied the *Army Manual of Hygiene & Sanitation*, there was a renewal of interest in it after a visit to the Army School of Hygiene at Ash Vale. It was a brilliant, cold morning and a very early start. We were courteously received and treated to an absorbing programme of well-illustrated lectures and films, a guided tour of their museum of pests and diseases, outdoor cooking arrangements, disinfestation units, sanitary layouts and water purification plants; the Manual was updated for us.

That evening, when we got back, Alison Fox, having served in Poland, Greece and other countries en route, gave us the benefit of her recent experiences, with many observations and hints that she had come across; the little details, useful and valuable information for relief workers we had not even considered. Feeling rather dead from a further batch of inoculations, some of us were too tired even to take notes. In bed that night, we heard on the wireless that the Government had announced that there would still be 1.1 million in Military Service by 1947, from a wartime peak of 5.1 million. These seemed astonishing figures.

Shortly after an unexpected, but programmed lecture from Audrey Ellis on Emergency Mid-wifery, including one of the first films I had seen on childbirth, there followed a very enjoyable day of well-planned practical exercises.

We were given various imaginary situations (no doubt drawn from experience) with which we might be confronted and have to face, such as delivering a baby in an ambulance on the way to hospital! Half an hour was given us, in pairs, to prepare and then we had to act. Though this caused much hilarity, it had a serious purpose, for in the afternoon, we were given a much larger scale emergency situation, which had to be acted out that evening before an invited audience of assorted and very different 'officials' at a social evening. 'They' judged it a success, though undoubtedly their comments and criticisms showed up our lack of experience and our naivety, but that in itself was helpful, as they played their roles and in different languages!

All this coincided with our barely completed and hastily cobbled-together reports on the surveys of our meals for the calorie values at Woodstock. The results revealed some wide variations and not a few curious anomalies. A difficult task!

On the last Sunday in February, a glorious spring day, I decided to go off to Kew Gardens without breakfast and arrived just as the gates were opening. With my Royal Horticultural Society card, I managed to get in at a cheaper rate and was confronted at once with a marvellous display of early blossoms – daffodils, snowdrops, crocuses, hellebores and scillas. I was astonished at so many different varieties. Everything seemed to be waking up and the birdsong, particularly the robins, blackbirds and thrushes, was magical. Different varieties of camellias were in bud and already showing colour, and the polyanthus beds were heavily scented. There were even early bees on the winter-flowering heathers. I could have spent the whole day there, but the gardens soon began to get crowded.

After briefly touring one of the tropical greenhouses, which revived memories of India. I left and took buses across London to Aunt Sylvia Brison's top floor flat in Neasden, to have lunch and tea with her. She was a favourite of mine and a retired Truby King nurse. Her flat had been my home during my short career in the International Ballet Company's School and the London Season at the *Lyric Theatre* in Shaftesbury Avenue during the summer of 1944. I was still able to get a really good hot bath there, and my aunt was much amused by my descriptions of Audrey Ellis' midwifery and breast-feeding talk and the exercises we were given. I finished up at Cecil Sharpe

House for a very enjoyable evening of National Dancing and Folk music, where there was always good company.

By now we were once again right out of coal slack for the boiler and relying on the wood and scrap we had brought over from Haddo House. As sparks sometimes flew, we carried out fire drills led by John Pettigrew and myself, both of us having had considerable experience of firefighting during the Blitz. The hostel really was bleak at this time and hot baths for washing at a premium. The Government was again appealing for everyone to save coal, since London coal yards were empty. The few electric fires we had were still working and we were assured that the spartan conditions and shortages were as nothing compared with what we might find in the field. The only thing to do was to put on more clothes and keep up the exercises.

We were further bolstered up by the step-mother of Sir Stafford Cripps, Lady Marion Parmoor, an amazing vital woman of 68 and a Friend, who limped into the hostel with a broken hip and a stick. She gave us an inspiring talk on the Quaker Peace Testimony. Without the pressure of taking notes for once, we were just able to listen and absorb the radiance coming from her.

Marion Parmoor was able to stay for supper and, in conversation afterwards, began to make us question our own individual commitments to peace-making, reconciliation and conflict resolution in international relations, whether we were Friends or not, for we would be representing Quakers. And this was a salutary exercise when we realised we would be asked such questions as "What are your motives for coming here to do this work? What's in it for you?"

Before going to bed, I just had time to read Vera Brittain's *Peace Letter*, for one or two of us were on her mailing list. One comment stuck out for me – that one reason for the world shortage of food was probably due to the fact that vast stocks of emergency rations and energy had been used, instead, for the production of synthetic rubber, after the Japanese had over-run and destroyed the rubber plantation areas in the Far East. I was finding it difficult to switch my focus of attention away even from Europe, let alone India and Palestine.

On a cold, wet and snowy day after lectures had been cancelled, a few of us took the opportunity of visiting the Russian Theatre Exhibition, which I immediately found fascinating. There were films of incredibly agile forms of Russian folk dancing from Gopaks and Cossacks, and classical ballet, of course. The latter included Ulanova in *Swan Lake*, of particular interest for me, and a special performance of the famous Lepechinskaya Puppets, which had never been seen in this country before, for good measure.

One of the exhibition rooms was full of a wide range of elegant photographs of ballet stage settings and productions in the great Russian Theatres. There was a crowd of ballet dancers and, to my surprise and delight, I met Barbara Barrie and Mavis Ray, two of the *corps de ballet* I had danced with in *Swan Lake* in the original International Ballet Company production at the Brighton Hippodrome.

In contrast, the following day included an all-day visit to school and adult feeding centres in South and East London, talking with the workers at all levels and discussing storage and hygiene, food poisoning, the re-use of 'leftovers' and prevention of waste. We were particularly interested in the use of modern machinery, including a huge steam dishwasher, and the stainless steel and other work surfaces for food preparation and cooking in large quantities.

By way of relaxation, we dropped off at the West End to see the brilliant David Lean film, *Brief Encounter*, and enjoyed a good weep! David Lean was an Old Leightonian and supposed to be a cousin on my mother's side of the family.

Somehow, we were given tickets for the afternoon performance of the BBC Symphony Concert on the next day at the People's Palace. We heard a programme that included Brahms' *Song of Destiny*, which Daphne and I had sung at Sidcot and was one of our favourite pieces, and Elgar's *Enigma Variations.*

That same evening, we all turned up at Friends House to hear Victor Murray's lecture on the Quaker Contribution to the Union of the Churches. He urged Quakers to take the lead in this movement. Afterwards, he reminded me that he had lived in the same bungalow as ours in Fox Hill Close, Selly Oak, and that the Thornes (Stephen Thorne is the Recording Clerk) had got engaged to be married there!

Two or three other Friends from Birmingham were also at the lecture, including Wilfred Littleboy and Robert Davies. They told me they had just said their farewells to my mother, who set sail for India on 25th February. So all our possessions were in storage – somewhere – and all the family were now independent. It was a strange feeling.

Just before the weekend and on 1st March, we heard that Magda Kelber had been appointed to lead the next team to Germany, at Solingen, and that Alice Eden and Kjell were to go with her. This was a sad blow, for there was no other man on the course, except for John, with whom I would rather work. It was an undoubted setback for the group and both John and I were disappointed not to be included, but we had been warned about such postings at a moment's notice and Louisa Roberts was tender about it after the House Meeting and the Devotional that followed. I soon realised that I was by no means ready to be posted anyway.

The News that evening was saying that German food rations would have to be cut by 1,000 calories. Having just done our own 'counts', we knew what that meant. In Britain, the Food Ministry had just issued a recipe for squirrel pie and bananas actually arrived in the shops!

Saturday March 2nd was a cold and miserable day with snow, but a small ration of coal had arrived. In an immaculate uniform, plus batman-cum-driver, Major, The Marquis Chetwynd, came to give us a talk and information on the Military Government set-up in Germany. He was the Military Commander for Kreis (District) Wesel and he described the ruins and devastation when they first went in, how the 'Mil. Gov.' dealt with it, and what they were still endeavouring to do a year later. He also outlined the political complexities of it all. He was a lovely man in a nest of 'conchies' and always referred to all Germans as 'the Hun'. He advised every woman to carry a gun: "She would look silly without one – so would I," he remarked.

That Sunday, I went to Meeting for worship at Friends House to meet two American Young Friend COs, Sam Snipes and Channing Richardson, the first to join UNRRA. They had been working for CPS camps for four years forestry work. Since they had only 24 hours in London, before moving on to Poland, I took them back to Woodstock for lunch – there was always something for extra and unexpected guests or visitors. John Hudson and I then showed them as much of London as we could and, in the evening, they took us out to dinner at the *Shanghai Restaurant* in Soho, which we often frequented after our evening performances at the *Lyric Theatre.* They were excited by the 'gigantic new airliner' in which they had flown over from Washington.

A couple of days later, a throat infection made me lose my voice. The whole morning was taken up with listening to Elizabeth Fox Howard, who came to tell us about German Friends and her work with them in Germany between the two World Wars[1]. Briefly, Elizabeth, Ruth, Margery and Joan Mary Fry were all great-grandchildren of Luke Howard, who had been Secretary of the 1914 War Victims Committee ('War Vics'). Elizabeth was frequently one of the hostesses at the Quaker Rest House, opened in 1933 near Frankfurt, and the winter refuge, St. Josef's Haus at Bad Pyrmont, a famous Spa town, which remained open until 1939 and reopened after the War. We had used her small book, *Across Barriers*, because there were German and English versions.

The story of her detention at the German frontier in 1935 and the confiscation of all her papers, with the names of Jewish contacts, will not be forgotten. Her colleagues, Corder Catchpool and William Hughes were implicated and questioned by the Gestapo. Elizabeth Fox Howard was to return as hostess once again in Bad Pyrmont shortly after the talk.

Unfortunately, my heavy cold and loss of voice prevented me from going with the rest of the group to the *Bedford* Institute the next day for a much larger exercise – making a transit camp for 500 refugees. So I had to stay back on my own, typing and getting my speed up, and had to rely on the reports of

[1] Ormerod Greenwood's *Quaker Encounters Vol.1 Friends Relief.*

others on their return. They had missed Winston Churchill droning away on the wireless in his characteristic voice, warning both the U.S. and Britain of the 'growing Soviet menace aimed at the whole free world and the spread of the Communist tyranny'. Some say that this was when the phrase, "The Iron Curtain" was christened.

While still feeling rather poorly and off-colour, some of the others and I had interviews with Dorothy and Geoffrey Smith about the future. It soon became clear that there was no prospect of getting out to Germany for at least another two months. Since Kjell and others had already been posted, we began to feel a little depressed, if not impatient, at the delay, because so many of the lectures and more inoculations were pointing us, we felt, in that particular direction.

Back in Woodstock that evening, we made a little music, drank mugs of *Fry's Cocoa* and powdered milk, and toasted a slice of bread with peanut butter. We roasted them over a cow dung fire and made delectable peanut and groundnut (Erdnuss, in German) butter long before it was ever heard of in England. Someone piped up and said, like everything else, it came from America just before the War; someone else was sure it had been introduced in a vegetarian restaurant in Birmingham 50 years before. Our hunger partially satisfied, most of us who were not car drivers, decided we had better opt for the next FAU Driving course at Mount Waltham.

Next morning, there was a long lecture from Leo Liemman. It was like a tap being turned on and left on. I simply could not follow and had to switch off. But in the afternoon, we were delighted to welcome Myrtle Wright and her friend Sigrid Lund from Norway, who particularly wanted to make contact with Kjell Nahnfeldt. Myrtle, I knew already. She had been at Woodbrooke for a year. Her mother and grandmother had both been born in India and, in the 1930s, as a keen Young Friend, she had visited India with Friends, met Ghandi and other political leaders and helped with reconciliation work. She had visited my parents while I was at the Downs School.

For four years, Myrtle, during the War, had found herself in Nazi-occupied Norway and, as a convinced pacifist, had lived with Diedrich and Sigrid Lund and their two boys. Shortly after her brief visit to us, she returned to Norway with Sigrid in the FAU, to help restore some order out of the chaos – she described – in Finnmark especially (where I had visited on my travel scholarship in 1938). She had received the King Haakon Cross for services given to Norway in the war years.

Myrtle Wright's *Norwegian Diary, 1940-45*, was not published until 1974, but makes fascinating reading. In 1951, she married Phillip Radley (Daphne's uncle by his first marriage to Christine Southall), and I worked under him, as a PE and Games Master when he was Headmaster of Ackworth for one term, when I came out of FRS.

Sigrid Lund[1] was another indomitable Friend, 11 years older than Myrtle; it was through Myrtle's influence that she finally became a Quaker in 1947, but she was a pacifist long before joining the Society. With the Women's International League for Peace and Freedom, in the mid-thirties, she had been active in the struggle for peace and human rights and, with the spread of Nazism, increasingly involved with floods of refugees. In 1937, she had been invited to join 'Nansenhjelp', an organisation led by Odd Nansen the explorer, who had attempted to reach the North Pole by drifting in his ship, the *FRAM*, and a former Nobel Peace Prize winner.

Sigrid, with a friend, was asked to go to Prague in 1939 and fetch a group of Jewish children back to safety in Norway, little knowing that three years later, the same children would have to be smuggled across into neutral Sweden. That winter, the War had broken out in Finland and Sigrid went as leader of a small team of medical relief workers, to help civilian evacuees, and experienced bombing and intense winter temperatures.

The Nazi forces invaded Norway in 1940 and soon Sigrid, Diedrich and Bernti, their oldest son, became involved in the underground work of the Resistance Movement, helped by Myrtle. But it was mainly about Sigrid's mission in 1942, when she helped rescue the children from the Jewish children's home in Oslo, her work with the Norwegian branch *Save the Children*, and her post-war concern for the voluntary relief and rehabilitation work in the devastated areas of Finnmark, razed to the ground by the Nazis in 1944, that we heard about and listened to with astonishment in the brief time these two were able to be with us. Lovely people! But there was a warning; the Germans just did not realise the strength of the feelings against the Nazis in so many different countries and it would take a long time to heal the wounds.

Roger Wilson gave us a very practical and helpful talk next day and quickly discerned the disappointment of some of us that we had not yet been chosen for Germany. He reassured us, but gently steered us to think about the other countries in need. Roger, who as a CO had lost his job with the BBC in 1941, had already been appointed General Secretary of the revived 'War Vics' (with its red and black star logo) to co-ordinate the existing relief services and to raise funds. Christopher Taylor was the Chairman. Together they founded the Friends War Relief Service, which was again redesigned and became the FRS, with Roger still as General Secretary. It was after the FRS was wound up in 1948 that he became Professor of Education at Bristol, following another Friend, Professor Basil Fletcher, who was my Professor.

---

[1] *Quakerism, a Way of Life*, Norwegian Quaker Press 1982.

Training Camp at Jordans

Training Camp at Jordans

We were all glad of a 'free' morning on the following weekend and took the train out to Seer Green, and walked to Jordans Meeting. Outside the Meeting House is the simple gravestone of William Penn. We walked on up through the orchard to the *Mayflower* Barn and the Guest House, where there was a warm welcome from Catherine Reynolds, the Warden, who had long been a friend of my mother's family, the Brisons. A most enjoyable evening of singing and country dancing had been arranged and there were wonderful log fires and the pungent smell of wood-smoke.

That Sunday morning Meeting for worship in the old 1688 Meeting House with local Friends was a deep and memorable one. It was a glorious sunny day, white with a crisp frost, as we walked down through the paddock and it was good to be back. Every summer term at Leighton Park, Reading, a group of us would cycle over for the annual cricket match on the village green and finish up at the swimming pool at *The Bell* inn.

The afternoon was spent at practical work in the Youth Hostel field, energetically putting up tents, digging refuse pits, water soak-aways and collecting fuel until darkness fell. We all enjoyed the clear country air. After supper, there was a further talk on the practical work planned for the following day by Jesse and Gilbert Wood, experienced members of John Saunder's Greece team.

We awoke to cold, crisp air – another glorious sunny day. Between us, we rigged up a field oven with a dustbin and trench fire and, with supplies provided, cooked lunch for everyone. In the afternoon, we set up a 'Serbian Barrel Disinfector' and a latrine. This was followed up by making a boiler with an oil and water flash-fire for washing-up water. All worked well and, as dusk began to fall and to the sound of birds singing, we began to cook supper. Eric Savage, another experienced FRS worker, came down from London to see how we were getting on. He had seen in the newspaper the headlines that Churchill, in Moscow, had been denounced as an anti-Soviet Warmonger. The fear and hysteria of Russia was growing.

March 12th was Daphne's birthday. The weather was holding good and we continued with our practical exercises and learning from the experience of others. One effort was very successful – Lazy Cook's boiler – which was duly christened 'Gilbo'. As soon as lunch was consumed, everything was dismantled, cleared away, tidied up and loaded. Turfs were carefully replaced and you could not tell (as dusk fell) that any exercise had been held there.

The day ended with another home-made entertainment: party games, singing rounds, folk songs, dances and a quiet period of thankfulness.

The next day we returned early by train to Woodstock. From the list, I saw that I had to prepare vegetables, which, with some willing help, I did in time to get to a lecture by Dr Kohle, who had been a Government official in the Weimar Republic before Hitler, on the German Social Welfare set-up, which had obviously been extremely efficient in the past.

It was quite an effort to switch after the lunch break to another lecture by Roger Soltau on Palestine. The kings of Egypt and Saudi Arabia were insisting that Palestine was Arab land and, in view of the hopes of the Austrian Jewish families – with whom I had been in Brecon at the *Tyn-y-cae* Hostel – whose dream was to get to Palestine when their men were released from internment, my thoughts began to turn towards the Middle East as a possible place for service. Roger was telling us about the Jewish terrorist activities directed against British soldiers.

Bertha Bracey came to supper and she gave us the evening lecture on Relief Work and refugees. Bertha, another dynamic Friend, was also a post-First World War relief worker in Austria during the famine period, when Austrian children had been sent to England. With 25 years of Quaker experience and service for individuals who had suffered in Germany during the Nazi period and again immediately after Second World War, she became involved in the rescue and emigration undertaken for the victims of Nazism. The Testimony to the Grace of God in the life of Bertha Bracey is to be found in *Quaker Work in 1989*, included in the documents of London Yearly Meeting and, for me, it is a most remarkable life. At the 'Stille Helfer' Quaker Exhibition in the Berlin Historische Museum in January 1996 – celebrating 50 years (and more) of Quaker Relief work, Brenda Bailey wore the CBE medal awarded to Bertha in 1944 by King George VI for her part in saving whole groups of Jewish children. In 1934, she had administrative responsibility for establishing the Quaker school in Ommen, Holland, for about 100 Jewish children, and she obtained permits for 10,000 Jewish children to come to Britain early in 1939. In 1945, just before the end of the War, 300 orphans were discovered in Theresienstadt concentration camp in the wake of the American Military advance. With the help of RAF Bomber Command, Bertha had them flown to a reception camp by Lake Windermere to be cared for.

All this had taken its toll on her health, but by 1946, the Friends Committee for Refugees and Aliens was being wound up at a time when she was actively helping with their rescue, immigration and repatriation. This was what she was telling us about and urging us, if we were posted to Germany, to take special care for them and others like them. This was of particular interest to me. Because we had maintained contact with the husband of one of our family's 'au pair' girls, who was a Prisoner of War throughout the War. One of the reasons why I wanted to go to Germany was to re-establish contact with all three women and their families. At this particular time, Bertha transferred her energies to the German Section of the Foreign Office and the Allied Control Commission, and she remained with them until she retired in 1953. To her, nothing was impossible.

Soon after this memorable evening, some of the group went to a concert in Friends House by James Ching and Winifred Roberts in aid of FRS, which was most enjoyable and had a warm reception. More and more of the lectures and discussions from Dr Eline Simon, Dr Audrey Ellis and Roger Wilson seemed to focus on Germany and German Welfare. Roger restored the balance somewhat by reminding us that, in actual fact, no European has any justification for trusting any German as such, because of what has been done in the name of Germany. This obviously does not apply to individuals that one knows of personally, but Germans have no right to expect more sympathy than anyone else. The German occupation also leaves the legacy of the enormous problem of those who collaborated. There were, in fact, more signs of suffering amongst French children than in Germany. Amongst 400,000 DPs in Germany, there were now 300,000 Poles on 2,000 calories a day. I had got to a point where I just had to stop taking notes.

In the middle of March, I played hooky and went off to the Riverside Film Studios, armed with an introduction to Sydney Box from Arthur Taylor, the film producer at *Cadbury's Bournville*, who had made the Leighton Park film in my last year there.[1] We had remained in contact. Sydney Box was not there, but out on location. However, his Casting Director did see me and showed me around the studios. He also asked me about my theatrical experience and ambitions. At this point, he was called away, but asked me to get in touch again when my relief service was over, or if I failed to be selected and he would arrange a screen test for me.

But, I think, as a result of this interview, any fantasy ideas of a career on the stage or in the theatre were finally buried. I had learned enough from my short, but blissful experience in ballet to realise I would never be a star in that particular line. And, though I had been compared as a vague look-alike to film star, Alan Ladd, it was crystal clear that it was not for me – not my way. I still loved to make people laugh, especially my mother, but I had to get it out of my system. I am still a bit of a showman though and enjoy the limelight, and I was encouraged by W.H. Auden.

So, I returned to Woodstock in time to join up with John Pettigrew to go off to the Wembley Ice Rink and, with Kjell, to see the England v. Sweden ice hockey match. It was very exciting and Sweden won 14-2, with obvious superiority. During the interval, there was some elegant exhibition ice dancing from the British ice-skating champions and a Swedish champion.

That weekend, a number of us went to the 'No Atomic War' Pacifist rally at the Westminster Hall, which was packed. Donald Soper was in the chair and there was a fine panel of very eloquent speakers who included, before lunch, James Hudson MP, Dr J.P. Hugenholtz, a Dutch Pastor, our Friend, Reginald Reynolds and Dr Alex Wood.

As I already knew Reg Reynolds, I must say a word about him at this point, because of his associations with India. Ghandi, back in 1930, had sent him, as a Young Friend of 25, to deliver his declaration of civil disobedience to the

[1] A copy of this film and a CD are available in my private collection.

Viceroy, and broke the salt monopoly, which had been denounced in the meetings of the British India Society a century earlier[1]. My father, too, was in communication with Ghandi on the salt monopoly. The original copies are in the Selly Oak College Library.[2] Reg is described as a tall, elegant and handsome young man by Marjorie Sykes and indeed, he was always a striking figure and eloquent speaker. He had first spent two years at Woodbrooke studying international affairs with Horace Alexander. He had then married the author Ethel Manin, and I have in my possession a letter from her, after my performance in J.M. Synge's 'Diedre of the Sorrows' at Leighton Park.[3]

But, to return to the rally at Westminster Hall. After the tea interval, during which there was much chatter with the speakers, Bertha Bracey opened the proceedings and was followed by Professor Norman Whitney (AFSC), Tegla Davies of the FAU and Canon Charles Raven, who left a very deep impression on me. It was an inspiring occasion.

On our return to Woodstock, I received confirmation of my full membership of FRS, plus the Quaker Star badge. Others also had already got the news and, of course, we celebrated. From the noticeboard too, we saw that volunteers were needed for famine relief in India.

That Sunday, the hostel was practically deserted. I overslept and failed to get to Meeting. I had been invited in the afternoon, with Marianne Beisinger, to the Pola Nirenska Dance Studio in Notting Hill Gate to meet a small select group of half a dozen people, including Adda Heynsan, who was Rudolph Labad's (Modern European Dance) pianist at the Sheffield course that Marianne and I had been on. They were a very friendly and welcoming group and we were invited to join them. For me, it was impossible, because my right leg in particular, though it was loosening up with regular exercises, was still not up to it, and, anyway, I was not free.

Marianne and I then went on to the German League of Culture in Hampstead, where they were putting on a performance of 'The Importance of Being Earnest' – in German. I knew the play well from Sidcot days, and Daphne had been in the play then, so to see and hear it in German was a great help.

We were now in the last week of the course. I introduced and chaired a talk by Harry Silcock[4] (a great friend of my parents) on the Worldwide Community of Friends, and he gave us a wonderful overview. Harry was the Congregationalist son of a Liberal MP and had joined the Friends Foreign Missionary Association in 1908, at the same time as my parents. He succeeded

[1] Ormerod Greenwood's *Quaker Encounters Vol.II1*, p.4. Marjorie Sykes *An Indian Tapestry*, p.238/9.

[2] Now in Birmingham University Archives.

[3] Hugh Maw, Memoirs, Vol. II, p.297.

[4] O.G. Vol. 3 p.140.

Henry T. Hodgkin as General Secretary in 1920, the year I was born in India, but he had also served as a missionary in China with Margaret (Standing), his wife. She was the daughter of a Madagascar missionary. Harry had established a Friends Centre in Shanghai in 1939 and, during the War, the burden of the relief work there had been borne, not by the FSC, but by the FAU[1], the revived 'War Vics' and eventually by the FRS. After the opening of Friends House and its International Student Club, Harry Silcock, as Joint Secretary with Carl Heath of the new Friends Service Council (FSC), had to deal with the flood of hundreds of Chinese and Japanese students in London, who streamed to Friends House for advice about accommodation and courses. Later it was Africans. In 1946, there was an appeal in The Friend for student accommodation, which brought in not a single reply. Myrtle Wright was the moving spirit behind the International Student Club and, later, with her husband, Philip Radley, ran the Student Movement House in Gower Street. So Harry was well placed, having travelled in so many countries, to give us a balanced and worldwide picture of the World Society of Friends.

That afternoon, we begin to switch our attention from the sublime to the ridiculous. I searched the local shops for artificial flowers for a ballet rehearsal of Phyllis Reith's 'Revue of the course', which she was preparing for the end-of-course party.

On the Tuesday that followed, after a lecture on 'Poland and the Polish people' by Dr Rose, most of us trooped off to Hampstead to the *Everyman Theatre* to see the pre-Hitler classic film, 'Madchen in Uniform' in German, which was useful. On our return, we were all vaccinated against smallpox – fortunately without side effects, John Pettigrew and I immediately left for the 'Save Europe Now' meeting in Finchley Road. It was organised by Corder Catchpool, at which both Vera Brittain and Victor Gollancz spoke with passionate conviction. I was able to talk with both of them and to Professor Whitney (AFSC), who was also there. My diary notes that the 'Face the Facts' group was <u>not</u> there, but I have no recollection of what this group was about. A retiring collection produced the sum of £200 towards the funds for COBSRA.

The atmosphere now at Woodstock was rather like the end of term and everyone focussed on Phyllis' *Revue*. Another lecture on Russia and her policies was politely attended, if sparingly, for our minds – mine certainly – were elsewhere. The rest of the day was a chaotic flurry of activity and preparations.

In the event, that evening the *Revue* went down like a bomb; the staff and guests generous in their applause. My ballet skit was highly complimented, as was the skit on the talk by the Army Kreis Commandant. In the dance cabaret, with clothes from the baling at the B.I., Kjell and I did a drag act with a wig, on the telephone, and together we did a 'Grand Opera' duet – 'Your Tiny

---

[1] Ibid. p.294.

Hand is Frozen' (La Bohême) in Italio-German! We really let our hair down. The 'spread' of food at the end was astonishing – what must have been, by intriguing means, somehow salvaged from rations and kind contributions.

The following day, I had to call quickly in to Friends House, as there was a message for me there. It was to let me know that both my father and mother had arrived safely and without incident in India. John Pettigrew came with me because there was a footnote from the FRS Office and, somewhat to our surprise, we were asked jointly to consider accepting famine relief work in India.

We hurried back to Woodstock, where 'spring-cleaning' of the hostel from top to bottom had already started. We both found it a difficult problem and, over 'break' and a lunch of left-overs from the party, discussed it with the others, then put it out of our minds for we all had a scheduled visit arranged to Wormwood Scrubs Prison. This was to be my first visit to a prison and of particular interest, because a number of 'conchies' known to us, who were absolutists, had spent time at 'the Scrubs'. As it happened, I found it absorbingly interesting, very depressing and acutely embarrassing. It was rather like going to the zoo and seeing the animals behind bars, the over-crowding and the military regime. I admired the work of the officers, but had little chance to talk with those in the over-crowded cells, or doing repetitive cleaning work, or to inspect the kitchens and workshops. Though we were shown the chapel arrangements, library facilities and an exercise yard, the visit was all too short. I must admit though, I was glad to get out, but with that eerie feeling of: "There, but for the Grace of God, go I." It was just as I had felt at Leighton Park after a visit to Reading Army Barracks – what lies behind it all?

The headline in the evening papers shouted out by the cockney news sellers was: "Nuremberg Trials! Nuremberg Trials!" Goering denies that he or Hitler knew of the 'Final Solution' regarding the Jews.

House cleaning and tidying continued. I had lunch with my brother and Sheila, his wife, at the *Shanghai.* Together, we went to see Sydney Box's film production, *The Seventh Veil.* The second film with it was *Defeated People*, about the British occupation of Germany.

That evening, the last meeting of the full course was held with the staff, who reviewed the course and we all expressed our thanks to them. It was an emotional time, but became more light-hearted as we produced some of the funny remarks overheard, repeated mimes, sketches and 'take-offs'; a joyous occasion that ended with quiet worship, which I for one was glad of, because of thoughts around the FRS offer of service.

Years later, my mother handed me back a typed airletter I had written to her on the following day, March 23rd, after my parents had confirmed their safe arrival. My letter explained the difficulty of the decision I had to make over the offer to work on the emergency famine relief in India. I explained that we had been given sparse details and that it might entail a further interview with FSC, which John and I thought we ought at least to ask for.

Since the beginning of the War, I had imagined myself going to an enemy country, or at least to some part of over-run Europe. It was true that I had signed a contract, but John and I gathered that it was likely to be administrative deskwork, rather than practical, and liaison at a high level between the Indian Voluntary agencies and Government. I also explained and outlined to them the reasons why I thought I might be attracted to go as they were already out there. We had also heard that the FAU were pulling out and the FSC were taking over. We were both apprehensive of taking over from such responsible and experienced workers. On the other hand, it was very tempting to leave a cold, damp and clammy winter climate for the hot and sunny one I had remembered from my childhood. The need was urgent and we would be expected to leave at once by special plane or priority passage. We knew of two or three others ready and eager to go. Also John and I had both wanted to work in a team, rather than take on rather isolated jobs. Another big consideration for us was that we were both engaged to be married. We had just signed up for the driving course at Mount Waltham and felt we badly needed to learn to drive and equip ourselves with those particular mechanical skills. My sister, Gill, was getting married the following week in Edinburgh, and Stafford and I had promised to give her away, and be best man respectively.

This all helped – to get it written down on paper. We both felt tugged in so many directions, but agreed that it was still a matter for further thought and prayer. As yet, neither of us had felt a clear call nor been shown the way. How does one discern God's will above one's own desires? It is so easy to deceive oneself.

Fortunately for us and those who were staying on and still without a posting, a 'retreat' had been arranged at Hampstead Meeting House, led by Corder and Gwen Catchpool and Joan Mary Fry. The theme was to be: "Christ and the washing of the Disciples' feet." None of us had been informed, other than informally, about our assessments on the course and, as one of the youngest at 25, I had assumed – in fact, already knew inwardly – that I was not mature and experienced enough for leadership of a team. The three leaders of the 'retreat' could not have been better chosen and were models of sympathetic, patient listening and discernment.

It was another lovely spring day. We moved to Kew Gardens for a silent retreat and enjoyed the sounds and scents of the Temperate Glasshouse and the wonders of the Alpine House. On our return, we finished with some recorded music and I shared some of mother's Pearls of Wisdom.

On Sunday, the following day, we joined with Hampstead Meeting Friends and it was decided to have a quiet afternoon, rather than a walk on Hampstead Common. The 'Retreat' ended with a delightful recital from a Dutch pianist on the Catchpool Grand Piano, and hymn singing. We had a good *ad hoc* choir and it was a blessed ending. By the end, both John and I had decided to turn down the India offer.

Sunday, March 24th, was the day the BBC began their first broadcasts in Russian and, on the Monday, course members and staff began to scatter early, some even before breakfast. A few of us went over to the *Bedford* Institute and baled clothes, having returned any that we had picked out or 'borrowed' for the revue and party! We had supper at the Queen Mary Hostel in Hoxton and this was followed by some country dancing arranged and called by Alice Scares and John Pettigrew.

Next day, I caught the train to Birmingham from Euston, having arranged with Dr Eileen Gittins (who had been at the Itarsi Friends Hospital and was my doctor) to pick up a suit for the wedding, which she had, amongst other things, kindly stored for me. On the way, I managed to call in once more at the Woodlands Hospital. I only just caught the next train to York, saw a bit of Bootham School and sent a telegram to Gill.

I could not afford lunch in the dining car on the train next morning up to Edinburgh, but had sandwiches that were not made with peanut butter and *Marmite* for a change! I was met by Gill, who had broken bounds to be there, at Waverley Station. I was taken to the Royal Infirmary to meet Dr Gordon Conacher, Gill's fiancé, and handed over to him. He is a Scottish Presbyterian and his father was a Minister.

I noticed that the crocuses were in full bloom and all was very colourful. Gill then officially left the Royal Infirmary and Gordon had to get leave of absence from Penicuik, where he had just been posted – a half hour bus journey away.

All was panic and confusion next morning. There was no sign of the wedding cake and Stafford had not arrived in time for the wedding rehearsal at St. Giles. This was to be my first church wedding, having previously attended only simple Quaker weddings and consequently was very nervous.

The weather again on Friday was brilliant and I went off early to meet Stafford from the night train and somehow missed him. So I rushed off to call for the wedding cake. Fortunately, it had arrived, so I took it by taxi to the *Chimes Hotel* where the reception was to be held. Only just in time I managed to get back to the church for the 11 o'clock wedding. It was held in the little side chapel with some 30 guests and friends. Gill, in Nahia's (Allen's wife) dress looked beautiful; Gordon and Stafford in full Officers' uniform were extremely handsome. It was a lovely simple, short service without hymns, but with readings and prayers while the couple knelt. Stafford gave Gill away and I passed over the ring without dropping it. Everything went without a hitch and, after the usual photo session, we left for the reception, which could not have been nicer. Everyone, guests included, radiated happiness. After the speeches, and Gill had changed, the couple left for a secret destination, covered in confetti – poured upon them by the hospital nurses and staff.

I had intended to spend the rest of my short leave in Edinburgh, or back in York with friends, but Stafford said he had booked to return on the night train, so I decided to join him. As everyone had suddenly cleared off, I helped to clear up and see to the wedding gifts and I must say I felt somewhat flat and very weary. Perhaps it was the inoculations.

As it happened, I just caught the night train, though there was no sign of Stafford, but I did manage to get a comfortable 3rd Class corner seat and a fair amount of sleep.

Tired and unshaven, I arrived back in time for breakfast at Woodstock, which was eerily bare, cold and quiet. But there was a wonderful, wonderful letter from Daphne awaiting me. The rest of the morning was spent typing a reply and giving a full account of the wedding to my parents in Sohagpur, which my mother kept and eventually returned to me before their death.

Mary Elwell and Constance Madgen were still around, so, in the afternoon, we went for a walk on Hampstead Heath together and had tea out. Back at the hostel, I had to stoke a dead boiler for a bath and then retired early to bed. Coal was still scarce.

That Sunday, the last day in March, was another glorious day and I had overslept – unusual for me. Someone else had stoked or revived the boiler and there was sufficient hot water to wash my clothes and hang them in the garden. There we were able to relax and listen to the pigeons, starlings and sparrows squabbling over nesting materials, and a pair of robins clearly marking out their territory, against the church bells and the subdued traffic noise.

That evening, we went again to Cecil Sharpe[1] House for country dancing and met up with Marianne and a crowd of my Loughborough friends and teachers, including Peter Hamberg and Peter Kennedy, who were at Leighton Park with me. Afterwards, we ended up at the Free German League of Culture for coffee.

It was here that I heard that, while I was away, in London the Metropolitan Police and Ministry of Food Enforcement officers had co-operated in a nation-wide sweep on black marketeers. Lorries, vans and cars were stopped and searched for eggs, meat and poultry, which were flooding the market and fetching more than double their fixed prices when sold 'under the counter'. Some shops and restaurants were also raided. The Enforcement officers had also searched the market stalls and barrow boys in London, where 'coupon-free' clothing flourished. The new nylon stockings were in great demand.

The League of Nations was finally dissolved. What would take its place? Life goes on.

---

[1] The original founder of the English Folk Dancing Society.

Chapter 3

Monday April 1st – I answered an appeal for help from the B.I. to go over and do a day's work baling clothes. It was tough and very dusty, physical work. I was really staggered by some of the clothing offered, which included a fine pair of whalebone corsets – Mae West style! We worked quietly and with short breaks, but I was whacked by the end of the day. I admired those other volunteers working at it day and night, but it was fun and I was able to offer another full day and then another – by which time I had doubled my daily output.

Thursday was another spring day. Daphne rang me up early and I went to meet her at Friends House. We took a tube to Baker Street, walked out to Regent's Park and took a rowing boat onto the lake for an hour, until the hailing call, "Come in No.7, your time is up." It was a blissful time, but all too short, because she had to be back at Friends House. I had lunch alone, feeling rather dead and cut off.

There were still a few about at Woodstock, including Kjell and Magda making last minute preparations for getting off to Germany in their new uniforms and looking rather self-conscious, but we had a sing-song that evening as some of the Mount Waltham people began to move in. The main news on the wireless was all abut the British Cabinet delegation to India, led by Sir Stafford Cripps, which had had talks for several hours the day before with Hindu leaders, Mr Ghandi and Dr Azad, the Congress Party President. The discussion had centred on Ghandi's demand for the establishment of an interim Government for India as soon as possible. That day, the delegation was to meet the Moslem leader, Mr Jinnah, for equally important talks, when the Moslem League was to present its case. India is six or so hours ahead of us in time – so they had probably had the talks and I eagerly awaited the next letter from my parents.

I had struck up a friendship with Bill Eltham at the BI and was attracted by his sense of humour. He had tickets for Max Wall in the Revue, *Make a Date* at the *Duchess Theatre*, which I found hilarious. He was a very funny man – my side ached. Bill took me to the Arts Club for supper and persuaded me to do another morning baling at the BI. That evening, quite a group of us went to Cecil Sharpe House again for square dancing. Mr Kennedy himself was doing the calling.

On the first Sunday in April, I went to Hampstead Meeting and met Richard (Dick) Harman, the Sidcot Senior Master, who was very good to me at Sidcot. He was up in London to see his daughter, 'Bunty', who was here for the FRS Representatives Conference and was a member of the Cologne Team, led by Michael Lee, and where Pat Radley, Daphne's cousin, was also a member. The Catchpool family was there, except for Corder, who had just gone out to Germany. On a quick visit to my Aunt Sylvia, I discovered on talking to Mrs Coates in the opposite flat, that her great friend, Joyce, who was at Bristol University with me, was now Sir Stafford Cripps' Secretary and was with the delegation in India.

Later in the afternoon, I transferred to FRS Hostel, Mount Waltham, 47 Netherhall Gardens, Hampstead, because the Driving and Mechanics course was due to start on the Monday. The bedroom I shared with John Pettigrew and two others was right at the top of this crazy old house, with a wonderful view across that part of London. There were only twelve of us on the course and four FAU instructors and four or five vehicles. The back axle of one of the *Austin* Ambulances had broken, we were told. Our German lessons were to continue, I'm glad to say.

Once we had got our learner's driving licences, our first driving lessons began round Hampstead. Though I was extremely nervous, made many mistakes, grasshopper starts and stalled the engine a good many times, I clocked up about eighteen miles. German classes were held in the garden, which was rather distracting, but made a change.

We soon had to get our hands mucky and learn to service the vehicles in even muckier overalls, as well as taking driving lessons. The classes on mechanics were excellent and we were particularly attracted to the virtues of using 'gunk' liberally before, for example, rushing off to the YMCA for a concert by the Dartington Hall Music Ensemble.

My great friend David Latoff (Webb) – now demobbed and back to dancing with the great Sokolova's daughter, Natasha, sent me tickets for the first night of the Jack Hulbert and Bobby Howes Show, *Here Come the Boys*, in which he is performing. I joined David's father and his wife, Babs Phillips, who was now teaching at the Sadlers Wells Ballet School. We had wonderful seats. It was a grand show, but the first night was not without its problems. The stage was too small and the curtains stuck. Backstage afterwards, we heard all about the problems. It was quite a reunion in David's dressing room, because David Davenport from Covent Garden, another ex-member of the International Ballet Company, came round as well. It was great to smell the grease paint again and, amongst the stars, who were there on the first night was Jack Hulbert's brother, Claude, James Agate, Lupino Lane, Manning Sherwyn and a host of others.

By the middle of April, I was beginning to feel much more confident with the driving, mastering the different gears and double-declutching. I was intrigued by one of our instructors who rolled his own cigarettes and this made me realise how very few of us in the FRS were in fact smokers. There also appeared to be few of us who were concerned with alcohol. At Mount

Waltham, I missed the communal typewriter and all my letters to Daphne and my parents in India had to be written in long-hand, which was a pity, as I soon began to lose my typing skills.

In Germany, 58 Matthausen Concentration Camp guards were sentenced to death and, at the Nuremberg trials, Nazi racial theorist, Alfred Rosenburg was explaining why Jews must be destroyed. In Geneva, the League of Nations was finally dissolved. President Truman in Washington promised to send a million tons of wheat a month to Europe and Asia and, barely a week later at home, our loaves of bread were to be cut by 4ozs and brewing by 15% to save grain. In Palestine, seven British soldiers were killed by Jewish terrorists.

Driving lessons in different vehicles continued each morning and I actually got down to 'decarbonising' the *Bedford* truck in the workshop. But the afternoon was free and I joined up with Biddy (Mabel Weiss) and Conny (Constance Madgen) of our Woodstock Training course for another afternoon at Kew Gardens. We had heard that the blossoms, and particularly the magnolias, were at their peak. Having passed all my RHS (Royal Horticultural Society) Teaching exams at Bristol, where we had our own gardens up at the Royal Fort, I became a Fellow of the RHS and received a free packet of seeds. I was always keen on collecting and growing tree seeds wherever I found myself, but through Jack Hoyland's influence, I was, all through the war, interested in growing vegetables (and keeping rabbits) to supplement our diets, along with any food for free – herbs, berries, roots, salad materials, nuts and fungi. Kew is wonderful any time of the year and, after sitting by the lake and admiring the reflections and a walk to the river and back, we visited Biddy's bed-ridden Aunt nearby. It was here that I learnt that Biddy had been appointed, with some other previous course members, to join the Brunswick team in Germany. I was glad for her.

Each of us in turn had our ups and downs about driving, but our excellent instructors declared that it was quite normal and there was none amongst us without hope! The *Bedford* was stripped down and its 'decarb' progressed painfully slowly. I wondered if we'd ever get all the parts back together again, but it certainly taught us all about engines and went well with the lectures. We learned to listen to the various noises coming from the engines and other parts, correlate where they were coming from and why!

We also had arguments and discussions. One of the first was on choosing or being chosen when and where we might serve. Who knew the best – the selection committee or ourselves? Another was on the black market in Germany. Were we justified in using the barter system and exchanging cigarettes – cheap from the NAAFI – for such things as cameras and watches 'as everyone else did' apparently. Fraternisation with Germans was still illegal. Where did we Quakers and Red Cross workers stand in our relationships while under Military Government regulations?

One day, I drove out onto the North Circular Road for the first time – north towards Mill Hill – quite an adventure and rather 'hairy', but I survived. I was shocked on my return to hear that David Bollam had had an accident with Alec. The car had skidded, turned over and slid along the road for about fifteen yards. We immediately went out in the *Ford* 15cwt truck to tow it back. They were shaken, but not badly hurt and there was not a lot of damage. The towing and hitching was a valuable lesson in itself. When we got back, we heard that John Murphy on the driving course had been chosen to go to Finnmark with the FAU team. We took him to Hampstead Everyman Cinema to celebrate and to see the French classic, *Quai des Brumes*, with Jean Gabin, in French.

When all the driving lesson cars were out of commission for one frustrating reason or another, I continued to work on the *Bedford* and then, with others, went to the fair on Hampstead Heath. It was one seething mass of people, noise, dust and colour. I was amazed to see on what a huge variety of things people were spending their money. Everyone looked so pale and unhealthy and the girls wore masses of make-up. It seemed like a *Vanity Fair* – money being made out of people's vanity, the gambling spirit and greed – things just out of reach and the craving for some sort of thrill, or something new. Shooting skills and imitation coconut shies, skittles and bowling for the pig, gold fish for prizes, strength machines – three goes for 6 pence – darts onto playing cards, four people a minute, 2/- a minute, £6 an hour – and I'm on 14/- a week! Something new – roll up and see! Is it male or female? Six legs, two bodies and one head! Look, the biggest and oldest rat in the world AND the smallest racehorse. Sandra, the wondrous fat, bearded woman. Joan, the pocket Venus dancer – a living contribution to art; the monkey that dresses up; the woman lion-tamer. Shrimps and snails in vinegar, 1/- a saucer! Roundabouts, swings, coloured electric lights; screams from the thrill machines, jazz booming from the loudspeakers, Bing Crosby crooning; Betsy Lee, Fortune Teller, daughter of the great Gypsy Lee, patronised by Royalty and positively no relation to anyone else with that name. In the next tent was Betty Lee – Palmist, granddaughter of the famous Gypsy Lee of Brighton. Jeering and booing from the boxing and wrestling rings and few volunteers; pickpockets about and Bobbies that looked the other way. Plenty of beer. George Fox's dismay sprang to mind and I retreated.

As soon as one of the *Austins* was repaired, we had to go out on a test run. John and I took it out to Mill Hill and, of course, we had our first puncture. Another valuable lesson and a ticking-off. We had not put back the spare tyre or puncture outfit, though we had learned how to change the wheel and tyres and mend punctures earlier on. So we had to abandon the car and return by bus, while the other *Austin* went out with spares.

That Sunday, we went to Hampstead Meeting again, eager to meet Corder Catchpool, home again after a fortnight in Germany, and we were inevitably invited back to lunch. Jean Catchpool and her brother, Neave, were also at home, the latter back from Bootham. I had missed them both while they were at Sidcot, but Jean had been there with my sister, Gill. It was a great time.

That afternoon, with Alec's help, I finally got the *Bedford* going and no bits seemed to have been left out on the benches. But it was clearly not happy. Everyone seemed to be away for the weekend and it was very quiet. There was a much more relaxed atmosphere anyway. The course was well planned, but the leadership was not intrusive and we often responded to the needs of the moment for the group. We took time off if we needed it, or made individual visits and received visitors. We were still a conscientious group when doing the domestic chores, though not the cooking. In spite of generous offers from the women, we did our own laundry and ironing, most of the men having sewing kits. I was glad of my training from The Downs and my parents to knit, darn socks and sew on buttons. John did a hilarious mime – threading a needle and sewing on a button on the wrong side of the garment. We kept pretty fit, with regular PE and country dancing. My leg was making slow, but fair progress and was less of a handicap. It was always interesting to see who were the 'Larks' and who were the 'Owls', especially in the small dormitories and with snoring companions. I was eternally grateful that I could take 'cat-naps' anywhere, at any time – a wartime habit and I seemed to have acquired a good in-built time clock.

Another evening's discussion with John M., Alice and George centred around Conscientious Objection, Violence and Force and Killing – animal, vegetable, making compromises and allowances, different customs, cultures and religions, rights and wrongs and should we be so judgmental of one another. I learned how prejudiced I was about Americans, or rather American tourists and films. I make an exception of Bob Hope. Now, there was a really funny man with impeccable timing.

Back to driving again and I had my first go in one of the *Bedford* trucks. It was very different and certainly much more difficult and clumsy. Having listened to it, I got back to work on the other one, took it out and made further adjustments until it was working perfectly. With Dick, I drove it down to the laundry where our linen was washed and he was satisfied.

A letter from Dad, in answer to one of my questions about the famine in India, said that he thought it was largely a put-up job by the press and was not bad in the Central Provinces at least.

At the end of April, it was raining and I was very discouraged working hard on decarbonising the other *Bedford* that I thought didn't really need it. But the frustration wore off when Bill Eltham took me out to the *Garrick Theatre* to see Beatrice Lillie's revue *Better Late*, which was brilliant and, afterwards, to a rather posh restaurant. We got into conversation with two amusing women, one of whom introduced herself as Miss Prichard and spoke Polish. I think she had had a good few glasses of wine, but she insisted on giving us the address of her bosom friend in Warsaw in case we might be attached to one of the Polish Relief teams. That was also the day when Magda Kelber's German team left for Solingen with Kjell.

At the weekend, I had Brian Taylor as my instructor in the 10-ton lorry and got on better. That Saturday evening, I had been given guest tickets to Covent Garden to see the Sadlers Wells production of *Nocturne, Les Patineurs* and *Dante Sonata* – a marvellous programme. I took Morna Smith, Alice and Conny with me. Harold Turner was at his best in *Patineur,* and, afterwards, I went backstage to see him and enquired after David Latoff. Harold said he was, rather sadly, reduced to one of the chorus now. I also met up with my older partner, Anne Negus – still such fun. Harold and Gerd Larsen took me home in their car. That evening late, Bernard Hayman, a cousin of Daphne's, who was a great friend of mine throughout our schooldays, rang up and wondered if we could meet. He's absolutely mad and single-minded about yachts. Not my line, but I went out to lunch and tea the following day – a Sunday – at his home and met Linda, his wife. I had a really wonderful time romping with their three adorable kids, Peter, Susan and Alan. They had a lovely house in East Finchley and the children were very excited when we found a blackbird's nest in the garden. I helped to bath them when they went to bed and we squirted water everywhere with rubber ducks. Afterwards, we sang some songs together – but Bernard had to go back to Newcastle. Apparently, Dick Steele and his wife live with them, but I was not aware of this, though he was one of our instructors.

It was back to intensive driving lessons on Monday in the *Austin* with Brian Taylor. I had two lessons. In a total of four hours, I covered 62 miles – four times across London to Wimbledon and back. This was very good practice because it was raining practically the whole time and the roads were very slippery. I grazed the back mudguard of a *Vauxhall* at Swiss Cottage, but otherwise escaped – it was a narrow squeak. I had no driving on the following day because I had to work on the *Bedford* truck to get it ready for convoy practice. By 10 p.m., I managed at last to get it going satisfactorily, but thought I would never make a good transport officer.

On May 1st, there was a whole-day trip in our convoy of two *Bedfords* and the two *Austins* to Luton, but, before we got there, we stopped for a picnic lunch (with the inevitable peanut butter and *Marmite* sandwiches) in delightful countryside. It was really refreshing to be out in the country again amongst the flowers and fresh green grass and to hear the birdsong.

The afternoon proved a very tiring one, but absorbingly interesting as we were taken round the *Vauxhall* motor works and talked with the workers on the production lines. The Company gave us a bumper tea, after which the convoy started back. I drove one of the *Bedfords* all the way.

In the evening paper, it was announced that Penicillin, the new wonder-drug and anti-biotic, would soon be freely available. But the main news indicated that fresh unrest was expected in the Holy Land, following the publication of the joint Anglo-US report on Palestine, which offended both Arabs and Jews. It recommended that the present British Mandate should continue 'until Arab-Jewish hostility disappeared', the goal being U.N. trusteeship.

Totally unexpected, 'Half Term exams' were sprung upon us. John Pettigrew came out top with 53% and I followed with 50% – rather low marks we thought and much room for improvement. "Imagine it," I wrote to Daphne, "I thought I had finished with exams for good. The instructors made some scathing remarks about Biology teachers knowing all about the insides of frogs, but nothing about the insides of a lorry! John and I were the only two on the course that had never driven a car, let alone a lorry before, and the only two to be allowed to take one out on our own. They seem fairly pleased with us, however, and with the fact that I had successfully decarbonised the two *Bedford* trucks with a little help, and which now ran extremely well, considering the treatment they get!"

A letter arrived from Münster in Germany from Toni Althaus, which from the postmark, I saw had taken a month and had been opened by the censor. Toni was one of the German *au pair* girls we had at Fox Hill Close. She was cautious in describing the conditions she was living under and the bomb damage, but had got an interpreter's job with Military Government, which carried a number of perks with it. Was there a chance of seeing me?

Saturday morning always seemed the best opportunity for doing the chores and, after a morning's scrubbing, Morna Smith, Winnie Wood and I took the afternoon off to go to Covent Garden again, as I was still able to get complimentary tickets with my Equity Card for myself and my friends. It was a fine matinee performance of *The Sleeping Beauty* by the Sadlers Wells, and the orchestra, too, was in fine form. I went round backstage afterwards to see David Davenport again, but it was so crowded. They were entertaining the members of the Champs Elyseé Ballet Company. So I withdrew and went round to have tea with David Latoff at the Saville Theatre. I did not stay for the evening performance, but met David again after the show and had supper with him and Natasha Sokolova at the restaurant opposite the theatre, much frequented by the theatrical fraternity. Frederick Ashton also came in for a meal and David introduced me when he joined us.

Ashton, now at the peak of his career as a choreographer, was originally schooled by Marie Rambert, as was Harold Turner. He spent his youth in South America and was educated at a Public School as I was, so it was particularly interesting to hear how he got on. He told me how he got started dancing by taking a lesson each week with the great Massine and then joined Ida Rubenstein's company. But really, he was a pupil of Marie Rambert, who had recognised his potential and given him the discipline and guidance he needed, and then the opportunity to perform. It was at the *Lyric Theatre*,

Hammersmith, that Ashton had made his début as a choreographer. Just when Pavlova had seen and admired his talent and was about to engage him in 1931, tragically she died. Ashton described the hard struggle he had had rather too late (as in my case) to learn dancing and to become a virtuoso. But Haskell described him as a competent and interesting dancer. He had also come under the influence of Bronislava Nijinski, a former dancer (with my teacher Idzikovski) in the Diaghileff Ballet, and Nijinski's sister. Haskell describes Nijinski[1] as "the only ugly dancer to find fame" and "the only successful woman choreographer in history; one who understood the systematic development of the male dancer." But, for me, Ashton had first appealed for his ballet *Façade*, with music by William Walton[2] and performed by the Sadlers Wells every season. *Façade* is a burlesque, with typically English characteristics and brilliant caricatures. This is why *Les Patineurs* also appealed so much, in which Harold Turner was the star and technically so exciting, like the Ice Ballets. Ashton was also the very opposite of Ninette de Valois, the other English choreographer, and so they made a wonderful partnership at the Wells. Both also had their empathic relationship with the conductor, Constant Lambert, who understood the relationship between ballet and music better than anyone else, and rather more so than his associate conductor, Julian Clifford, who was our conductor for the London Season at the *Lyric Theatre*.

For me, this was all like a flash-back in the life I had left five years previously, at the height of that London season in Shaftesbury Avenue. It was well past my normal bedtime these days. David took me back to his charming flat in Holland Park and we reminisced and gossiped until 2.30 a.m. before finally bedding down.

As it was Sunday, we had a glorious lie-in and finally David cooked some breakfast and made hot coffee. Though in time for lunch on arrival back at the hostel, I was not hungry and still emerging from a ballet fantasy world of which I was no longer a part. So I had a quiet afternoon reading and writing letters and slowly coming back to earth.

Once again, it was back to the grind on Monday, but it was an invigorating morning. I went out for a long driving lesson with Brian into the country around Barnet. Later that afternoon, I drove the breakdown van out to rescue Liz and Brian, who had become stranded without petrol. On our return, I found a note from Morna Smith, to say that she had been appointed to the FRS team in Dortmund. Another one settled.

To my great joy, I was allowed to drive solo in the 10-ton lorry on the next day. So I took Morna with me and drove 20-odd miles out in the now-familiar Mill Hill direction and brought her back to Haddo House, where we had supper with Conny, Biddy and Idwal Harry. We ended the day with a 'flick',

---

[1] Haskell – Balleto Mania – *Gollancz* 1934.

[2] Walton was also a CO.

Swiss Family Robinson. Amazing how all their needs were miraculously provided and near at hand! We preferred the book of childhood days.

I slipped back into the ballet world, however, for lunch the following day, with David Davenport, now with the Vic Wells Ballet, at an Italian restaurant, frequented by dancers and others from Covent Garden. He introduced me to another member of the company, Jean Beddels, who had her Pekinese pup with her. To my surprise, Michael Yates was also there – another Old Downian of my time, now production manager at Covent Garden, and a beloved friend of W.H. Auden.

By now, our driving training in the big lorry at Gordon House included manoeuvring between spaced bricks and parking, which was challenging. The classic FAU tale was told, after I had gently bumped a hidden, low brick wall, how, on one driving course, the FAU instructor had shouted to his learner-driver: "A little bit further, little bit further – come on, a little bit further. Too far!" Luckily for me, there was no sign of damage to the wall or the vehicle, but eyebrows were raised. In the German class, we were encouraged to visit the *Everyman Theatre* again, to see the film, *Maskerade*, in German. It certainly helped because I was able to understand quite a lot.

In early May, the rhododendrons at the bottom of Mount Waltham garden were beginning to come out and the Copper Beech trees were colouring beautifully. The scent from the lilies of the valley was heady. I picked a bunch and took them over to my Aunt Sylvia in her top-floor flat and begged a bath. She was as delighted with the lilies as I was to wallow in a good hot bath. She has promised to leave me, in her Will, an antique dressing table mirror, with a drawer, and a First Edition of A.A. Milne's *Now We Were Six*. She had forgotten that she had already given me the latter for a Christmas present in 1927, but I was pleased about the mirror – "for when you get married" – and I was glad to be considered her 'favourite' nephew.

Next day, I was given an assignment to drive across London to the Fulham Road in the huge *Bedford* on my own and pick up a spare part, or something, from a certain address. It was showery and the traffic – mainly buses and taxi cabs – made me nervous. However, all went reasonably well and I found the address down a narrow side street, which fortunately did not necessitate turning the lorry round (or backing). On the way back, I was humming a nervous little tune as I approached Marble Arch and attempted to get into the right lane. Having been unable to get off at the right turning because of the horrendous tooting and tight gaps that the taxi cabbies were giving me, I had to go round again. Suddenly the engine coughed and stalled. Clutching the crank shaft, I jumped out of the cab and tried to start the engine, crimson with embarrassment and from the effort of cranking. The bus drivers seemed less concerned than the taxi drivers, who shouted and yelled a veritable torrent of abuse, with cracks, advice and ribald comments. The engine showed no signs of life and I had panic thoughts of a hernia.

"Run out of gas?" shouted a passing cabby.

Now there's a thought, it struck me while I was wanting to give the truck a hefty kick for conking out just there, of all places. So, I ran round to the back and removed the jerry-can of petrol and poured some into the tank, which certainly sounded pretty empty when I gave it a tap. I started to wind the heavy crank handle again – thankful that I had at least remembered to put the gears into neutral. I knew it would take time to pump the petrol through and it did. Then suddenly there was a spark of response and, finally, it spluttered into life again. It was only just ticking over, so I dashed back into the cab and began to pump the accelerator gently, though it was hard to hear anything above the traffic noise. Having passed the turning up Edgware Road, I was aiming to drive along Oxford Street, then turn left into Baker Street. My knees were shaking, but, by using the indicator, mirror and horn, and being a large vehicle, I was able to creep into the left lane and get out of it. No further incident occurred and I arrived back in one piece, happy to have carried out my first solo assignment and the lessons learned from the experience.

It was John's turn in the afternoon – though with the *Fordson.* He decided to take Brian and myself out to his home in Welwyn Garden City. It was my first visit to Welwyn and a lovely place, larger and more spacious than Bournville, it seemed; a warm welcome awaited us in his home.

For no reason that we could tell, there was a pep talk from Alec next morning, in which he informed us that it cost £5 10s a week to keep each of us there. I forget the reason for this – perhaps we had failed to sign out, or sign in, or something. In any case, I had been invited (and signed out) that Saturday morning to go out for lunch, to Morna Smith's home in East Croydon. We had planned to go to The Oval to see the Indian Test team v Surrey. The Indians' last wicket stand of 190 was very entertaining, to the frustration of the Surrey bowlers. We joined Jimmy Brown, the oboist (an old Sidcotian from the same form as Daphne), for supper at the *Shanghai Restaurant* – going 'Dutch'. On our return to base, we learned that Diana, Conny and Albert had been appointed to the new Poland FRS Team.

The evening news was full of facts and figures of the nearly 50,000 Service divorce cases still outstanding in the Courts. Hartley Shawcross, the Attorney-General, had announced the immediate appointment of 35 legal teams to deal with this major social problem, because the cases involved around 80,000 men and women, as well as many of their children, many of whom were having to wait at least three years to have their lives sorted out. This was a poignant reminder for me, since my brother, Allen, after the British retreat from Dunkirk, found his wife was pregnant by another man and had left. Allen got his divorce and had remarried Nahia, a Lebanese girl from Beirut. He had returned to his old job at *Cadena* in Bristol after being demobbed. I knew also of several other families that had been disrupted in this way and, in many ways, it was a repetition of what happened during and after the First World War.

By this time, both John and I were feeling a bit low, though he was more convinced than I was that he had made the right decision not to serve in India. Monday morning was on us again and Brian went with me for my first go in the powerful *Fordson*. I did some 35 miles in the Hatfield and Watford direction. That evening, I went to Molly Lake's Ballet Company performance at the *Embassy Theatre* and was unimpressed. However, I went backstage to chat with Angela Bayley, who had joined this company from the International, and who was delighted to see me.

Back at the hostel, there was a message that I was wanted for an interview at Friends House the following afternoon. So, after another driving lesson on the Bedford in the morning, I left for the interview, along with Kathleen Gough, a teacher eight years older than myself, who spoke fluent German and a little Russian. The interview with Amy Lewis, the overseas Personnel Secretary, and Geoffrey Smith, did not last long. As soon as it was over, I rushed out of Friends House to the Post Office next door and for 6d bought an airletter and wrote the following on May 13th, in time to catch the post:

"Dear Mum and Dad,

Three days after my rather depressed letter to you, I now have wonderful news as I really think I have been given the pick of <u>all</u> places to go to. I have been asked if I would be willing to go to Berlin! At the interview today, I was told that a small FRS team is being selected to join the Berlin FAU team, which has been there since August 1945 and we will be expected to take over from them because the FAU are pulling out. The only other person from our Driving course is Kathleen Gough – she will probably be our team leader – and would be grand to work with. Of course we both accepted at once. Two others have also been selected: Edith Snellgrove (36), the Leader of the FRS team in Walcharen in Holland, another fluent German speaker, who had been on a previous FRS course, and Margaret Watts, an Australian Friend in her middle fifties, a former relief worker after the First World War. Those FAU members, who wish to remain in Berlin, will become members of the FRS team until their term of service ends. I do feel it is a great honour to be the first man-Quaker from FRS to get to Berlin.

At the interview, Amy Lewis and Geoffrey Smith told us quite frankly we were picked not for team work, but as individuals with strong personalities and particularly for possessing the necessary tact to handle the touchy and delicate situations with which we will be confronted, and be able to get on with anybody. Apparently, we are very lucky to be allowed into Berlin. It is a very complex and tricky situation there to work under the four Powers in four different sectors. Our work is to be general welfare work with the Germans, but with a special emphasis on Youth organisations, besides making personal contacts and working with the German Quaker group there. Perhaps Corder has had something to do with this. There will also be a continuation of the distribution of clothes, food, Red Cross Relief supplies and some work under the Public Health Department with Displaced Persons (DPs). We shall be working under the Education and Religious Affairs Department of the Military Government, as well as 'under the Red Cross' umbrella. We would also be under the close eye of the Russians. We will have to work towards a closer understanding and cooperation between the existing Communist, former Nazi and Christian groups and organisations – together with different loyalties that exist in the minds of the young people, including those as yet untouched or unattached to any Youth activities. The FAU have already established good relationships and connections with the Churches and it will be our brief to build on these.

I am to get leave from June 1st and assemble at Gordon House, 159 Highgate Road, NW5, from June 11th to 25th, to get my kit and equipment ready for a target date of sailing on June 25th.

While in Friends House, I saw Amy Montford and told her, and I happened to meet Marjorie Sykes, who had just met you in Delhi, before flying back on the 'plane with 'Unity', the famous Panda for the London Zoo!

I am expected to attend Yearly Meeting on the 22nd and shall meet Hans Albrecht (Clerk of the German Y. M.), who will be there. John Pettigrew was interviewed on the same day and was appointed to do Youth work with the Cologne team, Phyllis Reith and Barbara Whitaker to South France to work with Spanish refugees. So I am very pleased, very happy and very grateful for this wonderful opportunity. An answer to prayer?"

And, as soon as I got back to Mount Waltham, I sent off a long letter to Daphne, in her last term at Sidcot, to share in my joy and happiness, which was taking time to sink in. My immediate reaction was to go over to see Corder and Gwen Catchpool and get their advice and contacts. I was also determined to try and make my German more fluent by working at Magda Kelber's excellent books – particularly her *Heute Abend*! But I was sad for those few folks still left in suspense, who had not heard. I now had to plan what to do with my embarkation leave.

But I had to put all this out of my mind the next day because, in a convoy of five vehicles, of which I drove one; we had to go to the *Ford* factory at Dagenham. The truck was mis-firing and not behaving well, so I had to try to signal to the others as instructed – as well as to Brian, who was guiding us on his motorbike and worrying about like a sheepdog. We stopped off in Epping Forest at a convenient spot for lunch and to make adjustments to the engine.

It was a simple matter, of course, John realised that he had not pushed the choke back in! It was no trouble after that. The life was eased out of us for that.

It was a lovely grassy, green spot, with the smell of the earth, and we watched a greater spotted woodpecker for a time and then took a PT class. John and I showed off a bit with a few handstands and handsprings.

I had found the *Vauxhall* factory at Luton very tiring and incredibly noisy, but Dagenham was on a much bigger scale, very impressive and far more interesting. We saw the great power house, the gas works and blast furnaces for smelting. There were huge men pouring the white-hot molten metal into moulds; pouring with sweat whilst breathing in (without masks) all the foul fumes and dust around. It was so hot and thick that it made me feel quite sick being in there for ten minutes. How long could these men last, I wondered? Gradually, all the various vehicle parts were being assembled together on moving lines.

Walter drove back with me after the visit, but now the steering got worse and we had less and less power from the engine. So we stopped, rather anxious that we were no longer in convoy, and let No.67 cool down for half an hour. Even then, we only just got back 'home', with the throttle pedal flat on the floor all the way. It was a great day and we all got safely back.

The main item of news from the wireless that evening, as far as I was concerned, was that Prime Minister Atlee had announced the plans for an independent and united India, but we were off to bed early, prepared to be up and ready at the crack of dawn, for another assignment. We had to get the *Fordson* and No.68 lorry ready to drive to Haddo House to pick up a lorry-load of bales of clothing. As this was our first chance to drive a lorry with a full load, we jumped at it. Once loaded by 8.30, John, Albert, David, Alec and I then drove on to Tilbury Docks and arrived at what we thought must be the dockers' lunchtime. Everyone seemed to have knocked off, so we had time to explore the Docks. I was particularly interested to discover the liners *Strathmore* and *Strathaird*, and the latter casting off, sailing and being pulled out by the busy little tugs. This brought back memories of my childhood days in India, because we had used these steamships ourselves. Sure enough, on enquiry, the *Strathaird* was just off to India. The mail takes at least three weeks 'overland' that way. Perhaps one of my letters was aboard.

The dockers would not allow us to unload the huge FRS bales, sewn up in hessian and I was particularly interested in their comments and general badinage as we stood by and watched. One looked me in the eye with a serious face and said: "More clothes for the poor fuckin' Germans, I suppose, <u>and</u> fuckin' food. Those fuckin' warehouses are full of the fuckin' stuff."

We could see that, and that it included some with Quaker stars labelled for Hamburg. Thankfully, they did unload the truck and we started to drive back through the docks, realising we were lucky because there <u>was</u> a partial strike.

It was Saturday again and we were confronted with an 'End of Term' exam. This time, with 47%, I did not do very well, but there were no comments and we did not see our reports. That evening, I pushed off to see Molly Lake's Ballet Company perform *Les Sylphides*, which I really enjoyed and afterwards slipped round backstage to see Angela for a natter. I was introduced to a very pleasant friend of Angela's – Marcia – and took her out for a coffee. She invited me to join her on the next day, because she wanted to go to a concert at the Albert Hall. It turned out to be a lovely sunny afternoon, so we changed our minds about the matinee concert and started to walk through Hyde Park, which was fresh and green, until we came to 'Speakers' Corner' and joined the various groups around there, to listen. Most of the time, we were attracted to hear Donald Soper, with his brilliant wit and lashing tongue, as he answered his hecklers, many of whom he obviously knew. I appreciated his pacifist views, but I don't think Marcia did. So we got a cup of tea from a stall and strolled off to see the tulips in Regent's Park, a gift from the Dutch Government, as a token of their appreciation for what Britain did for them in the War.

Back at the Albert Hall, we got seats (which Marcia paid for) for the evening's concert without difficulty and heard Telemanyi, the Hungarian violinist, playing the Beethoven Violin Concerto, and a Mozart Symphony, which we both enjoyed. Marcia had arranged to meet a crowd of her friends at a Chinese restaurant afterwards and invited me to go along with her, as she had no partner.

The driving course had not finished yet, so it was back to work on Monday. I had to take the *Fordson* out manoeuvring all afternoon, round certain pot-holey roads in Hampstead. In the evening, there was an excellent talk from David Hughes on a transport officer's work in a German team.

I had to drive over to the FAU hostel in the *Fordson* on the following day and drove up Oxford Street to Marble Arch (without trouble) and Hyde Park Corner to the Albert Hall again, with money in my pocket to buy tickets for the Menuhin Concert. Bill Eltham, keen as ever on revues and shows in the West End, took me to *Sweetest and Lowest.* It was not a good show, but I saw from the programme that Barbara Barrie and Rex Reid, who were with me in the International Ballet, were now in this show, but did not get backstage to see them.

By now, the Yearly Meeting of the Society was gathering together at Friends House and a couple of us went to the Swarthmore Lecture by John Hoare, the subject of which was 'The Warrant for Youth's Search'. I could not afford to buy the book on sale immediately after the lecture, which I found challenging – though rather hard to keep awake! But it was grand to meet up with old friends, and especially Younger Friends of my generation, including George Gorman, Ted Milligan, and Mary Hooper, who spoke to me.

The Thursday sessions were the ones I particularly wanted to attend. For the Friends Service Council, Carl Heath spoke on the worldwide work and service of Friends, which included the latest developments in India. It was especially interesting to hear of the diplomatic service of Horace Alexander, Ranjit Chetsingh and Agatha Harrison in India, helping both the Cabinet Mission and the Indian Leaders with the negotiations – acting as intermediaries. Carl Heath gave his talk under four main headings, which I recounted in a letter to my parents: (1) The Evangelical purpose – that cares for individuals, (2) Relief Work, (3) Going as servants and learners and not as authority, and (4) Participation in Politics as part of the politics of the Kingdom of God.

Roger Wilson spoke on Germany in the evening and appealed for more volunteers for FRS. The Junior Yearly Meeting was on at the same time and there were a number of scholars from some of the Friends Schools, including Sidcot. I was sad that Daphne was not included because of exams. Amongst those I did recognise were Dudley Barlow and Pat Thorne. I learned that Dudley was training with the FAU, with the two from our course who were going to Finnmark. Dick Harman was in charge of the Sidcot group and he invited me down to Sidcot at Whitsun to play for the Old Boys' Cricket team. I hoped it would be a chance to see Daphne again.

In the session on 'Peace and Conscription', there was an interesting discussion, but it produced a statement that I thought was woolly, negative and not nearly strong enough – and I said so, hoping for something more attractive and constructive instead. Bevan Whitney immediately supported me in this, but, because of the time factor, the meeting was adjourned to the next session. In the interval, I was fortunate enough to meet Hans Albrecht – the Clerk of Berlin Monthly Meeting and Germany Yearly Meeting, I believe. We fixed up to meet later, as he was only there for a short visit.

The Education session was also a very interesting one for me because it was an address by 'The Duke' – my old Headmaster at Leighton Park – Edgar Castle, and also by Kenneth Barnes, the Head of Wennington School.

Margaret Watts was also there and we met after the Education session, which was good because we would be working together in Berlin. She was charming and friendly and immediately remarked, "Oh Hugh, did you know we are distant cousins? My maiden name was Thorpe!" So we got on like a house on fire. She explained that she would not be coming with us to Berlin, because she was on the next training course at Woodstock and had not had her inoculations yet. Also, she would not be taking the driving course because Mount Waltham was closing down; I had been on the last FAU driving course there. I told Margaret I had become very fond of the place, especially the garden, which had grown wild and was full of cow-parsley, clover, ox-eye daisies and ragged robin, so that, on all the tables, there were jam jars full of them about the place. I also discovered a robin's nest in the ivy, which everyone wanted to see. The bird sat tight on every occasion, with its little beady eyes unflinching from the frequent invasion of its privacy.

I was surprised at the number of people who, hearing that I was going to Berlin, gave me addresses and names of contacts there, begging me to take letters, parcels and other things for them. I also had invitations to visit Woodbrooke and other people in Birmingham on my embarkation leave.

Victor Gollancz[1] had written a letter, published in the *News Chronicle* and the *New Statesman*, to which I responded, asking if I could help. On my return to Mount Waltham, there was a very friendly response from him, in which he affirmed that I could help and a request that when I got to Berlin, would I keep him informed of our work, as well as the state of affairs out there. Corder Catchpool promised similarly and I knew that he, Vera Brittain and Victor Gollancz were all in close touch.

At the Young Friends Meeting, George Gorman asked me to step in for someone who had dropped out and talk for fifteen minutes on 'what Quakerism means to me'. The Small Meeting House was packed with Young friends between the ages of 18-35, one or two elderly Friends and a good sprinkling of Old Sidcotians. I was told it was good practice for Germany, where I was bound to get a lot of requests to do the same thing – and probably in German!

All FRS and FAU members still around, and as many Staff as we could find, were invited to a farewell party at Mount Waltham towards the end of May, which John and I organised along similar lines to the Woodstock parties. We warmed up with a few silly games and, after a snack, had a dance cabaret. The new rage in dancing from America just now was the 'Jitterbug', but it hadn't caught on amongst our lot yet. John and I put on a couple of acts, one of which was a wrestling match entitled: 'Unarmed combat for Quaker Relief Workers, needing the aid of the Friends Ambulance Unit'. This involved pulling each other's hair, noses, ears, neck and toes out – and anything else handy – with suitable grunts, groans and grimaces, eventually knocking out the referee. We climbed out of the ropes and up onto the balcony that ran round the huge central hall, switched off all the lights for a blackout and, while John disappeared down the back stairs, I threw a dummy body into the hall with a blood-curdling scream. When the lights were turned back on, John was seen to be lying dead on the floor with my foot firmly planted on his chest in victory.

The other sketch, on the spur of the moment, was of John giving one of the girls a driving lesson. Again, with a wig and some 'drag' clothing, I was the girl. Both sketches went off well, but we were too exhausted for any encores!

An FAU member read out an Army 'Red Tape Glossary', which was in current circulation and is worth recording here, because, as he said, we're bound to come across it in the field:

---

[1] The publisher in the 'Save Europe Now' Movement with Vera Brittain.

"Under consideration" – Never heard of it.
"Under active consideration" – Will have a shot of finding that file.
"Has received careful consideration" – A period of inactivity covering a time lag.
"Have you any comment?" – Give me some idea of what it's all about.
"You will remember" – You have forgotten, or never knew because I don't.
"Transmitted to you" – You hold the baby for a while, I'm tired of it.
"Concur generally" – Haven't read the document and don't want to be bound by anything I say.
"In conference" – Gone out – I don't know where he is.
"Kindly expedite reply" – For Heaven's sake, try to find the papers.
"Passed to higher authority" – Pigeon-holed in a more sumptuous office.
"Please take appropriate action" – Do you know what to do with it? We don't.
"Filed" – Permanently dislocated.

It can be seen from all this, as I wrote in my letters, that Relief Workers were not serious all the time!

But we had by no means finished yet. Monday was spent getting all the vehicles ready and serviced for a 'long trip' the next day, somewhere on the Southeast Coast, starting at 7 a.m.

Immediately after breakfast, at 6 a.m., we were given our sealed orders and told not to open them until we arrived at a certain place. The five vehicles were to proceed by different routes and meet up at a certain spot, Bramber in Brighton, at 12 noon. We each had a task to carry out on the vehicle on the way. In our case, this was to overhaul and check the entire fuel system with the engine cold. Promptly at 7 a.m., we all set off. I was allocated the *Fordson* with John as a co-driver and a couple of passengers. The weather was mixed, with showers of light rain and bright intervals. We had a good run, completed that task at coffee break and enjoyed the lovely woods we passed through, with the rhododendrons in full bloom.

John took over for the last 30 miles and I the map reading. We got lost at one point and then suddenly saw one of our lorries go past along the main road we were approaching, with one of the cars behind it carrying all the instructors. We would have been penalised if they had seen us, but, fortunately, they did not. Rather to our surprise, we were the first to arrive, only one minute late. The two lorries arrived twelve minutes late and "EXB" with the three girls arrived, after engine trouble, 90 minutes late, to the boos and cheers of the rest of us – ravenous for the picnic lunch. A wonderful, sunny and breezy afternoon was spent on Brighton beach and the front, with a stick of Brighton rock. I had to go to the *Brighton Hippodrome* to see what was on, because this was the theatre where I first performed in *Swan Lake* with Mona Inglesby's International Ballet Company in 1941. John Murphy and I ended up with an 18-hole putting match. I had longed to have another go on the ice rink, where I had spent many happy hours and learned to skate when staying with my cousin, John Allen, on the farm at Henfield, outside Brighton, but there wasn't time.

At 5.30, we started back in convoy, much refreshed and elated. The sea breezes had blown away the fumes from the lorry exhaust and we were eager to get home. But the route turned out to be rather different from what we expected. Brian, on a motorbike, led us off onto a cart track right to the top of the South Downs. The track was so steep it meant we had to double-declutch through the gears right down to 1st gear, which produced quite a bit of 'angst' and excruciating grinding noises! At the top, we stopped to change drivers and admire the tremendous view across the rolling green and chalky slopes down to the sea.

The girls took over and slowly and cautiously, in low gear, we crawled downhill and back to the main London to Brighton road. As the traffic of outer London increased, we were asked to take over. Half the skill, we found, was to judge the traffic lights ahead, so that the whole convoy of six vehicles could cross together and not get left behind; or, if they did, to let them catch up by careful use of the mirrors and signalling from tail to nose. We got back just before lighting-up time, weary, but elated. Dick, the boss, was very complimentary and said that it was the best bit of convoy work he had seen on any course, which pleased us, because we had rather got the impression that we were a dud lot.

All the vehicles had to be thoroughly cleaned the next morning and left absolutely spick and span for inspection. A wireless was on in the workshop, and while we were working away and asking each other questions for the tests on Friday, we heard the announcer telling us that, as the western nations were mobilising against the threat of world famine, the British Government was preparing to ration bread for the first time. John Strachey, the new Food Minister, told the Commons that a decision to ration would be an assurance of 'security for our daily bread'. Supplies of butter and other fats were also threatened. The peacetime loaf, already darker than the wartime 'Victory-bread', the announcer informed us, would be rationed on the basis of energy consumed. The workers in heavy industry would get more than clerical workers and others using less physical effort.

That evening, Brian, Albert, John and I drove down to the Land Girls' hostel again for a social – games and dancing. For the first time, we tried out the 'Jitterbug'.

Sure enough, on the last day of May, a Friday, we had our final driving test. Much to my surprise, I came out top with a B1 grade. John and Albert also achieved B1s, Walter a B2. Mary and Di got C1s; Alice C2 and poor old Liz, a

C3. I blushed when Dick said that they had wanted to give me an A for 'an almost faultless performance (to the loud hoots and guffaws from my colleagues), but went on to say that they could not do so, as an A grade is only awarded after 18 months of lorries the size of buses. Personally, I was far from satisfied – it had been raining and I thought I had made too many mistakes. I also commented on the course and said I was just sorry that we had had no practice in real winter conditions, or with skidding – apart from theory. We all gave a big vote of thanks to our patient and long-suffering instructors, all about to end their service. It was indeed, we felt, a right good course. We had prepared a number of ash trays out of old piston heads as souvenirs of the course and to present to the few smokers, or to leave about in the hostel, instead of the old scallop shells. The evening was rounded off by a visit to the *Everyman Theatre* to see *Le Roi S'amuse.* In my pocket was my report for German, also top, but thankfully not publicly announced: "Has made great progress by hard work and native wit," whatever that meant. Since the course cost the FRS £6 a week for each of us, I hoped I had justified the cost, though paying myself.

Chapter 4

On Saturday June 2nd, the course finished. A few of us went off in 'CLL' and 'EXR', as we refer to them, to see Morna Smith off to Dortmund – very smart in her Quaker grey uniform and red and black star badges. On the way, I ran out of petrol, but fortunately there was some in a spare can.

Feeling gloriously free and independent, I went to help Linda Hayman with Peter's birthday party, to which a group of about a dozen five-year olds had been invited. It was a wonderful house for games and 'hide and seek', and Linda put on an amazing spread, but was short of milk.

"The milkmen are on strike," she said, "and are demanding a weekly wage of £5.4s.6d.

For a present, I had taken Peter a delightful little book called *Peter the Dragon*, that I had picked up in the Friends House Book Shop. Linda was mad with Bernard, who was absent. Apparently, he had joined a Repertory Company.

Marcia knew it was my birthday on the following day and that I had promised to spend it with my Aunt Sylvia, so she had arranged to take me with a group of her friends to see the 'Ziegfield Follies'. Very impressive and, for once, I knew no one in the cast, but that did not spoil a wonderful evening.

On the Sunday morning of my 26th birthday, as there were only a few of us left, I got up, made breakfast and went to Hampstead Meeting with the hope of seeing the Catchpools, but without success. I had then to cross London, via various bus routes out to Aunt Sylvia's flat for lunch, a quiet afternoon writing letters and tea. Again a hot bath was sheer luxury. After supper, I returned once more to Woodstock to welcome the twenty new members of the XIth Training course. They seemed a very nice lot and much the same age as our group, though with fewer teachers and one or two hospital-almoners and nurses. It was another chance to chat with my cousin, Margaret Watts. I discovered that, during the First World War, while Friends in England and Australia were very concerned about the trials and tribulations of Conscientious Objectors in Australia and New Zealand, Margaret was working with Arthur Watts, who at the time was Secretary of the Australian Freedom League[1], which was helping the COs. They got married and, in 1918, came to London when Arthur became Secretary of the Friends Service Committee, the specially instituted wartime committee of Young Quakers of Military Age, and he was one of the defendants in the Guildhall trial of 1918. After the War,

---

[1] O.G. Vol.1 p.167.

Arthur was a leader in Russian Famine Relief and they went out to Russia together. Margaret was reticent about what happened there and her experiences. She simply said that Arthur fell in love with Russia and Communism and out of love with her and she had to divorce him. Arthur stayed on in Russia for the rest of his life, as an engineer under the Soviet Government. Margaret had returned to Sydney, Australia and worked in Social Welfare.

Another member of the course was Nell Lunnen, who was at Sidcot with my sister, and it was good to meet up with her too.

I started off early on Monday morning towards Hendon. It was a windy, but glorious day and I started to thumb lifts in the direction of Birmingham. By 9.15, I was lucky enough to hitch a number of short lifts, one of which was from an RAF Officer on his way to pick up his demob suit. We entered into a long argument about the black market in Germany. He thought the black market in food ought to be stopped, but that cigarettes should be used to swap for luxury goods, such as cameras, binoculars and watches, as it was the only way for the ordinary persons to get reparations out of the enemy! He was not in the least prepared to consider the moral issues that we had discussed on the training course, or that the cigarettes were getting into the food black market anyway. The whole concept of demanding reparations remained unresolved by the time he dropped me and turned off. I continued to be lucky with lifts and reached Birmingham and Selly Oak by lunchtime.

There were many visits to make and the first was to Frank and Hilda Butler in Witherford Way, by the old Post Office. They had been like second parents to me. Frank was for many years the Secretary of the Friends Institute in Moseley and my father often worked with him there when he was on furlough. He was still in great demand for his conjuring and Magic Circle shows, and Hilda, though unwell, was always warm, hospitable and full of fun. Vera, their daughter, was also an active Young Friend and had been at Yearly Meeting.

I soon went on to the Education office at *Cadbury's* Bournville to see Cyril Harrison and Jack Herbert, my previous employers, to settle up one or two outstanding bits of business, including Pension payments. They confirmed that the Government does not recognise FAU or FRS service as War service. They were eager to hear about my posting to Berlin, provided me with references and testimonials, and gave me reports on all that was going on in the factory, the Youth Club and the Day Continuation School. Two returning demobbed Army PT instructors had been given my job.

Jack Herbert was the brother of Roland Herbert, the greatly loved and respected teacher at Sibford. Jack was a marvellous personality and a great sportsman at Bournville. He was a tremendous support to me on many occasions and, with his wife, kept open house in Northfield, where one was always more than welcome. I joked about my time at *Cadbury's* and the availability of scrap in the factory shop for employees. While the advertisements were saying to the general public: "Our milk chocolate is wonderful, unfortunately *Cadbury's* are only allowed the milk to make an extremely small quantity, so, if you are lucky enough to get some, do save it for the children," they assured me chocolate would be included in food packages.

Next came a flying visit to Cotteridge and 107 Middleton Hall Road, Daphne's Grandfather's house, where the Southall family had moved to from Oxford, after Kenneth's early retirement. It was in the process of being redecorated. It also had a wonderful garden. I could hear a chiff-chaff singing, and a cuckoo beyond the main railway line. Back again to the Woodlands Hospital, Northfield, to visit Ronny – the only patient in my ward who was still there after his horrendous accident. I found him quite cheerful and just beginning to walk again, but he still expected to be there for a further three months, which would bring it up to a year, poor fellow.

Woodbrooke College was as welcoming as ever and Ernest and Olive Ludlam were the Wardens. I think Francis Knight and David Wills were still Fellows, but Hugh Doncaster had succeeded Gerald K. Hibbert as Reader in Quakerism. I was invited to supper by Konrad Braun, the former High Court Judge in Berlin, who was living in Holland House – the Woodbrooke Annex. He put me up for the night in Jack Hoyland's bed, as Jack was not using it that night, though I was glad to see him again the next morning.

Konrad had a lot to talk about and gave me the addresses of his friends and relatives, including his mother, in Berlin, as well as much information to try and absorb before I got there.

One of the few students at Woodbrooke this term was *Egil Knudsen* from Bergen in Norway, where I had stayed with his Quaker family at the end of my Travel Scholarship in 1938 – when he was only thirteen. He spoke English with barely a trace of an accent and said his sister was trying to join FRS. The Finnmark group was hoping to visit the family on their way north into the Arctic Circle.

The other good news at Woodbrooke was that Leslie Gilbert from Bootham was joining the Staff as Old Testament tutor. He had taught my brother, Allen, was a great cricket enthusiast and an excellent wicketkeeper.

After the Devotional next morning, which for me was a very much needed quiet time, I left and took the tram out towards Rednal and started hitch-hiking again down to Bristol. As it was raining hard and lifts were rather few, I stopped off at Gloucester, by the old Quaker firm of Bryant and Mays that made matches. I had better luck after lunch and soon passed Thornbury Cricket ground and Down End, the scene of W.G. Grace's (the grand old man of cricket) triumphs from the age of fifteen. I had played many times on this ground, both cricket and hockey, for the university and loved it.

One lift took me over Durdham Downs and down White Ladies' Road to the university, two minutes walk from Allen, and Nahia's flat. I was for the first time an uncle and was anxious to see my niece, Leila Maw. The flat, at the back of the *Cadena* in Berkeley Square, was being altered and decorated and was very spacious. It looked out onto the Cabot Tower. Leila was a perfectly sweet baby, smiling and gurgling away while we had tea.

One of the first things Allen said to me was that he had met Nada my former fiancée. She had recognised him in the café and spoken to him. Allen thought that she wanted to make it up with me, or at least apologise for her behaviour of a year before. She thought he had been rather rude to her – which was a pity, but rather typical of my brother. With her very good Biology degree, she had got a research job in Bristol and, over coffee, she now appeared to be a chain-smoker, which I found very sad and hard to believe.

All this was soon forgotten, as I went out to my Uncle Edward Grace's farm at Dundry, outside Bristol, to see my Aunt May, and told her all the news.

During the air raids on Bristol, the farm had been used as a 'dummy airfield' to attract the German bombers away from Bristol itself. It had partially worked and several sticks of bombs had been dropped there. All the craters had been filled in by now, with the exception of one, which had been made into an excellent dew-pond for their herd of pedigree Friesian cows that supplied milk to the *Cadena* café and restaurant. The farm was one of the first to start an electric milking parlour and everything was doing reasonably well. There was talk of Bristol expanding even further than the reservoirs in that direction. In May, the Government had announced plans to spend £380 million on creating twenty new towns, which, it was hoped would house over a million people – houses for all-income groups, not just the working classes.

Fortunately I did not bump into Nada the next morning, but, over lunch at the Union, I did meet up with many of my old university friends back from the War, studying again, now called 'mature' students. Many of the 'freshers' of my last year at the university were now involved in their 'finals, or in their post graduate education year up at the Royal Fort. I was particularly pleased to meet up with Penelope Jenkin, Quaker lecturer in the Zoology Department.

I drove my Aunt round to the shops in her old wreck of a *Talbot*, which was emitting clouds of smoke. I longed to decarbonise it, having learned to do just that. She generously lent me the car to drive over to Churchill in the Mendips. The object of my journey was to go out on a horse ride with Faith Tronson, who had stables there and had given several of us, on the staff at Sidcot, riding lessons. Faith was a remarkable person, who owned a riding school and was a most unlikely teacher. She is an elderly retired Opera singer and former mistress, we were informed, of Ivor Novello and had appeared in his musicals. So she was full of stories and scandals about the West End shows and theatre world, of which I was familiar – if only on the sidelines for a short while. She loved to talk about this when out riding.

Faith had remembered my birthday, as had her young assistant, who would eventually take over the riding school from her. It was a glorious day. I was riding on *Royal* and the route took us up 'Stoney' valley, in all the fresh green and limestone glory up to the Mendip hills. As usual, *Royal* attempted to grab a mouthful from the odd over-hanging branch of the Yew trees and I had to remind him we didn't want him poisoned. Once again, my batteries were recharged and refreshed.

Finally, I took the car back to the farm and had time for a walk on Dundry Hill, overlooking Bristol. The fine view reminded me of the time when, standing there with Allen after sunset one Sunday during the War, we had heard the air raid warning sound and I had dashed back on my bicycle and up to the Victoria Rooms – our Union building, on fire-watching duty, as the first incendiary bombs began to fall before I could get my tin helmet on.

I was enjoying this first week of my leave to the full, but it was clear, when going around the shops with Aunt May, that Britain, and Bristol for that matter, was going through a difficult period of austerity. Petrol rationing was still in force and clothes were still on coupons. From birthday gifts, I had a little money in my pocket and, in trying to look ahead, I found that most of it and my few coupons were gobbled up when buying a pair of leather lambs' wool-lined driving gloves and waistcoat to wear under my uniform. I had lunch as usual with my Aunt on a Thursday at the *Cadena* and Nahia joined us. Allen, as manager, hovered in the background on his rounds and came over to speak to us briefly. Bread was still severely restricted in quality and the rationing of bread and confectionery flour was about to be introduced. We had chosen the fricassée of chicken. Allen asked us if it was satisfactory.

"Yes," we said, "delicious."

"Well, it's mostly rabbit disguised to look like chicken," he said in his characteristic way, knowing that Nahia would be amused. They had met in Beirut, while he was in charge of the Army School of Catering in the Middle East Catering Corps and he knew all the tricks.

Nahia was still fairly new to the austerity and rationing in her new country of adoption, though philosophical about it. But the conversation did make me realise that, during the five months of my training courses, we were to some extent protected, unaware and mostly uninvolved with the queues and shortages after years of wartime rationing. Our ration books were held centrally and 'they' just got on with it. Milk, eggs and oranges were distributed and obtained according to supply. One tin (four pints) of dried milk per person every eight weeks was allowed. Of the basic foods, the weekly ration during the war had varied from a shilling to 2/2d worth of meat; four to eight ounces of bacon; one to eight ounces of cheese, two to four ounces of tea, and eight ounces to a pound of sugar. Nearly every other comestible had a value in 'points', of which the monthly allocation had varied from 16-24. 'Personal points', governing chocolate and sweets fluctuated between 3 and 4 ounces. Soap was limited to 4 coupons a month[1].

Housewives such as Nahia (comparatively well off) still had to be careful, and rations were already beginning to fall below the wartime average. It was depressing and began to look worse. External pressures seemed to be diminishing Britain's food supplies. Dried egg powder had vanished from the shops in February. The *Daily Mirror* asked its readers to choose the dollar imports, in which they would most readily accept a cut: cheese, dried egg, films, fruit, grain, meat, tinned and powdered milk, or tobacco[2]. I was not a *Mirror* reader, but the readers voted overwhelmingly for a cut in films, with tobacco, fruit and milk next on the list. The dried egg appeared back in the shops.

In 1945, there had been poor harvests and I have already referred to the world food crisis, alarming the U.N. The whaling season had been as poor as the harvest, so the fat ration had to be reduced. There were still some 400,000 German prisoners of war in the camps, of which our artist friend, Hans Riemenschneider, was one, and the Government had appealed to the farmers to sow grain in the spring of '46. Hans had been among the POW labourers promised to them. We had all been encouraged to go on digging our gardens and allotments, to reinforce the green vegetable supplies. In the countryside, there was still a lot of military litter: concrete tank traps and rusty, twisted metal – pill boxes; anti-aircraft and lookout posts in the middle of cornfields, which I had remembered from my duties in the potato fields of Cornwall. Europe was short of eight million tons of wheat. During the height of the War, 240,000 acres of land (not counting the concrete) had been covered by airfields and that land was, as rapidly as possible, being returned to the farmers. The Prime Minister was urging us <u>not</u> to send food parcels to Europe, but to eat less ourselves. I enjoyed the fricassée of rabbit (or chicken), but wondered what would it be like in Germany when I finally got there. I did not feel undernourished and, as Churchill had pointed out, bread had never been rationed, even in the darkest days of submarine warfare. I do not remember people going hungry and I had always been fond of bread and soup. There was still waste; bread was always unwrapped when we bought it, but now the loaf was shrinking in size.

That particular evening, I went for a walk with Allen and Nahia up through Clifton and past the great Redlands Church to the Clifton Suspension Bridge, to see if the tide was in. Bristol was still a busy and important port, but that tide was out. Only recently, someone had jumped off the bridge.

The following day I went up to see the University Education Department at the Royal Fort, to see Professor Basil Fletcher, who was also a Quaker, and

---

[1] *Age of Austerity* ed. Michael Sissons and Philip French. OUP 1963, p.23.
[2] Ibid. p26-27.

tell him of my appointment to Berlin. He gave me a very helpful and confidential report on the state of Youth work in Germany and he wanted to be kept in touch. I had been eternally grateful to him for many things, but two in particular. One was to arrange a teaching practice term for me at Gordonstoun School, which had been evacuated from Elgin in Scotland to Wales. This was after a lecture from Kurt Hahn, an experience that had pointed me in the direction I had wanted to go in teaching. The second was the teaching practice he had arranged for me at Sidcot School, and then allowed me to stay on and take the full-time teaching post there, following the sudden departure of the PE and Games Master. This had certainly changed my life and was one of the turning points. Basil Fletcher was able to give me the latest news of the Outward Bound Movement and schools, and that an Outward Bound Trust was being set up to carry on Kurt Hahn's pre-war German refugee work.

There was a garden party up at the Royal Fort for the Education Department, with excerpts from *Richard III* and *The Importance of Being Ernest*, given by the Drama Department, but I left early to catch a bus over to Langford and another ride with Faith. This time we rode over Blackdown, I on *Bletso*, who just would not respond and did not go well. But, it was a marvellous evening and the view over the Quantocks, the Bristol Channel, and the Welsh Mountains beyond, was superb. I wanted to take it all with me. Somehow, I could not put it into context that evening, when I heard on the wireless that Britain and the U.S. had agreed in principle to an eleven state Federation in Germany, whatever that meant.

Up at the farm the next day, young Robert Grace[1] came to show me his collection of birds' eggs. So we went round the farm together, looking for nests. We took a twelve-bore gun with us, but there was very little game about and he only shot a rook – not enough even for a rook pie. I remember my father telling me stories of his young days in Needham Market – and rook pie. Robert tied it to a fence to deter other rooks, which were regarded as pests, in the elm trees.

Garth Kew, who had left Sidcot before Daphne, a talented clarinet player and a good friend of ours, fetched me in his car and took me home nearer Bristol, for tea with his family. His father was a Director of the Bristol City Football Club and was away with the team in Denmark. So I took Garth and Stephen Eisler with me back to Manor Hall, where there was a Sunday evening gramophone recital. They have always had a fine collection of classical 78s there.

Why Sidcot Old Scholars' cricket match against the School and Staff was on a Monday, I did not fully understand, but I had been invited to play and it was a chance to see Daphne again, if only briefly. It was a blustery, cold day

---

[1] He got into contact with me once more in 2006!

and a long time since I had had any cricket practice. My leg was not fully back to its former suppleness. We had lunch in the School and then proceeded with the match. Old Scholars won the toss and were put into bat. I was put in at number 10 and, when the score was 96, I was called on to bat and take the score above 100. I managed to score two runs off the first ball before being caught by Thomas Tregear, off the bowling of Dick Harman (RAH). However, we won as the school side was quickly removed for 48 runs. I had already been invited to Prefects' Tea and was able to see Daphne for a short while there and say farewell. The Old Scholars and Staff put on an impromptu entertainment that evening and I contributed my Conductor's skit, with the help of Garth Kew. It was good fun. But it was with a sense of anti-climax and sadness that I caught the bus back to Bristol.

The next day was my last day of leave, so I took the opportunity of going up to Henleaze to Mrs Hicks, the wonderful old lady, a retired Missionary in China, who was my Guardian when I first went up to the University. She still had some of my possessions, including a tea trolley I had made in the Woodwork Shop at Leighton Park. It was Mrs Hicks, who had introduced me to the actress and film star, Mary Morris, whom I met quite often during the West End season of the International Ballet, and with whom I had been, as her escort, to the premier of the film, *Pimpernel Smith*, with Trevor Howard. Mrs Hicks looked not a day older and was full of life and interest. She asked after Mary Morris, whom she had first met on the Trans-Siberian Railway, returning from China, and she wanted to hear all about my posting. From her, I learnt the latest news about my first girlfriend, Pat (a descendant of the explorer, Captain Cook), who had jilted me in favour of a fellow student by the name of Law, which was easy to remember. The sad news was that John had been blinded in the war, but they were still together.

Having said my farewells to Allen and Nahia, who were also keeping many of my Biology text books in case Daphne might need them, I was only just in time to catch the three o'clock express train back to London, as the guard blew the whistle and waved the green flag. A delightful young couple, with a 5-month old baby and a little lad of 3½ were somewhat surprised to see me scramble into the carriage as the train began to move. And there were two girls, it turned out, who were returning to St. Christopher's School, Letchworth. We soon got talking about military service, conscription, pacifism, education and social problems. When I started talking about my posting to Berlin with FRS, the girls, both Vth formers, pricked up their ears at once and joined in. They knew all about FRS and, in fact, the school had actually supported and raised money for the training of three FRS members. We compared notes on the running of Sidcot with St. Christopher's, of which they were very proud and happy. Their father had just been demobbed, I discovered, and had been given a three-year education grant to study industrial design. He was one of well over a million men and women coming out of the Forces and the Government was faced with a huge housing shortage.

Time passed quickly and I was back in Gordon House in time for supper. John Pettigrew had arrived before me, having said his farewells to Jane and was officially engaged.

Our Quaker grey FRS uniforms were all ready when we went together next day to pick them up from the Haddo House depot. Of course they did not fit and I thought we looked quite absurd. So I suggested to the others that we took them round to the *Co-op* and get them altered, which we did and then began to look around the shops for the list of equipment that we needed to take with us. We needed to remember, as someone once said: "A uniform changes an individual into a type.". Back at the hostel, there was a huge pile of mail and letters to answer and requests to take food parcels out to relatives and friends in Berlin.

"It will be quite impossible and heart-rending to refuse some of these requests," I wrote to Daphne, "and we will simply not have room to take everything. But I promised each one in writing to do what I could (legally or illegally!) when I got to Berlin, even though it was still forbidden for the military to fraternise with the Germans. I assumed that, under the Red Cross, this did not apply to us. Rumours from Berlin indicated that the FAU totally ignored that ruling anyway."

By now, I was calculating how far my remaining clothing coupons would stretch. My Aunt May had got some grey wool and was knitting some socks for me and I wrote to Daphne, who was an expert knitter, to ask, if I got some grey knitting wool on coupons, could she find the time to knit me a long-sleeved pullover after she had finished her Higher School Certificate exams. In any case, I sent my Aunt six of my remaining Board of Trade clothing coupons to get some wool – out of my birthday money – and explained that it only cost a penny halfpenny to send letters to anyone in the Forces. My address was to be simply 135/Relief Section/FRS, BAOR.

The office at Friends House provided us with a float of £19 each with which to go and get the Macintoshes, shoes, boiler suits, pullovers, etc. on our lists that would not be supplied by the Army. I had a final typhus injection, which fortunately was painless and had a long talk with Ken Wildman, just back from the FAU team in Berlin. He was able to give me a lot of useful information, not only about the members of the team there still remaining, but also about the work they had started and the complex Military Government set-up.

We were directed to the Army Equipment Depot in Marylebone the next morning, to collect the rest of our standard equipment, which included kit bags, camp beds, black boots, berets, etc., all of which had to be labelled. After further, rather unsuccessful shopping, I decided to visit Marianne, who was ill and off work, and her Jewish friend, Ruth, to say farewell.

From then on, we were all marking up our equipment with stencils and paint and labelling everything with marking ink and name tabs. But there was time to pick up Ruth and go to see *Spring Awakening*, a play in German put on by the Free German League of Culture at the Free Austria Centre. I could understand it fairly well now, but soon got lost with the speed of delivery of the German language. Afterwards, we strolled in a gang down to Piccadilly and Trafalgar Square to see the lights.

The next few days were a whirlwind of preparation, assembling and checking our clothing and equipment, ready for the departure date, and more last-minute shopping. In the evening, we relaxed, listening to gramophone records, going out to meetings and farewell parties. John and I managed to get to the 'Germany Under Control' Exhibition, where we could have stayed much longer. My brother, Stafford, and his wife, Sheila, had a party at their flat. David Latoff and Anne Negus took me out for an evening at the Monte Carlo Ballet, but I did not find it memorable.

I spent most of one whole day queueing for the renewal of my passport and, when back at the hostel, dying all the khaki webbing and hanging it up to dry – thankful that I was not in the Army, with a Sergeant watching and inspecting. I had my final typhus jab, the ninth injection and I hoped the last.

At last we got a message that our uniforms had been altered and were ready for collection. At the same time, I got a message asking me to go and meet Guy Clutton Brock of 'Christian Reconstruction in Europe', recently back from Berlin, where he had been in touch with the FAU team. It was immediately clear to me that I was talking with a remarkable man. Guy explained that he was between two jobs. He had been for a short period in the Control Commission for Germany, which was in overall command. He had had special responsibility for the schools and education in the British Sector of Berlin and for Religious Affairs, a new department that had been recently set up, but which was made much more complex than in the British Zone of Germany, because of the four-power administration of Berlin. I explained the brief I had been given and was able to ask him questions. In the all too short time available, Guy gave me a great deal of helpful information and encouragement and was extremely friendly. He also gave me a number of contacts and hoped that I would support the ecumenical work and not just the Quaker group in Berlin. The International Fellowship of Reconciliation also needed support, as well as the reconciliation work and contacts renewed by Bishop Bell of Chichester. I wished I had met this great liberal-minded and deeply religious man earlier. He was now on his way to Africa and service in Rhodesia.[1]

---

[1] See his book *Cold Comfort Confronted*, 1972, on Rhodesia. Molly was born 3/2/02. She died 27/4/13 aged 101.

On leaving Church House, I went off to collect my uniform and also my military passport. When I got back, I learned that Kathleen Gough, whom I was expecting to travel with me to Berlin, had not returned from leave because she was ill and would have to postpone her departure. This meant that I should probably have to travel on my own. Word also came through that my brother, Stafford, had been posted to West Africa of all places and was on embarkation leave. I thought how sad this must be for Sheila and also Gill and Gordon, who were coming up to London on leave, but had to cancel it.

Our target date for embarkation, Tuesday 25th June, was rapidly approaching and our last weekend was upon us. On the Saturday, we trouped off to Friends House for a final briefing, paper work and the last cash float. This was very welcome as there was very little left in my Post Office savings account. I still have the papers with me. They included my FRS Members book, signed by A.J. Brayshaw, the FRS Assistant Secretary on 25th June. This declared, in three languages – English, French and German –

> "That the bearer of this letter was a member of the FRS, which is the relief organisation of the Religious Society of Friends, commonly called Quakers.
> The members of the FRS express on behalf of the Society the desire to do all in their power, in the spirit of Christian Love, to alleviate distress among our fellow human beings without regard to race, creed, or nationality.
> We therefore entreat all to whom the bearer may come, to aid him in the fulfilment of his mission."

Since it was like a third passport, I was to keep it always with my two passports and, when travelling, always in my pocket, for it contained my birth date, nationality and National Registration number, FRS Overseas number, Field address, personal money account and dates of all inoculations. In the pocket provided, there was also my British Red Cross Commission Civilian Relief (attached Foreign Office, German Section) Certification card, Passport Number and Military Entry Permit No., signed by the Deputy Commissioner HQ5, BAOR. There was also my Control Commission for Germany Driving Permit (not valid for private purposes!), but only on duty, and was renewable, signed by a (retired) Brigadier.

I had to blow some of the money straightaway on a ticket at Lord's to see the beginning of the Test Match, before going round to the *Saville Theatre* to have tea with David Latoff.

My goal on Sunday was to get to Meeting at Hampstead and a final chat with the Catchpools, who gave me letters for Berlin. My last lunch with my Aunt Sylvia, Ruth Lidbetter and Mrs Coates was memorable for the fact that I was treated to strawberries and cream. This was a real luxury, as soft fruit was rarely to be found. I could not stop for long because I had tickets in my pocket for the afternoon concert at the *Albert Hall.* So I took the bus across London and met up with Marcia. Yehudi Menuhin was playing the Brahms Violin Concerto and that too was a treat and much better, I felt, than his interpretation of the Elgar Violin Concerto. We had tea at Marcia's place with a few of her gang, in which I was beginning to feel a little out of place. I knew Marcia was a Socialist, but I hadn't realised she was a Communist Party member. I was taken off to a Communist Meeting to hear John Mainfield speak on Germany, which turned out to be a valuable experience and I got a very different perspective.

By the end of Monday, everything was packed and bundled into the three massive kit bags and a rucksack. We were twiddling our thumbs and listening to the news on the wireless. Having considered what money was left in our purses, we learned that *Morris* car prices had risen. A two-door saloon was now to cost £270 and a four-door version £290. John and I looked at each other and joked. On fourteen 'bob' a week, it would take a good long time to save up that amount, let alone anything for getting married! I heard also that in India the Congress Party had rejected Britain's independence plan, and I wondered how the Delegations and my parents were getting on.

Just as time was beginning to hang a bit and we were trying to stuff in every bit of extra gift food as possible, news came through that there was a delay of possibly 24 hours, for 'technical reasons out of FRS control' and we must stay put.

I busied myself with letter writing. Letters were still coming in thick and fast. I heard from my parents that my mother, who had been seriously ill, was better and feeling more cheerful. I had letters from our former *au pair* girls in German to decipher, but with little news. Victor Gollancz and the 'Save Europe Now' sent me a 15lbs parcel of food, with the good news that the ban on food parcels was soon to be lifted and that 1lb parcels could be sent to civilians. Edith Snellgrove was unable to get to Berlin for about a month and there was a possibility that one of the AFSC volunteers, now at Woodstock, might be able to join the team after the training period. Up to this point, there had not been much summer weather and it was all rather wet and windy.

*****

Here my diary ends and I started my German Journal, for we left the following day on June 26th. I was leaving a drab and austere Britain, still struggling to clear up the shambles of V2 and other bomb damage of war. In Bristol, Birmingham and London, I had seen whole estates of 'prefabs' springing up everywhere, to relieve the housing shortage. Over 150,000 Poles were asking to stay in Britain, rather than be returned to Poland. The family I had met in the train, like many thousands of others, was living in cramped, parental, borrowed, or rented rooms. I sensed a lot of stress and strains, rootlessness and even despair, as people were struggling back to 'normal' life, or picking up the threads of their old lives. The camps that soldiers and airmen had occupied during the War were rapidly emptying and the accommodation going to waste, as families searched for just somewhere else to live. Our own spartan conditions in Woodstock and Mount Waltham seemed luxurious in comparison. These were the conditions that gave rise to scroungers, spivs and black marketeers. What must it be like in Germany, I wondered? No one seemed quite sure what the restrictions were on occupying old Army camps and, at about this time, the squatters were beginning to move in. The more local Councils and police struggled with the squatters, the more publicity it gave them and the idea caught on. Empty houses and flats around us had begun to be invaded. I had picked up some of these murmurings at the Communist Meeting I had been taken to by Marcia, on their well-organised grapevine. At least they were taking notice of the plight of the homeless, both in Europe and at home. I began to understand why Marcia and her friends were starting to quiz me on the matter of civil disobedience. People were already thinking ahead, as I was, over clothing and the coming winter. Many of the properties occupied had no water, electricity or gas. It was fairly common, too, to find people hoarding goods and food, and the spivs were hawking the new luxury nylon stockings that everyone was after. The police were harassed and the general public seemed sympathetic with the squatters. Hostels began to be set up, but the authorities also began to see that that camps were useful stop-gaps, although some, as I knew, were still occupied by prisoners of war.

A new black market was a rising for building materials and labourers for repairs to deal with the inevitable shortages. I was also aware of the many FRS workers in the various Quaker-run Centres, Depots and Hostels, both in the London area and in the provinces in Birmingham, Bristol, Liverpool, Manchester and other places, were not only backing up the overseas work, but also facing many of these problems at home quietly and efficiently, with dedication and out of the limelight. They, too, were wondering about life after FRS and FAU. I cannot thank them enough for all the backup, encouragement and support we received.

Just at this time of flurry, doom and gloom, there fell into my hands a list of what I called 'sic Milk Jokes', that restored one's sense of humour, and which I took with me to Germany, knowing they were untranslatable into German. Later, I learnt that the Germans have a totally different sense of humour from the English.

Does anyone still remember free school milk, cod liver oil, *Marmite*, concentrated orange juice, Rose hip syrup? Well, here are a few 'extracts from the various letters sent to various ministries during the last War', and should be preserved:

"Please send me a form for cheap milk, as I am expecting mother."

"Please send me a form for supply of milk for having children at reduced prices."

"Will you please send me a form for cheap milk, I have a baby 2 months old and I did not know anything about it until a friend of mine told me."

"I posted the form by mistake, before my child was filled in properly."

"I have a baby eighteen months old, thanking you for same."

"I had intended coming to the milk office today, but have had 15 children this morning."

"Milk is wanted and father is unable to supply it."

"I have one child nearly 2 years old, and am looking forward to an increase in November. Hoping this meets with your kind consideration and approval."

"I have one baby fed entirely on cows, and another 4 months old."

"Will I be able to have milk for baby as my husband finishes his job as night watchman next Thursday?"

"Sorry I have been so long in filling the form, but I have been in bed with my baby for 2 weeks, and did not know it was running out till the milkman told me."

"This is my eighth child. What are you going to do about it?"

"I cannot get sick pay, I have six children. Can you tell me why this is?"

"Sir, I am forwarding my Marriage Certificate and 2 children, one of which you will see is a mistake."

"I have no children, as my husband is a bus driver and works day and night."

"In accordance with your instructions I have given birth to twins in the enclosed envelope."

"You have changed my little boy into a little girl, will this make a difference?"

"In reply to your letter, I am glad to say that my husband who was reported missing, is now dead."

"Unless I get my husband's money I will be forced to live an immortal life."

"Please send me my money, I have fallen into errors with my landlord."

"My husband got his project cut off 2 weeks ago, and I haven't had any relief since."

"I cannot get eternity benefit in spite of the fact that I saw the Insistence officer. I have 9 children. What can I do about it?"

"I want money as quick as I can get it. I have been ill in bed with the doctor for 2 weeks, but he doesn't seem to do me any good. If things don't improve I will have to send for another doctor."

"Mrs Brown has no clothes, has not had any for a year. The Clergy have been visiting her however."

"Re your dental enquiry – the teeth in the top are alright, but the ones in my bottom are hurting me terribly."

I have gone into considerable detail about the training we were given, the dedication of those who gave it, as well as the great fund of experience of those workers from the First World War and thereafter. But I have made too little reference to the spiritual preparation that was behind the service of all the workers, whether they were Quakers or not. We were not concerned with who was what, Friend or non-Friend, for we shared a common purpose and strong bonds of fellowship.

In 1920, the year in which I was born, there took place in London the first World Conference of Friends, numbering a thousand English speaking Quakers. The First World War was over and they came together to discuss the future implications of the Quaker Peace Testimony. In 1946, we were engaged in the exercise once more. The strong pacifist traditions of the Society had been strengthened again by war, and now imprisoned COs were being released from prison. How could we maintain and uphold the Peace Testimony and take an active part in peace-making and reconciliation? Up to this point, we knew where we were and, though we may have felt a 'peculiar people', the Society of Friends was a part of the Christian Church, with an emphasis on inwardness, freedom and activism that rejected the more outward forms and authority of the other Churches. Christianity itself seemed to be changing and, under the leadership of George Gorman, Young Friends were being looked to for maintaining our distinctive testimonies, to the forefront of which was the Peace Testimony, along with the other Peace Churches, such as the Brethren and the Mennonites, particularly active in America.

In the spring of 1946, as I started my FRS training, Carl Heath, who in 1918, dreamed of starting Quaker Embassies (soon to be called 'Centres') in Europe and later the great cities of the world, was the General Secretary of the Friends Service Council. In 1933, both FSC and Meeting for Suffering had become actively involved in the rise of Hitler and the sufferings of the Jews, and the Berlin Quaker International Centre had been set up, with Corder Catchpool at its head. Carl Heath had reviewed Hitler's *Mein Kampf* in *The Friend*, the tone of which "was one of perplexity rather than downright condemnation.[1]" In Meeting for Sufferings at the time, the epigram was quoted with approval; "Hitler was born, not in Austria, but at Versailles." And we were made very conscious of this during our training.

With a view to reactivating the Friends World Committee for Consultation (FWCC), Carl Heath had appointed an *ad hoc* Interim executive Committee in

[1] O.G. *Quaker Encounters Vol.1*, p.260.

May 1946[1], which was predominantly European. Hans Albrecht, whom I met prior to leaving for Berlin, and Regnar Halfden-Nielsen, with whose family I stayed on my Travel Scholarship in 1938, from Denmark, were invited. The officers of the Committee also included the Elkingtons from U.S., Leslie Shaffer from the Paris International Centre, Errol Eliott from U.S. and Bertram Pickard from Geneva, all of whom I was to meet later, in addition to Fred Tritton, Barrow Cadbury and Harry Silcock, the London Officer, already well-known to my family, who had visited India, China and the Pacific. In their Meetings, there were long discussions on '…the special message of Quakerism to this generation and (the means to) communicate it…'[2] One could not help being aware of this enthusiasm, which was reflected in the Meeting for Sufferings and Yearly Meeting reports in *The Friend*, while we were in training.

The first European Conference was held at Ommen in Holland in April 1947 while I was on leave from Berlin in the Harz Mountains, with the Goslar team. The theme then was 'The Spiritual Need of Europe and the Responsibilities of Friends'. By this time, other FRS teams and certainly ours in Berlin, were becoming more and more aware of the spiritual hunger of Europe, rather than physical hunger and need for relief, as we were, in Britain and Europe, emerging from one of the bleakest and coldest winters on record.

My little pocket New Testament[3] that I took with me, given to me as a parting gift at the Christmas of 1927 by 'Grannie' Anna Evens in India, in Matthew 10 v.16 reads: "Behold I send you forth as sheep in the midst of wolves: be ye therefore wise as serpents and harmless as doves." So the Peace Testimony continues to be the predominant one in our lives.

In our Meeting for worship and quiet times, while training and at Hampstead and Friends House Meetings on Sundays, both vocal prayer (which was frequent) and ministry on this theme was often heard. Active peace making and reconciliation, together with the other relief organisations, churches and faiths, was encouraged, as were relationships with the military authorities, as well as the defeated enemy. No one wins a war. One could not help but be involved politically and with political parties as well. But there were other testimonies to uphold also, and foremost amongst these was our social testimony. For me, this had for a long time been of great importance, as I felt it to be also amongst my own generation of Young Friends. It reflected perhaps a swing away from the evangelical orientation of my parents' generation. It was clear, I think to all of us, that we were not going abroad to 'convert the heathen', nor in any way to proselytise for Quakerism.

---

[1] *A History of FWCC Quakers Worldwide.* Herbert Hadley p.31.

[2] Ibid. p.32.

[3] Given to my grandson Philip Coventry in 2006.

Alastair Heron, another FRS member working in Germany, summed up the period of Quakerism between 1920-1945[1] as: "…a time for slow and relatively uneventful internal development. This contrasted with the troubled and uncertain times in the wider society. But it started with a prolonged exercise on the revision of the part of its *Book of Christian Discipline* concerned with doctrine. The outcome established the acceptance of the 'liberal' position. By 1945, most of the previous leadership had gone and a new wave of men and women with different backgrounds and experience had come in." I would put this period as ending a year or two later, but certainly my parents were beginning to reflect this change.

Their first *Book of Christian Discipline of the Religious Society of Friends*, which they grew up with in their respective Quaker families, was published in 1883. When they returned home to England with me in 1923, their *Book of Discipline* was being revised and was finally published in 1925. So this was the version of my childhood and growing up, for the next revision was not approved until the Yearly Meeting of 1960. Mother was very involved in this revision and I have her original draft copy. She was familiar with it and often quoted from it in her ministry. It was the 1925 version I grew up with and loved, and took to Germany with me. Its purpose was to keep us aware of our inheritance and, from the writings of early Friends onwards, aware of how we have been led into the service of Truth.

Another of the testimonies was simplicity and in the chapter on the *Abundant Life, the Yearly Epistle of 1691*[2] is quoted, the advice to Friends to take care to keep to truth and plainness of language, habit, deportment and behaviour… Simplicity does not mean ugliness or dullness. My parents used plain language and, throughout their lives, used 'thee' and 'thou' to each other. In my letters to Daphne from the time I left Sidcot in 1944, I was also in the habit of using 'thee' and 'thou', which I welcomed in the study and use of the German language.

In this same chapter, there are a number of headings and sections on the Arts and on Recreation and Amusements. Painting, Sculpture and architecture, Music, Literature, Drama and Self-Expression and Sacrifice[3]. There was nothing about the Dance, but the word 'Sacrifice' intrigued me. The date of the paragraph – 1925 – indicated when it was written or sanctioned to be included. I will quote part of it: "There are many voices today which call us to enjoyment, to self-expression, or to contemplate and share in the beauty of creative art. These things need to be subordinated to the service of the Highest, and sometimes in that service they must be given up. There are some too who, listening to the still small voice, which makes it clear to them a duty

---

[1] *Quakers in Britain – A Century of Change. 1895-1995.* Alastair Heron.

[2] *1925 Xian Practice Pt.2* p.78.

[3] Ibid. p84.6.

that may not rest upon all, will forgo pleasures and activities in themselves good, for the sake of other claims."

And in section four on Drama: "Friends have refrained in previous generations from supporting the theatre, and even from encouraging the amateur performance of plays, having been led to take this attitude because of the undesirable associations of the stage, the doubtful character of many plays and the dangers connected with the actor's profession."

This was certainly not true of Friends Schools where all the arts were encouraged, and were flourishing at the Downs School when I went there in 1929, under Geoffrey Hoyland, and with the full encouragement of Dorothea Hoyland's mother, Elizabeth Cadbury. But outside the Friends Schools and amongst the Society in the 1940s and wartime, many of these ideas prevailed – the theatre was still considered 'not quite nice'. So that, when I joined the International Ballet Company at the beginning of 1941, soon after my tribunal as a CO, I detected feelings of conflict amongst older and 'weightier' Friends and was eyed with some suspicion. I was quite relieved that 'disownment' from the Society had been laid to rest, even though it had only been used in the recent past, for failure in business or marrying out; rather than from 'disorderly walking'. But my short theatrical career was frowned on by the few for I must have been one of the first Quakers ever to appear on a West End stage in a professional Ballet Company. My parents, though puzzled, did not quite know what to make of it, perhaps because of the sexuality stereotypes particularly associated with male dancers. But this was overcome after my mother came to see a full performance and met some of the company backstage afterwards. She thoroughly enjoyed the show and the people in it.

During the period after the end of the Second World War, there were changes in attitudes, and the Friends Fellowship of the Arts was beginning to make headway, and this alone deserves a fuller recorded history. Alastair Heron's *Quakers in Britain. A Century of Change*[1] declares: "This quarter-century started with high hopes, passed through a period of relative stability and came to a turbulent close. The effects upon Quakers in Britain were to some extent inevitably a reflection of what was happening in the wider society of which they were but a tiny part. After the War, Quakers made a fresh start, along with everyone else, and during the 1950s resumed familiar ways and events, enlivened by the experiences of younger new-comers."

For me it was certainly a new start. The 'Fellowship Hymn Book' of my youth gave way to 'Songs of Praise'. I took with me two lines from well-known hymns, which I was to hum frequently when driving alone. One was Martin Shaw's tune to Goethe's lines: "Everything changes but God changes not; The power never changes that lies in his thought:

---

[1] *Quakers in Britain.* Alastair Heron. p.48 Part III *Brave New World 1946-69.*

Splendours 3 from God proceeding,
May we ever love them true,
Goodness, truth and beauty heeding
Every day, in all we do."

The other hymn, which everyone knew: H F Lyte's *Abide with me*, contained the line "Change and decay in all around I see; O thou who changes not, abide with me."

Steamships, trains and engines were giving way to diesel, electric and the jet engine. The wireless was turning into radio; the age of television began and the plastic age started. Electrical gadgets replaced 'chars' and servants. Antibiotics, such as penicillin, revolutionised medicine. As the number of real 'weighty' Friends decreased, in society individuals began to increase in *avoir dupois.*

The 1960 revision of the *Book of Discipline. Christian Faith* and *Practice in the Experience of the Society of Friends*[1] says: "Our peace testimony is much more than our special attitude to world affairs; it expresses our vision of the whole Christian way of life; it is our way of living in this world; of looking at this world; of changing this world."

It was with this vision that I set out on a great adventure that certainly changed me and, with the hope that at least I might take one small step towards changing the world, just as an ordinary citizen of the world. But there were still questions I asked myself.

Can one ever be fully trained for a task like this? Do I really measure up to the qualifications of a good Relief worker? How on earth did I arrive at this point? I took a deep breath…

The next version of our *Book of Discipline* was approved by Yearly Meeting 1964, at which both Daphne and I were present, and in full agreement, though there were still some who were unable to find unity with Chapters 22, and 23.45, of what is now *Quaker Faith and Practice*, since when there have been some revisions.

Roger Wilson's definition of a Relief Worker is worth quoting:

"A Relief Worker is one who goes about doing good, the sort of good that requires a lot of going about."

Think about this as you read my diary. Is it relevant now?

---

[1] Extract 624.

SECTION II

GERMAN JOURNAL
THE LOGBOOK AND DIARY
OF A FRIENDS RELIEF SERVICE WORKER

PART 1

BERLIN WITH F.R.S. 135

JUNE 26TH 1946 – JUNE 6TH 1947

Let your life speak.
George Fox

What you are doing may seem insignificant,
but it's terribly important you do it.
Mahatma Gandhi

Contents

Introduction

It was never the intention of the writer that this journal should be published. It was compiled mainly as a daily record, and aide-memoire, for reporting back to many enquirers and in response to numerous requests for talks and reports. So it is by no means a highly polished or finished professional article.

Fifty years on there have been requests from family and friends, and from Germany, for me to resurrect it, and print it up.

Soon after my appointment as Headmaster of Sibford Friends School in 1956 Frances Naish, then living in retirement in Sibford Gower, asked me for any typing and secretarial work that she might help me with. She had recently retired as the Warden's secretary at Woodbrooke College, Selly Oak, Birmingham, and was in poor health. I am greatly indebted to her for the many hours she spent deciphering over 700 pages of my appalling handwriting and spelling to produce two 300-page copies of my journal, which she thought ought to be published.

Now, 50 years on, I am equally indebted to Brian Micklethwaite for offering to use his technological skills and PC to get the whole thing into a more readable form and layout. His interest and suggestions too have been a great encouragement.

The diary was written under difficult conditions, often late into the night, or up to one or two o'clock in the morning after a long day's work, often by candlelight because of numerous electricity cuts, and with cold fingers. So the reader is asked to be tolerant of its many defects, mistakes and omissions. It is primarily a description of the daily work of a Quaker Relief Worker and an attempt to describe and comment on some of the events of the post-war period in question, as seen through the eyes of a C.O. and a privileged Young Friend of 26. My reactions, attitudes and opinions of course reflect my background, upbringing and education. These were more intimately reflected in my many letters to my parents, Geoffrey and Mildred Maw, and to my fiancée Daphne Southall. Also there were articles to "The Friend", and other journals, the Press, broadcasts on the German Radio, and in official reports, some of which had to be confidential. Some expressions of opinion, personal and team difficulties had to be omitted for obvious reasons. Some of these were trivial, but others very much more serious.

Since I also wanted to include a historical perspective, I have made a few changes to the original by way of additions and omissions, so I hope it will not be too tedious for the readers. At the age of 75, I am glad to note that at least some of the arrogance of my youth, pompous, 'do-gooding' and judgmental attitudes and political naivety, have been rubbed off and softened by experience. I have been encouraged to include names, because names have so often been left out in official reports, and I feel they ought to be included for the record. They have contributed so much – without them I could not have achieved anything. It may seem like "name dropping", but my contacts are very precious to me and were made possible because of my very privileged position, membership of and work for Quakers. These names should not be forgotten in both countries. They are part of the history of the times and I learned so much from them. Their names are to be found in the Index.

Part II will record my service with the Cologne F.R.S. team 125 from September 1947 to March 1948. In between these two parts I wrote my American Journal, June – August 1947, which is to be found separately. I was one of an invited delegation of British and Irish Young Friends to the American Young Friends Conference at Earlham College, Richmond, Indiana. My particular brief was to report directly to Young Friends in the U. S. on Quaker Relief work in Germany; to appeal for funds and relief supplies; and to contact A.F.S.C. (the American Friends Service Committee) in Philadelphia to appeal for more American Relief Workers for Germany. The editor of "The American Friend", Errol Eliott, then asked me to become a reporter for the journal for the next six months until my service came to an end in Germany. I was also reporting for *The Friend* and *Peace News.*

None of us working in F.R.S. could have achieved what we did without the training that was given to us, and I intend to add to this Journal some account of the training my particular group received from January to June 1946 at Woodstock in London, and from which I have benefited all my life.

1 have always enjoyed writing and receiving letters. Both my parents were always marvellous letter writers. I regret having kept so few, especially when we were separated and they were working as Quaker missionaries in India, where I was born a birthright Friend on June 2nd 1920. In that month:[1]

> "At a meeting of the full Board of the American Friends Service Committee (A.F.S.C.), Hoover's proposals were accepted." (Herbert Hoover was then Head of the American Relief Organisation and future 31st President of the United States, and was himself a Quaker)... and by the end of June 1920, more than a million German children in 1,640 centres were receiving a supplementary meal, organised by a small Quaker team supervising 40,000 German assistants."

In Germany in 1946/47 I found exactly the same moral issues as described in J.O.G.'s book, i.e. that:

---

[1] *"Quaker Encounters Vol. 1 Friends and Relief", J. Ormerod Greenwood, p221, 223.*

> "Although Hoover was actuated by genuinely humanitarian motives he was driven also by that hatred of communism which infected the Allied governments and which has proved such a powerful and disastrous force in American politics ... If hunger was the ally of communism he was prepared to use food as a weapon against it, and he was prepared to use hunger as a lever ... and in Russia the whole issue of relief became a matter of political controversy." (See pp 22/23, August 7th and 8th in this Journal.
>
> However (p223):
>
> "In the summer of 1920, the British Friends decided to set up their own feeding scheme in Cologne, with co-operation of British officers of the Rhineland Commission, and *Paul Sturge* was detached from the Scheme in which he was working, to organise this project with the aid of a German Committee and using American supplies paid for by British contributions. After five weeks' preparation feeding began on 2nd December 1920; before the end of the year 12,000 children were being fed; and when the peak was reached in July 1921, nearly 30,000."

This action[1] was remembered by many individuals we encountered in both Berlin and Cologne in 1946 and 1947, and meant that we had a virtually "open door" everywhere we needed to go, and maximum co-operation.

In 1930 while I was at the Downs School, the Preparatory School run on Quaker lines by Geoffrey and Dorothea Hoyland, I kept a sporadic diary, and a precious autograph book, and started the habit of keeping a journal and a Day Book.

Whilst at Bristol University taking a degree in Biology during the war years I registered as a C.O. when I received my Call-up papers. Though not an absolutist, to my surprise my Tribunal gave me complete exemption to carry on with my training for teaching, and relief work in the vacations.

In May 1945 I attended Yearly Meeting in London. Suddenly in one of the sessions some words spoken by another Young Friend, Ted Milligan, hit me like a blinding light and the call to join the F.R.S. became a clear imperative. I knew this was what I had to do. My hope was that I might be sent to Germany, and, I know not why, to Berlin. Perhaps it was because, all through the war, Hitler epitomised for me the voice of evil.

At the time I was working at the Bournville Day Continuation School and in the Youth Club with Arnold Edmundson ("Eddie") – as a P.E. and Swimming Instructor for *Cadbury's*, Bournville. As soon as the V.E. Day celebrations started I handed in my 3 months notice and applied to join F.R.S. I was given an interview and accepted on the condition that when trained and

[1] *"Quaker Speisung"*

assessed I would be willing to serve anywhere where there was the need, including in this country.

Later I read in The Friend of 30th November 1945 Robin Whitworth's reflections while in charge of the F.A.U. overseas relief work:

> "Germany is prostrate, and the Germans know they are beaten. Their minds are empty, but they are not cowed. 'We must work and work and work' they say. In the midst of such fearful destruction caused by British bombs, it might be expected that they were filled with hatred for us. But even in heavily bombed Hamburg and the Rhur there is a remarkable absence of resentment. The people feel they have been saved from something terrible, and are thankful that they live in the British Zone. They feel themselves in a spiritual vacuum... No matter how democratic Germans may now wish to be, they have forgotten the art... and have little understanding of the extent to which their name is hated throughout Europe."

Having experienced the heat of the German bombing of Bristol (Winston Churchill was the Chancellor of Bristol University) I understood this feeling of hatred. But Berlin with the 4 Powers had even greater needs and difficulties.

Whilst I was working out my 3 months notice I played hockey for *Cadbury's* and Worcestershire and was very fit. Unfortunately, whilst playing rugby in the Old Leightonians match against the school, both knees were injured and I developed cartilage trouble. Fortunately I was able to carry on for a while, but finally had to go into the Royal Orthopaedic Hospital, The Woodlands, at Northfield, Birmingham, across the road from the Manor Farm where the F.A.U. members were being trained, and over the Christmas period.

In those days the operation was an extremely painful one and my right leg was in plaster for a considerable time. I had to learn to walk again and I became severely depressed for various reasons. I was afraid that my career as a P.E. teacher was finished, that my ballet dancing days were over completely, and that I might no longer be acceptable as a relief worker if I could not pass the final medical examination and complete the relief work programme.

However after a short period of skilled physiotherapy and an undertaking that I must exercise the leg for at least 2 hours a day, morning and evening, I was able to start the F.R.S. training course with sufficient confidence. I kept up the exercises for a whole year while I was in Berlin, but never in fact was able to return to full mobility in my right knee or sit in the relaxed Lotus position I had learned in India.

My parents, with whom I was living at the time, were delighted that I was now off their hands, because they too were leaving for India for their last period of service with the Friends Service Council. My brother Allen had a distinguished career as a Major in the Army Catering Corps, and my brother

Stafford also as a Doctor was in the RAMC. My sister Gill was a fully trained nurse from the Woodlands Hospital, Northfield, working in Edinburgh and engaged to a doctor.

It should be emphasised that my part of the work in Berlin and Cologne was only a very small one in the overall work of the two teams and of the total service given by many other men and women in F.R.S. A full account is to be found in Roger C. Wilson's "Quaker Relief", George Allen and Unwin, 1952. On pp 246/7 there is the following reference:

> "In Berlin where the problem of juvenile delinquency soared to enormous proportions under the combined influence of social collapse, inadequate housing and occupation, Hugh Maw found scope for his gifts of sympathetic understanding for boys and girls in their social setting, in a far reaching investigation which led on to a multitude of local efforts to mitigate the dangers to youth."

It goes on to record our efforts in Cologne also, where:

> "... a rather different kind of youth project was begun. Contact with various organised youth groups showed the team that those within their sphere were well catered for, but there was a vast youth population outside them whose evenings were spent in pubs and dance halls, at street corners in furtive black-marketing, or filching coal briquettes from railway dumps and wagons. The problem was the more urgent because work, as ordinarily understood, was becoming a fool's choice when there was more to be gained in half an hour on the Black Market than by a week's employment."

The rest of this account will be quoted in Part II as seen from the F.R.S. office at Friends House by Roger Wilson, the Chief Executive Officer. It is worth including some of the Foreword in Roger's book (1952).

> "This account of Quaker Relief Work during and after the 2nd World War is not a 'history' in any substantial sense ... it is far too short to allow any assessment of the significance of the Quaker operations, either in relation to contemporary events generally or in relation to the life of the Society of Friends in the twentieth century. Should anybody wish in the far future to make such assessments, this book will provide only some of the raw material. Far more valuable will be the wealth of memoranda poured out for internal consumption by members of the Service, for whom a sense of divine guidance and of religious concern were no substitutes for an effort to think straight about the principles and practice of relief work. These memoranda, together with a good deal of official and semi-official correspondence and much frank contemporary note-making will, I believe, yield in the fullness of years a clear insight into the way a substantial group

> of youngish Friends and near Friends thought in the 1940's. But this material is too controversial and too intimate for immediate use..." "...In my own view, the question of HOW we accomplished our work is of more ultimate importance than what we did in the field."

To this I must add that our work was only made possible because of the daily and weekly Quaker Meetings for Worship both during the training period and in the field. I was under concern[1]. My concern was tested by my Quaker Meeting (Selly Oak). Members of Warwickshire MM had supported me at my tribunal, as had Redland Meeting in Bristol. Throughout my 2½ years of Service they upheld me in their thoughts and prayers, and corresponded regularly with me both overseas or on leave, and cared for me afterwards.

With their help I was enabled or 'liberated' to search for and try to follow the Will of God, and I was able to say with complete confidence "Here am I, send me." (I Samuel 3, and Isaiah 6, v8).

Roger Wilson gave us, during training, one definition of a Relief Worker which I have never forgotten: "A relief worker is one who goes about doing good, the sort of good that requires a lot of going about!" He reminded us also of Francis Howgill's words (1656):

> "Why gad you abroad? Why trim you yourselves with the saints' words when you are ignorant of the life?"

and I had to wrestle with these questions. George Fox's words of the same date:

> "Let all nations hear the word by sound or writing ... Be patterns, be examples in all countries."

and which ends with:

> "Then you will come to walk cheerfully over the world, answering that of God in everyone",

were constantly before us, as was the Quaker Advice to "live adventurously".

1 took with me always 2 or 3 books: my Bible, given me by my parents in 1939 (and a pocket New Testament given me in India in 1927). In the flyleaf I had inscribed a quotation from St Jerome: "To be ignorant of the Scriptures is not to know Christ." Secondly the 1921 edition of "Christian Life, Faith and Thought," part of the then Church Government from our Book of Discipline, and an English-German dictionary. But during this time I was heavily into the

[1] *The special Quaker use of this term is to denote 'a divine imperative laid inwardly upon a person'.*

books of *Harry Emerson Fosdick*[1]: "The Meaning of Prayer" (1915), "The Meaning of Faith" (1943), "On Being a Real Person" (1943), and "On Being Fit to Live With" (1947), and received much inspiration from him, especially after I entered into correspondence with him and received an invitation to visit him at Riverside Church, New York, in 1947.

1 was also in correspondence with *Phyllis Bottome* a prolific writer of the period, and with Quaker connections. Her Penguin classic "The Mortal Storm" was an inspiration to me, as was her biography of Alfred Adler (she was a student of his). These books helped to guide me to 'life after F.R.S.'

But most of all I must pay a tribute to *Vera Brittain* and her books "Testament of Youth" and "Humiliation with Honour". She was a prolific letter writer, friend of Friends and of *Corder Catchpool.* From 1939 onwards she supported and upheld me and encouraged me as a young conscientious objector.

Unfortunately very few of their letters have survived, but the above books and authors, my family and my fiancée were my constant companions in my thoughts and prayers, and always a source of inspiration and support.

Roger Wilson dedicated his book "To the wives and families of members of the Friends Relief Service who often bore most of the hardship while we had most of the fun!" and similarly I dedicate my journal to them.

This brings me to the point where I must also pay tribute to all the members of the Military Government whom I encountered in transit, in the British (and Allied) Zones and Sectors of Berlin, and the civilian members of the Control Commission who patiently tolerated us, gave us their protection and ultimately their full support. As one high ranking officer said to me: "We are after all just ordinary people, perhaps from very different traditions and starting points, but all of us are working for peace and against the forces of evil."

> In his book "A Great Time to be Alive", Harry Emerson Fosdick wrote: "To defeat a nation with our armies and leave it crushed, rebellious, resentful, angry is not to conquer it. It will not so stay defeated. Real conquering is ultimately a spiritual matter, the inner conquest of a nation by persuasive forces of justice, fair play, goodwill, until the nation's soul voluntarily surrenders to a world policy that is good for all."

At the end of the war I heard Winston Churchill on the radio say "The only worthwhile prize of victory is the power to forgive and to guide."

Vera Brittain in "Humiliation with Honour[2]" wrote:

---

[1] *Fellowship of Reconciliation (F.O.R.)*

[2] *1942.*

"There can be no better contribution to real victory than the attempt, however limited in scope, to rescue individuals from spiritual darkness and physical pain. To help them find in defeat or exile a new and deeper level of experience is itself part of the endeavour to maintain those religious and social values by which democracy has lived."

I believe that unless the cycle of war is broken, each war begets another and the cycle can only be broken by individual acts of individual people – one step at a time, in the footsteps of Jesus of Nazareth.

"Seek love in the Pity of other's woe" wrote William Blake in 'William Bond' and, in the same vein, "in gentle relief of another's care. In the darkness of the night and the winter's snow. With the naked and outcast. See love there."

1 took with me also two prayers, which I quote in full. The prayer of St. Francis:

"Lord, make me an instrument of thy peace!
Where there is hatred, let me sow love;
Where there is injury, let me show pardon;
Where there is doubt, faith;
Where there is despair, hope;
Where there is darkness, light;
Where there is sadness, joy."

And the prayer of Abraham Lincoln (1809-65) from his second inaugural speech as President of the United States:

"Grant, O merciful God, that with malice toward none; with charity to all; with firmness in the right as Thou givest us to see the right, we may strive to finish the work we are in; to bind up the nation's wounds; (to care for him who shall have borne the battle and for his widow and orphan); to do all which may achieve and cherish a just and lasting peace among ourselves and with all nations; through Jesus Christ our Lord, Amen."

And for a text and a talisman the words of Joshua 1, v9:

"Be strong and of good courage: be not afraid, neither be thou dismayed: for the Lord thy God is with thee, whithersoever thou goest",

and the words of Micah 6 v8 went with me:

"The Lord has shown thee, O man, what is good, and what the Lord doth require of thee, but to do justly and to show mercy and love constantly, and to walk humbly with thy God."

Such words, and the Quaker star[1], were my guiding lights.

For the next 2½ years of Service I received 10/- (about 50p in today's money) a week in material terms and all else was found. This period was not recognised by the Government as pensionable for superannuation purposes, but I was content to forgo this. But what I gained in spiritual terms and what treasure I found I hope I have made clear in this journal: the "that of God" in so many people, events and the things that happened by more than chance. Someone also once said:

> "A uniform changes an individual into a type." There is some danger in this truth in my experience."

[1] *The origin of the red and black Quaker star which I was proud to wear is described on pp 60-61 in J.O.G.'s Quaker Relief Vol.1. Further references are to be found in this Journal in Part II under Sunday December 14th 1947 (The Friend December 12th). And in 'Craftsman and Quaker' by Leslie Bailey, p.56.*

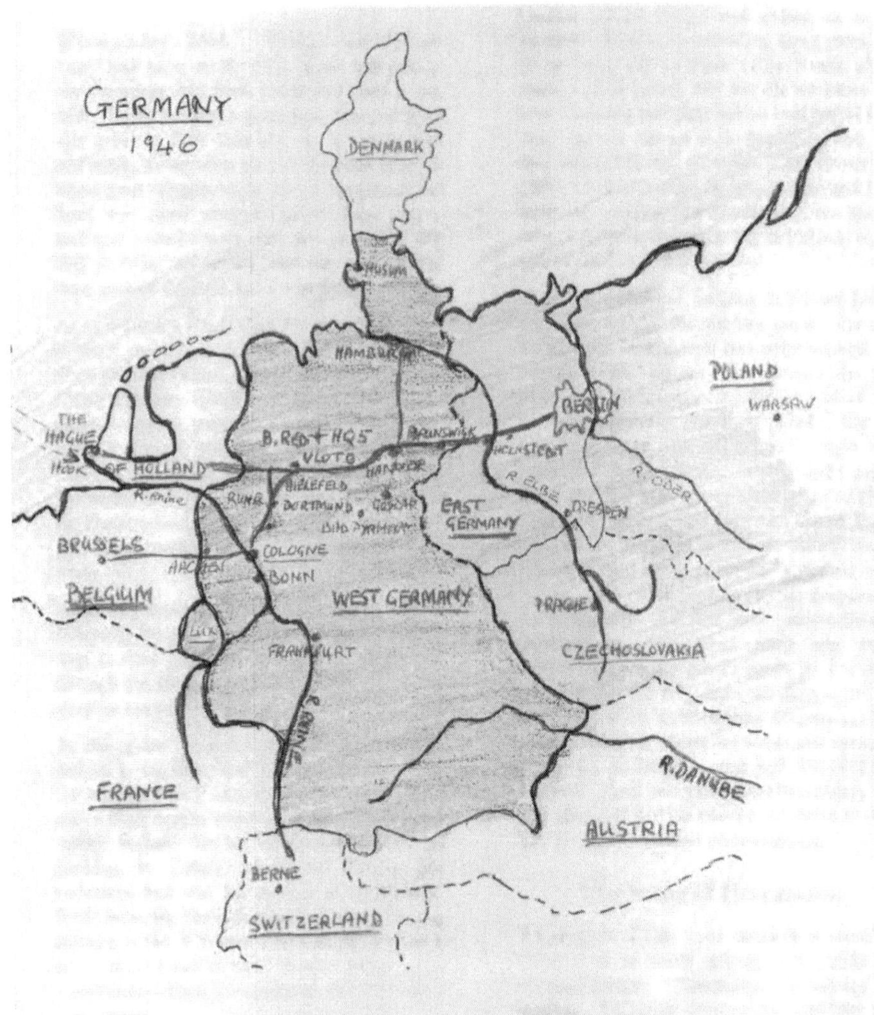
GERMANY
1946
DENMARK
HAMBURG
THE HAGUE
HOOK OF HOLLAND
B. RED + HQ5
VLOTO
BIELEFELD
DORTMUND
R. Rhine
BRUSSELS
COLOGNE
BONN
BELGIUM
WEST GERMANY
EAST GERMANY
BERLIN
POLAND
WARSAW
R. ODER
R. ELBE
DRESDEN
PRAGUE
CZECHOSLOVAKIA
FRANKFURT
R. RHINE
FRANCE
R. DANUBE
AUSTRIA
BERNE
SWITZERLAND

June 1946

To Germany

Wednesday 26th. Though our "Target Date" had been set for 25th, at the last minute our departure had been postponed until a day later. It was perhaps a good thing because there was precious little time anyway to get packed and ready, so we were glad of the extra time. It was a great struggle to get all our equipment and food into three army issue kit bags and a rucksack – made more complicated by the fact that so many last-minute requests to take food were pressed upon us, and it was hard to refuse.

At 11 o'clock a F.R.S. Unit *Fordson* truck came to fetch us and our kit, and whisked us away from Gordon House – the assembly centre – to Victoria station. There were seven of us in all – *John Pettigrew*, going to Cologne; *Walter and Alice Southwell*, going to Brunswick; *Maurice Ginat* of the French "Secours Quaker", going to Dortmund and *Hetty Tinkler* also from one of the Dutch teams; *Alice Scares*, going to Goslar – also as a replacement. All our papers were ready.

A military leave train took us down to Dover. Gradually the grey sultry drizzle of London gave way to blue sky and sunshine as we passed through the lovely orchards of Kent where the cherries were being picked.

At Dover we were shot through the Customs and on to the boat, and in part separated from our luggage which caused some anxiety. There was a fresh breeze coming up the Channel and 'white horses' for an otherwise uneventful crossing to Calais, where we finally got ourselves and our kit ashore at 4 o'clock. From here we were shepherded along by the military to No. 4 Transit Camp where we had a four course meal in the Officers' Mess. My 'rank' was evidently considered the equivalent of a captain.

Perhaps the worst bit of the whole journey out was carrying all our kit along the length of a very long platform to our compartment at the end of a long leave-train. We found we were only one carriage away from our girls who had been taken to their own transit camp. Each lot of us had a compartment to ourselves. We had also included in our party two "S.C.F." (Save the Children Fund) girls, who were to join their own Red Cross Relief teams.

Just as we were leaving Calais on the eight o'clock train, Maurice sighted two of our Quaker Relief trucks and called us to the window. They were travelling along parallel to us on their way to Paris. Our frantic cheers could not be heard, and not till we came to a level crossing and they had to wait for us to go over did we attract their attention, and then they waved us out of sight. One driver – of "HGC" – the *Fordson* on which John and I had done our training and driving test, we thought was *Ted Harris* shortly going to Poland, to join one of the F.R.S. teams there.

The strip system of farming in France looked very neat, and all the produce good. The little farmhouses looked neat and whitewashed, and though it was all very flat scenery the pink glow of a perfect evening sunset looked very lovely. Gradually the light faded. We had supper together with hot coffee brought from home in Thermos flasks. Walter and I passed away the time with a very close game of chess. Gradually we followed our route across France and on into Belgium before we turned out the light and tried to sleep. It was a perfect starry night. We were woken by a corporal at 1 o'clock for hot tea and sandwiches at Schamerbeek, just when sleep had come. Walter and I were awake again at 4 o'clock when it was the first light of dawn again. It was flat, rather uninteresting country and we tried to discover where we were, and found we were still in Belgium and just crossing into Holland. Here everything was beautifully neat and luxuriant and the houses, all made of those tiny toy bricks, looked clean and trim.

The Scene of Devastation

Thursday 27th. At about 8 o'clock we stopped at a small station just inside the German border. The change was abrupt and marked. To begin with things were not neat and well kept. There were the faded blue-green uniforms of the German frontier police about, and children on the line.

Maurice and I began to talk to our first German civilian – he was friendly enough, but he began at once the inevitable complaints, begging and whining we had been warned about. He and his friends were grateful for the cigarettes we gave them. They were rationed for cigarettes and even then they could not get their ration, and when they could they were made of half rose leaves and hay – very little tobacco, and burned away in no time. Were we rationed for bread in England? Not yet, but it was coming on July 15th. They got only 2½ lb. a week. Potatoes were unobtainable, yet across the border in Holland there were plenty but the Dutch would no let them have any. Others came up and stood at a respectful distance, also with that "cigarette hungry" look in their eyes, and yet too proud to beg.

The train went on. Bomb damage was at once apparent on each side of the line. At *Münchengladbach* we got the first sight of what our bombers had done – it wasn't a pretty sight! There were children now with haunting faces on the station, 50 or 60 of them, looking up and crying "nix Brot" ('no bread') and wandering expectantly backwards and forwards. Whenever a soldier threw them a sandwich they put it quickly under their coats, and were on the lookout for more – or they would dash for the paper bag and dash off with it triumphantly – never sharing. Or they would rush away in fear whenever a guard, a British Tommy or other official-looking person came around – they would sneak away and hide – rush after the train and wave an aimless hand and cry "nix-bread". It reminded me of the seagulls following the boat across the Channel – their behaviour was almost identical when scraps of food were thrown to them.

In France and Belgium the children had smiled when they waved, and it was a different kind of wave. In Germany there was no smile but a wave to attract attention and this haunting cry. They did not stuff the food into their mouths. It was an organised family scavenging operation.

The train waited a few minutes before going into the bombed station at *Krefeld.* Then hordes of children converged around the carriages and the cry now changed to "nix-bre-ead". Five per cent[1] had bare feet, another five per cent carpet slippers – most had home-made wooden sandals with thin straps to hold them on to the foot. Few had boots or shoes.

---

[1] *This 5%, on second thoughts, may partly be normal in summer anyway.*

The train pulled into Krefeld and troops disembarked for breakfast served by German waitresses. We had the best porridge I have tasted for a long time, real meaty sausage, peas, fried bread. Pure white bread and any amount of butter, marmalade and sugar. I felt embarrassed and guilty eating the stuff. I felt, both in the mess and on the train where Germans looked on, as I did when going over Wormwood Scrubs prison – acutely embarrassed and uncomfortable. I did not know where to put myself or where to look, and there was a look in their eyes. The loudspeaker blared "It is strictly illegal to give food to German civilians. All ranks found doing so will be severely punished." Nevertheless food continued to be given to the children wherever possible.

The devastation from Krefeld to *Duisburg, Essen, Dortmund* and that part of the Ruhr has to be seen to be believed; it cannot be described adequately. The worst bombed part of Bristol between Temple Meads and around Bristol Bridge might just come up to it, only there there has been some attempt to clear it away. In the *Ruhr* it is like that for mile upon mile with no attempt at clearance. Almost all the way at 10 yard intervals, and more frequently around the devastated stations, the children keep up that haunting cry. There's a look of disappointment in their eyes when the train has passed and they were not among the lucky ones. Eric says that there are quite a lot of accidents to these kids, who watch our trains so closely they do not see a train coming the other way. Here 10 per cent are without shoes. It may be a ruse to get more pity – but it's hardly likely. Even mothers here and there swallow their pride and stand with a baby and a basket hoping for some morsel to be thrown to them from the conquerors passing by. One hates to be seen patronising or giving, yet one hates not to give. One gives all one can and then gets what's going at the N.A.A.F.I. canteen to throw overboard. Still the men half look at you, all their desire being for a cigarette.

Burnt-out and blown-up rolling stock rusts where it was hit in the sidings. All the way along on each side of the line the fields, gardens, sidings everywhere are pock-marked with bomb craters in which weeds have grown – some sort of cultivation is going on around them. No longer neat strip fields. There are crops, but not so luxuriant as in Holland – an obvious lack of fertiliser – particularly potash and sulphates, I would say. The potatoes have poor heads, often look blighted, yellow and full of virus. Yet there's lots of colour. John and I saw many flowers we'd have liked to examine more closely, and a few strange birds as well. The railway embankments were often blue with the stiff spikes of borage, or purple with vetch, or yellow with trefoil and corn marigold, blue with scabious, or rust-red with sorrel.

But how will the ruins ever be cleared? Sporadic patching-up was going on. Factories looked cold, lifeless and at a standstill. We crossed the Rhine slowly on a bridge that was undergoing repairs. The industrial area looked like parts of Birmingham or Wolverhampton, Sheffield or Manchester, but imagine it all – rusting girders, shattered concrete and no intact pane of glass, bricks everywhere.

We stopped at *Münster*. In great haste I wrote a note to *Toni Althaus*[1] and gave it with a parcel of food to one of the station officials. He looked honest: he promised to deliver it. I think he will. I tipped him the usual cigarettes. He was pleased, friendly – there seemed to be an understanding. I longed to stop and see her, but the train moved slowly on. Perhaps I shall get back later.

---

[1] *Toni was one of our 'au pair' girls, pre-war, in Selly Oak.*

After Münster it was more normal farming country again and better crops – a relief after the devastation. Somewhere among the ruins of Dortmund *Morna Smith* was working with an F.A.U. team. The teams at Cologne and Solingen weren't far away. I knew a little of their conditions now. I thought Osnabruck was undamaged from the outside, but that was just the houses on the perimeter. In the centre again every house was a burnt-out shell. Occasionally a civilian train would pass – old carriages and cattle trucks pretty packed with refugees. On stations the civilians looked tired of eternal waiting, resigned and apathetic.

At last we got to *Bad Oeynhausen* where we had to disembark. *Tom Noel* was there to meet us and *Deryck Moore*, an O.S. of my sister Gill's time at Sidcot (F.A.U.). A Bedford 3-tonner truck took us the four miles to *Vlotho* – the Area 5 H.Q. of B.R.C.C.R. We had tea at the Hotel Koch's and afterwards a wonderful and welcome supper. Shown our billet – another good Pension with a nice garden. We found H.Q.5. was full of Quaker gray uniforms. There was *Roger Wilson*[1] to greet us, and *Eric Cleaver* who got us out here; *Elizabeth Fox Howard* and *Bill Brown* were over from Bad Pyrmont – the former on her way back to England after being first hostess at the Rest Home. *Joshua Watts* was also there with the F.A.U., and *Priscilla Lewis.*

Vlotho appears to be a beautiful little unspoilt town, undamaged, and in lovely country overlooking the River Weser where the Germans only blew up the main bridge. Sleek house martins have built their nests in the concrete recesses, children don't cry for food, have good shoes, and wear neat white stockings.

Visit to Quäkerhaus Bad Pyrmont

Friday 28th. After lunch there was a Meeting for worship in the little chapel led by Roger Wilson, which consisted of six F.R.S. members, two S.C.F. and one Salvation army team member.

Deryck drove Roger, Hetty Tinkler, Maurice and me over to Bad Pyrmont in the Humber staff car. It was a lovely drive through beautiful Westphalian country, well cultivated but not flat. The beech woods were particularly beautiful. The women on the farms seem to work very hard. Quite often we saw barefooted children (seems fairly normal). Everyone drags a little handcart, and outside each village house is a neat round pile of chopped wood, stored for winter use.

We went first to the B.R.C. Rest Home where *Miss Locke* is the warden, then on to our own No 1 Quaker Rest Home where *Margaret Colyer* and *Lilian Piper* are the present hostesses. We had tea there and then Bill Brown and Margaret took us up to see the famous Quäkerhaus where we met *Leonhard Friedrich*, a German Quaker who married an English wife Mary. Their daughter, now Brenda Bailey (married Sydney Bailey) was at Sidcot in Gill's time. I also met another Sidcotian at breakfast, Priscilla Lewis, who is working in the Red Cross. Leonhard showed us round the meeting house which has been redecorated and is beautifully modern and very well designed. We walked back to St Joseph's House (The Rest Home) hoping to see *Pastor Mensching* who was expected, but he did not come. So we went down to have a look at the little town which is famous as a spa. One is at once struck by the great number of one-

---

[1] *Head of F.R.S.*

armed or one-legged German soldiers who are there and walking about on crutches[1]. We saw also the beautiful avenue of trees which divides the whole town down the middle like a hair-parting, and we walked through the park gardens and saw the moat round the Schloss. We finished up with a cool drink at the B.R.C. Rest Home. Bill seems very popular everywhere and he is always greeted with a smile. Apparently he has a lovely tenor voice and does a lot of singing at clubs, churches and concerts etc. He was asked by the Town choir to sing with them in a performance of Beethoven's Choral Symphony recently, which was a great honour. He was once a soloist in St Martin's and also a soloist at many Friends Schools concerts.

Back to Joseph's house for supper. Nuns do all the domestic work. Interesting talk with Herr Dr. X, in German, who turned out to be a biology teacher in Hannover who has suffered a great deal from our bombing raids. He went into the complicated details of what he had specialised in, which I gather was the sex cells and reproduction of the Axolote (salamander)! The German was a bit too difficult and technical for me. There were about half a dozen people staying there for the ten days' complete rest – all victims of Nazi oppression and with sad histories:

two women teachers, one D.P. who had been put to work in a shell factory and her arms became poisoned. They were swollen up and in bandages; she could hardly lift them. I wished my German was better so as to be able to understand and converse more freely, just when we were beginning to get to know them. We left soon after 8. The Friedrichs gave us some fresh strawberries to eat on the way.

Visit to Pastor Mensching[2]

Saturday 29th. After breakfast Deryck took me over to Protestant *Pastor Wilhelm Mensching's* house at Petzen, just the other side of Minden. It was a beautiful drive to Minden where we crossed the Weser by temporary bridge, as the main bridge was blown up but was being gradually jacked up again by sappers.

The F.A.U. boys were going over to say goodbye. Pastor Mensching, a well-known pacifist, and his wife received us with a great welcome, and there was an exchange of letters and parcels which obviously meant a great deal. We were offered beautiful big ripe cherries from the garden.

Then we walked down the lovely garden while Pastor Mensching talked. He led us to the red-currant and raspberry bushes, and begged us to eat the ripe fruit.

I found him a very lovely man – unassuming, humble, generous and kind, and full of Christian love for everyone and full of gratitude. Though he himself has passed through great personal sorrow over his own family, he is full of hope and activity for the future. Their daughter suffers from epileptic fits, the eldest son suffered in the last war – is now nearly blind. Another son was badly wounded in this war, and their only really healthy child was killed in 1944.

---

[1] *The Germans, without penicillin, frequently amputated, and at once, where often modern methods of treatment in Britain saved the limb.*

[2] *Pastor Mensching had been a* FOR *member before the war, and Hitler, though the* FOR *had been pronounced illegal, had not succeeded in destroying it entirely. After attempts were made to trace the members of it, who had survived concentration camps and torture, Mensching had been under the close scrutiny of the Gestapo for 13 years, but nothing had induced him to acknowledge the Nazi salute. He won the respect of even the most aggressive local Nazis by his steadfast stand for humanity.*

Pastor Mensching preferred therefore to stay quietly at home and work in his parish, and to continue quietly writing, which he believed would do a great deal. He would thus carry on his international pacifist and F.O.R. work from home. He was at present trying to get the 4 powers[1] to recognise and allow the F.O.R. to resume. The difficulty was that if it was started in the British or American Zones, Russia would be suspicious, but not, he thought, if it first started from the French Zone. He hoped to approach the Inter Allied Control Commission and later on he started 'Friendship House'.

Mensching also spoke about de-nazification, a problem that was worrying him greatly. It was no good, he felt, putting the young Nazis in camps where they only got worse. The thing to do, he said, was to employ them in jobs or get them to live in houses as servants with the right people of the other persuasion. He gave us an example of what he himself was doing. They had a girl as a servant living with them who was a Nazi. She had given so much trouble that they had come to the point of dismissing her, but at that time she had become converted to Christianity and it had given him great joy. He gave us other examples of girls and boys who were formerly Nazis, and who often have more initiative than others, gradually coming round by such treatment and becoming interested in F.O.R. pacifist literature, and in Sunday School classes. This was the kind of positive work that he wanted to see Germans do, and not simply the dismissing of all Nazis from their posts. The Bishop had repeatedly asked him to come on to the Church committee for de-nazification but he had not joined the committee for that reason.

There was a very lovely peaceful atmosphere as we talked in the warm sunny garden amongst the flowers and fruit which he was so happy to share with people of all nations.

On the way back we drove up to the top of a hill just outside Minden where there is a colossal statue, the Rote-Denkmal[2] – to Wilhelm dem Grossen – one pillar of which had been damaged by American shelling. From the top there was a wonderful view. Towards the North were miles and miles of flat plain, and to the South rolling wooded hilly country – a complete contrast, and with the Weser flowing past below us with brown bridges at regular intervals. Some girls were singing part-songs to the accompaniment of a mouth organ.

At lunch we met *Jean Low* of the Dortmund team, and *Dennys Berry* ex F.A.U. who knew the Samsons in London.

Later I went up the hill behind H.Q. where there is a Jugend-Herberge[3]. There is a wonderful view over the town, of the Weser and surrounding countryside.

Watched a little lizard only a yard away, beautifully green on the underside and brown on top, with little white and silver flecks. Also watched a wasp gnawing at wood for its nest, and three beautiful Red Admiral butterflies sunning and sporting together.

There was a party on at the Mess this evening to celebrate the first anniversary of the coming of B.R.C.C H.Q. to Vlotho – so besides an extra-specially good dinner with wine, there was a fine cake with a single candle in the middle. *Colonel Gidley-*

---

[1] *Great Britain, France, Russia and America.*

[2] *Red Statue.*

[3] *Youth Hostel – now a training centre for Youth Leaders.*

Kitchen[1] made a speech, which included welcomes to new personnel and farewells to many F.A.U. boys, to which *Michael Rowntree* replied.

I was taken to the station for the 10 o'clock military night train to Berlin. Having just settled in a compartment at the rear of the train, the R.T.O. very kindly gave me a sleeper right up in the front, so I hastily transferred all my kit. I found myself sharing a sleeper with *Captain Taylor*, the personal protector and driver of *General Erskine* and a Brigadier who had a sleeper a little way down. Taylor went off for a few drinks with the Brigadier. He came back about midnight exclaiming he'd put much too much on board today. He thought he had better get his "pea-shooter" out just in case the Russians "tried anything". They didn't search the train, as they used to, since it was locked[2], but still, with a General – !! "You can't be too careful!"

Arrival in Berlin

Sunday 30th. *Rosamund Wallis* joined the train at Hannover just after midnight. An otherwise undisturbed night. We were called twenty minutes before we reached Berlin and found, when dressed, that it was a beautiful sunny day. As we got in to Berlin I was surprised at the sandy nature of the soil. It seems a wonder that anything grows in the soil. The Berliners were up early watering their gardens. I was also surprised at the fir woods that are everywhere.

John Fleming, F.A.U. leader of the Berlin team, met us at the station with one of the *Austin* Ambulances, and we first took Rosamund Wallis to her billet, and then went back to have breakfast at the Ruhleben F.A.U. H.Q.[3]

Our H.Q. is a fine house in the Spandau area of Berlin and just by the entrance to the Freyberg Barracks used also after the First World War as a prison camp for the internment of 4000 British men and boys. The Swiss Jewess *Dr Elizabeth Rotten* is said to have visited and distributed 'Quäker Speisung' there and elsewhere in Germany[4]. There is a 'Biergarten' right opposite my room, and a considerable amount of traffic and trams passing on the road. It also possesses good parking space for our vehicles and a small garden. There are altogether 14 on the domestic staff which is going to be difficult, as Roger Wilson says the number must be cut down, and the unit says it can't be.

Spent the morning unpacking and getting straight. Afterwards we went to the Grunewald station to meet the Red Cross train bringing back over 500 children from Austria where they had been evacuated for safety three years ago. They were brought back by the Red Cross and mostly by the initiative and organisation of the F.A.U. Chalked all over the carriages were numerous pictures of Berlin and Austria and such words as "Endlich nach Muttern" and "Endlich nach Berlin". The German official representing the evacuees welcomed them and issued instructions from a loud speaker van. He seemed to go on and on interminably, and he packed in a lot of propaganda

---

[1] *B.R.C. Commanding Officer.*

[2] *At the border of the Russian Zone at Helmstedt.*

[3] *I was the first F.R.S. member to arrive in Berlin to start the takeover from the F.A.U. team, and so was regarded with some suspicion in my Quaker grey uniform – they were in Khaki uniform.*

[4] *From "Quaker Encounters" Vol. 1 by J. Ormerod Greenwood, p215. Though Quakers in May 1920 opened their first Speisehalle for 125 students in Breitstrasse. Dr Schairer, with the support of Albert Einstein and the Oberburgermeister of the city, the scheme was extended to feed 750 – J.O.G. p224.*

for the Democracies. We weren't sure whether this was more to impress us than to benefit or indoctrinate the children. The children all looked well and very healthy and brown. Many of them came and shook hands and bade farewell in a very friendly way to the F.A.U. boys including *Colin Prior*, who were themselves pretty exhausted after the three day trip.

I was then taken for a tour round Berlin by John Fleming through all 4 sectors to see the sights. Berlin really is in a terrible mess. I did not see one building undamaged, and most were just shells. All the famous buildings were total wrecks. (60% destroyed).

When we returned I took over the *Austin* ambulance and tried it out for myself. Got on alright and liked it. After tea I took out the *Fordson* 15 cwt. that has been allotted to me. It has a V8 engine and is a beauty with a colossal acceleration and gets up to 50 m.p.h. in no time: easy to handle and manoeuvres well. I had only recently passed the F.A.U. Driving Course.

July 1946

First Assignment

Monday 1st. The entire morning from 9.00 till 1.00 was spent in a F.A.U. Section meeting at which we discussed various domestic matters such as cutting down the domestic staff, which numbers 13 or 14. We had reports on work being done and to be done, and the future of the team and its work was also discussed. We had a lengthy discussion on the employment of Young German Quakers as full members of the team, and the various consequences our choice of personnel might have on the Berlin Quakers. There appears to be a split amongst them and the situation is a very delicate one.

In the afternoon I drove John Fleming round Berlin in the *Fordson* and we distributed food to 'non-Mosaic'[1] Jews. This is a monthly distribution of the contents of Red Cross Invalid Diet parcels supplemented by other foods, and soap. It goes to -

(a) 'Catholic' or 'Orthodox' Jews, of whom there are 4000 approx., and this distribution has aided 120 individuals with the greatest need. The food represents about 140-260 extra calories a day.

(b) 'Evangelical' or 'Liberal' Jews, of which there are about 12,000 registered, of which about 800 have been issued with food. Now about 180 people get 180-220 calories extra daily.

(c) 'Dissident' Jews looked after by the Quaker Buro with about 2000 registered. 210 issues have been made, providing 80-120 (and now dropping to 60) extra calories daily.

It involved pretty heavy work carrying large boxes of food up flights of stairs in hot weather to the various offices. The women receiving the stuff were always very pleased and glad to help, but they were particularly enthusiastic about the soap. Women certainly work hard in Germany, particularly the older ones in their characteristic dust caps. They look tired and listless. It is noticeable how hard they work, both in the country on the farms and also in Berlin itself where they shovel rubble, or pass bricks, or carry stuff about all day in the dust[2]. So many men or husbands are still missing, P.O.W.s or absent.

---

[1] *I was told. I have yet to learn about these classifications, but I felt this was the kind of work I came here for.*

[2] *These women are either Nazis, or women working for the heavy workers' ration card.*

The Writer

The Team's Billet - Ruhleben

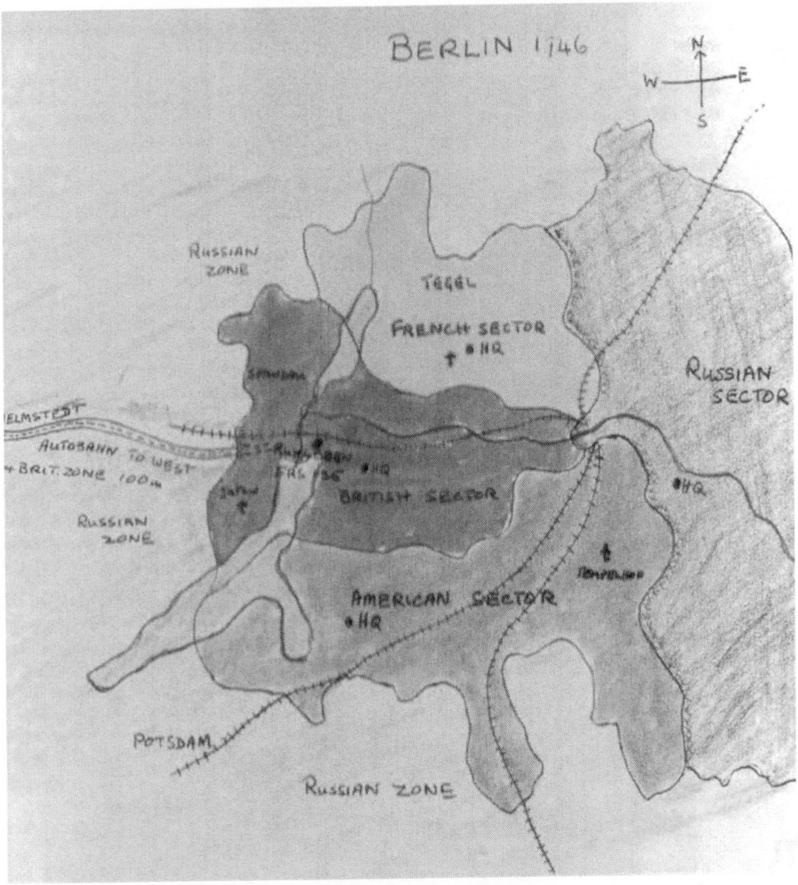

Berlin Sectors 1946

135 RELIEF SECTION
Friends' Relief Service

Freyberg Barracks
Berlin-Spandau (Ruhleben)
Charlottenburger Chaussee

U-Bahn Ruhleben
Straßenbahn 54
bis 2. Haltestelle

Tel. 93 51 42
Sprechstunden:
9–12 2–4

John Fleming (Acting Leader)

Brian Burtt (Transport)
John Seed (Red Cross Supplies)

Ethel Snelgrove, Harold Ridgley
John Downing

Some of the Staff. Hasso Wolfing, our driver/mechanic, is second from right

View from my bedroom window

Team Transport

John Seed in the VW

500 children, wartime evacuees, returning from Austria to Berlin

Saying farewell to the FAU, and Colin Prior on the right

Distribution of relief supplies

Distribution of relief supplies

After the Battle of Berlin, 1945
(Photos by Manfred Durniok)

(Photos by Manfred Durniok)

More Reichstag ruins

I drove 30 miles on this trip alone just round the Berlin streets. It was a good opportunity to get used to driving on the right hand side of the road.

P.M. went to a British military cinema to see "Song to Remember", the life of Chopin. I've never heard Chopin played so beautifully. It was good relaxation.

An atomic bomb was exploded in the Pacific today.

Distribution of Relief Supplies

Tuesday 2nd. I spent the morning on my first solo job – to load up the ambulance with food and take it to the Quaker Buro where I again met *Hans Albrecht*, the Berlin Quaker, and Clerk of the German Yearly Meeting.

My next call was to a hospital where again they were particularly glad to see the soap. Passed a graveyard for tanks.

In the afternoon I acted as chauffeur, and took various people to do various jobs. Colonel Gidley-Kitchen came to lunch and *Pastor Winterhager* from the Russian zone, who speaks perfect English.

After supper I went to call on the *Keups*. They are a lovely family. Later *John Seed* joined me there and we talked of the English and Russian occupation. People do not feel hostile to the English but they still shrink in deep fear from the Russians. We spoke of the soap rationing. The soap ration for one month fits exactly into a Bryant and May matchbox, but they have had only 3 since the end of the war. It is poor quality and smells of plasticine. I did not hear them complain. They shared some fruit with us which had been illegally smuggled through the Russian zone. They spoke openly of buying potatoes on the Black Market. They had great admiration for the work and writings of Victor Gollancz.

While I was waiting today outside the Jugendamt[1] small boys rushed up and offered me souvenirs for cigarettes. There were iron crosses and badges from Wehrmacht uniforms, postcards and stamps.

Wednesday 3rd. During the morning went out with John Seed to Spandau hospital with *Ingela Keup* as interpreter. Greatest shortage seems to be of Insulin and Morphia. We could provide some of these things and a small supply of Penicillin for V.D. cases has arrived.

Prepared parcels of food from the stuff I had brought over from England for various people. It is impossible to go and find each one, as one is not allowed to park military vehicles in the streets. So I shall have to inform them and they will have to pick up the parcels here.

I quickly noticed in a few people (Germans) the tendency to 'use' us in some way. Often the cases are pathetic enough. Often they have been recommended to come to us. Perhaps they will bring us a large basket of fruit and then ask some big favour e.g. transport to the West; or they will bring us a pathetic story and beg some sort of aid. It is hard to refuse or comply, and it is often inconvenient to comply. One does not know where to draw the line. But I feel that there are times when we must just say 'no', against our inclinations, recognising that we did not come here for this sort of work. There is the danger that if we accepted all such requests we would develop into either taxi agents or a parcels service or furniture removers!

---

[1] *Youth Office.*

A woman came up to me while I was at the curb in the ambulance and asked me if I knew where in the British zone she would get food for her dog. They had enough for themselves but they could not get food for the dog anywhere and guide dogs are very important.

First Reactions

As a newcomer I find John Seed's attitude interesting towards the Germans. On the road as a driver he has little patience with civilians who do wander about the road very carelessly and apathetically. To me their minds are so obviously pre-occupied with thoughts of how to get the next meal. Also their reactions and reflexes are very noticeably slower than English people's. I would undoubtedly put this down to lack of food. John has the same attitude towards drivers of other vehicles and carts. They too are inclined to wander about and only after persistent hooting will they suddenly swerve in or out. He shouts at them. He once walked out of a "No exit" at the Spandau hospital. I remarked on the fact, to which he replied that he always used it. It was quicker and more convenient. "Who won the bloody war anyway?" was the attitude he took, at least on the surface. I was somewhat surprised and I have also heard him use that phrase jokingly when the cooks replied they could not get a meal ready at a certain time. I was new and found myself becoming critical and judgmental of my seasoned and hardened fellow workers.

This afternoon I went to the D.P. and P.W.X. camp at Spandau to pick up an ambulance case for the West End hospital. Ilse K., the nurse, sat in front with me and chatted away in a friendly way and in good English. She told me how she had lost everything to the Russians. She was rather emotional and apt to take certain little things about the F.A.U. team too seriously, just as I was myself.

Thursday 4th. Went down to a paper factory in Wilmersdorf and took a 15 cwt. truck. Took on a load of paper, and took it up to the French sector to a printing firm where it is to be made up into Bibles. It was excessively hot and I got pretty well roasted in uniform and with the heat of the engine as well.

Spent the early part of the afternoon fetching the mail and parcels (of which there are generally 2-3 sacks full each day) from the Forces P.O. Practically all those parcels contain food and are illegal.

At tea we had rather a special cake as it was John Seed's 20th birthday. Afterwards Les Butler, John Fleming and I went up to the Olympic swimming pool for a dip. The beautiful open air bath was being cleaned. The bath was empty and there was a gang of about 30 women on the job of scraping the bottom so that the blue tiles gleamed again. It must have been swelteringly hot for them – some looked sunburnt. Very boring and monotonous work, like the Children of Israel, I thought.

Had a refreshing swim in the indoor pool and then went outside onto the grass in the sun where there was a lot of gymnastic apparatus and instructors to be used. Rather warily because of my knee recovering from a cartilage operation, I tried a few hand springs and back flips into the sand pit. An instructor and a German girl then demonstrated and helped me with some ring work, which was new to me and very interesting. I learnt a lot of new swings – twists and turns, and hope to continue some time. It will provide relaxation and help to keep me fit and in training.

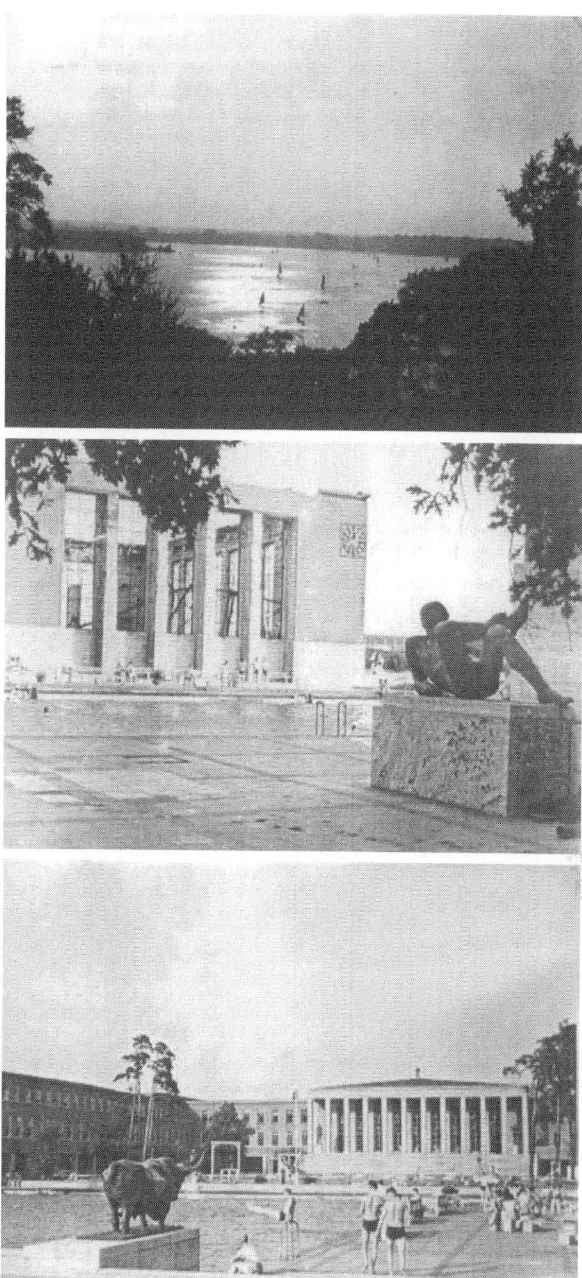

Lake Havel and Olympic Swimming Pools

Friday 5th. Got up today feeling very weak and sick. One was sweating with the dry heat by 7 o'clock in the morning. Had no energy at all and ached rather – probably stiffness from yesterday's swim and the first real bit of gymnastic exercise since my operation.

Went with John Seed to the West End hospital to distribute cigarettes, sweets and supplies to the D.P. patients and T.B. cases. Among the patients, many of whom looked in a pretty bad way, and a few who had a leg missing, there was a Chinese, an Italian and several Poles.

Continued to feel thoroughly unwell all day and could only drag myself to get the post in the afternoon. Sent out some letters to get people to call here for food and messages brought from England.

I Learn about Education

Saturday 6th. The team spent the entire morning on cleaning and servicing the vehicles.

In the afternoon I went with Ingela and Jappi to *Prof. Rheinsteins'* (Professor of Law at Chicago University) group in the American sector, where young Germans can meet to talk and discuss problems freely. The subject for today was Education. I was the only English representative, though there were several Americans there.

First some young German boys from a 'Gymnasium' (high school) spoke. He told us of the Volksschule – which is free and takes the ages of 6-14. Some at 11 go on to Secondary Schools where they paid 20 M. a month[1]. They started with Latin and in later years Greek, English and finally Russian are added. Among other subjects they learnt German Literature, History, Geography, Music, Science and Maths. In the non-classical school there was English main language, Latin and Natural Sciences. Secondary School ends with a certificate of maturity after 10 forms or grades (Matura). 5 to 6 lessons a day. 3 hrs in the afternoon. Boarding schools were rare. Some grants for talented children of poor families are available. Scholarships scarce and rather given by personal favour, it was hinted.

In Berlin most of the teachers appear to be caricatures of their profession, and there is only very rarely the close personal contact that their parents had in their own school days. Rarely a friendship between student and teacher, nor would teachers stand up for the students against the authorities. There was not enough 'civil courage' among teachers. Difficulties could be got over in the teachers with courage and personality. So in schools a complete break with the past is needed. One reform, at present being attempted, is to get rid of the Gymnasium with its humanistic programme on the classical side. Thomas thought it would be a great pity to get rid of this type of school from which most of the greatest German artists and writers had come. Does the Russian inspired "Einheitsschule" (comprehensive school) with its uniform method of training offer a good alternative in education for the Germans, he asked? He pointed out the danger in this type of school of trying to adopt a Western or an Eastern, in preference to a German orientation. It would not be good to separate

---

[1] *Also Commercial Schools.*

talented children from the others. There is now a surplus of teachers in the High Schools and too few in the primary schools. As they had a different training they could not be swopped over. Reforms are being started where they are not necessary and are merely artificial. Students, he said, perhaps surprisingly, want to have less to do with politics in schools than formerly. Many are disgusted with the school because they still have to write essays on Politics, Trade Unions, etc. Some even have had to learn names of defence council of Nuremberg Trials. It is terrifying to see tendencies growing up similar to the past period where minds are forced into strait jackets and narrow lines, and the distrust when the students produce any ideas of their own. He gave an example of how an American journalist had been to the school to talk about the Nuremberg trials. Afterwards he was asked some delicate question by a student who was afterwards arrested. On the whole, he continued, the subjects taught were quite enjoyable, but he urged that Mil. Gov. officers should take more interest in schools and come into them unannounced, so that the lessons would be unrehearsed. He hoped in this way that some of the desires of students could be heard and something done. To me this was extremely interesting, and suggests a possible line of work. So much for Berlin (Russian sector?). They were very interested and keen on the ideas of Prof. Grimm and other "German experts" which have been suggested, though not yet adopted by the authorities in the British zone (Western zone?). In Berlin tradition is thrown overboard. It was pointed out that the mere act of overthrowing a tradition simply because it was a tradition was very dangerous. Good tradition is of great value. In the Western zone the policy is more one of recognising traditions and to reform where necessary. The "Gymnasium" is encouraged.

After graduation it is possible to go on to university but in between there is an opportunity to study German philosophy for half a year.

One interesting point that came out in discussion was that no one wants to be a teacher. Teachers are so disliked. They are officers and officials (civil servants) of the State and therefore have no freedom of their own.

The Americans gave a brief résumé of Education in the States, and I was asked to follow on "Education in Britain", and was asked about Quaker Education. Prof. R. who was born and brought up in Germany, but who became an American, summed up the differences between the education he had had and that which his son was now getting in America. He said that at his son's age he knew three times as much in the way of facts, but what he did not have was his son's ability to stand on his own feet, his ability to tackle problems single-handed, to hold views of his own and to stand up and defend them. His son was learning a better art of living and more how to become a good citizen.

It was such a lively and fruitful discussion that it was decided to continue on another Sunday.

First Visit to the Ballet

In the evening Les Butler took me to see a "Grosser Balletabend"[1] by the Städtische Oper Berlin Ballet Company. They did quite a long programme of small ballets and divertissements, mostly of a character nature, with very little classical technique. This is largely due to the fact that they simply cannot get adequate bloc shoes. The German

[1] *Great Ballet Evening.*

ballet shoes are made of cardboard and are so unreliable and soft. *Margot Ufer* – Les' fiancée – is one of the principal dancers, and has a very pleasing personality and a perfect softness and gentleness about her dancing. She is also a sweet person. Les introduced me to her afterwards and to "Puma", her teacher, and *Erwin Bredon* the principal male dancer who is good but too small. We had a drink in the theatre canteen where musicians, singers, and dancers, stage hands and friends can all meet. Afterwards we went out to Margot's and her parents' little house in the woods close to the Havel Lake – very lovely. Had supper there with them partly provided by Les.

Sunday

Sunday 7th. Went to Quaker Meeting in the morning held at Jebensstr. There was a large gathering, most of whom, I gather, are "friends of Friends". About 10 people spoke, some not more than a few words. I could not follow all that was said. It was rather emotional. One man caused some disturbance by almost having a fit. Afterwards transported a load of Friends over to their Monthly Meeting place.

In the afternoon went a long walk with *Friedel Bialke*, one of our staff, through the woods to the Havel, and heard something of her experiences in the war. On my way home picked a lovely bunch of wild flowers.

Monday 8th. Spent most of the day wading through a lot of 'Mil. Gov.'[1] Education and Religious Affairs fortnightly reports, and some of *Roger Newsom's* on the contacts he had made in the Youth Work line – so as to be up to date as much as possible with the job I shall probably have to take on from the F.A.U. after they withdraw. Spent a considerable time going to the A.P.O. and Mil. Gov.P.O. to pick up the large number of parcels which come to us daily – medicine, food, and "comforts".

In the evening John, *Brian Burtt* and I were invited to supper at the Keups in Charlottenburg. They are a lovely homely family. We took rations along with us. There is a charming custom in Germany which I met for the first time after the meal at Bad Pyrmont, and after meeting on Sunday, and after the meal here of, for a moment, holding hands in a circle – as a kind of grace in brotherly love.

After the meal the Keups showed us photographs of their former very lovely estate in Mecklenburg which was seized by the Nazis. They had a huge ducal "Schloss"[2] with a lake in the middle of three adjoining estates totalling well over 3,000 acres. There was a great deal of woodland and they had over 300 deer, and stables of the most beautiful horses. They fled from the Nazis to Paris, where, after internment, they lived for a time. Then they came back to Berlin, where their flat was bombed and they lost everything. Fortunately they were able to get their present flat furnished, which formerly belonged to a Turk.

Tuesday 9th. Spent the morning taking 2 little children from the Spandau D.P. camp to be X-rayed at the West-end hospital for T.B. Waited there for them, and watched the sad cases going in and out of the hospital. One little Arab boy, who talked English, came

---

[1] *Military Government Admin. HQ.*

[2] *Castle.*

with us. They loved the ride and seemed very happy and shouted "Herr Engländer, Herr Engländer"!

In the afternoon went round on odd jobs – delivering letters and parcels to various Red Cross organisations and friends. Took Wulfin, our young German mechanic – with me to give him a driving lesson and he did improve a lot.

Wrote letters to *Ninette de Valois*, *Marie Rambert*, *Mona Inglesby* and *David Latoff* to appeal for bloc ballet shoes for the Städtische Oper ballet company here, who can do no classical work because of the shoe shortage.

A Russian soldier came in at 10 o'clock to ask for "Benzine"; he spoke good German. Fortunately it was all locked up, but we had some filthy petrol mixture Brian called "Bullsch", used for cleaning cars and gave him a Jerry can full of that, with which he was most pleased, and promised on his return to bring us "Schnapps". All very friendly! Another one was in earlier asking the way. He said he understood German but not ours! So much for our contacts with the Russians so far!

Visit to D.P.Camps

Wednesday 10th. Some of the I.V.S.P. team came round, and we loaded a huge barrel of cod-liver oil onto their truck. They took me to their D.P. camps. Jack showed me round. The main one is a transit camp for refugees and D.P.s from the Russian zone and New Poland, in transit to the British Zone. There are about 7,000 in a barracks which normally houses 2,000 people, so the rooms are grossly over-crowded. I looked in many rooms where they have wooden double-decker bunks. Less than 2 ft. apart. The blanket problem is a difficult one because they'll cut them in half and hand back half or any dodge to get away with them. They are up to every trick under the sun and will sell and traffic in railway warrants.

We saw them having a substantial midday meal of a good thick meat and vegetable stew, and also saw the bread they got – a good brown, and a hefty ration. Saw the kindergarten and children's play-centre at work and a well conducted hospital with fewer patients than I expected. In one of the other camps I asked to see the cases of scabies which they are continuously treating, about 180 cases, in – spite of a shortage of Benzol benzoate. I asked about V.D. and was told that the figures were very low. All are inspected on entry into the camp, de-loused and dusted with D.D.T. The camp leader had been arrested for black marketeering by the German Police in a raid and Mil. Gov. were in the process of electing a new "leiter" (leader). I.V.S.P. had installed wireless into the horizontal wards and were preparing a very nice old people's home.

I also watched the distribution of clothes to needy people and children in the camps. I've now seen the whole process from the beginning. I have collected clothes in Birmingham, baled and sorted them at the Bedford Institute; taken them down to Tilbury docks in a truck, seen them arrive here in Germany, unpacked and distributed them to needy D.P.s.

Thursday 11th. Went to the station at 7.30 with *Harold Ridgley* to meet *Margaret Watts* off the Berlin night train. She joins our team.

Margaret is an Australian Friend from Sydney who worked here and in Russia after the First World War, and is a relative of mine.

Ambulance work all morning, and went in search of *Horst Brasch* of the Frie Deutsche Jugend, without success.

In the afternoon collected a mail-sack full of large food parcels. Went to the Czechoslovak Military Mission to get visas for entry into Czechoslovakia for two of our Goslar F.R.S. team. Successful. Tried again to contact Horst Brasch. Eventually found the new H.Q. of the F.D.J. but not Horst Brasch – established contact, however.

Supper with the I.V.S.P. team to meet them socially and to discuss what part the 3 relief teams can play in helping with the summer holiday play centres to be started by German authorities for 8-18's in August.

Friday 12th. From an address I had been given in London by his wife, I went to see *Max Schwerdtfeger*, an artist of some repute in Berlin. He was a tall thin man with a quiet sense of humour. It was a fascinating flat full of interesting subjects and objects. There were many of his own paintings about the place which he showed me. He paints in two very distinct styles. One is of straight-forward but very attractive landscapes – the other very modern and abstract in complete contrast, more imaginative, phantastic and witty. I was invited to come again one evening and to take Les Butler, also an artist.

On the way back had a long talk with a Mil. Gov. officer (Cook) in the car park at Wilmersdorf. He noticed my uniform and was very friendly – wanting to find out where we lived as he and the padre he helped had a great admiration for the Quakers. His admiration for the conduct of the Germans in their plight was also great – of their lack of complaint and their cheerfulness. He told me he did everything in his power to help individuals and families with food and clothes. He bought all the food he could for them in canteens – all his money went that way. He seemed quite amazed how like us the Germans were, and one couldn't help treating them as human beings just like ourselves and as individuals whatever they had done. I went away feeling glad that there were such men in Mil. Gov., who when they went back to England also helped our cause.

In the afternoon Hasso, our mechanic, and I went to Spandau Hospital in the ambulance to take a young Russian Mother and her baby to another hospital. The baby was minute – mother very ill suffering from septicaemia. I sympathised, my Mother was also ill when I was born. Spent the rest of the afternoon and evening seeing the people for whom I had brought parcels of food from England.

The most interesting person was Horst Brasch – publicity agent for the Frie Deutsche Jugend. He had himself recently come out from England where he was one of the leaders of the Free German Youth in Hampstead, London, and German representative at the World Youth Congress – the opening rally of which I attended at the Albert Hall. He was very depressed at the attitude he had found amongst his own fellow-countrymen and youth. He found that the majority of youth expect another war and very many of them hope for it as their only salvation. They hope that they will join with the western Democracies in war against Russia, and in fact the tragedy is that they rejoice to see disagreement amongst the Allies and anything against Russia. At the back of their minds all the time is the idea to get back the German territory ceded to Poland.

There is still a great deal of Nazism in the youth which will be desperately difficult to eradicate, and instead of looking to and building the future, and the students, instead of being alive and seeking new ideas they are turning back and looking for the old ideas. He is amazed that people grumble so much. He himself says that it is possible to live on the rations and black market, and in uncomfortable surroundings – "with a little idealism one gets used to it and one doesn't mind", even though he himself from every point of view would wish himself back in London. But he says, "people forget what things were like;

how a year and a half ago they were starving and praying for peace, and now when they have bread and peace they forget what it was like and say it was better under the Nazis. People don't realise for instance that in Paris as regards food they are as badly off, if not worse off. There, of course, you can get plenty on the B.M. One can here, one has to live." He made one suggestion that the British Sector should bring out a Youth magazine or paper similar to the American one, or particularly the Russian sponsored "Der Staat" which contained very little politics.

Saturday 13th. The usual morning of maintenance and servicing of our vehicles.

P.M. Went to the Rheinstein[1] group again with Ingela Keup[2]. It was transferred to another group led by Capt. Stern. Professor R. spoke on the English Constitution and Democratic Government in England. He spoke in German for about an hour, and then there was time for questions and discussion. Afterwards an argument arose between the R. group and Captain Stern about the different methods. Captain S's idea is that German education has been all wrong and so he has got a group of Young Germans together to "re-educate" them. His programme is all cut and dried – so many lectures and weeks on the process of de-Nazification, so many weeks on Democracy, etc. etc. implying that he has the only way and the right way. R's group is more mixed, other nationalities being present and talking in English with more of the idea that we can all learn from one another. We did not finish till well after 6, by which time I was exhausted.

Sunday 14th. A glorious hot sunny day. There was no Quaker meeting in the morning. Relaxed. In the afternoon went to Havelsee by train with Friedel to have a swim and sun-bathe[3].

In the evening went to hear the Städtische Oper but the opera was cancelled and the ballet was put on instead, so Brian and I stayed to see the performance. Met *Mark Baring* who is touring with ENSA's "London ballet". He danced with me in the corps de ballet in the first London season of the International ballet at the Lyric in London in 1942.

Assessing the Needs

Monday 15th. In complete contrast a welcome day of rain, which cooled things down, and was badly needed by the vegetables, and will swell the grapes growing on the side of our house. Drove right down into Zehlendorf in the American sector with Margaret Watts to take a week's supply of food to 40 children and 10 adults being looked after by the Austrian repatriation committee. U.N.N.R.A. has now stopped food supplies to these people. The Americans have ceased allowing any more people into the transit camp. So it is a grave problem for these people to know what to do with the many people trying to get back to Austria. Ex-P.O.W's and D.P.s are repatriated straight to

---

[1] *Prof. Rheinstein – U.S. Mil.Gov.*

[2] *One of our interpreters.*

[3] *I was astonished to find some crayfish near the edge. Friedel made a face as I picked one up and it waved its claws. "They have grown fat on the bodies of dead soldiers and Berliners who drowned in the War – do not touch them. Put them back!"*

Austria and often their wives and children are left stranded here and cannot get back. At the moment they have to be turned into the street.

From 12 – 2.00 Margaret and I inspected some feeding centres in the Friedrichshain-Bezirk, where the child-feeding scheme run by the Swedish Red Cross is already in being. With F.R.S. help it has now been possible to extend the scheme to feeding pregnant mothers of 5-7th month's stage. Their diet is supplemented by a meagre meal of soup. Large quantities of this nourishing pea and ham soup concentrate (Vato) is taken to the Swedish kitchen where it is cooked and sent out with the children's soup to these various feeding centres. It was our job to see that the German welfare authorities thoroughly understood and were getting on with the job. We found things running more smoothly and better organised than we expected for the first day. There was at each place a pleasant, keen and efficient staff of women to do the job. We saw that the right number of women were getting the food, checked lists, asked whether anyone was collecting the food for those mothers who, on presentation of a doctor's certificate, showed that they were too ill to get the meal. The soup was disappointingly thin, and the only problem that arose was what to do with those mothers who were working and could not come and collect the stuff.

P.M. I went a round to the Swedish, International, French, Dutch and Swiss Red Cross organisations, Mil. Gov., I.V.S.P., and Salvation Army with minutes of the Food Sub-committee.

Went to supper at the Keups again with Margaret, and spent another delightful evening with them.

Feeding Centres

Tuesday 16th. Took *Jane Leverson* of the Brunswick F.R.S. team to the Polish Consulate to get her a visa to go to Poland, where she is to join the 1st F.R.S. team there. We managed this without difficulty, and then took her on to a friend.

Picked up Margaret and Ingela Keup our interpreter and went to the Tempelhof area to inspect more of the feeding centres. Again we found capable and interested women in charge. The universal complaint was that the soup was too thin, and that if it continued so, for many mothers who had to come a long way for it, they just would not come, and on looking at and tasting the soup I could not but agree that it was not worth it. I discussed the problem with a Swedish Red Cross worker at one of the places and we agreed that if possible the soup should be made half as thick again. I talked with some of the women who were all extremely glad to have the extra soup, but hoped it would be made thicker. This we have promised to do and the S.R.C. have added biscuits to the meal as well. Owing to bridges being down and streets blocked (from the bombing), we drove, in all, 38 miles, mostly in Russian and U.S. sectors, so we did not get back for lunch till 3 o'clock.

Set off straight away afterwards to get a Movement order for Brian from "Q movements" Mil. Gov.

In the evening took Les to see the ENSA "London Ballet". In spite of a very small stage quite a good show. Went round to see Mark Baring afterwards and then took him to supper with Margot Ufer. Finally delivered all the parcels I had brought from England.

Left to right: Hugh Maw, Bob Byrd, Brian Burtt, Edith Snelgrove, Kathleen Gough (Leader), John Seed, John Bourke and Margaret Watts

Child Feeding Programme with the Swedish Red Cross

Left to right: Edith Snelgrove, Bob Byrd, Kathleen Gough, John Seed, John Bourke and Margaret Watts

Captain Dale (Salvation Army) and Herbert Dobbing (FRS) inspecting Holiday Play Centres

A huge grasshopper, bright green and nearly 2 inches long, suddenly flapped into my room today and seemed somewhat stunned to find itself in such unusual surroundings!

Wednesday 17th. Took 5 more large sacks of the concentrated Swedish soup round to the Swedish Red Cross kitchen in the French Sector (Wedding) in order to make the soup for pregnant mothers thicker. It is a very fine modern kitchen with enormous steam electric soup cauldrons. Cooking is done by the Germans. Delivered relief parcels to the Quaker Buro.

Hordes of flying ants, in their nuptial flights, settle on my windows at night. Hot and dry.

Les was telling us of the enormous job he has discovered:- the welfare of unmarried German girls landed with British babies, for whom no welfare is provided. Many of these girls are genuinely in love with the British Tommy who may have gone off back to England. Many of these soldiers on returning to England change their minds. Perhaps if the ban on such marriages is lifted, the problem may ease. One example he gave us was "like father like son". On visiting the house he found photos of the man everywhere. The girl informed Les that the man spoke fluent German. How? His father had been in the Rhine occupation-army after the last war and had married a German girl then.

Thursday 18th. Took *Thea Wilmer* and Mark Baring of *Nat Dolsky's* London Ballet to see the Städtische Oper Ballet class at 11 as I had been invited to come along by *Jens Keit* the ballet master. It was a very good class and extremely keen and hard working. Their bar work was particularly good. 8 of them had had an invitation from Nat Dolsky to come and see the show and they were so pleased.

Thea and Mark came back to dinner with us.

In the p.m. Margaret and I went to the Zwölf-Apostel-Kirche to hear *Karl Barth* the Swiss theologian speak. The church was packed, all very eager to hear him. We had been given tickets and sat right in the front row. The speaking lasted 2½ hours and towards the end it became very difficult to follow but I managed to get the main gist of it. I was asked to send copies of the speech to Carl Heath and H.G. Wood.

Friday 19th. Kathleen Gough, Edith Snellgrove and John Downing arrived this morning from Vlotho and London to join the team. We are now complete.

Went on a hospital round at the West End. Took Ingela with me to help interpret. Took Red Cross parcels to D.P., and T.B. patients, cigarettes and sweets, and heard which ones wanted clothes. One of the doctors, a Palestinian, also asked for a suit, food and cigarettes. One gets the feeling that when one is brave enough to ask and gets it, the others then try to do the same. I had an enormous number of requests, quite a few of which I suspected were not in great need. It is extremely hard to judge the genuine cases. I found it an exhausting business.

Took another load of Swedish soup across to the soup kitchens.

P.M. gave Wolfin another driving lesson while doing various delivery jobs.

In the evening was invited out to supper with her to Margot Ufer's with John S., Puma and Erwin Bredon one of the leading dancers. It was a most amusing evening and I had the first real good laugh since entering Germany. I suddenly realised this strangeness to hear myself laughing again – a reminder of the grimness of Germany's state and the tasks ahead.

Puma is a wonderful mimic and it was an evening of ballet anecdotes.

R.A.H.[1] sent me a wonderful parcel of food and clothes. With it I was able to help a woman who came to see me today. She had heard of me through someone I had been able to help. This was to help a baby that had been brought to Berlin by its aunt – the mother having died due to the birth, on her way to join the father in a different part of Germany, could not get exit permit to leave Berlin and so could not get food for the child. It was 11 months old and a baby of this age should be about 20 lb., but this one weighed 13 lb., and was getting practically nothing.

Saturday 20th. An interesting afternoon with *Miss Mary Bailey's* student group. They are mostly from the theological college. Their views about Karl Barth's speech were, that though he was very good and had many important ideas and suggestions to make as the result of much thinking, yet it was experience from outside. It was not from inside experience such as *Pastor Niemöller's* who had himself suffered. Both had escaped to Switzerland, so they felt he could not really feel and sense what the Germans had and were experiencing now under the Russians. They felt he was not *the* great leading light, and that he did not fully understand the feeling that there was another form of totalitarianism under the Communists. Pastor Winterhager bore out much of this at supper when he said that he (Barth) did not realise the religious force behind Marxism. Another woman who also heard him bore this out too but thought that through his isolation he would also have a more detached and wider view of things. Barth, I understand, has not come back to Germany to take up a professorship at Bonn University. Letters from the Sadlers Wells, New York, and Marie Rambert Ballets to say that there was no hope for ballet shoes from England. Shoes are used till they are worn to shreds in England and they are very hard to come by. By Customs law the New York Ballet must take back the exact number they brought. *Mona Inglesby*[2] wrote to say she would try and send me some but could I send her silk stockings if she asked nicely!?

Heard it said today that there is a large section of the Church which believes that the world and man have reached the last days and look for the return of Christ. Reminiscent of Christadelphians.

Monday 22nd. Entire morning given over to a section meeting. The first of the whole group together.

Spent the afternoon giving Wolfing a driving lesson in the *Commer*, and Edith and Kathleen in the Ambulance.

Mary Bailey[3] of the Mil. Gov. Education and Religious Affairs Department came to supper and afterwards to talk. She gave us some idea of the set up in Berlin and then some lines of work that she thought we might usefully do. She is a teacher from Keswick and formerly had applied to do relief work with the Guides. Since she could not get her release as a teacher, the only way of getting to Germany was with Mil. Gov.

---

[1] *Dick Harman (Senior Master at Sidcot).*

[2] *Director of International Ballet Co. and my former employer!*

[3] *Who succeeded Guy Clutton-Brock (who had been so helpful to me and who had left to serve in Africa – Cold Comfort Farm).*

in this capacity. My first impression on meeting her with the theological group on Sat. was not too favourable. But as a result of this talk it seemed as though her arguments and judgements were sound and shrewd on the whole, with only minor disagreements. It was interesting that she appealed most strongly for fair-play to the Russians and thought it was more important to get on successfully with them than it was to make the Germans happy and satisfy them. Possible lines of work: a youth group here of an educational nature. Renewing contacts with the Youth Committees and Clubs already in existence. Finding out what is being done for youths who have just left school. Visits to large factories to discover what youth Welfare and educational work is being done, etc.

Jewish terrorists bomb King David's Hotel (British H.Q.) in Jerusalem.

Entertaining Guests

Tuesday 23rd. Main event of the day was entertaining to supper *Pastors Grüber*[1], *Weckerling and Rackwitz* and their wives – all the three were very different but distinct characters. Rudolf Weckerling is young and speaks fluent English, and from all accounts is one of the finest and best known personalities in Berlin. He is the Protestant Pastor of Spandau and is very interested in Youth work, a close friend of *Bishop Bell* of Chichester and the Fellowship of Reconciliation. I also talked with Pastor Rackwitz who was keen on my suggestion of getting an English group such as the Rheinstein group, as international as possible, or of ourselves going to speak with representatives of the other allies to speak to groups in his Parish. He is a tall quiet grey-haired man, and a member of the S.E.D. – the "united" party, and the F.O.R. which they are hoping to start in the sectors – a curious mixture.

I did not get a chance to talk to Pastor Heinrich Grüber much. He does not speak good English. White-haired, has been in concentration camp. Brusque and with rather blunt manners. Another friend of Bishop Bell in touch with *Bertha Bracey* in London.

Rather a tense moment when Margaret began to play the piano, and when asked to play Chopin waltzed off into a Prelude and forgot it half-way through!

Wednesday 24th. *Theresa Hoene* (German Quaker) called for her luggage and I took her right up to the north of Berlin in the *Ford* as far as the Russian border. She lives just the other side. I managed to find some food for her children at the special request of the Catchpools, whom she adored. She was living in Bad Pyrmont in safety and good conditions, her husband is a prisoner in Russia. She felt called to come back and live in the Russian zone[2].

We entertained *Ingeborg Stelten*, a Norwegian war correspondent, to lunch. She has been to Woodbrooke and at one time or another has had considerable contact with Quakers, and so looks up the Quaker teams when she can find them. We found we had a good number of friends in common, such as *Myrtle Wright* and the *Lunds* of Oslo. Norwegians are still very bitter about the occupation.

She remarked on the incredible amount of self pity of the Germans and how they expected to have things done for them. They are only too ready to talk unfavourably about the Russians. They do not realise their guilt, and they still think that no-one can

---

[1] *Propst (Provost and Archdeacon).*

[2] *I met Theresa again in Philadelphia, U.S.A. in 1989.*

be as bad as the Russians have been. She points out to them the sensible conclusion to Germans that she would rather have a Russian occupation than a German one. The Russians are a primitive people and therefore one could forgive their actions more easily but it was not so easy to forgive such uncivilised and primitive behaviour committed by a highly civilised nation such as Germany.

Kathleen, Edith and I went to visit the Waldschule in Grunewald. This is a German sponsored experimental school where young German children of about 9-14 are sent for three weeks to this beautifully situated school in the woods by the Havel lake. The idea is that it should be a complete contrast to the type of Nazi school of iron strict discipline, and that the children should have a taste of real freedom. In the morning there are freer and enjoyable lessons in the open air. They get extra feeding, and the afternoon is free for them to do what they like. Parties are made up to go bathing and to play games, walks, digging and so on. We joined one party going down to bathe – about 30 small girls about 9 years old. Played games with them in the water and helped to teach them to swim. It was a wonderful hot day. Children all look very happy, well, and brown.

In London the Foreign Secretary Bevin said the Big Four must unite to govern Germany. Shinwell warns that there is not enough coal to get through the winter.

Thursday 25th. Spent the morning going round in the Big 3 ton *Commer* delivering the salvage that Brian had brought up from Vlotho. Took it to the Salvation Army team, the I.V.S.P. team at the refugee camp and the Frauenausschuss[1]. It consisted of canvas, ground-sheets, army battle blouses and trousers, stoves, boots, etc. for distribution.

Took Les Butler to tea at Max Schwerdtfeger's – the artist. He showed us his paintings. There were the old ones – many of which I liked – particularly some of the landscapes, and then a huge pile of new ones of modern style – grotesque, bizarre and crude – seeing so many, as Les said after tea, made one feel rather sick. One felt the man was rather on the scrounge for all the cigarettes and stuff he could get, though I rather like him. His wife is very grateful for getting letters and parcels through. Max said the Nazis didn't allow him to paint anything original in the war. His wife was a Jew and got to England, now trying to get back. Les says it was a good thing he wasn't allowed to paint anything more than copies!

In the evening Margaret and I gave a talk to the Berlin English Society on Quakerism. I spoke on it of England and Margaret of Australia. Kath, Edith and J said they thought it was an extremely good meeting. John said he'd been to many in the 8 months he's been here but this was best and showed most interest. Usually they are rather cynical. Quite a few questions at the end, would have liked more, and expected to be challenged more. Given tea afterwards and RM. 100 for expenses or to be used for our work.

There was that evening one of the most glorious golden sunsets I can ever remember. It lit up all the ruins of the city and made it look like a stage setting – made everything strangely beautiful in spite of the awful chaos and destruction.

The first sub-surface atomic explosion is detonated at Bikini atoll.

---

[1] *Women's Committee.*

Meeting Berlin Quakers

Friday 26th. Entertained the main Berlin Quakers to supper in order to get to know them. Had the *Halle* family, the *Hoffmans*, *Martha Rohn* a dear old lady I fetched and took home by car, *Elizabeth Abegg*, white-haired and angelic – the Clerk, and *Thea Horleborg* one of the leading Young Friends, rather a more informal friendly evening than with the Pastors. Discussed our work and theirs. John D. and Edith went with Red Cross train of T.B. patients to Schleswig Holstein.

Anglo-U.S. panel recommends the partition of Palestine.

Saturday 27th. Another very hot day. Kathleen and I had a wonderful swim in the Olympic open-air park which looks beautiful. Did some P.T. on the lawn with some P.T.I. s and did my first cartwheel backward somersaults since my operation on the cartilages of both knees (Christmas 1945, Woodlands Orthopaedic Hospital, Northfield, Birmingham). So I really feel encouraged to know that my right leg is really almost back to where it was before. Slight stiffness and a little weakness left.

News that- Toni Althaus[1] received the parcel I left for her when coming through Munster. Also news that Morna Smith had visited Lena Riemenschneider.

Sunday 28th. A quiet morning reading up the Mil. Gov. Education and Religious Affairs monthly reports, to get a general picture. They make fascinating reading as a history of events in Berlin since end of war.

In the evening most of us went to a special concert for British troops by the Städtische Oper Orchestre under Arthur Rother. The programme opened with Wagner's "Flying Dutchman", and then the IIIrd Act of Tristan and Isolde with the Opera soloists Gunther Treptow as Tristan and Kirina Kutz as Isolde and Hans Heinz Nissen as Kurwenal. I thought it exceptionally good, and a very musical, sincere and sensitive performance. After the interval came two Debussy Nocturnes, Fêtes and Sirenes with choir, and lastly Dvorak's 4th Symphony – one of my favourites.

Summer Play Centre Scheme

Monday 29th. *Herbert Dobbing*[2] senior French master at Ayton School, arrived to pay us a week's visit. He came round in the p.m. with Kath and me, and Captain *Dale* of Salvation Army, and Beryl of I.V.S.P. team, on an inspection of the Summer play-centre scheme which we are interested in helping. This is a German operated scheme whereby 40,000 children 7-14s are taken out of the centre of the city to these play centres for extra food and recreation. The one we saw in Grunewald had 900 children, and lovely playing fields. There were 36 staff which included voluntary teachers, student teachers, helpers and older 'Gymnasium' boys and girls to assist. The children were all extremely happy and friendly, crowded all round us and took hold of our hands and sang songs. The other centre we saw had packed up because of the rain.

Brian went off early this morning to accompany Pastor Grüber by air to London. He was chosen as he was due for leave. John D. and Edith back from Schleswig Holstein after a successful trip – having hitch-hiked back.

---

[1] *Toni Althaus and Magdalena Riemenschneider were our prewar 'au pair girls'. Lena was married to Heinz who was a P.O.W. in England for most of the war.*

[2] *And later H.M of Brummana High School, Lebanon.*

Took H.D. round in the car to see some of his friends and a bit of Berlin.

Tuesday 30th. Went round again to several of the feeding centres to see if the pregnant mothers' scheme was working satisfactorily. Found the whole thing going badly. The soup was still far too thin, and half a litre is too much in such liquid form and was inclined to make them feel ill at night. They asked again for less and thicker soup. The German authorities had muddled up the numbers and sent too many mothers along to the centres and so there was often not enough soup to go round. It seemed hardly worth while continuing if it was going to be badly done.

Kathleen and I went along to the Grunewald Waldschule again where, with the Hauptschulrat and others, we were the honoured guests and given the front row of seats at the farewell concert of this lot of girls and boys. They gave a very good little show – sang songs, reciting poetry, little plays and scenes in verse, puppets etc. with complete self-confidence. The children were perfectly sweet and seemed very happy. K. and I noticed that the children that came from the poorer districts of Berlin, where some of the heaviest bombing had been, showed it markedly in the mature ageing of their faces far in advance of their actual age.

We were able to take them some medical supplies, soap and towels, of which they were very badly in need.

In the evening most of us went to see a performance of Shaw's "The Apple Cart" produced by Basil Dean by an excellent ENSA company at the Städtische Oper. The show was an experiment, in that it was the first time that a German audience was invited. Half the theatre was reserved for Germans who had to pay and half for the British troops which, as usual, was free. We are still not supposed to fraternise!

Later in the evening we came out into the Reichskanzler-platz to try and take photographs of the fantastic N.A.A.F.I. building with its neon and flood-lights wasting electricity.

First Trip Across Russian Zone

Wednesday 31st. Started off on a long trip to Vlotho at 9.30 a.m. First of all picked up *Annie Halle* one of the Berlin leading Young friends who lives in Zehlendorf in the American sector. She had passes to go to Vlotho for a conference. Had on a full load of furniture to take to Hannover for a German family.

Arrived at the British check point on the Autobahn at the beginning of the Russian Zone at 10.20. It is exactly 101 miles through the Russian zone down the Autobahn to the Russian and English frontier posts or checkpoints at the other end. I picked up *Herr Schaffner* – chief engineer responsible for the Penicillin factory in the British Sector of Berlin who wanted a lift as far as the border where a car was waiting for him.

Halfway down the autobahn we stopped to stretch our legs in the Russian zone. I brought out my thermos, some biscuits and chocolate. Herr S. told us how 80% of the penicillin made in the factory in the Russian sector went to Russia and only 20% to civilians, but that in the factory in the British sector the reverse was the case.

Hitler's Network of Roads

The autobahns are amazing uninterrupted, two-way, concrete highways which run right across Germany, this one down to the Ruhr and Cologne. No minor roads come into it or go off. They all go over the top in neat little concrete bridges. It does not go through any main towns but misses them by a few miles, and the "Ausfahrt" and "Einfahrt" or exit and entry to these main places go off at an acute angle and a wide sweeping bend right round and underneath, rather like a clover leaf pattern. The whole thing is built for speed. One sees very few houses.

Mostly through the Russian zone the Autobahn runs through beautiful wooded country, mostly fir and pine woods mixed with birch and occasionally oak woods. Flat country with quite often a half mile stretch of farm land neatly cultivated. Mile after mile I kept up an average speed of about 38 m.p.h. One could not easily tire of the beauty of the different green colours of the woods and fields, and the splashes of yellow, gold and brown of the ripe harvest which was being gathered in. Brighter splashes of colour were made by the wild flowers, bright yellow, blue and pink, with here and there butterflies which are rarities in England – such as Swallowtails and Camberwell Beauties.

The *Commer* was running beautifully and as we went along we waved to all the Russians and Russian trucks, mostly one pulling another as they went past. Generally they just stared at us and did not respond.

At 2.20 we arrived at last at the Russian check point on the far side where we had to have our papers examined and the truck was inspected. The Russian Corporal was asleep on a bed in the control hut. He refused to be woken. The soldier repeatedly shook him. An officer arrived and took down details. 3 Russian soldiers then searched the luggage of my two civilian passengers.

They came upon a box of Annie's modern American sanitary towels. They must inspect. They took them to pieces like children playing with new toys. Ah, at last they understood and sniggered and hastily shoved them back. What was her occupation? Children's nurse and nursery teacher. Ah she had children of her own? No, she just worked for children. She was not a mother herself then? No. Time she was. The barrier was lifted. We passed through into the 50 yds of no-man's-land to the British barrier where we went through the entire process again, though in a more dignified and efficient manner. Once more the barrier lifted. Herr Schaffner was met by his wife and car.

I filled the truck up with petrol and oil at the relief garage and had a cup of tea and a bun at the N.A.A.F.I. Canteen and read yesterday's newspaper. Shinwell, in Britain, warns there is not enough coal to get through the winter at home. From about here the woods give way to farmland. They seemed to be fine crops of grain that were being harvested. Away on the left we passed Brunswick. One has to slow down at practically all bridges. They were nearly all blown up and have been replaced by temporary ones – Bailey bridges which rattle and squeak and groan as one goes over, and which hardly seem safe. These have to be negotiated at 5 m.p.h. in 1st gear.

We left the Autobahn to call in at Hannover. Had tea with our team there, which included *David Hughes*. Did not stop long as we had the load of furniture to dump. It took some time to find the place. The street addressed on the envelope was non-existent – there was not a house left standing. We then discovered that the address was wrong but was probably another street with a similar sounding name. After picking our way through the ruins of still uncleared streets, we found the firm. By the time we got there all the workers had gone home and of course there was nowhere to put the stuff. After much argument and telephoning, it was settled and a place was found. With the help of another man I then had to unload the entire truckful of heavy furniture and put it in the store. It was getting late, we still had a long way to go and I admit I was getting pretty impatient. However the job done I recovered my sense of humour and politeness. Soon after 7 o'clock we left on the last stage of the journey. The country now gets more and more beautiful as you approach Vlotho. With wooded hills, colourful valleys and lovely wide sweeping views as one gets higher. At one place there is a series of parallel, narrow, single-track temporary bridges where the original ones were blown up. They look and feel perilously unsafe. Left the autobahn too soon and got onto a very bad narrow country road and did not realise until too late that we were the wrong side of the river and had to go all the way back to the autobahn, then over the bridge and round to Vlotho. Finally arrived, pretty tired at 9.30 p.m. exactly 12 hours from when we started. Distance of about 250 miles. During the meal, which was waiting for me I had a chance to talk to Tom Noel. Afterwards he took me up to the F.R.S. billet which is right up on the hill behind H.Q.

August 1946

Relief Supplies

Thursday 1st. After breakfast unloaded the rest of my load of parcels, and 2 drums of oil, and began to load up again with stuff for the return journey. Called in at the Red Cross garage for 2 new tyres for the Mercedes. Another load of stuff from *Pastor Fischer* for two pastors in Berlin, and finally 30 large tea-chests full of Red Cross food parcels, some Penicillin, mail and so on. I had hoped to be off by 9 or 9.30 at the latest, but owing to people's general inefficiency, and 'take it easy' policy I didn't get off till 11.30, too late to get to Brunswick for lunch. The truck had a very heavy load on – there being no space for anything more, and up the hills it was heavy going to begin with. I was a bit nervous of the tyres bursting as they are none too good. Also the red ignition light was now on all the time and the vehicle not charging. I decided not to do anything but carry on at a speed just below 30 m.p.h. and get it seen to at Brunswick.

Again lovely country. I longed to stop and take photographs but it was a dull day and visibility not too good.

Finally arrived at Brunswick just after 2 o'clock, where I saw *Mabel Weiss* in the Polish D.P. camp, and she took me over to the F.R.S. hostel where I was welcomed by good old *Alice Southwell* and Walter and given lunch. Walter took me down to the P.O.L. Garage where I filled up with petrol. Back again to the D.P. camp garage where Walter got the Polish Mechanics to fix the ignition light so that she was charging again. It was the old trouble with the Automat. She was distinctly less noisy when this was put right. After a nip of tea with the team, Mabel very briefly took me round the camp, and showed me her Nursery School, which was extremely clean and good, and well equipped, I also saw the kitchen and the chapel. The Poles have made a most striking altar out of Spam tins. She says that their services are a very real part of their lives and very moving. Met *Beryl Wood* the leader, *Lawrence Speak* and *Idwal Harry*. They hoped I could stay the night but I felt I had to get back. I rang up the Frontier Check point to see if I was too late to cross into the Russian Zone and was told that 6 o'clock was the official closing time but they allowed half an hour's grace. They said it was about 45 minutes' run from Brunswick I decided to leave at 5, but actually did not get off till about 5.15. I made a slip on the way and so did not get on to the Autobahn until 20 min. to 6, to discover it was still 18 miles to the frontier. To get there by 6 meant going at about 60 m.p.h. With the engine now going beautifully I decided to risk a burst tyre and go at 45 m.p.h. to get to the frontier in reasonable time. It rather meant "flogging" the vehicle to go over 40, but she seemed to take it comfortably. Had to slow down to 5 m.p.h. again to go over the bridges. Finally got to the frontier at 6.15. Only 2 min. at the British post, and was let straight through the Russian barrier without being searched.

Then began the long 3 hour monotonous trek. For mile after mile I kept up a steady average speed of 35 m.p.h. The road was practically deserted at this time and hardly any traffic. Occasionally a small pathetic civilian family group would be sitting, tired, at the side of the road. I must have been almost their last hope of a lift at that hour, and it was awful each time to have to sweep past and ignore their appealing looks. The sky was very dark and overcast. It gave one an almost eerie feeling to be reliant on one's engine. I felt anxious and vulnerable and found myself thinking of all the things that might happen if the engine failed or I ran out of petrol. I must have gone over careful petrol-mileage calculations a dozen times to assure myself I had enough. Actually I knew I hadn't got a great deal to spare. I found myself watching the signposts and milometer and making calculations of how much further it was, exactly how long it would take me, at my average speed. All the time I was listening most carefully to the engine and watching the oil-gauge and ammeter anxiously to see if there was the slightest change. She continued to purr along beautifully. It seemed almost too good to last. Fortunately the strong head wind I had encountered on the way down was now helping me from behind, so that even with a heavier load I was able to get a higher m.p.h. out of her.

As I found myself getting nearer the frontier post I felt my spirits rising and my speed increasing. There was a wonderful sunset behind me, reflected in the tree tops and occasional vivid glimpses in the driving mirror – a brilliant deep orange red which gradually deepened until violet and mauve rays entered in, and when the sun finally dropped behind the trees it quickly began to get dark. Sooner than I expected, and I confess, to my relief, I rounded a corner to arrive at the frontier post. I got out of the cab to report to the Military Police. It was cold and I felt pretty stiff as I had not stopped for a rest this time.

The first question the Red Cap asked me was whether I had had any trouble with the Russians en route. I replied that I hadn't, and asked if there had been any. He replied that the English driver in the truck in front of me had been attacked by an armed Russian who had stopped his vehicle. The driver was asked if he had any more soldiers in the back, and was then threatened that if he didn't get out of the cab he would be knifed. On getting out of the cab the driver had kicked the Russian in the face so that he lay sprawling in the road. The driver had kicked him thoroughly once more in the face, jumped back into the cab and driven on. I felt somewhat thankful the experience hadn't happened to me, and wondered what I would have done under similar circumstances. I saw no Russian lying in the road, but I did see an armoured patrol car with a jeep full of armed Americans, before and after, tearing down the Autobahn in the opposite direction.

I had arrived at the British barrier at 9.15, exactly three hours after I entered the Russian zone. Got into the centre of Berlin at lighting up time and home at 9.45 just as the team was beginning to think about 'phoning up'. A good hot meal waiting.

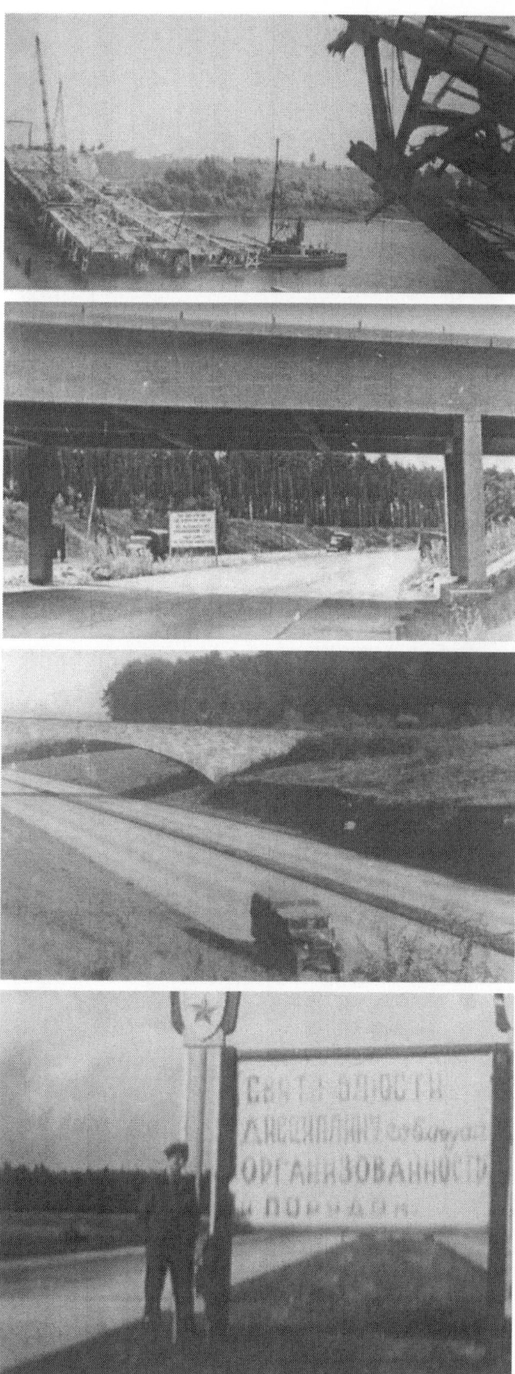

Autobahns

Delivery to Hospitals

Friday 2nd. Took Herbert Dobbing and Edith with me on a delivery round – supplies to 3 hospitals. At the West End hospital Edith was able to speak to some of the D.P.s in their own languages, Italian, Dutch and Polish. It obviously meant a lot to them. I always find this going round as 'Lord Bountiful' embarrassing, depressing and tiring. On to the Kinderkrankenhaus[1] where we handed over stores to Ruth, who then showed us round the hospital and gave us a cup of tea. At present a large number of children with T.B.; dysentery not so bad as last year when they were dying at a rate of 34 per week, quite a lot of Diphtherias and chicken pox, and measles. Also 20 cases of Malaria. How they do need this food, and how pleased they were. The nurses too need it. Pale and thin often, and doctors and nurses understaffed and few.

In the afternoon went off with Margaret to inspect more Play Centres in the Neukölln district. All had too many children, and not enough organisation or helpers. It is difficult to organise play for children from 9 a.m. to 6 p.m. without giving them a lot of extra food. They only get so little. However they are kept off the streets and in the open. Not so easy in wet weather. It is good that "Gymnasium" and "Hochschule" boys and girls are helping. I tried to encourage them in a job which surely must put them off ever wanting to take up teaching.

In the evening the team was entertained to supper royally at the Salvation Army team's house which is now only 10 min. away, beautifully situated and quiet, just by the Olympic Sports Club in the woods.

Sunday 4th. Ann Hodgkin, Roger Newsom and Malcolm Sadler were here from the Goslar team. At Meeting met Mrs Francis Bolling whose husband is an American War correspondent living in Berlin. Hoping to see more of them.

In the evening a few of us went to see a special performance for the troops of "The Barber of Seville" by the Städtische Oper Co. Kathleen and Anne were bored stiff probably because they were tired, and walked out. I enjoyed the performance, which though it was not first class and had not got the great singers was nevertheless a good and interesting performance both musically and artistically.

Bank Holiday

Monday 5th. *Eileen Groves*[2] was to have come to see me from Minden for the weekend but no C.C.G. personnel were allowed up to Berlin for this weekend for "swanning" as such leave is called. Anne, Roger and Malcolm were up here for a "conference".

Most of the team took a holiday. Edith and I took the ambulance and went to see Pastor Weckerling to talk over our youth project. We saw the Jugendausschuss Jugendheim that is being used as a feeding centre for 6-9 year olds and is being repaired with aid of some young girls employed by the Jugendausschuss. The place was apparently a "Schloss" (castle) that once belonged to an "English Lord" who gave it to a

---

[1] *Childrens' Hospital.*

[2] *Eileen and I grew up together in Kingsmead Close, Selly Oak and played much tennis together.*

dancer called "Petipa"[1] after whom the place is named. There is a big room upstairs with concealed lighting which lights up a pale blue ceiling in which golden stars are set. In this room they show fairy tale films to the youngsters.

We went to look at a large wooden hut building which had been used as a Youth club, but the leader had been dismissed, Pastor W. thought because of his refusal to join the Communist party which dominates the Jugendausschüsse. It was an excellent place down by the river. To get there we had to go across a very sandy part and the ambulance got stuck. I could not get out and the wheels just stuck, whizzed round and sank deeper and deeper till the back axle was right down. We tried to dig her out and put bricks underneath but to no avail. In the end we had to telephone for a rescue squad to come and pull us out. In 25 min. John Fleming and Wolfin appeared in the 15 cwt. with boards. We dug again and put the boards underneath and tried to back out. She moved at last only to get stuck again, finally hitched onto the 5 cwt. and both together we got her out and onto firm ground.

Out of Bounds

As it was such a hot afternoon I decided to take the afternoon off. So I went a walk through the woods at the back of our house and through the barracks by the shooting ranges to the Olympic Games stadium and took a lot of photographs. I went up the bell tower which is very badly damaged and has a bulge and is open through the middle. Poked about in the rooms where wireless apparatus and debris were mixed up with burnt uniforms and papers, bits of flags and so on. Picked up several sheets of note-paper of the Nationalsozialistische Deutsche Arbeiter Partei. It was a very queer feeling to wander about in these deserted rooms where drama had been played. In one place there were reports of wireless broadcasts in English and English Newspaper cuttings about shipping and industrial figures. One I remember being underlined was that the "Normandie" had been taken over by the Allies as a troopship and might be used as an aircraft carrier.

It was an odd sensation to walk about this huge deserted stadium, having seen the film of the games, and to stand on the very rostrum where Hitler had delivered speeches and received great ovations[2] as seen on the news films.

Finally had a swim in the sports club and did some P.T. again on the lawn. Met Major Smith, O.C.,P.T. in Berlin and a Colonel who was O.C.,P.T. of Rhine Army.

Tuesday 6th. Took Hasso, the mechanic, and Harry who arrived today out on a driving lesson in the 3 tonner. Having given them all the practice and coaching I could, I then put them in for the Army Driving Test. The corporal who came out with us to test the lads was a very decent fellow. We were all very pleased particularly Hasso, that they both got through. They were both extremely grateful. Hasso had set his heart on getting

---

[1] *I assume this was one of 2 brothers Marius and Lucien Petipa, the most famous, and one of the founders of modern classical ballet. According to Arnold Haskell: "In 1847 Marius Petipa, real founder of the Russian Ballet, goes to Russia (St. Petersburg). He was a Frenchman who became a Russian. He headed the dance company for 50 years, composed 54 ballets, including Swan Lake. D. 1910".*

[2] *I still have these souvenirs. I was told that this bell tower was strictly out of bounds to British troops and in danger of collapse. I did recognise that I was a member of the Forces.*

through. Spent the afternoon giving Harry practice on all our different vehicles. He will now be able to drive the women round and do odd jobs on his own.

Lord Haw Haw[1] and Rumours

We were all invited in the evening to go down to the "Terrassen am Strandband Wannsee" where we were entertained by Students of Berlin University English Society, who gave us a programme of music and singing followed by an open air performance of "A Midsummer Night's Dream" which was beautifully done, and with great vitality and enthusiasm. The play was interrupted by a thunderstorm and had to be removed indoors. A beautifully situated spot, with a wonderful view over the lake. In the course of conversation we talked about "Lord Haw Haw" on the wireless. I explained how in England he was never taken seriously and we turned him on as a joke, and to have a good laugh. One or two women expressed extreme astonishment that we had been allowed to listen to foreign stations and Lord Haw Haw. "That's democracy," said one of the girls triumphantly and she proudly told us of how she illegally listened to the B.B.C. during the war. Most of these students have only had the year from the end of the war in which to discover all the literature and plays that were banned during the Hitler regime. The difficulty now was to find the copies.

Rumours of wars still seem to be rife. Here in Berlin, of course, there are many stories of the evil of the Russians, fear of Russians, and suspicion, as bad and often worse than in Nazi times. Jappi says that still the anxiety and uncertainty of living in the Russian zone outside Berlin is ever-present behind the whole of daily life. The Russians are incomprehensible and you never know what they may do next. They may pick out a bus load or a cinema load of people and transport them en bloc as they are, to work on the land or something (uranium mines?) for a couple of days and then come back. Meanwhile their relatives know nothing of it. This happened to her some time ago. It is not so frequent now. But there are still many stories of people disappearing for good and not being heard of again. The latest of these is that officers and prisoners of war repatriated and released are being kidnapped in the Russian sector and disappearing, on the assumption that they are British agents.

Les told us of one woman he went to see whose door was barred and bolted and who was living in fear of her life. She lives in the British sector and yet she was being thoroughly badly treated by the Americans and the French. Her husband has been taken off to Russia and she has heard nothing more from him. The Americans now boycott her and accuse her and her husband of being Russian co-operators. She is in mortal fear, worse than in Nazi times. There are stories of American soldiers disappearing or being arrested as spies. Roger Newsom told Harold Ridgley that an American colonel who had given him a lift on the autobahn had told him that a lot of these stories of Russian kidnapping of Americans was a put-up job to stir up feeling, and that there was a definite anti-Russian campaign to stir up this ill feeling with a view to it leading up to war with Russia before she got the Atomic bomb secrets! It does

---

[1] *"Lord Haw Haw", William Joyce. fascist Director of Intelligence in the British Union of Fascists until 1937, when he formed the more openly pro-German National Socialist League. On the outbreak of the Second World War he went to Germany and regularly broadcast to Britain, being known as Lord Haw Haw. He was tried for treason at the Old Bailey in 1945 and was hanged (Hutchinson's New 20th Century Encyclopaedia, 1964).*

seem also that food is being used for political ends. Russia wants to feed her zone the best, to get the October elections in her favour – so that if America offers to bring food in to Berlin, Russia threatens to withdraw all her food supplies. It all seems incredible. Some examples are first hand, but for most stories we ask if they actually saw the incident or knew the person, and they do not have first hand knowledge.

Wednesday 7th. Spent another morning going round with Kathleen inspecting more of the Childrens' holiday play centres. The 3 we saw seemed to be better run, probably because there were fewer children at each place, i.e. about 300. Organisation better. When it rained there were films and shows for them indoors, singing and stories. Keen staff co-operated with the Frauenausschüsse. The extra food was excellent. They were very pleased to have had sweets given to them. The place in the Tiergarten had its own individuality. There was no playground but they made little Indian huts and wigwams among the bushes.

Scavenging

In the afternoon I called at an army engineers' Storage Depot on the scrounge and managed to get 4 crates of broken glass sheets for one of Pastor Weckerling's Church buildings which he hopes to convert into a Youth club or kindergarten. These large pieces of broken plate glass can be cut to fit the windows. I also managed to got some roofing felt to patch up the roof above the boiler room of the Jugendheim in Spandau (Petipa's house). The carpenter was very pleased that I could get some, and told me that the 10 cigarettes I'd given him the previous day had bought the Plaster of Paris necessary to finish another job. Pastor W. was very pleased to get the glass. "A real bit of practical relief work" he said. Unfortunately, cigarettes are the universal black-market currency.

While we were dealing with the glass Kathleen was talking over with Helga Weckerling the results of K's talk to 20 women in Spandau on "Women in England during the War". K. had felt she had not been a success, and Mrs W. was disappointed and told her that her description had the result that the women remarked that it was very similar to being under the Nazis. K. had not stressed sufficiently the moral difference behind the two sides – how England had been totally unprepared for war and joined all these organisations voluntarily and because they knew they were right and fighting for the right against something evil. I began to realise some of the problems that Pastor Weckerling must have in his parish of Spandau (where *Rudolf Hess* was eventually imprisoned[1]) as a pacifist and member of F.O.R.

Hunger – A Political Weapon?

Thursday 8th. I was interested today to read on the front page of "Soviet Weekly" of July 18th the following headline:

"Hunger as a Political Weapon. What is wrong with World Food Relief?" By A. Gorodstsky, as it bears on what I wrote on Aug. 6th.

"The deficit in the world food balance is variously assessed. Politics colour opinion to a certain extent. There is here and there a tendency to 'lay it on thick' in assessing food requirements particularly in the case of countries which the U.S. and Britain are interested in supplying.

---

[1] *After his life sentence on October 1st.*

Bell Tower

View of Olympic Stadium from Bell Tower

Rostrum at base of Bell Tower where Hitler gave speeches

Army Games – Berlin Olympic Stadium

Helga and Ruth Weckerling…

…with Mary Bailey

This applies chiefly to the western districts of Germany", and, ... "in the hands of Britain and the U.S. food has become a most important political lever. Indeed the foreign progressive press asserts that, at the present stage in world politics, it is the most important political tool of these two countries. Foreign democrats regard the food policy of reactionary circles in the U.S. and Britain as an instrument of political pressure analogous to the "atomic policy" though at another level".... "Hoover used his tour.... for open anti-democratic, anti-Communist and anti-Soviet propaganda. (See Introduction).

The food policy of Britain and the U.S. is bent either towards giving direct support to reactionary groups in power in various countries, or towards using relief as a means of applying pressure to democratic governments in the interests of reactionary elements. Food relief for Greece is a most striking example of this ..." from "Izvestia".

Entertained the I.V.S.P. team to coffee this evening. They are an extremely nice, friendly, natural lot and everyone felt quite at home. It turned out, extraordinarily enough, that one of my best friends at Bristol University in the early days, *John Richards*[1], is *Margaret Richards'* brother. I was his guarantor at his tribunal in 1940 and often used to go to concerts with him, and even went to their home in Gloucester. She is extraordinarily like him. Some of the team knew *Anna Crosfield*[2]. The Richards family had camped on the same field as our family at Bosiney Bay in Cornwall.

Democracy or Communism?

Friday 9th. Read *Guy Clutton Brock's*[3] fascinating diary of his German visit in April for the World Council of Churches, and for Reconstruction in Europe. He made an exceptionally fine report full of real Christian suggestions. I think his visit will have done a lot of good. I was glad to have had a talk with him before I left London, and to have met him, and to be working with his great friend here, Pastor Rudolf Weckerling.

Kath, Edith and I went to Rudolf's this evening where he was entertaining German and English guests one of whom was Padre Neil, an army chaplain. The subject as usual turned to Democracy and Communism. Germany was not yet ready for democracy, she had been used to dictatorship for centuries – to being told what to do, and not having to express her thoughts freely or take responsibility and make decisions. The great problem for Germany is Democracy or Communism. She is not really ready for the former and yet she could not stand more totalitarianism. With Communism that totalitarianism already exists in the Russian zone and to a large extent in Berlin. If you become an official under the Russians you are more or less forced to become a member of the united (S.E.D.) party. There was no freedom or liberty. There was a sense of disappointment and disillusionment to find that after all the Western Democracies aren't so Christian after all. So in the British zone there is considerable anti-British feeling. This is not so in Berlin where undoubtedly and without bias the English Mil. Gov. is the most popular. Russia is feared and hated and there is the desire to join with the Anglo-Saxons in a holy war against Russia as the only salvation and the only hope for the future, the only way out of the hopelessness.

---

[1] *One of the few pacifist students at Bristol University. John died c.2004. Margaret Richards (née Cutforth), who became a Quaker at Warwick Meeting, died Oct. 2011.*

[2] *P.E. teacher for girls at Sidcot with me. Married Michael Rowntree.*

[3] *Former Head of religious affairs Dept. and member of Warwick Meeting.*

It seems amazing that people who have been so bombed and who have lost so much could desire another war so soon. What has happened? What they have passed through does not seem to have sunk in. As Rudolf said, they are like deer grazing; when the storm comes they shelter in the rocks, when it has blown over they will come out and continue as before remembering little of the storm, its significance or what it has done.

Evangelism or Food?

As another German said to me the German nation has not had to suffer enough and has not been brought low enough to realize what has happened, otherwise she could not think of war again. The Church has little influence and poor attendance mostly. The church has not the inward authority and vision to put the gospel into modern terms that will appeal to the majority of working people. As Guy Clutton-Brock emphasised – Evangelism is needed, desperately, more than food.

We finished the evening with a reading from the Bible, a prayer and some hymns.

There seems to be so much writing to do, so many letters to answer, so much to learn, facts to find out and confirm, and to report and send home. I wish I had a better knowledge of the language and could talk more easily to people. But there isn't time. As it is I haven't been to bed before 12 since I can remember. It's becoming a habit – I survive on cat-naps.

Deportations of Children

Saturday 10th. The question the Germans are asking, and it is a difficult one to answer is: "You blamed us during the war for not rising up against and resisting a Totalitarian regime. Now when we are again under a Totalitarian regime equally as bad if not worse, why do you not encourage us to resist it, why do you not help us to resist, and fight against it yourselves?"

A prevalent attitude among the people seems to be "roll on the 5th Reich, the 4th is as bad as the Third".

I made the following translation from the German (British Controlled) paper "Der Kurier" of Aug. 8th:

"A delegation of mothers from the Province of Brandenburg has come to Berlin to appeal to the International Red Cross, the Protestant Bishop, and the World Council of Churches Relief Committee, because thousands of 13-17 year old children have been deported from Brandenburg Province in the last month.

The children were seized from the streets, the mothers report; the parents have since then received no sign of life from them. The delegation of mothers has produced a list on which hundreds of parents have registered.

The children were carried off, according to a Reuters report, by Russian troops and Russian secret Police. In 6 Kreise of the Soviet Zone there are practically no children left between 13-17. The delegation of mothers explained that the children were placed into groups from each village, without luggage and just as they were. They were taken by lorry to concentration camps in East Germany. The women who had thrown themselves in front of lorries were driven away by the guards with shots fired into the air. People have, so it is said, seen the children in camps surrounded by 4 rows of barbed wire and being guarded from observation towers.

It is impossible to send letters and parcels to the children. With an inquiry the parents were referred by those belonging to the Russian local Kommandantura[1] to the Kreis[2] party control of the S.E.D. where they did not receive any help."

Also young people who were in the anti-fascist Youth movement were included in the compulsory deportation. In the opinion of many parents the children were removed to camps to have their world-outlook trained[3]. Also officers of the Russian secret police have said to the mothers, according to the Reuters report, that the children had been taken away for their education and would stay away for 2 years. From a report in the French News Agency "France Presse" which itself included a report from the Daily Mail, it is a question of a "political removal from school" or a training on different lines, after which the children will soon return. The Berlin Correspondent of the News Chronicle explained that the report of the mothers was being confirmed by Bishop Dibelius and the Int.Red Cross. The children were being seized village by village by the Russians and taken into concentration camps, and this correspondent stressed that it was only a question of a few belonging to the former Hitler Youth!

Some of the mothers came to see Leslie about this and we are going to try and take it up with Mil. Gov. It has profoundly disturbed people of course and it is hardly tactful to tell them that the Russians are doing exactly what the Germans did to young people of other countries such as Poland, though I did hear that remark made by a German. "It is so silly", she continued, "the Russians are doing the same wrong and bad things that we did and making the same mistakes."

John S. and I were invited to a party in the evening of some young students in a cosmetic factory in the American sector. We got so involved and interested in our discussion that food and dancing and the party were temporarily forgotten. This was a group that, apparently, had suffered much under the Nazis. Margaret, for example, whose parents were Jews was not allowed to study in wartime and was made to work in a factory. It was refreshing for me to find a group that was so balanced and perceptive in its judgement, and who put internationalism above nationalism; who had a distinctly pacifist outlook, and who did not think the Russians were all bad. They had not been allowed to dance in the war. John and I agreed some of them would make good members of our proposed International Youth Group.

Sunday 11th. Heard for the first time a concert by the Berlin Philharmonic Orchestra conducted by the young Rumanian *Sergiu Celibidache.* Here is a very fine orchestra and conductor. They gave us a most incredible performance of Shostakovitch's 5th Symphony which was quite unforgettable. I have never heard such incredibly soft pianissimos or loud double fortes at the climaxes. I have not been so excited or so moved by any music or performance for a long time.

Interviews that Spoke to Me

Monday 12th. Had two interesting interviews today. The first was on an introduction from Corder Catchpool to *Dr Sofie Quast*, head of the office 'Archiv für

[1] *Commander's Office or H.Q.*

[2] *District.*

[3] *Brainwashed.*

Wohlfahrtspflege'[1]. Here they have all the records of social welfare in Germany. They interest themselves not only in all German but also in international welfare work of a non-political nature. It seems that it is an organisation that will be of the greatest help to me in Industrial Welfare and Juvenile Delinquency.

Dr Quast told me one interesting sidelight on the deportation of children – see Aug. 10th. This has been going on for some months from the Russian zone (not sector) and of even younger children, but the English controlled German papers have only given it publicity now so that it can do its work politically with regard to the coming elections.

Family Breakdown

The second interview was with *Herr Wittkowski,* head of the Spandau Jugendausschuss or Youth Committee, who seems to have a great concern for Youth in his area. He is to let us have a programme of all activities and all Jugendheims, so that we can visit when and where we like without warning so that nothing can be specially prepared for us, and we shall see good and bad as we find it. He stressed that we could help with material things but also on the intellectual and spiritual side. He gave us examples of how the present set up can affect morals. Young boys have been sent to pick up and collect cigarette ends. They have been encouraged to steal food or cigarettes by their parents and told that unless they bring the stuff back they will not be given any food. This came out at court when a young boy who had been caught with a gang he'd been told to join. Young girls are sent out by their parents to fraternise in order to get the soldier's cigarettes and soap. The implications and results are frightening and vast.

Went out to join with the I.V.S.P. team's effort to teach some German Youths cricket! They had already had one previous attempt, and had got about 20 youths for the second try. But it was rather a cold windy evening, and it certainly was not a success and after about an hour they lost interest and as soon as they had had a bat, ran off to play football. The difficulties of explaining the game and showing them are impossible, I thought, for they have no idea of bowling or of hitting a ball[2].

The Russians Hit Back

Tuesday 13th. It appears that in the Russian press and Radio, attacks have been issued on the reports of deportations of children. The Russians accuse the British of bribing the German papers to print such rumours in order to influence the coming elections. The statements however are such that they do not deny the truth of the accusations but are so worded that they get round the whole business. John Fleming and Kathleen today went to the Security branch of Mil. Gov. for further facts and to see if anything could be done. It is now really too late. The whole thing is a great embarrassment to the British authorities who are, I really believe, honestly trying to co-operate with the Russians, for they know that such suspicions reverse any progress that is made. It also becomes easy for the Russians to say: "Oh well you have a camp for young girls". It is true but they happen to "be diseased" – one gathers they have V.D. and it is an isolation hospital.

---

[1] *Welfare Archives.*

[2] *Some weeks later, by a roundabout route, I received a warning that the Russian authorities regarded these attempts as 'military exercises' and that they must cease!*

Today took medical and first aid supplies down to the Childrens' holiday Play Centre at Wannsee where they have 800 children. The Sportleiter[1] and the Red Cross nurse were extremely glad to see the stuff – it was exactly what they wanted.

I Am Given an Assignment

Had an interview with Mary Bailey, Religious Affairs Dept. Mil. Gov. to get more details of the survey she wants me to make on Juvenile Delinquency. It sounds most interesting, but she hopes I can do it in three weeks. I hope to get into the Law Courts and prisons and reform schools. Hope to make use of Dr Sofie Quast whom I met yesterday.

Paid a call on *Charlotte Falkenthal,* friend of *Dr and Mrs Ruben*, and took her a parcel of food on their recommendation. She is a most charming woman and spoke German both clearly and slowly so that I found her both easy and natural to understand and talk to. We had a most interesting conversation for about 1½ hours, over some tea. She has some beautiful books. Out of 10 rooms of furniture she now only has enough to furnish one room, the Russians had the rest.

John D. and Les went down to the 'zone' in the 3 tonner for salvage. Team difficulties over the N.A.A.F.I. Poor Kathleen tired and depressed.

Saturday 17th. *William Hughes* arrived to join the team. He is a wonderful old man of 74, full of life and vigour and a grand sense of humour. He was a First World War veteran relief worker and had been thrown out of Germany by the Nazis. Kathleen and I went down to meet him on the 7.30 train and I backed into a *Volkswagen* and crashed its window!

Sunday

Sunday 18th. Quite a crowd of us went to Meeting. For the first time I was able to understand most of what was said. Met quite a number of American Quakers there with whom we hope to have further contact.

Later in the day Hans Albrecht rang up inviting me round to his house to meet *Sam Snipes* who was passing through Berlin on his way back to Munich from Poland. He was one of the first C.O.s from the C.P.S. camps in America to join UNNRA. On his way over to Germany by air he had 12 hrs in London, in which I had met him at Friends House with his friend *Channing Richardson* while I was training. I had spent the day showing them "Woodstock" and London. Our last words were: "perhaps we shall meet in Berlin". This was before I knew I was going to Berlin. And here we were, meeting for another 12 hrs. or so actually in Berlin.

At Hans Albrecht's house Sam spread out a map of Poland and showed us his route and all his adventures on the way. He had met the 2 Quaker teams in Poland, one of them included the people we had trained with at Woodstock. It was great to see him again – as he is quite one of the finest young men I have ever met.

Einstein deplored the use of the A-bomb today.

---

[1] *Leader.*

Dr Sofie Quast

Sofie and Peter in the garden

Ilse Abshagen
(student interpreter)

Nabbed for Speeding

Monday 19th. Spent the afternoon showing Sam round Berlin. Had him back home to tea and then took him down to the Anhalter station – centre of Berlin. On the way I was nabbed by Military Police for speeding down the Kaiserdamm on wet slippery roads. Admitted I had no excuse, and was let off! After some difficulty owing to bridges across the canal being blown up we found the Rail Transport Officer (R.T.O.) only to learn that it was the wrong station and that we had to get right down to the station at Wannsee in the far tip of American sector in 25 mins. to catch the train. That was over 10 miles which demanded that I should have to exceed speed limits again. The *Fordson* is inclined to skid like mad on these wet roads, but I decided to risk it and kept up 30 to 40 all the way and had to go over red traffic lights. Just as we were coming to within 1 mile of the station petrol gave out, but fortunately I was able to switch over to the reserve tank and she picked up. Roared up to the station and just made the train.

Over 3,000 killed as Hindu – Moslem riots broke out in Calcutta today.

First Discussions on Youth Problems

Tuesday 20th. Attended a meeting of the Archiv für Wohlfahrtspflege Welfare workers at Dr Quast's home and met there *Dr Thoran* who is to be my interpreter on the job, *Dr. Rengier*, a Catholic and head of a college for social education, and *Dr Klapper*. I was presented with the provisional programme mapped out for me for visits and talks with all people and institutions connected with Juvenile Delinquency.

We discussed at some length the problem and state of young people in Berlin and of delinquency in particular. They are all extremely keen to help me with the survey. The discussion inevitably turned to the Russians and to Communism, and to the fact that the Germans have no hope under present conditions. Totalitarianism still gives them no freedom. Dr Quast herself gave an example how she could have telephones, money, support and everything she had not got now and wanted, if she joined the Communist party. She had asked for all these things from British Mil. Gov., and they know that it is an organisation working for the Allies but nothing is done. As usual argument got hot and excited and it was often hard to get a word in edgeways, and to quietly put our Quaker Relief point of view. A session of nearly 3 hrs, which anyway seemed to make us all keen to start.

At the Nuremberg Trials the prosecutors reject Rudolf Hess's plea of insanity. He continues to be imprisoned in Spandau Jail, within sight of my window across the Russian controlled railway yard.

Visit to a Juvenile Court

Wednesday 21st. The entire morning at Lichterfelde, in the American zone, attending the Juvenile Court with Dr Thoran. It was most interesting. 5 cases were heard, 4 boys and a girl all about 16 or 17 years old. 3 of the boys were up for driving offences and were let off with a caution. Under the Nazi laws of 1943, which are still the basis that is used in the courts, fines have been forbidden. In the case of the 4th boy he was imprisoned for stealing Allied clothing.

The girl's case was an interesting one. Her mother was a labourer, i.e. cleaning debris all day, father dead. Past history revealed she was a prostitute, had been before the courts before and sent to a corrective educational school which had failed. She had run away from a hospital while being treated for V.D., in itself a punishable offence. She lived in a small garden hut with a girl friend for which they had stolen coal for cooking, and to which they had invited Americans. She had already been under arrest for 2 months. The judge gave her 6 months in prison, and they are now making an appeal.

I talked with the Judge who seemed to be a very sound man, genuinely concerned with youth welfare and corrective education. I asked him a lot of questions, and the jury, prosecuting counsel, and defending counsel or Fürsorger from the Hauptjugendamt, and they were all glad to help my survey.

Juvenile Crime Statistics

In the afternoon I had a 2½ hour interview with *Herr Beuster*, head of the Jugendgerichtshilfe of the Hauptjugendamt, to get facts and statistics for the report. It was incredibly interesting. This department concerns itself with the social relief work on the legal side for "Youth in Danger", as they are called. The principles are based on the American and English probation system. Youth courts are now obliged to ask for the help of this organisation when dealing with juveniles. They help to prepare reports on each case brought before the court; on the background of the delinquent, conditions of family and home life, education, behaviour in community, and all other circumstances that may lead to a judgement of his/her psychological, intellectual and physical condition and character qualities. They also find out about his parents, school and the Youth movements he belongs to. These people really have the same rights as the defending counsel. The judgement (and sentence) must be in agreement with them.

They also visit prisons, speak to the youths and find out why they are there, and help them to have their cases heard at the earliest opportunity. Though the judicial side rests with the judge, their work is more to help with the re-education and corrective educational side.

I got the follow interesting facts and figures from Herr Beuster:

Continual rise of juvenile crime from 1918
During inflation Peak period 1923
Yearly average 4600 cases 1928-32
Number considerably decreased after 1933
2800 case per year and steady increase 1933-36
Rose by about 1,000 a year from 1936-39 till more than before – about 6,000.

Herr Beuster thought that even in spite of better economic conditions it is the normal tensions that exist within the body of the nation and under the surface that are responsible.

At the beginning of the war numbers grew only very slowly.

1939 – 4200 cases
'40 – 5200 cases
'41 – 6000 cases
'42 – 7600 cases
'43 -'44 – bombed, no records

Since the end of the war they are incredibly high and on the increase.

From Nov. '45 – 480 cases
Jan. '46, – 660 cases
Feb. – 800 cases
Mar – 925 cases
April – 1000 cases
May – 1600 cases
June – 1800 cases
July – 1800

and if they go on at this rate in 1946 the number of cases will be round about the staggering figure of 18 thousand altogether.

The ratio of really serious crimes has increased alarmingly. For example in the last 4 weeks the number of murders committed by juveniles has equalled the total for the past 4 years. Among the 1000 juveniles awaiting trial are 15 murderers who have robbed in addition, and among these 15, are young girls of 15 and 16 years of age.

Whereas in former times there used to be crimes of every sort now they seem to specialise and narrow the field down to crimes against property and persons – robbery and murder. There are now, for example, very few who have committed arson or political crimes, whereas during the war about 10% on average were political crimes committed by anti-Nazi youth. In 1940 more than 50% were political crimes such as sabotage.

Herr Beuster was certain that crimes against property would diminish when economic conditions improved. The value of life has so much diminished in consequence of war and present conditions. He stressed the point that these young people are not anti-social. In the first place hunger is the cause. They steal to get bread, and often where bread has been stolen they have left butter or sugar or dried milk which were side by side with the bread. Therefore they cannot be counted as real criminals. The reversion to primitive living conditions is responsible – continual hunger, often no homes or lodgings, or they don't feel at home with parents, one or other of whom may be dead or missing, the other working all day, or there is a divorce.

The Youth have no opportunity to join sports organisations or gymnasiums for these are forbidden by the Kommandantura. They loiter in the streets or go to Cinemas and dance halls, craving for cheap excitement. They are not so interested in films because German films are all out of date, and foreign films are in a foreign language which they do not understand. The Youth are lethargic and have no special interests. When these officers go to see the boys in prison and ask them about their home or school life they will always answer, but ask them what their special interests are and they are stumped for a reply. They have none.

Characteristic feature of youth, he says, is that they are suspicious of all they are told. In the last 12 years all that they were told was wrong. So now they don't accept anything. The uniforms that they wore in the Hitler Youth took all authority away from parents. To punish the youth was going against the Führer personally. Also the sudden change in political attitude of the parents shows the youth that the parents lie and have lied.With bombing and war experiences they are prematurely adult.

They do not appreciate liberty of the press. One paper says one thing and another the exact reverse. Therefore both are liars. With no knowledge of the outer world youth has been deprived of opportunities to develop mentally and at a rate comparable with their physical development. Seen now in their present attitudes it will take a long time to get back to their former freedom intellectually. For them all values have been destroyed, and must be rebuilt and must come from within themselves. But how? I ask myself.

General demoralisation of the population (Herr Beuster's views continued): The Black Market[1]

The decent honest worker who is keen on his work and has vision and hope in the future works all day for a very small salary. All round him he can see people buying and selling in the black market who do no work, but make far more in one day than the honest worker can in one month. The honest worker who is conscientious has dry bread to eat – the other eats well. The young people see this state of affairs and think the honest worker is dumb and unintelligent for doing his work conscientiously.

It can be said in favour of the Nazi government that they had the power to stop such rackets as the Black Market. The Allies far from using such power foster the Black Market and largely support it. Now children under 14 take a prominent part in Black Market dealings.

They get a great deal of encouragement from adults and parents.

Family Disintegration – Demoralisation of Youth

V.D. is common amongst girls of 12 and 13 and has been found in children down to 8 years of age. Only British soldiers are kept away and severely punished if found with them. Americans and Russians are beginning to follow the British example and often search the quarters of their soldiers, and finding children there give them up to the German police. Beuster stressed that the German courts should be empowered to hold the parents responsible for such conduct of the children because in so very many cases it is the parents themselves who force the children to do these things. He knows of cases where girls of 13 always have a Russian with them. They are not personally interested in the Russian but the mothers are – for the cigarettes! Boys of 16 bring Russian soldiers home to their sisters in order to get food and cigs, for themselves. The Americans do punish the parents in such cases. Normal family life in Berlin has become quite the exception. This also is true of other large German cities, he says.

Another interesting fact to note is that only the smallest percentage of the criminals were Hitler Jugend in Nazi times – which was because they were fully occupied. That occupation is now missing. Beuster feels frustration in not being allowed to get young people together in a group to talk to them because it would be condemned as a "new" organisation by Mil. Gov. Sports organisations too are prohibited – as encouraging militarism! Russians are afraid of new resistance movements or a political movement springing up. Beuster can only get the youth together when they are in prison, for talks and games!

---

[1] *After the end of the War the Deutschmark lost its value rapidly and a thriving Black Market economy was flourishing by the time I arrived. It was not until June 1948 – 3 months after I left Germany – that currency reform took place to restore confidence.*

Little Hope For Youth

Thursday 22nd. In the morning Dr Quast took me to the Soziale Frauenschule or Women's' Evangelical Institution at Johannesstift where she had a class of first year women students training for social welfare and social relief work, as it is called. Here, for 2 hours, I discussed and answered social welfare questions and youth problems and the problems of life in Germany today, and in England: emigration, the Russians, food, and the Christian basis of life, Quakerism and so on. They were a very friendly, keen and interested group. It was good to see it, but once more I felt powerless to offer them much hope.

As I am finding everywhere else they stressed this opinion that there is no hope for young Germans. They themselves stood very little chance of getting employment. For most young people there was no possibility of professions or at least not the right ones for them. For intellectuals and professional people it was even more hopeless.

One met the accusation again:- if the Allies have no common policy as to what they want to do, how can the Germans know what to do?

Before the war their standard of life was very high. Now they say it must be lowered to the Russian standard and so the youth say that if it has to be lowered any further than it is now then there can be no hope, because now it is hopeless.

They, too, said how difficult it was for honest people. That it was easier to sell a sack of potatoes on the black-market. You could get more money that way than by working conscientiously all day.

In the afternoon Dr Quast and Dr Thoran accompanied me to the Bezirksamt or Town Hall of district Wedding, the poorest district of Berlin, in the French sector. We took Dr Quast's two dear little fair-haired boys Peter and Paul with us. It was a great treat for them and they were very excited with the ride. All German kids love a ride.

Here in the Jugendamt I was introduced to *Frau Klappe* the Leitender Stadtvormund or Berufsvormund (Professional Guardianship for Youth) and another man in the same office.

Orphans of War

There are only 4 full-time and one half-time Guardians in this district to look after welfare of 6636 children. These are mostly illegitimate children, orphans and refugees. It is their function to try and get the fathers to pay. The mother has to look after the physical side of the child's welfare whereas this department is responsible for them legally until they are 16. Where there are no parents they have to try and find foster parents. The lower-middle class are the most willing to adopt. There are plenty of volunteers for the younger children because the extra ration card is valuable to them, whereas there are few volunteers for older juveniles because they just cannot feed them on the ration card.

Frau Klappe herself gets a salary of 650 RM a month, and after taxation and rates are deducted it comes to 350 RM a month or just over £2 a week, which hardly pays for rent. Fürsorgerinnen[1] get RM 220 a month and Ration card 3, yet it is essential that they keep healthy for this strenuous work.

[1] *Welfare workers (women).*

The Facts of Juvenile Delinquency

The Kommandantura has ordered that no leniency be shown to juvenile delinquents and here in the French sector punishment is often very severe and often more severe than for adults, and quite a number have died from T.B. in prison even before trial, they reported. Here the youths are arrested and put into an air raid 'Bunker' now used as a prison. This office tries to prevent pre-trial imprisonment and tries to keep them in Jugendhilfsbund and Bunker rather than in prison. In the two former places no record is kept so they are not 'branded' as they are when they come out of prison.

They pointed out again that the first stealing is as the result of a real need. They then see how easy it is, and how easy it is to make small fortunes on the Black Market and so they develop into real criminals. They should be brought to trial as soon as possible and not left in the prison atmosphere, often with older criminals. Effects of punishment seems to be zero, for as soon as they come out they start again. Large increase in gangs consequently.

I asked what she thought was the influence of the Church. She seemed to think it was growing. Whereas formerly it was a particularly anti-church district in 1933, now a great number of parents are baptising their children. There is a need for more pastors and more active ones. But the attitude towards death was interesting. Nowadays at funerals very little emotion was visible. Death seemed more of a friend.

Unemployment

While discussing delinquency we got onto the question of unemployment. Whereas last year there were 4000 unemployed boys there were now 319 but a lot more girls. There was the organisation known as the Jugendnoteinsatz which got them jobs as semi-skilled workers, and the girls sewing. Since January they have been compelled to take part in this emergency work and those not wishing to work got no food card. But that still did not prevent them from not turning up, for they could live quite easily on the B.M. without food cards. For this work the Komandantura or County Council pays them 35 pf. an hour but later could not afford it and they get now a small lump sum or aid. They tried to give them some education, or send them to the people's high school (Volkshochschule) to keep them off the streets. When they finally got employment they got 72 pf. an hour. But the chief difficulty now is that there is a great shortage of all materials to carry on this emergency work and crime begins to take its place.

The young people are taken round the factories so that they can see the different jobs and what they would like to do, and the factory Youth Welfare committees inform this office when vacancies occur. I asked if they thought young people here also wanted to emigrate but they said not.

Disappearing Youth

Then almost by chance came the stories, rather hesitant at first, of the French Foreign Legion, and I saw the proof in an actual letter from a boy who had escaped, got back to Germany and had given all the details. It seems that often these young criminals are given the opportunity, prior to the trial, to join the Foreign Legion in order to escape punishment. Many are forced to do so. Those who have committed the most serious crimes are glad to escape punishment. Some want to join for adventure, and as an escape from the hopelessness of the present situation. Boys of 16 are made to sign a declaration that they go willingly and voluntarily, and that they are 18 years old. If they are under 18 they are given a new birthday and have to stick to it. These boys then make propaganda to other boys to join them, who are outside. They are given a good uniform and transported through the Russian zone in closed wagons, and on reaching the French zone have the good uniforms exchanged for old tattered ones. Former SS types who wish to 'disappear' are also offered the same advantageous facilities, and so Nazism, violence and a spirit of war is once more fostered in this way.

I was able to talk also to Herr Förster a young 22 year old lad who was head of the Jugendausschuss. Very likeable and efficient and with the light of enthusiasm and hope in his eyes and obviously doing great work.

More and More Facts Come to Light

Friday 23rd. Went to the Jugendausschuss of Charlottenburg to interview Herr Pankow. On the question of delinquency he had some interestingly different shades of opinion. On the whole this is an upper-middle class district.

He said that as the Black Market was getting more and more difficult the young people took to stealing what they wanted (Thus indicating that B.M. was not wrong). Money was scarce. So one lot takes to work and the other to crime. Often, he said, it was the parents' fault. They sent the children to the B.M. to sell cameras, and to the barracks to collect cigarette ends. Children do not have the difficulty that adults have in coming into contact with soldiers in order to get their cigarettes, so the desperate parents send the children out. Everywhere there is this universal craving for good cigarettes.

Also he said the difference between anarchy and democracy is not clear to youth. They think that now they are 'free' they can do what they like. This means they can vandalise property if they like, without getting punished.

Hunger, he emphasised, not only induces stealing to satisfy that hunger but it also brings on a craving for other things such as tobacco, and it brings out the primitive animal instincts. Sports organisations alone won't cure this for they haven't the energy for sport. Boys want to go to other zones to see if it is any better there. Berlin is like a prison to them. In all zones there are rumours of Foreign legions American, English and French, though the latter has the worst reputation. He is convinced that there must be an American Foreign Legion as the boys talk so much about it, are so keen on it and say it is the best. He has even talked to a couple of boys who claimed to be back on leave from Bavaria, and one proudly showed off parts of his uniform. They can't forget their uniforms, and can't wait to get another. The police too are so desperate to get back into uniform that they can't wait even if they have to, but get hold of one somehow, even if it is not issued by the police office! And they are proud when they are back in uniform.

He pointed out that many of the very best people in Youth clubs belonged once to the former Hitler-Jugend and Bund Deutscher Mädchen. One youth even belonged to the secret police but is now ready to co-operate and to be convinced that the other side is right. They are outspoken and frank about it.

We arranged that I should go along to some of his clubs to see them and talk to the young people myself.

Youth Welfare Work

I then had a 2½ hour conference with Fr. Dr. Quast, Dr Thoran, *Frau Dr. Meyer-Kulenkampff*, expert educational adviser to the Schulamt, *Frau Ziesler*, leader of Family Welfare work in Charlottenburg, *Frau Dr. Coler*, Leader of the Johannesstift school of social education, *Frau Dr Bourbeck*, same, and a pastor, *Frau Ellenbeck*, secretary of that college. It was a somewhat imposing array sitting round the table, and a rather sticky beginning but they soon warmed up. After a bit of 'bluffing' and a few general questions I managed to find out who they all were, and that they represented the training of the social welfare or social relief work training for Fürsorgerinnen. I was then able to get this side of Youth welfare work cleared up and understood. Whereas in England we have various specialists such as the Probation officer going to the house, here the Fürsorger has all these jobs rolled into one and is able thereby to have a more intimate contact with the family, and be a better case-worker and deal more efficiently with their problems as a whole. This system needs a lot of people. That was one of the chief troubles and therefore one of the chief disadvantages – there were not enough people to do the job properly and those they had now left over were often the wrong people.

Responsibility for the material well-being of the community, they stressed, was destroyed by the Nazis. The conscience of the nation must be awakened to regain it.

Dread of the Russians

We then went on to discuss the *Einheitsschule* which the Russians have introduced into their zone and was wanted throughout Berlin. The discussion then rather strayed off the subject, as we expected, and centred upon the Russians. It was again pointed out to me that England was not sufficiently aware of the danger of the Russians who were doing exactly the same as Hitler had done, making all the old mistakes and were clearly aiming at world domination. We managed to get back to education. Before 1933 schools were purely educational. Then after '33 they became political but they had a cultural background. But now it is even worse as they are purely political and the teachers have no cultural background. At present under the Russians there is no possibility for the Germans to show authority, no government, no democracy. The Head of the Schulamt, for example, who is leader of all educational questions declared publicly that it did not matter to him whether people could not spell or use proper grammar as long as they had the right political views. Members of the S E D openly say that the elections in the Russian zone have already been decided. In the Russian zone pastors even have to submit the text of their sermons to the Russian commander. One recently contained the word 'king' and was suppressed.

With difficulty the discussion was drawn back to the church. All were convinced that the only hope was a reversion to Christian ethical standards. "We Germans", said Dr Meyer-Kulenkampff, "are very sorry for ourselves but the great need is not for more material help – you give that as much as you can, but for more spiritual help", she emphasised, "what is needed is more spiritual awareness of all nations. To my mind it is Christianity that is in danger – that is the important thing, not that Germany be pitied." There spoke a very fine woman. They were all remarkable women, full of energy, courage, determination, and sound pre-1933 sense. They asked me to stay to lunch which I did, and the conversation was pleasantly trivial and one could relax, for it had been an exhausting morning. We returned to Dr. Quast's flat to discuss next week's programme, and then I went to her garden with the 2 children.

Some of us passed a very pleasant evening with the I.V.S.P. team in country dancing and singing. 5 of us ended up by singing some very beautiful Bach chorales. It was very lovely.

First Hand Experience of the Black Market

Saturday 24th. I decided during the morning that the only way to get to know about the black market and its effect on young people was to go into it myself, and if necessary take part in it. So I invited two young German friends of mine to come with me and help. During the morning I fitted myself out with not too smart civilian clothes, so that after dinner when I dressed up even the staff thought I looked thoroughly German but begged that I should be careful in the Russian zone.

Brian dropped Hasso and myself at Reichskanzler-platz where we met Joachim and set off together by underground to Potsdamer Platz in the American sector. It was the first time I had been in the Berlin Underground. Long waits, crowded trains and very little politeness. A German woman was quite astonished when I, presumably another German, offered her my place. Only Allied soldiers did that- yes, Russians too! The people looked undoubtedly pale, and an almost permanently solemn and worried expression is becoming engrained. The smell in the underground is not very pleasant, and is not made any fresher by the bad breath of so many people. It is quite often extremely unpleasant to have a conversation with a Berliner for this reason. Conversation is in low tones and serious, and laughter seems to have almost vanished. The ruins look awful from the train. Berlin was 60% destroyed.

At Potsdamer Platz there was no sign of the B.M. only small stalls selling a few things such as scent, cheap wooden toys and small domestic utensils etc. So we went to the Brandenburger Tor where the B.M. used to flourish but apart from a few men waiting for soldiers it had also moved from there to the Alexander Platz we were told. It was a fine feeling to be able to walk about without having any special notice taken of one, because normally everyone looks at what is for Berlin, a new uniform, the Quaker gray and mine was the first one to be seen in Berlin (the F.A.U. were in khaki).

We walked on together past the ruined cathedral, Schloss and Rathaus; to Alexander-platz, and one could see the Black Market there at once. Small groups of people hanging about, talking in low voices and moving on. We got closer and began to watch. A row of country-looking people were sitting down on a ruined wall, with goods – probably farm produce, concealed in little black bags. One or two old men and young boys were doing their best to exchange one or two cigarettes. Gradually one could spot bigger deals going on in cigarettes, a whispered word, a tilt of the eyebrows, a nod or a flash movement under the coat. One followed, saw the discussion – prices not good enough – cigarettes not good enough – neither party satisfied, moved off, tried again. Small-time men were trying to interest Russian soldiers in pens, watches and small things. There were no Leica cameras and silk stockings being visibly displayed as they were, I'm told, after the collapse. For the bigger deals you want to go into the small cafés. Time was getting on and fascinating though it all was – we wanted to see everything and so moved on towards the more ill-famed parts of Berlin. I passed a place where Russians were having their great-boots polished – the expression, or rather lack of expression on the faces of the German onlookers was interesting but we didn't stop because Russian secret police were moving about with their green lapels, and we were warned of German plain-clothes detectives being about. We looked at some of the cafés, but they didn't seem "low" enough and so moved on up Grenadier Str. We overheard a man with a white cap telling another of some women he had in the back room of one of the houses, and their "prices".

We caught sight of B.M. activities again in Mulackstrasse, one of the streets with the worst possible reputation in Berlin. As soon as we got into the street we were suspect, and as soon as we got up to the groups to see and listen, they broke up and things vanished as though it was a casual talking group breaking up.

Further down the street we came upon a scene such as one sees only on the films or reads about. There were one or two of what I would call perfect specimens of prostitutes. The scene was theatrical and like the ballet "Miracle in the Gorbals", or "Big City". All types, sizes, and ages of prostitutes, ditto men; small groups of black-marketeers and a group of flashily dressed, long-haired loud-mouthed spotty boys with sordid, coarse laughter and a racing bicycle; a skinny dog chewing filth in a street – old people who were "past it" leaning out of the windows watching – one feeding a tame pigeon on the window-ledge. Joachim got so excited by this scene and it aroused his journalistic urge so much that he must take out his camera in the middle of the street and snap a "prima" prostitute. We were immediately the focus of all attention and though one could not see it one could feel a growing hostility. Joachim wanted to go into the bier café outside which they were all standing. But it was a bit too 'hot' for me and I could not risk any trouble. So we retired to another dark and dingy café, it was deserted but we had a fruit drink and tried again – walking up and down the street. Small deals only were going on in fruit and cigarettes – it was too early in the evening. We watched the fascinating scene for quite a time wishing we could talk to the people on the 'set', but it was impossible. They all knew each other and were intimate, we were outsiders. Amongst all this there were small children playing on the pavements and doorways. What a future for them. But you could find this in any big town or city if you knew where to look, I was told.

Pretty tired we took the Underground back home. They were visibly relieved to see me, eager to know what had happened, and what I had got on the Black Market etc. Pastor Weckerling and his wife were eager to know what had happened at supper and later Dr Quast and Dr Thoran, when I went round to see them. They were delighted to receive small parcels of needy things I took them from a parcel sent by *Millicent Sturge* from England.

Sunday 25th. The newspapers reported that in the U.K., the Black Market in nylons, chocolates, perfume and other scarce goods was flourishing.

First Prison Visit

Monday 26th. Met Dr Thoran and Dr Quast after lunch and went with them to the Fichterbunker in the American sector. This is a kind of prison for first offenders in a disused air-raid Bunker of a wrecked gas-works. We were received in the Prussian military fashion (clicking heels, handshake with bowed head) and taken down into the Bunker to meet the Governor in his office. Hardly before we started talking the lights went out and the rest of the interview took place by the light of oil lamps. This is a common occurrence – it happens several times a day, maybe for several hours, and when it happens the cells are plunged into darkness and the air-conditioning system, also lacking current, packs up, and as there are no windows the air soon becomes warm and foul.

I took *Ilse Abshagen*[1] along with me because I thought it good for German students to see these things. The governor seemed a simple man and doing his best under difficult conditions considering he had no special training for the job. He had one or two good ideas which he was attempting, but I doubt if they were original and he was able to say most of it off 'pat', and often his statements did not tally with our conversation with the boys afterwards. At least the food was fairly good and they could have hot baths when they liked – but the rest was pretty awful. The idea is that children convicted of minor first offences are sent here for 'punishment' during their free time at week ends, short-term confinements and longer term arrests of up to 4 weeks for "corrective education". They are supposed to suffer no stigma by coming here and not to lose their jobs because no records are kept, in theory. We saw records however and many of the boys told us they had already lost their jobs.

We interviewed first the three girls all in solitary confinement in pitch dark cells. They were cheerful girls and a very nice sort – not at all my stereotype of 'criminal'. In fact few are – because in all cases the theft was out of real need. The story in each case was interesting and typical of the majority – stealing ration cards, father dead or a prisoner or divorced.

We were glad to get out into the fresh air and talk to some of the 50 boys. We picked out two of the most interesting from their empty cells where we had discovered in one some good paintings and in the other some music. The artist was a lovely looking lad, in for forging bread coupons. He was 15. "Well what else can one do when one is hungry?" was his remark. He told us of his plans to study art. The musician was a young swing fiend who played in a band and a music college – he said his friend had stolen 20 loaves of bread in exchange for this boy's leather wind-jacket. The musician had been caught with the stolen loaves.

We talked to a group and put general questions to them about their homes and interests. I took an instant liking to these boys – they were sincerely disturbed at being there and wanted to get good jobs. Most of them had fathers missing, or foster parents, or family troubles. Few wanted to emigrate or join a foreign legion. They showed me their shoes which were in a terrible state and their clothes in rags. They apologised and did not like to be seen so shabby. Most of them were just walking about in the desolate bombed shell of the gasometer, some shifting rubble for others to shift back later. Some attempt at little gardens. They were eager to talk to us. We would like to have stayed on but it was getting late and they had to go below for their meal. One hopes the governor is right and that there is really an 80% success in re-educating these boys and girls. I doubt it even though they are good type and easy to deal with.

Drove back to Ilse's house as it was getting late and I did not have time to go home to change. So put on a suit of her father's and went with her to visit two youth clubs in the Charlottenburg district. I was really too tired to pursue my researches very seriously at this stage. In the first club they were preparing for a dance and in the

---

[1]*Interpreter student at University (Languages).*

second there was a small group of the student type sitting round reading Thomas Mann, and all listening most attentively and seriously. It all seemed very earnest.

At the Nuremberg trials Schreiber reveals that the Nazis were poised to begin germ warfare and experimented at Dachau.

Tuesday 27th. Spent the morning at Mil. Gov. house getting permission to visit the two main prisons. Much to my disappointment I was given permission for myself only and not allowed to take any German or even women members of our team with me. I also had to be accompanied by *Lt. Stirum.* This was all rather depressing as I knew I should not be able to take my own time, see what I wanted or get true answers. In all cases they would tell the officer what they thought he wanted to know and not the real facts or what they thought. However I considered myself lucky to be the first civilian allowed in. I was told the French Red Cross had been round, otherwise no one else.

In the evening, by invitation, Kathleen and I attended a meeting in the Spandau Rathaus on "Peace, no more war". We thought it a worthy cause and dashed down there 10 mins. late, only to find we were practically the first there. Greeted by *Herr Lemnitz* the speaker whom I had met previously. Eventually half an hour after the set time he started to speak to the 18 young people who turned up. Frankly I did not understand a word or I was too tired to concentrate. It didn't sound as though it was what I expected to hear and indeed Kathleen informed me afterwards that it was a passionate appeal for no more war except a war against capitalism, and that he was rather embarrassed by our presence. To my surprise, after a few intelligent questions by the young people the meeting broke up after only 75 minutes, so we were able to return home where Edith had collected up a group of young German friends of ours for a singing evening. Pastor Winterhagen was there and in his element as happy as a child to be able to sing again.

He told us he's standing as a Christian Democrat in the elections and fairly certain of getting in, in spite of violent S.E.D. press attacks.

Wednesday 28th. Eric Cleaver and *Lettice Jowitt*[1] arrived by the night train for breakfast. They came to settle some of our difficulties and domestic problems which could, if we allowed them, easily occupy our entire attention. Our staff must be halved.

I went to pick up Lt. Stirum. He greeted me in his office in a raging temper because his car had been stolen the previous evening and had been found bashed up at Spandau. So I had to take him to the Charlottenburg prison in the 15 cwt. truck of mine.

Another Prison Visit

Spent the morning going over this prison which is very cramped and small. There were only 21 Juveniles there and I interviewed each one. Amongst them was a young girl of 16 who was serving 4 yrs. for having murdered her foster parent. This foster parent had apparently nagged at the child telling her repeatedly that she was bad and a thief etc. until in the end out of sheer desperation she had murdered the woman. She seemed such an innocent sweet-tempered child and incapable of such an act.

---

[1] *Sister of the Lord Chief Justice in Atlee's Government.*

Fuel shortage

Stealing coal brickettes
(Photo by Manfred Dorniok)

Checkpoint Charlie into the Russian Sector

Russian HQ

U.S. 'legal' barter market

I talked also to two other girls who had attempted murder – one who was in a remand home and had attempted to murder the director with a knife.

Practically all the other cases were young girls who had stolen food or ration cards. One girl was an abortionist, having been pregnant from a British soldier. I felt very much ashamed as Lt. Stirum persisted in questioning the reluctant child and that the offender had been British. I saw the look in her eyes. I was glad she'd only been given a few months.

The cells were small and cramped – generally 3 to a cell, so that they had little room in which to turn around. Most of the girls seemed a very nice lot, just a few looked really bad. In practically every case there were family difficulties as before, or food and housing shortages. They get half an hour's exercise a.m. and p.m., a book each a week, but very little work or education. Visits by Fürsorgerin and prison chaplain, and 1 friend per 6 weeks to visit them.

All were fairly satisfied with the food. Wardresses seemed a fairly nice lot. I was shown the kitchen and tasted the food, a sort of soupy porridge. The immediate need seems to be to provide them with occupational and sewing materials.

I was glad to get out of the place as it did not have a fresh smell, and also the breath of Lt. Stirum was 'of the morning after the night before'.

Back to an early lunch and afterwards a team meeting at which future policy was discussed and various pieces of information and views aired by Eric and Lettice. She is an amazingly fine woman and always a source of inspiration.

Had to go at 3 o'clock as I had an appointment to see the Remand Home in the Protestant Religious community at Johannesstift. Took Ilse along as well as I thought it would be good for her to see such a place. She was most interested as it is indeed a model home and filled me with admiration and hope for the future. Here real trouble is taken with the boys to give them an apprenticeship. Saw over the woodwork shop and admired the beautiful furniture they are making. Saw the bakery where the young apprentices make beautiful bread under a first class teacher; also the engineering shop where much is done for those interested in that line.

It was such an interesting place and in such lovely surroundings that we decided to see as much of it as possible. So *Frau Ellenbeck* who is the secretary of the community and a wonderful-looking and active person showed us round and took us into their most beautiful central church, in which music students were practising on a lovely undamaged organ. It was hard to tear oneself away from the strains of a Bach prelude and fugue.

We also saw the old people's home where white-haired elderly people were happily spending their last days in comfort. A lovely garden to sit in, beautifully comfortable beds to lie on and all that they could want. One dear little old man showed me with great keenness the salad he was making out of wild plants and weeds and was thrilled when I could tell him the names of one or two in German and Latin.

In the Cripples' Home we found the most hopelessly deformed children laughing and happy, and so excited that an 'Engländer' had come to visit them.

We came away feeling that here was a wonderful piece of work – something that was good and right and beautiful, and a model for Germany's future. Why? Because there was a real religious spirit and motive behind it. Here they lived for each other and for the community and not for themselves.

Took Eric, Lettice and William Hughes down to the station to catch the night train to Vlotho. They all managed to get sleepers as they have the equivalent rank of major.

Thursday 29th. Went to the Hauptjugendamt again, this time to see *Herr Friedlander* who is in charge of all Remand Homes in Berlin. He told us that there were 35 Juveniles per week going into Remand homes, and 4,000 in them at present. Most of the girls that go, he says, have V.D. from Allied troops. Many more homes and better teachers and trained helpers are wanted.

Exploration of Hitler's Chancellery and Bunker

As we finished this interview early we decided to go into Hitler's Reichskanzlei which is on the other side of the Wilhelmplatz square, from the Jugendamt, and stretches 140 metres backwards from the square.

There was a large notice in German saying no German civilians allowed in, but we walked past the Russian guard with Dr Quast talking English, and with a smiling greeting to which he responded.

It was awe-inspiring to be in this place where so much of the world's history has been made, and the fates of millions sealed. Here one could see all the signs and remains of where the last drama of the Battle of Berlin took place. Little did I ever imagine that I should one day stroll about in the very place where the madman Hitler stormed and raged about, and that in the afternoon I should visit the prison where the Generals who plotted Hitler's murder were imprisoned and shot. The Reich Chancellery buildings are huge and spacious inside.

One can imagine something of the awe and fear of a minor official or statesman as he walked down the huge passages and halls to the presence.

We went into Hitler's study, which is now bare. John Downing who went in soon after the fall told us of what it looked like then-papers and documents all over the floor – contents of safe still intact and furniture about. Now just a few ashes in the fireplace. All the beautiful panelling has been stripped from the walls and doors, and the marble has gone. There is just a trace of the blue tiling of his private bathroom, and little sleeping and rest room off one corner. Every possible thing has been removed as a souvenir. We went into the other huge room, which Mussolini had used and waited in.

We wandered through the rubble and weeds and remains of a once proud and lovely rose garden towards the bunker or bolt hole where Hitler and Eva Braun met their ends. We were shown the spot just outside where the bodies were burnt, and it appears to have been left very much as it was then – there is all sorts of burnt rubbish lying about, bits of machine guns, a burnt Jerry-can full of bullet-holes and so on. We went down the stairs of the bunker lighting matches in the pitch darkness but the iron door was locked – one could see a light on inside through the cracks. I took photos.

Hitler's Reichkanzlei (from Wilhelm Platz)

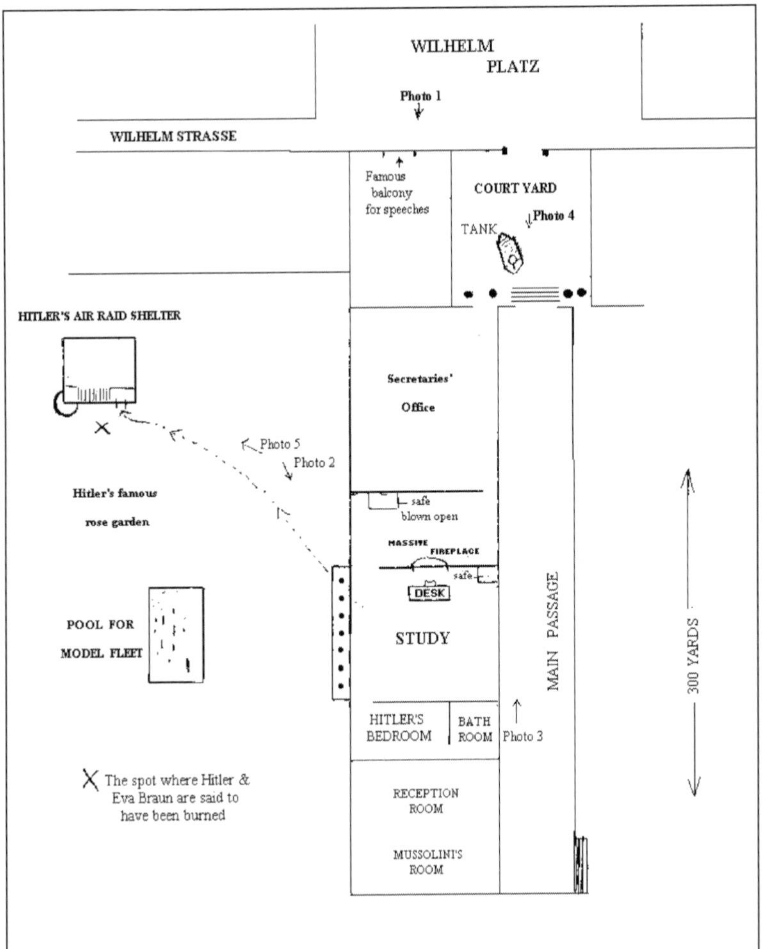

WILHELM PLATZ

Photo 1

WILHELM STRASSE

Famous balcony for speeches

COURT YARD

Photo 4

TANK

HITLER'S AIR RAID SHELTER

Secretaries' Office

Photo 5

Photo 2

Hitler's famous rose garden

safe blown open

MASSIVE FIREPLACE

safe

DESK

STUDY

MAIN PASSAGE

300 YARDS

POOL FOR MODEL FLEET

HITLER'S BEDROOM

BATH ROOM

Photo 3

X The spot where Hitler & Eva Braun are said to have been burned

RECEPTION ROOM

MUSSOLINI'S ROOM

Diagram of Hitler's Chancellery

Entrance courtyard to Reichkanzlei
Battle of Britain tank

Outside Hitler's Study

Long corridor to Hitler's Study

Hitler's Bunker (possibly exit)

Another Prison Visit

In the afternoon I picked up Lt. Stirum again and we went to *Plözensee Prison* near the French sector, where 640 young convicted Juveniles are imprisoned. On our arrival there was a great deal of saluting, jumping to attention with click of heels and shouting, and jingling of keys, or "Ja, Herr Oberleutnant" or "Nein, Herr Oberleutnant", etc. We did a rather hasty inspection. I was shown the least bad offenders and the worst – the murderers among the Juveniles. In all cases questions put to the boys had very much the same answer as in Charlottenburg, except that the murderers talked more willingly, openly and almost laughingly about the deed and how it was done. Conditions did not seem too bad – less overcrowding and more cleanliness than in Charlottenburg. Saw a little more of the attempt to give them some employment – glove-making, toys and cabinet making etc. Saw also the brand new kitchen, just built, which was very modern, and food better or as good as outside rations. I felt that most of the boys could be successfully re-educated and helped if there were the proper facilities -but present conditions only increase the negative tendencies and trouble. I didn't feel as depressed, though, as when I came out of my Wormwood Scrubbs prison visit.

Facing the Realities of Life

Friday 30th. Woke up to find it was pouring with rain. Yesterday Dr Thoran told me that he could not come with me today as he had to go out with his two boys to dig up tree stumps to provide fuel and heating. He had booked and paid for a small truck to transport the wood, "What if it rains?" I asked. He shrugged his shoulders. "If it rains, it rains. Tomorrow is the only time we could book a truck – we shall have to dig the wood tomorrow or have no fuel on which to cook or heat the house when it gets cold."

When I went out in the ambulance at 9 o'clock it was pouring cats and dogs. I thought a lot about Dr Thoran this morning as he has a weak heart anyway. I did not meet him till the following Tuesday evening when he told me that of course they had got soaked to the skin and the little one had caught a cold, but they had managed to get a good truck load of 15 or 16 tree stumps which would last them probably half the winter if the weather was fairly good. His case is only one of many. You can see old people digging away for stumps in the woods, or collecting toadstools to eat. Imagine how much worse it is for those old couples who have no son to help and who have to drag a tree stump at a time back to their homes, if they have one, in a handcart. It may take two days work for one old man to dig out one tree stump and he would have to sleep near it to guard it during the night. There is no coal unless you send out the young people to steal it. During the same afternoon we went along a street down which a coal truck had just rumbled. All German transport is on its last legs and this one left a black carpet of small bits of coal no bigger than walnuts all down the street. All the inhabitants of the street poured out with shovels and brooms to get what they could, and when we came back along the street later on, it had been swept clean. It was quite amazing. No speck of coal was left.

You can see the same thing when a horse-drawn cart goes down the street. Everyone watches for the precious manure to drop. The moment it does so some little boy or old man will rush out with his bucket and spade – manure means better food – one doesn't know quite why except that it produces magic results with the vegetables in this barren sandy soil. People become so easily entirely food and fuel conscious –

that it becomes the major problem, and this preoccupation excludes all other things. They want these things badly now, and behind it all there is the thought of winter ahead. They want to save a little if it is possible for that dreadful future. Autumn has crept in amongst us stealthily and without us realising it. One can see with a shock that the trees have turned quite yellow and the ivy and mountain ash quite red and orange. As one sweeps down the road in the ambulance, particularly at night, one notices the leaves falling and swirling up off the road as they get caught in the head-lamps. Yes, people are feeling the cold already – with lowered resistance and little warmth-producing food it's easy for cold to creep in especially if you have bare feet. Gooseflesh is a common sight.

An Unexpected Visit to the Russian Kommandantura

This morning I visited a Hauptpflegeamt – a kind of shelter for 'girls in danger' – orphans, refugees, prostitutes – any young girl without a home picked up by the police or sent there by the Jugendamt. Very few of them had a decent pair of shoes.

We had a great deal of difficulty in finding the place which was in the Russian sector. We landed up eventually outside the main Russian Kommandantura. While I waited outside, Dr Quast decided to go in and ask, as she thought, if the Arbeitsamt (Employment Office) was in the same building and they should know. There were Russians everywhere – red flags and pictures of Stalin and Lenin. One would have thought it would have only taken two minutes to find out. After she had gone for half an hour I began to get worried. After all the stories one has heard one cannot help feeling a little apprehensive. I thought it high time I went in to find her in case she had been arrested. I frankly admit I was scared, but as I walked up the steps with as bold an air as I could, I saluted and smiled at the armed guards hoping I'd see them again shortly on the way out. I got right into the building without being challenged and started to make enquiries in German. All the Russians stared at my strange uniform. Eventually an officer challenged me and beckoned me and an interpreter into his office. We passed through another office and I was followed by a troop of armed soldiers. The officer sat down put his feet on the desk and did not offer me a chair. I explained in my best German that I was looking for a little dark-haired woman – Dr Quast, who had come in 30 minutes previously to ask a question and had not reappeared. The officer did not know anything about her. He left the room. Another officer took his place. The whole conversation was repeated. Several other officers and men poked their heads round the door, stared at me and closed the door again. More armed soldiers came into the office and the officer started to talk to them. The German interpreter beckoned to me to come out of the room and I gladly slipped out without the officer being aware of it. We went to a room crowded with waiting Germans and shouted for Dr Quast, no reply – somehow I was shown out of the building and with considerable relief saw Dr Quast standing by the car and wondering if I had been taken off by the Russians. She was just coming in to ask for me, having been down the road to the Arbeitsamt to find that address. We finally got to the Home, where there was an extremely pleasant woman in charge who gave us facts and figures. But by this time unfortunately it was time to leave for home before we could see over the place.

During the afternoon we paid a visit to *Professor Gottschalk's* Child Guidance Clinic in Wedding. It is the only one of its kind in Berlin and he is about the only man left doing this kind of work for the whole of Berlin, all the other clinics having been bombed and the best people, most of whom had been Jews, had left long ago.

I thought he was a very fine man. It was a beautiful clinic, in a hospital. During the past year he has had to deal with a thousand cases between the ages of 2-20 who need psychiatric treatment. It was interesting to know that he too had been allowed to talk to all the cases in Plötzensee Prison including the young murderers. It was interesting to hear his views about them. He thought that the figure for V.D. amongst youth was between 30-40%, which is terribly high, if true.

Farewell Party for F.A.U.

This evening we gave a farewell party to the old F.A.U. members who are leaving. They invited their own guests, and we had about 20 young people. Valentine the cook produced a most wonderful and colourful 'pre-war' spread. It seemed all wrong to eat so much and such a good spread with people around so short of food. But at least it was mainly Germans getting the best of it, and indeed they stuffed themselves to capacity. It was Valentine's last effort too. He was pastry cook to a Nazi General in Norway, and gave us his notice because he wants to cook for a greater number of people, and just cakes – his speciality, so we had to let him go, and he now has the job of cooking for the B.A.O.R. Berlin wives who have just come. I was not in the mood for a party having had enough on training and was in a more serious mood. However it did go well and though I was feeling dog-tired myself I joined in and enjoyed myself. After some games and dancing the party adjourned to the dormitory for champagne and other drinks, I made an excuse that the servants should be taken home as it was after midnight, and so I took them home through quite a heavy fog.

When I got back the party had come downstairs and they had started dancing again. I had some really enjoyable dances with 'Jappi'. These girls, starved of dancing for years, do love to do it now, but unfortunately most of the boys can't dance. We went on till about 3 o'clock when they went home at last.

Saturday 31st. As it had not been really possible to see over the Hauptpflegeamt yesterday, I went again this morning with Margaret and Dr Quast. There were 3 sets of about 20 girls. We went to each group and heard them sing beautifully, including "You are my sunshine," especially for our benefit. We spoke to each lot about England and answered questions. Most of them wanted to come to England as domestics. We found them a much better type of girl than we were led to expect. They were most friendly and eager to learn things. Most of them were just sitting around a table with nothing to do, so our visit was a great event.

In the evening another party . Did not really feel like going but as we had promised Joachim, Brian and I went. As it turned out it was mostly talking and a bit of dancing, and was not too bad, and we managed to get away by 10.30.

One little girl there, who had been to England, Annemarie, told me it was hard for her to believe that we had come to Germany because we wanted to help, of our own free will, voluntarily and without pay. Such a thing was quite strange and new to her, and she found it hard, she admitted, not to suspect some ulterior motive behind all our actions. It was quite amazing to her that we were able to criticise the other allies and particularly the actions of our own Mil. Gov. as well as our own Nation, so openly and freely without getting into trouble. There must be some ulterior motive in it. She found it wonderful to be in such an atmosphere, but felt a little afraid and a little guilty at finding herself one minute so happy, so free and so much in agreement with her English friends, and the next back in her family trying to convince them. Was it just the enthusiasm of the moment? Her attitude gave me much food for thought.

The U.S. Barter Market

One of the Rheinstein group of Americans was there, and was telling us all about the wrongs and unfairness of the open legal barter market that the Americans had set up in their sector in Leichhardtstrasse: it was nothing but a Black market made "legal" and organised. There were 50 Germans there to every American, and they were selling their most valuable silver and china, and cut glass, cameras, watches and silver fox capes and their priceless porcelain – things that must be "their life's blood", he described it, "for a few cartons of cigarettes or food. The Americans were just sending home for cigarettes and sending all this spoil back home in exchange. Wasn't that morally wrong and dreadful? Ought it not to be stopped?" He went on to tell us what he personally had been able to get there and for how much! It was all news to the other American who decided that he too must write home for a few cartons – to see what he could get – a silver fox fur for his wife for a few cigarettes – why, it was unbelievable – what he'd wanted for a long time. Brian and I decided we must go and see this place for ourselves and try to get some photographs.At Nuremberg: The War Crimes trial ends; only Hans Frank, Nazi Governor of Poland, pleaded guilty.

September 1946

Sunday 1st. We were invited out to tea this afternoon by *Claude Shotts,* the American Friend representative on the C.R.A.L.O.G. and C.A.R.E. food distribution committees, to meet *Julia Branson* of the A.F.S.C. along with other German Quakers, and to hear her talk on some of her experiences on visits to American relief teams in Italy and elsewhere. We went straight on afterwards to a lovely concert by the Berlin Philharmonic at the Rundfunk (Berlin's broad-casting station) where we heard the first performance of Prokofiev's "Romeo and Juliet", and Brahms' 1st Symphony. It is a very beautiful hall in white, but looks rather like a swimming bath.

The Law Courts

Tuesday 3rd. Went to the Central Amtsgericht or Law Courts in the centre of Berlin to see *Direktor Franke*, the distinguished Juvenile Court Judge responsible for the 1923 Laws. He was a sombre quiet man in black with rather a feeble ageing voice but with an understanding sympathetic smile.

He begged that we should use our influence to get P.O.W.s released and to secure more food for the adolescents to help combat the crime increase.

As we had very little time we made a further appointment and were invited to the juvenile court sitting on Thursday.

Went once more to the Catholic Frauenbundschule to speak to and have a discussion with Dr Quast's class of 6 social workers in training. It was an interesting little group and I had considerable help from them.

They stressed the need for a levelling out of economic conditions between the Allies and the German people. It was very difficult to get willing co-operation from Germans if, when they were hungry and in material need, they saw us living in plenty. Only if we were ready to make that sacrifice would they regard it as a real willingness to co-operate on the part of the Allies!

In the afternoon we had an interview with Frau Ziesler head of the Family Welfare work in district Charlottenburg, and 3 of her helpers – a Fürsorgerin, a Gerichtshelfer, and the head of the Pflegeamt[1]. It was a most friendly, frank and interesting discussion, valuable to us all.

They stressed the point that it was the lack of light in the evenings which drove the young people out of doors as well as the over-crowded conditions of home life, with up to as many as 6 families in one flat in their district. Another problem too, which I have seen in England is that many of the 18s-21s were in the army and had attained some rank. Now they are not satisfied with just any labourer's work, but even though they may have had only elementary education, they now want only the higher official positions, and quick money. Mostly they have very little hope for the future, so that even "good class" boys are getting into trouble. Parents have no authority over their children.

After this interesting discussion one of the women took us to see her Pflegeamt where there were about 90 girls. In contrast to the one we saw at PrenzlauerBerg this one had a lovely building formerly part of a hospital, and they had much more to do in the way of knitting and sewing, games and reading. I did not take to the girls so much as at the other place perhaps because the group was bigger. One invariably gets better results from small groups, and more contact with individuals.

In the evening we went along to Dr Quast's house again to meet and talk informally round a cup of tea with some of the people we had met in official interviews during the past week, such as *Prof. Gottschalk*, Herr Beuster and other social welfare workers. They said that by the time I had finished my researches I would be one of Berlin's experts on Youth Welfare, because no other person had such an opportunity to go round and talk with anyone they pleased, especially Germans!

Remand Homes and Approved School Visits

Wednesday 4th. A very busy day rushing round in a tearing hurry trying to fit in everything and everybody. Drove altogether 90 miles within the boundaries of Berlin. A *Mr Crawford* of the Y.M.C.A. turned up wanting to see Youth work, and so I took him with me on my visits to two remand homes in Tegel in the extreme North of the French sector.

The first was 'Grünes Haus', where there were 80 boys between the ages of 9-19. The house itself had been bombed and burnt out – so they were carrying on in overcrowded conditions in wooden huts. Much to our surprise we came upon one boy talking perfect American English. He was in style a complete "Yank". They have here a wonderful garden where they can do most of the work – some are apprenticed to outside firms. The dormitories were overcrowded and one, belonging to the youngest group, was absolutely filthy and smelt abominably, indicating a high proportion of bed-wetters. I asked about this and treatment.

[1] *Nursing Office.*

We saw one pathetic class of nine-year olds learning to read and write. They look pathetically small and undernourished for their ages, with that wistful, lean and hungry look – paleness of skin, on which one can so often see the gooseflesh of sheer coldness. What it will be like in winter heaven knows! There was very little for them to do in their free time in the way of games, etc. Lots of relief work could be done here. This was a City Council home. In contrast we went on to see a Catholic home. And what a contrast! It was in ideal woodland surroundings by the lake, and with a lovely garden. They had a most scrumptious modern building, originally built as a nursing home in 1929. Then the nuns took it over. It really was a beautiful place – wonderfully clean and full of a quiet, calm, caring atmosphere. The quiet devoted service of nuns is most striking. I always feel that if there is a nun connected with any piece of work it will always be thoroughly well and efficiently carried out. The children looked bright and happy and were well but simply dressed. It was a special festival day and so everywhere there were decorations of lovely flowers and leaves. We saw them having a good meal, and the tiny tots asleep. We were shown their beautiful modern church, and also their concert hall and stage. A sewing room had 30 electrical sewing machines. Then there was the bakery and laundry, so they were practically self-supporting. What a contrast!

In the evening some of us went down to Zehlendorf where the Berlin Philharmonic was giving a public concert in the Freilichtbühne or open-air theatre of a large private house with a wonderful garden, and lawn sloping down between trees to a lake at the bottom. Acoustics were surprisingly good. The programme included *Bach's Brandenburg Concerto No.3*, Haydn's *Clock Symphony* and Beethoven's 2nd. The place was packed, but with surprisingly few Allied troops. The concert finished just before the rain came on.

At the Juvenile Courts

Thursday 5th. Attended the Juvenile Court at Neue Friedrich Strasse where Direktor Franke was the Judge. Heard altogether 5 very interesting cases. First was a boy of 18. He had stolen 18 pairs of shoes from a shop which had no window panes, only shutters, and had been caught for selling stolen clothes on the Black Market. He was also in prison-hospital with V.D. and the court had proof that he was using a false name and papers, though he would not admit it. His case was adjourned until his alleged father was called as a witness to own or disown him.

The second was a girl of 17 who was ill with glandular trouble and had impetigo on her face. The mother looked ill in the extreme and was continually breaking down in tears. The girl was there on 4 charges of stealing bread and ration cards for bread. She was continually hungry. The food office had taken the equivalent amount she had stolen from her mother's personal rations so that she was practically starving. This, I'm told, often happens. The parents are held responsible and punished, so that they starve. Allies say punishment must be severe for such cases. She was sentenced to only 2 weeks at the Fichtebunker as it appeared to the court this was a case of real hunger and illness.

The third was a boy of 20 who had stolen a typewriter and an overcoat from the office where he worked to get more money. He was an orphan – his parents divorced when he was 11 years old, and he had had no foster parents. He was now living with a girl and was hoping the court would declare him of an age to marry. He had also been in hospital with osteo-myelitis and remand homes most of his life. He was given 3 months at Plötzensee, and went out in tears.

Two boys then came in together full of confidence. One was an army deserter. He sold things to the Russians and got a lot of money. Lived alone in Berlin, had no parents then, but they came back later. Had been adopted by a foster-parent but had stolen things from him. Between them they had 8 charges of stealing and Black Market activities. The step-father of the other boy was there and denounced him as impossible; he had tried everything without success. He had found him jobs but he would not work. Franke asked him why he didn't work. "Why should I?" the boy replied, "no one in our street works!" It also came out that he had stolen 2 bicycles from the street. They were both sentenced to imprisonment in Plötzensee.

My opinion of Franke was that he was not such a good judge in practice as his writings and talk were in theory. This opinion was later confirmed by Dr Quast and the Jugendamt officials at the court, but he was obviously under great pressure.

During the afternoon went to see a "compulsory attendance" school in Wannsee run by *Herr Baruch* who had himself been in a concentration camp. There were 80 young boys from 6-14. I felt he was doing very good work under difficult conditions. He had many good ideas on education, and aimed at teaching them some responsibility. I felt he had a real idea of "the ideals of democracy." A lovely big house in need of repair must be terribly cold in winter. Only been going a year. Large number of absconders at first, now only very rarely. Problem of large number of bed-wetters and how to keep beds, linen and mattresses clean and dry. The children were quietly playing games and reading or singing. They sang us songs and 3 little mites played to us on recorders. They all looked incredibly small, pale and thin and undernourished. Quite the worst I have seen. My visit was a big event for which they had obviously prepared – but they were very shy. It was all too 'official'. I longed to be able to help them. All so wistful. Very few had shoes – most looked cold.

Brian and I took the evening off to see Noel Coward's 'Private Lives' which was being played at the "Jereboa" theatre. It is now possible to take German guests to theatres and cinemas, which is a big step forward.

Friday 6th. Went to the South Eastern extremity of the American sector nearly 16 miles away, to visit the Tannenhof Remand home for girls. The place had great possibilities, but again is understaffed and with no materials or means of employing the girls, some of whom we saw working lazily in the garden.

On the way back the truck broke down and I had to be rescued by Brian.

In the evening I was invited to a farewell party for *Dr. Manotti* at the International Red Cross, and to meet his successor. It was a very sober and distinguished affair with *Dr Melvin* there – Head of the Public Health Dept. of Mil. Gov. *and Maj. Boyce* Head of Welfare. We all had some extremely good games of table-tennis which I haven't had for a very long time. Back at 2.15 a.m.

Edith Snellgrove and John Seed away at the Red Cross Regional Conference, and Kathleen had to rush off to England because her father was dying. We are a very reduced team, sometimes only 4 or 5 of us left to cope.

First Anglo-German Wedding

Saturday 7th. John Downing got legally married to Marion. He must be about the first Britisher to marry a German girl in Berlin. They are having the church wedding on Wednesday. Pf. Rudolf Weckerling has agreed to use his church.

In the afternoon I went to see the preliminary rounds of the Inter Allied European Sports Championship at the Olympic Stadium which was a colourful and exciting affair.

The Nine Nation Games

Sunday 8th. During the afternoon quite a few of us went to see the finals of the Inter Allied European Sports Championship arranged by the U.S. in which nine Nations took part. It was a very colourful and ceremonious occasion, which I photographed.

General Joseph T. McNarney and other distinguished guests drove up the approaches between flags of all nations and between two lines of guards, and American mounted troops. Inside the stadium, which was almost full with about 90 thousand spectators, we saw the procession of the teams, and this was followed by a colossal artillery salute. Then a fanfare of trumpets announced the arrival of the torch bearer at the East Gate, in white, who ran round, up to the west steps and lit the brazier – the traditional Olympic opening ceremony.

Finally the events began. It was all most exciting – the 5000m run I shall never forget when the Czech runner *Zatopek* raced ahead at a colossal pace outstripping everyone and kept it up for 12 rounds. He caught up and passed at least the last 5 men and was ¾ of a lap in front of the 2nd man. He was the only man in the Czech team and got a tremendous ovation from the crowd.

U.S.A. and Belgium seemed to pull off most of the best results.

Life in the Russian Sector

Monday 9th. During the afternoon went to see a Catholic remand home, Don Bosco, in the Russian Sector run by *Father Klinski*, a very fine energetic little man.

He was telling us of the difficulties he had experienced during the 12 years of the Nazi period – how they had struggled to keep it a non-party religious home. The Gestapo were continually onto him, accusing him of being a pacifist and anti-Fascist. It was difficult enough in those days but now he is reluctant to admit that under the Communists it was even worse, and that was saying something.

Now the O.G.P.U. are continually at him saying that the discipline is so strict as to make the place almost a military organisation. "Put a pistol into the boys hands", they say, "and you'll have trained young soldiers". So the O.G.P.U. have taken away all gymnastic apparatus and have searched the library, and have cross-questioned the boys. The trouble of course is that it is a religious home and Religion is "against" the Communists as it was "against" the Nazis. Now boys over 16 have to leave because they are accused of being "secret" soldiers! The Russians are also trying to get the director of the place removed because he was a padré in the army.

Father Klinski was very worried about the situation which was coming to a climax and we took him to see the Bishop. He was enthusiastic in his praise for the British who were setting up a new home for the over 16's for him in British sector.

The "Kulturkampf" he warned us is rising again, and people are already saying that it is worse than being under the Nazis.

Another example: Dr Quast teaches at a school in Potsdam. She invited us to go and talk to her class which was impossible unless I went in civilian clothes, as Potsdam is in the Russian Zone, and the risk would be too great. So she invited her class to come and meet me one evening in her home, whereupon the director of the school dismissed her because I didn't come to the school to talk and with herself able to be present. Dr Quast's students have since informed her that the directress has reported her to the S.E.D. party. One of the boys who stood up for Dr Quast and said it was wrong for her to be dismissed has been expelled. Other teachers have warned Dr Quast not to go back into the Russian zone, as the Russians may get her. She dare not take the risk, because her husband has already been taken by the Russians and she has had no information as to his whereabouts and whether he is dead or alive. She has Peter and Paul to support. Already one teacher has disappeared from there and has not been heard of since. By this Dr Quast has lost about 300 R. marks a month. She shrugged her shoulders.

I picked up today in the garden a magnificent Privet Hawk moth larva that was lying motionless in my path. I put it in a large jam jar with some lilac leaves, as there is no privet about and for a day it did not move or eat. It then proceeded, very cleverly in the usual way to change its skin. And as soon as it had wriggled out of the old one it began to eat the leaves ravenously and almost visibly swelled. It is now a beautiful fresh yellow green with fine purple and white streaks and a magnificent black and white posterior horn. The Abshagens found another one in their garden and kept it several days for me on their balcony. Then by mistake Hans dropped it and it rolled down the roof into the gutter, and was lost to sight.

Also had a grand rabbit chase in the garden by torch light and almost caught the little beggar but he was too elusive and got through a hole in the fence into the barracks.

Interview with Women's Criminal Police

Tuesday 10th. After another short interview with Direktor Franke, the Juvenile court Judge, when we discussed his cases, we went along to see the head of the Weibliche (Women'*s*) Kriminalpolizei. We had to have a signed paper to get into the building and when we got to the department we were made to understand that we were kept waiting because the Leiter was a most important person. It was somewhat of a shock to find that the head of this department was a young woman with dyed hair, plucked eyebrows and painted cheeks and nails, who, in short, spoke and looked to me like a tart!

She first "hummed and ha-ed" and was not at all sure of her ground or what she should or could tell us. Then decided she had better take down our names and details of who and what we were. After this she excused herself, which it appeared to us was an excuse to get further permission to give us the information we wanted and show us what we asked to see. The whole atmosphere was one of suspicion and of being on their guard. We rather enjoyed it – but wondered if we should get out of the building. It appears that there are 28 of these female kriminalpolizei who are separate from the actual women who walk the streets in uniform. These are in plain clothes and supposedly used for probation and welfare work. It appears that most of them have not been trained as welfare workers, but have come from different professions and occupations and have only had 8 weeks' special training. Most of them appear to just sit about in the offices.

It then appeared that there was a sort of 'Pflegestelle' or secure shelter on the premises for girls and boys where they were mostly not kept for more than 2 or 3 days, though some in fact were kept longer, up to several weeks awaiting trial. We asked to see it. She must come with us, and in our interview with the women in charge of the girls' side she was there to see that what was said was correct, and put off certain of our questions, or would not answer, and avoided others. The girls' place was a dingy well-barred room with tiny closed windows and cramped double bunks, with a dirty floor hastily just washed before we came in, and which stank.

We were taken downstairs to the dungeon by an evil-looking bowing and scraping warder. The door was locked behind us. We were shown into a stuffy dingy room where there were 25 double bunks. At least the hay in the mattresses smelt sweet, but the beds were only about one foot apart.

In another room over 80 dirty, badly dressed, pale, long-haired boys were imprisoned. The room was bare except for a few tables and benches. The crowd milled round us. I found a young boy who spoke perfect American, so I pushed aside to talk to him and Dr Quast got hold of the woman and engaged her in conversation so that she should not interrupt me or hear what was being said. Dr. Q. told me afterwards that the woman had said we mustn't believe a word the boys said because they always told a pack of lies.

The boy told me he'd been in for 16 days. Had committed no crime, but had been put in there because he'd been found on premises where he should not have been and had declared himself an American citizen. He had no parents and had been living with and working for the G.I.s and he wanted to go back to them. He wanted to go back to America with them to start to learn something and get a job. He liked the Americans not because they gave him chocolate but because they promised him work. He hated being in this place because all the other boys were dirty – he liked to keep clean and they all talked about escaping and what they would do when they got out. They only wanted and planned more crime, but he wasn't interested but wanted to start to learn a trade, so he felt rather unpopular with the rest of them. He pleaded with tears in his eyes for me to try to get him back to the G.I.s.

During the late afternoon a visit to *Frau Thorbecke's* girls' home. A good place with the usual difficulties: roofs that let the rain in, no window panes, under-staffed and under-fed, skin diseases from vitamin deficiencies, little employment for the girls, no sewing materials and shoes.

Youth Employment Problems

Wednesday 11th. Went to see the head of the Youth Department of the Arbeitsamt or labour exchange, to hear some of his views and problems. We decide that he was a good man for the job, but with rather more organising efficiency than practical ability, and with rather totalitarian methods, with which he likes to draw a democratic parallel – describing himself as the King and all his committees as the parliament.

Since the end of the war there have been 35,000 unemployed youths of which 20,000 have been found employment or apprenticeships. There are 3,000 apprenticeships available which no one will take because in these cases the work is too heavy or too dirty for boys and girls to undertake willingly unless they are given more food, shoes and clothes to do the job. Partly the problem is that those employed only get between 40-60 marks per month in wages, whereas a girl who doesn't work but goes with an Allied soldier and gets one cigarette a day only from him and sells it for 10 marks on the Black Market can earn 300 marks a month this way. Usually she gets a great deal more. So why should they work? The other way is too easy.

During the afternoon a most interesting visit to *Frl. von Estorff*, a Fürsorgerin at the Gesundheitsamt (Health Office) Wilmersdorf. Here we were shown the consulting rooms and clinic for T.B. cases, V.D. cases, massage-therapy clinic, infant welfare, and pregnant mothers and marriage guidance bureau. All beautifully clean and white, with a most interested and efficient staff. Was shown a large number of interesting X-ray photographs of T.B. lungs. In the courtyard was a Russian soldier's grave, and Frl. von Estorff told us something of the drama that went on in the courtyard during the battle of Berlin. One wing was burnt out and the building was pock-marked with bullet holes. Russian soldiers had found their dead comrade in the courtyard and had taken it that the inhabitants had killed him, so they ordered them all out of the cellars and lined them up to be shot when an officer came along just in time and stopped them.

She promised to arrange that I should go on a police-raid when they brought in a batch of young people for V.D. examination and that I could put on a white doctor's coat and watch the whole procedure.

The First Anglo-German Wedding

John Downing got married this morning to *Marion Neuer*. It had been arranged that an Army chaplain should marry them at 11.30 in Pastor Weckerling's church. The story had got into the papers that "Capt." Downing was getting married. Then the trouble and publicity started. The chief Chaplain rang up and everyone wanted to know how a British officer was getting married. Finally *General Nares* himself intervened and forbade the wedding, and reminded us that we were "Camp followers" and were subject to military law. John P. and Harold went off to fix it with the General who would not see them, so they spoke to his colonel. It turned out that it was possible to go ahead with the wedding if a German pastor took the ceremony so off they went to ask Pastor Weckerling. Meanwhile all the German papers and English correspondents were ringing up Reuters, the Kemsley Newspapers, The Sketch and so on, and they all wanted to get the story and photographs at the church. The street was crammed with people as it was an historic occasion, the first of its kind in Berlin and I believe only the second in Germany. Pastor Weckerling conducted the ceremony in perfect English. There was to have been a reception in our house – but that was forbidden, and so we had to take all the food and stuff down to Marion's house and hold the reception for them there. It was a wonderful spread. But I regret all the publicity it has caused and we have yet to see the results and consequences.

In the evening we invited all the American Quakers living and working in Berlin to coffee. Nine very different and very pleasant Americans turned up, including Claude Shotts and Julia Branson, Landrum Bolling, who is a war correspondent, and his wife, *Roger Thorpe* working in the Finance Dept. of O.M.G.U.S., an elderly Quaker *Walter Mohr* representing C.R.A.L.O.G. in the British Zone, *Caroline Yerks*, also in the Finance Dept., and *Sergeant Jannssen*. I managed to get the Bollings interested in some of the bad things and things I had found that needed looking into in the American sector, such as the Fichtebunker, the 'American' lad in prison, and the home at Wannsee.

Thursday 12th. Went far down into the Russian sector to see a large municipal remand home. A grim place for the most difficult girls in the city. Again too few staff and all very ancient. The girls too were a very shifty-looking and difficult lot. The majority had V.D. but were not as infective as those who are sent to hospital. Came across some of our Quaker food that we apparently supply to this place (distributed through the churches). Quite a few refugees or expellees from the East, including a large number of very old women. These were a friendly smiling lot who seemed very content.

German papers with the accounts of John D.'s wedding sold out.

Harold Ridgley and John Fleming left by the night train for England.

Friday 13th. Visited 3 remand homes today. The Catholic one was good, the municipal one bad, and the Protestant indifferent.

In the Catholic home there was again a very wonderful atmosphere. The Oberschwester who took us round, we were told, had got up from her sick bed to greet us. She was indeed a beautiful character in her picturesque black and white nun's habit. Whereever she went she cast a loving spell around her and was always greeted with a "Grüss Gott" and a smile of welcome. The small orphans flocked around her and took her hand. She was very gentle with them. All the girls' faces were open and friendly and sincere. I felt that this home was doing enormous good. The place was beautifully kept, clean and fresh, flowers everywhere artistically arranged. Many of the girls proved their conversion and devotion by staying on, becoming nuns and helping with the new girls as they came. These group leaders were all lovely people. We met several very old nuns who had come there as girls and stayed all their lives, in this very sheltered and isolated community.

The Protestant home was in the Russian sector, and again was doing very good work, devoted people in charge, battling with primitive conditions i.e. no glass panes in the windows. But here too the children looked happy and well fed, for besides extra Swiss food they also get extra food from the Russians.

The small municipal home was a bad one, in a shocking building -no bed linen. There was a young and inexperienced, obviously easily influenced leader in charge – one or two boys were smoking. But one was struck by the fact that they were a grand set of boys but rapidly going to seed. Such a lot could be done for them that wasn't being done. It is pitiable.

Had a talk at lunch today with *Mrs Giles* of Durham university sent out under C.C.G. to lecture on Youth Welfare. She had been sent to us by Mil. Gov. to make contact with us over Youth work, and was eager to hear what our views were and of our work.

English Papers full of J.D.'s wedding.

Saturday 14th. *Ron Hadley* arrived for the day to do various jobs. During the morning took him down to the F.I.A.T. building to see Claude Shotts, Walter Mohr, and *Herta Kraus.* I also had a job there making enquiries for the papers concerning permits for Pastor Mensching, *Charlotte Friedrich* and *Hedwig Braun*[1] to go to England. No luck with first two, but the last had just been granted.

---

[1] *Konrad Braun's mother.*

John and Marion Downing…

…with Pastor Weckerling

…and friends

Visit to the American Barter Market

During the afternoon went out onto the Autobahn down to Wannsee to test the new little *Austin* P.U. (pick up) that Brian brought up for us from Vlotho. She goes beautifully and will be a great help to us. On our test run we called in to see the American Barter market in Leichardtstrasse. We found two long wooden buildings with American armed guards outside each entrance. Germans and Allies go into one building and deposit their goods which are valued and exchanged for B.U.s or *Barter Units.* For example, an American, for a carton of 200 cigarettes, gets 95 B.U.s. They then go into the other 'store' where all the goods are displayed, and labelled with a ticket with the price in B.U.s. A wireless 390 B.U., a typewriter 270 B.U. and so on. I haven't seen for a long time such a display of luxury goods. The Germans are not allowed in all at once – only a few at a time. Those waiting queue up in a sorrowful-looking line. Their expressions were tired and worried and their reactions were revealing to watch as the satisfied Americans walked past with "reparations", while the Germans were queuing for food, soap, shoes etc.

On the tables and shelves were radios, typewriters, Hoovers, electric dryers, cameras, field-glasses, expensive clothes, silk stockings and fur coats, mats and rugs, embroidery, linen – beautiful cut glass and porcelain, silver ware, everything to tempt material greed. The best looking German girls had been put in neat blue overalls and were serving behind the counter.

For Brian and me it was a dreadful sight to see – we felt guilty at even being seen in the place. I asked a guard whether any young people came to the place as we had not seen many. "Oh yes", he said, "quite a lot of even small ones. Anyone can barter here."

"Do you think the stuff they bring here can have been stolen?' I asked. "We don't ask where they get it from," he replied. "If they steal from each other that's O.K. by us – it doesn't affect us."

In the evening I went to a fine concert in the "Rundfunk" where we heard the Berlin Philharmonic play a modern piece by Hindemith, and Schumann's beautiful Piano Concerto, and the finest performance of the Tannhäuser Overture I have ever heard. Afterwards went back to the Abshagens and we talked about India, and got onto poetry. They then asked me to read to them which I did until after midnight. A happy evening.

Sunday 15th. Attended a Youth meeting during the afternoon down in Kladow got together originally by an R.A.F. chaplain and German pastors whereby the Protestant Evangelische should meet and talk with the British. We were invited by Pastor Weckerling. A very large crowd of fine young people gathered together and took part in talks, discussions, singing and a service from 2.0. – 8.0. There was a really fine, sincere atmosphere about all that was said and done – which I found most encouraging. The German pastor who spoke gave a passionate appeal for Bible study and "Bible-work" and for putting God and His word at the centre of all that we did in our daily lives. They were also planning the form which Church Youth work would take and what the young people could do personally for the service of the community.

Monday 16th. Saw *Stadtrat Geschke* at the Magistrat (City Council House) today, who is the present head of Youth Welfare for the whole of Berlin, but he had little of interest or anything constructive to say. I didn't take to him or anyone in his office. Hoped after the elections he would be replaced, as Sofie suggested.

Called in to see a Municipal home on the way back. It was, in contrast, the first good one of its kind. Formerly a Protestant hospice it had been taken over as a co-educational home for young apprentices, students, and homeless children between 14 -18 years. The outside of the place was decidedly "Red." The inside was not so and we found a good atmosphere, probably due to younger people being in charge.

At supper I received an urgent 'phone call from *Waltraud Hielscher*, a girl who had come to us for help and who had heard me speak at yesterday's youth gathering.

As it sounded urgent I went along straight away, as it happened to be my only free evening in the week. It was urgent as the girl was in a very bad state psychologically. She explained that because I was helping young people in moral danger she had asked for my help, as she was at breaking point. The long and the short of it was that life was not worth living – nothing she did was any good or had any success – her life was useless and unworthy to be lived and had no meaning. She wanted me to give her morphia with which she could go to sleep and never wake up, as she had not the courage to take her life any other way, though she had thought of it many times. I began to feel very inadequate.

The situation was somewhat delicate and obviously needed careful handling. I offered up a silent prayer for some miraculous aid. A refugee from Silesia where her parents were, she had drifted to Berlin to look for relatives. They were missing so she had no friends. She went to school where she also had no friends, no decent clothes and all the things a young girl longs for including of course a boy friend. So far she had refrained from going on the streets to pick up a soldier. But now she was at breaking point, and didn't see what was so very wrong about doing that – since it got you the things you wanted.

The girl seemed one mass of fears and with a persecution complex – she could trust no one. She took instant dislike to certain people – Pastor Weckerling, of all people, for one, and everyone was against her, looked down on her, spied on her and talked about her. She had lost all belief in God and Christianity. She tried to go to Bible class, to church, to read the Bible and pray. She tried to make new starts but they never turned out and what one heard in church and read in the Bible were just empty phrases with no meaning. There was nothing to live for, no hope for the future she said and so she begged for morphia.

At 11 o'clock I was exhausted and could not take any more and left. I had given what advice and help I could to steady her, but did not feel it was very successful. Margaret then took over the case, after I had talked it over with her. She had success.

Tuesday 17th. In the morning saw two Protestant Remand homes, the first a small one and the second larger. In the first one again there was the same lovely atmosphere as we found in the Catholic home, though it was smaller and much more primitive. The leader was a very fine woman and I liked the other sisters. The girls obviously had to work very hard and looked pale and thin. We did not take to the leader of the other home, which seemed strict and lacking in any friendly, homely atmosphere.

I felt extremely tired today and had headaches, which indicated there must be a storm about.

Spent the afternoon going back and forth to the Travel Bureau in the F.I.A.T. Building to get Pastor Mensching's travel permit to England. Finally put them on the night train, to the relief of everyone.

A Musical Evening

Went up to Hermsdorf in the extreme North of the French sector with Ingela and Ilse who had invited me to attend one of *Prof. Jakobi's* musical evenings. He is Music Prof. at the Music High School and had collected some of his pupils together, not more than a dozen. We talked in the garden and ate apples, a nice friendly atmosphere with some good (but rare in Berlin) laughter, as the Prof. has a fine sense of humour.

In his charming house we listened to the lively trios of Corelli and Handel for flute, violin and piano, most beautifully played. Unfortunately I had to leave early, but was invited to come again to sing old English madrigals.

We had *Willi Wohlrabe* to supper. He is a Quaker and one of the 2 Directors of Education in the Russian Zone. I liked him from the beginning. He is absorbingly interesting – has much to say and has a lively wit. By 10 o'clock I was quite exhausted and had to go to bed, and sure enough at 1 o'clock there was a colossal thunderstorm. I don't think I ever remember seeing such lightning or hearing such thunder, or such rain and wind. I thought of all those houses with leaking roofs.

We Watch an Operation

Wednesday 18th. Attended with Margaret, *Mrs Piano* and *Miss Jowett* of B.R.C. an operation at the Charité Hospital performed by *Prof. Sauerbuch's* assistant. The Prof. himself was most pleasant to us. We put on white coats and masks and were given positions where we could see from a yard away all that was going on.

A canalisation was being performed on the stump of an arm to which, eventually, was to be fixed an artificial forearm. A flap of skin was cut away, the outer edges of which were sewn together forming a tube, which was then pushed beneath the exposed muscle. The exposed muscle was then covered by a piece of skin removed from the thigh.

Much to my surprise, having seen worse operations in the R.I. in Bristol where I helped in the theatre during air-raids, without turning a hair, I had to sit down to prevent myself from fainting, felt sick and broke out in a cold sweat.

We then went to the clinic where we saw all stages of the process from a 12 day wound practically healed, to a complete and perfect tube, and finally to the fixing of the artificial limb onto small ivory bars running through the two canals on each side of the stump. Some of the patients had learnt to manipulate their wooden hands and fingers so perfectly that they could pick up a match from the floor, tie shoe-laces or thread a needle. It was truly remarkable and wonderful. I nearly went out a second time and had to be ministered unto, covered with confusion at such weakness of the flesh! Margaret never turned a hair though she was adequately forewarned and armed with a bottle of smelling salts.

Dr. Quast and I had been invited to a Kinderfest at the little Remand home school of Mr Baruch in Wannsee. The children were all dressed up and waiting and sang, and did a little fairy-story play. They then sat down to a huge plateful of raw vegetables – 3 tomatoes, a white and a black turnip-radish, 2 carrots, a pear, a beetroot, 3 biscuits and some roasted nuts in sugar. It was more than most could manage. I managed to find about 100 bars of chocolate, so that each could have one, and they were delighted. I also took them some sugar and milk and a bar of soap, of which they are so short.

Mr Baruch, who is a Jew, lost his wife in the concentration camp at Theresienstadt. Another man and his wife who were also inmates with him were at the party and showed us the numbers branded on their arms. This little school obviously lacks the loving influence of a woman. The massive Alsatian dog looked the best fed of anyone there. During the evening *Landrum Bolling* came to give a talk on "An American Idea of Individual Freedom", to which we invited a number of English-speaking German friends of ours. It was an interesting talk and a good discussion followed, the whole evening being greatly appreciated. Hungry for more.

First Secondary School Visit

Thursday 19th. I went to visit my first big secondary school in Berlin this morning – a Vocational school of about 450 pupils in the American sector. The headmaster and staff were beyond my expectations -average age only about 40, but the school buildings were deplorable, particularly the classrooms. I went to observe about 10 classes at work. In every one the windows were boarded up with occasionally a whole window pane to let in a little light. There was a howling gale outside and rain was blowing in. It was cold and miserable. In most rooms the electric light – a single bulb, was on. In one classroom which adolescent girls had to work in all day, there was no electric light, rain was coming through the roof, so that in front of the teacher's desk there was a large puddle. No glass, girls had to tilt their books towards bare gaps in the boarded windows. Not enough boarding, some cardboard and old Biological diagrams of germinating beans filled in the gaps. Yet in spite of all this the teachers and pupils were cheerful, working hard and learning. We saw mostly English, shorthand, typing and economics classes. I spoke for about 10 minutes in the senior English class about similar schools in England.

We rushed home to put on warm clothes – it really was a wintry day.

Friday 20th. A very interesting interview with *Oberstaatsanwalt (Public Prosecutor) Scheidges* in the Gerichtsamt. He was a tall distinguished man with a monocle, and wearing the tweed clothes of an English country squire, and deaf. Found he was one of the best men we have met and with the most constructive, practical and really sympathetic ideas for the corrective education of delinquent youth.

During the afternoon went to visit 2 more Remand homes in the sector. One was supposed to be the Catholic Bahnhof's Mission (Station Mission), where young homeless girls in moral danger are picked up off the stations and given a home. It turned out to have lost this function and was just a glorified hotel. The second we visited was a Protestant home for old people and working girls. It stank in more ways than one, and the atmosphere was without love or caring, and an awful apathy.

During the evening went to a "Bunter Abend" given by the girls of Frau Thorbecke's home. They gave us a good hour's entertainment of lovely singing, dancing, 'acrobatics', miming and recitation. It was then announced that I had brought a large crateful of woollen balaclava helmets, which could be unravelled and knitted up into gloves or pullovers. I also took them a large supply of knitting and sewing needles, wool, buttons, thimbles, cotton, nails to mend furniture and vitamin tablets, all of which they are so desperately in need. The news was greeted with cheers, wild clapping and much joy.

A musical evening with Professor Jakobi
(extreme left in top picture and middle right in bottom picture)

Saturday 21st. A meeting with Pastor Weckerling at his house, and Herr Wittkowski – Head of Spandau Youth Committee, to discuss Rudolf's proposed Youth club. We went to inspect the club which needs wood for the roof. The main purpose of the meeting was to get W.'s support so that it could be on an official basis. The idea is to have City, Church and British support, co-operation and interest. W. jumped at the idea and promised his support. He wanted it used during the day for workrooms for unemployed and as a youth club in the evening. I promised to try and supply tools, material, games and a canteen and also said I hoped it could be made into a neighbourhood centre for parents as well.

W. then came home with me to fetch some ping-pong balls for his "Tisch tennis" groups, stayed for tea and a long conversation about Youth problems.

In response to a letter, I called on *Heinz Worner*, a German, just back with his wife and children after 7 years' exile in London. He was a well-known sculptor before he left and did a lot of underground anti-Nazi work.

I also met at his flat *Jan Petersen* the author of "Our Street", "Gestapo Trial," etc., published by Gollancz. He was back only 3 days. I had met him before in the Freier Deutscher Kulturbund in Hampstead.

We had a most interesting talk about conditions in Berlin. They told me that the reaction of the German people on their return was interesting. The Berliners could not understand why they had come back, and were surprised that they had had such good treatment in England and been equal and free citizens with the English. The thing these returned refugees felt most was the lack of decency and politeness in Berlin amongst the inhabitants compared with what they had been used to in London. They were loud in their praise of all that had happened to them in England. The conversation inevitably drifted towards the Russians, and to my surprise I found they were very Communist, and pro-Russian and that their views were interesting and undeniably sound, since one cannot help but admit that the present policy, or lack of policy of the Western Allies is disastrous.

I took Jan Petersen on with me to the Bollings who had invited me, and any friends I cared to bring along, to meet some Americans for supper. I met the first American who wasn't a Quaker that I warmed to and with whom I had anything in common. Some German girls were also present and it was interesting material for Jan who is commissioned to write another book for Gollancz.

Monday 23rd. For the first time the three Berlin relief teams, Salvation Army, I.V.S.P. and F.R.S. got together to discuss how they could co-operate, and thereby economise in time and labour seeing that our numbers are now so reduced. It was a happy and friendly occasion and it seems that much good should come out of it. We decided to make sub-committees from members of each team so that the work of each could be co-ordinated and kept together.

Prison Hospital Visit

During the afternoon I went to see the prison at Alt Moabit[1] with Dr. Quast and Dr Thoran through the kindness of *Oberstaatsanwalt Scheidges.* I particularly wanted to see the prison hospital where prisoners who are sick are sent not only from this prison but from others also, and because there were youths there as well. I was apparently the first British civilian to be admitted and to see the appalling sight, and only about the second or third British person to have shown any interest. It was absolutely incredible! I did not believe that such conditions were possible outside the concentration camps, and in Allied occupied territory. I was shown first the T.B. patients -thin, emaciated, pale and dying. Then I was shown the cases of hunger oedema, malnutrition and undernourishment, and I saw my first cases of real starvation. One had seen the film of Belsen and one had seen pictures in the newspapers and Gollancz publications of 'living corpses'. Now I saw them with my own eyes in this ward. The worst, an old man, was only skin and bone – the typical flat posterior – just flabby skin where his rump had been – the gluteus maximus muscles completely absorbed. Hollow sunken cheeks – the bones and vertebræ of his whole body plainly visible. He could speak a little English and he begged me to do something for them. He had been for 11 months, mostly on card 5, but now card 3[2]. He had murdered his wife. I didn't know this until the doctor said to me: "You've just shaken hands with a murderer." I had not thought of him as that – I saw a man dying from starvation – just able to stand up and with just strength enough to take off his prison pyjamas to show us his emaciated body. All of them had loose folds of skin and no visible trace of muscle left. I was horrified.

Two prisoners told me they had been in a concentration camp, but they had got more food in the camp, and that it had been better for them there than in this prison hospital.

I saw the diabetics. Insulin only made them worse because there wasn't the food to do any good.

I saw the V.D. cases, maniacs (one in a straight-jacket) and the mentally deranged patients. The doctor pleaded for food, for medicines, for penicillin. I saw the kitchen, with flies walking over food that made me feel sick to look at. I arrived at the time of their evening meal – a bowl of coffee – one large hunk of bread smeared with margarine, and they don't get the margarine every night.

Where oh where can one get the stuff to heal their bodies and minds and the stuff to heal their spirit? John tells me he has only 8 million units of Penicillin that I can have. I believe it's illegal to possess it. Sent by a kind doctor in London. But food? As I left the prison hospital some of them shouted through the window, "Please, Please try and make the food better".

Tuesday 24th. Went to see the Pflegeamt down in Zehlendorf with Dr. Quast. A very fine woman, *Frl. Excener,* is in charge. Only a small place and part of it is a V.D. Clinic belonging to the Gesundheitsamt. They examine at least 150 cases a day of

---

[1] *This was the prison where so many of Hitler's prisoners of conscience were sent, and where Pastor Poelchau F.O.R. was the prison Chaplain as well as at Tegel prison. I was shown the iron rings in the wall and manacles on the floor.*

[2] *The ration system Card 1 was for most needy cases, progressing down to Card 7.*

suspected V.D. Girls who are rounded up by the police in the raids are taken there for the night and examined next day. We saw several that were still waiting at 11.30 a.m.

A *Dr Siemsen* telephoned and asked for an interview as she had heard I was interested in the problem of prisons. So I went to see her in her office in the Kammergericht (Superior Court of justice) to hear all the things she wanted for the prisons. Took Penicillin to Moabit Prison. Heard that the prisoners were very elated by my visit and had said now that the Quakers have been we shall get food.

In the evening another meeting at Dr Quast's of people interested in our problem, *Scheidges, Frl. Lowenberg*, leader of the dreadful Tannenhof Remand home and other social welfare workers. A very profitable discussion.

Took some footballs to the Don Bosco Home.

Wednesday 25th. Went to the Catholic Frauenbundschule to hear the reports and discussion of the practical work done by social welfare students training to be Fürsorgerinnen[1]. They seemed a very fine lot, very genuinely concerned for the care of Youth in moral danger.

Spent the afternoon seeing over a child welfare clinic and hospital in Wilmersdorf. In spite of the fact that they are short of everything from nappies to bananas there was a very happy atmosphere in the place. Great number of T.B. children – some minute prematures and only one or two with V.D., thus dispelling the rumour that there are great numbers of such infected children.

Arrived back to find that Mary Bailey of Education and Religious Affairs Department and *Major Williams* in Charge of Prisons had both rung up about my visit to Moabit Prison. It seems there's a row brewing and I should have got permits!

The Row Over My Prison Visit

Thursday 26th. Phoned up Mary Bailey at Mil. Gov. and found out that I was in hot water and that the trouble was over Moabit prison. So, having told her exactly what had happened and, with her blessing, I rang Major Williams and asked straight away if I might see him. Went to Mil. Gov. When I went into the office he was engaged but Lt. Stirum was there. He was, I could see, pretty cross and told me I'd let him down badly; that I knew perfectly well what the rules were for being allowed into the prisons and that I had committed a very serious breach of etiquette. I then had a chance to explain to Major Williams how I had got in and what I had done. He informed me that he had got the report from the doctor that I had asked for and that it would be translated and passed on to me. However he never let me see this report! He was very decent about the whole affair. That I should have got permission was obvious – afterwards. It did appear, however, that the information that I had got and what I had seen rather softened things down, not that they had anything to be ashamed of, he explained, but that simply it had been impossible to improve conditions any more. But if a reporter, say of the "News of the World" got in, they might make a scandal out of it that would be bad for all of us, and that was undesirable. He asked if I had already made a report. He would be interested to see it – see how it tallied with a similar report he had. Of course all reports had to be passed by him. In any case, he said, you could not trust what the Germans told you because they would always try and get something extra out of you if they could. As it

---

[1] *Welfare workers.*

happened he had informed the prison officials that the Kommandantura was raising the rations for prisoners especially for sick prisoners and particularly for T.B. patients, and that drugs were available if they would only make application to the Public Health authorities. It was cheering to hear they are to go up to ration card 2. I only hope it is true. I pointed out that we were here to help him with prisons if he needed food and drugs.

I then got permission to take Charlottenburg prison juveniles a supply of mending materials and knitting wool, etc., for all of which he was very pleased. The discussion became quite friendly and the air cleared. Even Stirum, as I went, was beaming all over, and informed me he was leaving the service for C.C.G. in the Zone. I left with a sigh of relief not only for myself, but that I had not got the F.R.S. team into further trouble at a critical time for us.

Spent the rest of the morning dictating my report and realising how difficult it was to get it in order.

An Evening Reception for Lady Falmouth

In the evening we were invited by *Miss Birkett M.B.E.*, Commandant of the B.R.C. Convalescent Home, to an "At Home" to meet *Countess of Falmouth D.B.E.*, a Commissioner of the Red Cross, who had just flown up from the Zone with Colonel Gidley-Kitchen who is now staying with us. All the personnel of the Relief teams and B.R.C. had been invited, and there was a large number of V.I.P.s there including *General Nares* – Commander of British troops Berlin and 3 Brigadiers, *Colonel Bevier* of Welfare Dept. U.S. Mil. Gov. who had heard about my Report on Juvenile Delinquency and was particularly interested. He hoped I would let him have a copy for 2 reasons:- one because he was interested personally and two, to show O.M.G. U.S. what "wonderful" work the Quakers were doing, in order to persuade them it was time they allowed American Quakers into the U.S. Zone. (Six months later, they were allowed in). He said he thought the Quakers were the only Christian people left on earth, certainly the only people who were in Germany for completely selfless motives. I also got in a very lively conversation with *Brigadier Whales*. It appears that he had arranged the accommodation at the Potsdam conference and therefore responsible for all that appalling luxury that was boasted about so much. He is also responsible for the Olympic Sports club for British troops – another luxurious place. Did I ride? Yes I rode. Well I must be sure to ring up for a horse – he rode every evening for an hour and hoped he would see me. His face was vaguely familiar. Was there a connection with this man, I wondered?

Lady Falmouth was perfectly charming and quite unassuming. She kept completely in the background but was so friendly, and talked quietly with each person. Colonel G-K. walked about in a very jolly way introducing everyone and kept saying to each V.I.P., "Oh you must come and meet my Quakers! There now! – we're all very international and friendly."

Some harmless-looking orangeade turned out to be a foul concoction and I was amused to see that John, Brian and I had all hit on the identical idea of 'watering' the geraniums, which we did. Elaborate snacks were handed round. It was a perfect evening as we stood on the balcony. There was a wonderful sunset over the marvellous view of the lake, which changed into all sorts of pastel shades, surrounded by the deeper colours of the woods. There were perfect reflections of the little yachts in the water.

Lady Falmouth's Reception

Edith Snelgrove, Margaret Watts and Pastor Weckerling

Meeting Archbishop of York, Col. Gidley Kitchin, Lady Falmouth and Adj. Dale

I found the whole evening intensely amusing especially as yesterday we had entertained the *Duchess of Mecklenburg* to lunch. When training as a relief worker one had never expected to 'hob-nob' with such people. The Duchess had been sent to us by Mil. Gov. for help with food and clothes, having first fled from Nazis to Hungary and then from the Russians back to Germany. Finally she was caught by the Russians and had lost everything. She was great. Margaret more or less adopted her.

Juvenile Court Cases

Friday 27th. Went to the U.S. Mil. Gov. Juvenile Court in Zehlendorf, which was due to start at 1.30. but it didn't. So while we were waiting for the Judge to arrive we were shown over the small prison at the back where a good number of juveniles were being held. 2 or 3 young fellows were cramped into a cell built for one. However conditions were not too bad.

At last *Major Sabo* the American Mil. Judge arrived and the Court began at 3.0. I was interested to see that the boy on trial was one I had spoken to in Moabit where he was being held for medical examination to see if he was mentally deficient. He was only 14½ and very pale – unfortunate parents and home life – neglect – and had absconded from his home and the various institutions he had been in several times.

The American judge was excellent and took infinite trouble, and relied for his judgement upon the advice of the German Youth Office and the doctor. The boy was given 5 years at an approved school. The procedure was a model for the Germans to follow for he was so good with the boy. The Germans were deeply impressed. I had a few words with the Judge afterwards. He was interested and friendly. Arrived back for my lunch at 6.0 p.m.

In the evening went out with 3 Fürsorgerinnen from the Wilmersdorf Gesundheitsamt to various cafés, bars and 'Tanz Locals' where they made enquiries about V.D. cases among the young people. No one objected to these personal questions, which was surprising, and those that had V.D. or suspected it were told to report at the Health office the next day. Some, who recognised the two Welfare workers as soon as they saw us arrive tried to escape. These of course are the most likely cases. They do escape easily. One couple disappeared and were at the next place when we arrived and were caught there. They have to report if ordered, otherwise the police are sent after them.

Saturday 28th. Lady Falmouth, *Miss Johnstone* and *Col. Stackpool* paid the team an official visit this morning to hear about our work. Since we are only 5 members at present we had little to show her. They were very interested in my survey and asked a lot of questions. They also went over to see our British Red Cross store. We all found them perfectly charming visitors who have helped us a great deal. Miss Johnstone, who is very high up in the Red Cross, is very widely travelled. She went to Russia as Mrs Churchill's secretary on their 'Aid to Russia' Red Cross visit.

Reactions to the Quaker Team – Crisis Point

Col. Gidley-Kitchen told us of the party's interview with *Brigadier Robertson* and Dr Melvin and all the people in Mil. Gov. to whom we are responsible. He told us that Melvin thoroughly disapproves of us – that no one will take full responsibility for us or make decisions as to what they want us to do. Melvin should but won't – says it's

Brigadier Hinde's job. Hinde says it's Melvin's job. Anyway, the reputation of the relief teams is in very bad odour, with Mil. Gov. due to John Downing's wedding, which has caused everyone so much trouble, as well as other small matters.

So Col. G-K. had asked him point blank, if he wanted the relief teams to leave Berlin. Melvin almost said yes, but said it wasn't his responsibility to make such a big decision. Said if it was the Zone he'd be glad to have us but in Berlin with the quadripartite administration, we were, by our "irresponsible actions", an embarrassment to him. Col. G-K. apparently stood up for "my teams" as he calls us all and said: "If my teams go, then all the British Red Cross supplies to Berlin go too." So it seems that the £2000 of Medical supplies we have just offered Melvin saved the day, for he could not very well order us to go under these circumstances, and he does need our supplies.

In the afternoon we were all invited again to the British Red Cross Convalescent Home to meet the *Archbishop of York* and to hear a programme by the Berlin Broadcasting Orchestra in the open-air. Lady Falmouth introduced all of the members of the Relief teams to the Archbishop who was dressed in-black with gaiters and appeared on his last legs. The poor man had to shake hands with so many people and he did not appear interested in any particular one. The programme of music was delightful. It was a gorgeous hot, sunny day, and we sat in deck-chairs on the beautiful lawn overlooking the Havel Lake. We began to relax.

A Tour of Potsdam

Sunday 29th. Much to our relief the perfect weather held good, because we had decided to go to Potsdam on the weekly C.C.G. tour. Two full buses left the Kaiserdamm at 2.15, and by 3 o'clock we were in Potsdam. "Potsdam," our leaflet tells us: "first mentioned in the 10th Century, is of ancient Slavonic origin. It is indebted for its splendour to William I and still more to Frederick the Great, who generally resided there. The whole area is similar to the Versailles Palaces in Paris." "Potsdam", the leaflet continues, "is the true cradle of the Prussian army. From Potsdam Frederick William I issued his regulations for uniformity of drill and discipline which he had previously tested on his gigantic grenadiers." We entered the park along an avenue of gigantic limes and then turning to the right suddenly saw a beautiful view of Frederick the Great's residence – the Palace of "Sans Souci".

"But first we see the 130 ft. high fountain," so the leaflet says. "Behind it stretches a broad flight of steps 66 ft. in height intersected by 6 terraces on which Frederick the Great cultivated vines and choice fruits. The former were visible behind the glass of the greenhouses which now protect them."

Masses of people were milling about: English, Americans, French, Russians and Germans – all seemed happy and friendly, but "Eugh!" remarked one little C.C.G. girl, "I can't help it but the Russian soldiers do look dirty little beasts". She shuddered.

We walked up the steps and into the palace (1R. Mark entrance fee) and had to put on great felt slippers over our shoes. With these one goes sliding about in a skating motion over the marble floors.

The interior is fantastic, and unless seen personally cannot be adequately described. Suffice it to say that the interiors of this palace are supposed to be among the finest examples of the then prevalent rococo style, and the furthest away from simplicity I have ever seen. It is a perfect representation of all that the early Quakers strived against – all the elaborate ceremony and outward trappings with which man surrounded himself in those days.

We saw Voltaire's room in the West Wing – the wood-inlaid and marble-inlaid floors, embroidered furniture, the gold and black squiggles and flowers and grapes – birds and monkeys all over all the walls and ceilings, the paintings by Watteau and Lancret on the wall, and ugly busts in the corners and fantastic glass pear-drop chandeliers.

We walked on round the park, past the windmill's burnt-out shell, and through the "orangery"; through vast Cathedral-like avenues of trees, past 'Belvedere' and round to the New Palace – deserted and ruined.

Time, we discovered, was getting on and we were further away than we had realised. Then began a long walk back through the lovely park full of vivid Autumn colours. We only just made the bus in time at 5 o'clock when it was due to leave, hot and perspiring, because to be left behind in the Russian Zone, as people have been, causes grave difficulties.

Heard a fine performance in the evening of Hindemith's Symphony in B by the Berlin Philharmonic at the Städtische Oper, with Ilse and Ernst. Siegfried Borries played the Mendelssohn Violin Concerto. It was quite a new interpretation to me – having heard Menuhin so many times – particularly the last movement which was played very staccato.

This was the first performance of the concerto since the war, when it was banned.

Had a long talk afterwards with Ilse, till about 1 a.m. She is sincerely troubled by what to believe in these days, and is very troubled in spirit, searching for faith and a purpose in life.

On my way back in the ambulance a rabbit darted out in front of me and must have hit the wheel, for when I stopped to see if I had killed or wounded it, it was lying dead in the road. I took it back with me and, early next morning, I skinned and gutted it. We had it cooked for supper giving our staff extra meat for their meal. It was a great prize!

Monday 30th. Second combined meeting of the 3 teams, this time at the Salvation Army's house.

We were given another account by Adjutant Dale of the interview between, Lady Falmouth, Col. Gidley-Kitchen and Mil. Gov. Apparently it was stormy and we were sailing very close to the wind. The rest of the meeting was devoted to the meetings of the sub-committees to elect chairmen etc. I was nominated chairman of the Youth Welfare sub-committee.

Luncheon party at the International Red Cross to which I was invited to represent F.R.S. It was a farewell for *Dr Lindt* of the International Red Cross, who is going to London to join the Swiss delegation there. Met his successor *Mr Myer* who was extremely interested in our work and asked for our continued co-operation and help.

Spent the afternoon trying to scrounge roof-planking and beams for our proposed 'united' Youth club in Spandau. Went to the same army salvage depot as the place where I got the glass, but this time without success – not a scrap of planking. Called on Pastor Weckerling to tell him the sad news. Must try elsewhere.

Hess got life imprisonment at the War Crimes Tribunal judgements and is to be moved to Spandau. With binoculars I could see from my room Hess standing on the balcony of Spandau prison guarded by soldiers to make sure that he did not jump off and commit suicide.

October 1946

Tuesday 1st. First meeting of our Youth sub-committee. We each outlined the youth work of our teams and made proposals for the future. There was good agreement and enthusiasm all round, but how much we shall be able to do, I don't know. We decided to continue to visit and support clubs, and help start the new Spandau club.

One of my ideas is to go into schools and talk to and have discussion groups with English classes, and to collect a panel of outside people in Mil. Gov. and C.C.G. willing to help here, and in clubs and remand homes. Quite a lot of work should arise out of my report – in providing materials to the remand homes for toy-making and the making of useful garments.

In the evening went out to Prof. Jakobi's home again where there was a lovely informal musical programme. We sang old English madrigals, John Dowland, Bennett, Purcell etc., and Bach Chorales. *Miss Pruss* played beautifully some pieces from Bach's 'Well-Tempered Clavier'. The flautist played part of his own flute sonata. The Prof. extemporised on the piano.

Today at Nuremberg it was reported that 12 Nazis were sentenced to death and that Hess got 'life'. 5 were jailed and 3 acquitted.

Wednesday 2nd. Was asked to attend a meeting with *Dr Strebel* head of the Education Dept. of the American Mil. Gov. 2 German Quakers, *Eric Mohr* and *Dr Thiemke* had been to him wanting English speaking people to go to their schools so that the pupils could practise English and learn "the right democratic ideals". I offered our services. Then discovered it was impossible to go ahead with this scheme because it was a Kommandantura decision that German teachers could start such discussions but outsiders must not go in. It was then decided to work through the Youth clubs in the Jugendausschuss, and this was gladly accepted by the American Youth Dept.

A very cold wintry day – really the first taste of winter. The flame colours of the trees are a wonderful sight and the leaves are being whirled away . There is general apprehension about the coming winter and its many problems.

Many Visitors

Friday 4th. Professor Jakobi came to lunch with *Monsieur Fataud* (French Mil. Gov.) and we fixed up for the latter to give a lecture at our house. Prof. Jakobi seemed to enjoy himself very much – he is a charming natural person, and we arranged for a musical evening either here or at the I.V.S.P. where *Basil Eastland* (who later joined Friends) is the leader and is very musical[1].

In the evening I went to Dr Quast where we had a meeting and discussion with Dr Scheidges and a few pastors concerned and interested in prison visiting and after-care of delinquents. I felt it was a most valuable and interesting evening. Stayed behind

[1] *Died of cancer in Birmingham in 1996.*

afterwards to talk with Dr Q. about the report which is occupying most of my time these days.

Saturday 5th. Went down to Charlottenburg station at 7.30 a.m. to meet John Pettigrew from the Cologne Team and Morna Smith from the Dortmund team who had come up to spend their 72 hr. leave with me. We had trained together. *Fred Tritton* from London also arrived and I took them all back for breakfast. Fred was a first world war relief veteran.

Miserable cold wet day. Spent the morning with John, Morna and Dr Q. at the Juvenile Appeal Court where we heard a couple of interesting theft cases of boys from a gang.

In the afternoon I took J. and M. round Berlin seeing the Olympic Games Stadium, the Russian sector, and Hitler's Chancellery. Finished up in the evening with a variety show at the Jerboa Theatre.

Sunday 6th. *Errol Eliott* (Editor "The American Friend") of the A.F.S.C. turned up for breakfast on a flying visit to Berlin to visit Quakers and teams. He had come over as a "war-correspondent," as the only method of being allowed over. He was telling me of the visit he had paid to the A.F.S.C. group in Lapland at Rovaniemi, just on the Arctic Circle. I knew the place before the war having passed through it on my travel scholarship. It was a beautiful city then.

We all went down to Meeting together, so there was a big group of English speaking Quakers there.

Hitler's Bunker

In the afternoon took Fred, Errol, J and M. again to visit the Chancellery as there was a chance of getting down into Hitler's Bunker. It is pretty bare now with very little furniture left. It was a weird feeling walking about in the depths of this bunker into Eva Braun's and Hitler's bedrooms and study etc. and to see the whole place black from the flames and still with that damp burnt smell about it.

Took J. and M. on in the car to John's friend *Gretel Sommer* in the American sector for tea and afterwards some music. We had to leave early because we had decided to go to the Opera. Heard a performance of Verdi's 'Othello'. Desdemona's voice was good but the Moor very poor, so that, while it was an interesting production, it was not the best singing.

There has been quite an uproar in Berlin as a result of the verdict on the Nuremberg trial prisoners. At a demonstration, which I did not see, there was a protest and death demanded for the 3 set free.

"If they are not guilty why should we be counted guilty?" seemed to be an opinion frequently expressed.

Our Sponsorship is Questioned

Monday 7th. Edith spent the morning with Dale and Douglas at Mil. Gov. straightening out our problems and getting our position clear. It seems that J.D.'*s* wedding is still causing a lot of headaches, and that the whole position of British Red Cross has had to be reviewed again. My Moabit prison visit too seems to have caused embarrassment, but Edith told me that as a direct result of my visit and report the rations had been raised to ration card 1. It should have been done some time before officially, but no one realised apparently that it had not been implemented.

It also appeared that Mr Myer of the International Red Cross had asked for our co-operation with a feeding scheme for adolescents as a result of my talk with him at the luncheon party a few days ago. That is cheering news.

Our position with Mil. Gov. seems to be a little more secure, and we are now definitely under the sponsorship of Public Health and Welfare Depts. and Education and Religious Affairs have thrown us over, which is a pity, though if they want us to do some work for them we are still at liberty to do so. My survey is safe.

In the afternoon took John, Morna and Ilse to see "Pink Strings and Sealing Wax" at a German Cinema, and then went down for tea to the Officers' Club at Gatow overlooking the lake. It was the first time I had been and there was no one else about, so we had a table by the most wonderful log fire. It is a sumptuous and luxurious place, beautifully and tastefully furnished and with lovely pictures. In large vases there were brightly coloured autumn leaves everywhere. After supper saw them off at the station in pouring rain It had been wonderful to have them and was just like old times back at "Woodstock".

Tuesday 8th. a.m. A long conference with Dr. Q. reading over my report and making last-minute corrections and additions. Had a bad cold and did not feel too good. Spent the rest of the day catching up on correspondence, and dosing myself with penicillin lozenges without the slightest effect.

Wednesday 9th. Gave a lecture on "The Religious and Social Work of the Quakers" at the Volkshochschule in Tempelhof. Since it was widely advertised by posters and announced in the Press nearly a hundred people turned up. When I arrived at the place it was in total darkness except for two candles one at the entrance and one on the speaker's table so that when I started I could not see my audience , what sort it was, or how many were there. Fortunately about half-way through the lights came back on again. I spoke for about 40 minutes and afterwards questions and discussion followed for over an hour! After a two-hour session the meeting was closed though I was ready to go on answering questions. There were a few pointless and rather silly questions, but the majority were intelligent and interesting and produced good discussion. Some were extremely difficult but I managed and there seemed to be a genuine sincere atmosphere of seeking and understanding. Had a cup of tea at a Friend's house.

Thursday 10th. Confined to my room all day with a very bad cold and slight temperature. Dosed myself with Penicillin Lozenges which at last took effect. Dr Q. came and we discussed the report all afternoon.

Got the truck and all my papers ready for tomorrow's leave trip.

At Nuremberg today the war crimes tribunal rejected pleas for clemency from the 11 Nazis sentenced to death. There seems to be little reaction to this news anywhere that I can detect.

On Leave

Friday 11th. Left our house at exactly 6.30 a.m. with Malcolm Sadler, of the Goslar Team, in "179" – my *Fordson* ('Liz') 15 cwt. truck. It was a bitterly cold, frosty and a thick misty morning – had on every stitch of clothing. Was over the Russian frontier at 7.0 a.m. and travelled West at an average speed of 44 mph along the autobahn. Still too misty to see anything. Later in the morning patches of mist cleared revealing beautiful autumn sunlit trees. All beautifully fresh and exhilarating. 'Liz' went perfectly, but at that speed makes too much noise for conversation. Reached the far Russian barrier at 9.15 (101 miles) and passed straight through to the English barrier of the British zone. Stopped at the 'N.A.A.F.I.' to get warm and have a spot of breakfast. Mist cleared and gave us a wonderful day.

Arrived at the Brunswick Team at 10.00 – saw Biddy, Alice, Walter and all the folks very cheerful and had a cup of hot tea with them. Left Malcolm there.

Spent an hour in a great long queue getting petrol. Left Brunswick at 12.15, and dashed on down the autobahn – stopping to take occasional photos on the way. Decided not to stop off at Hannover. Had my lunch on top of a beautiful hill with a lovely view over the Westphalian plain – just before Vlotho. Decided not to stop off at Vlotho as I was behind time a little.

Left the Autobahn again at Herford, a quaint little country town, to get more petrol – doing about 10 miles to the gallon. On again down the Autobahn and then left it at Redda to branch off to Münster. A lovely tree-lined country road with charming little Westphalian villages. Finally arrived at Münster just as it was getting dark at 6.0 p.m. about 300 miles.

Soon found Toni's[1] house, and had a meal, and got down to talking. Toni did not seem much changed after 13 years. I recognised her but she saw little likeness in me. Her parents were there and also her brother and sister-in-law and nephew, all very kind and friendly to me. Most of the houses round them were pretty badly damaged and still unrepaired. A bomb fell in their own garden blowing up a large apple tree right over the house. But their house has been repaired, luckily, and redecorated. Toni works at the Salvage Depot as an interpreter, and is in charge of the girls (350 of them) who work there. She is on very friendly terms with "the Major" who seems to have got repairs done and who seems to have given her food clothes, wireless etc. and everything for her comfort. She talked mostly of "the Major" and never mentioned her 1st cousin to whom she is, it seems, engaged, but who is a prisoner in Russia. She spoke, of course, bitterly against the Russians, and had little to say for the British administration. Toni seemed much more serious than of old and her face rather bitterly-lined and cynical.

Saturday 12th. Went along to the Salvage Depot after breakfast to pick up Toni, who then walked me round Münster. It must have been a wonderful old place. It is now so hopelessly 'kaput'. The streets, formerly narrow enough anyway, are made *even* narrower by still uncleared piles of rubble and little train tracks. Some active clearing up by gangs of prisoners in some parts – with busy little puffing engines and trucks full of rubble. The Cathedral is not totally, but practically all destroyed and though they are

[1] *Toni Althaus – one of our pre-war German au pair girls.*

beginning repairs, I can't see that it will be any use. No laughter or smiles on the people's faces. My uniform was quite new and they stared at me as if I was a Russian.

At 11.45 left Münster and carried on down Route 54, finally crossing the autobahn again to Dortmund, and arrived in time for lunch with the F.R.S. team. Some difficulty in getting to the team's billet. Dortmund is at once depressing from the moment you enter it. Again "ganz kaput'. But being industrial as well it is dirty and smoky. The roads are frightful and so are the gray-black ruins everywhere.

The F.R.S. team lives in two small adjoining suburban and rather "slummy" houses, even more primitive furniture and cramped than ours. There is however a very homely friendly atmosphere about the team. They are quite international with English, Irish, Scotch, German, French and American members.

A little *Volkswagen* and driver were waiting to take Morna and me the 80 miles on down to Cologne. As we sped down the autobahn mists appeared again. Many more diversions in the road which had been frequently bombed here, and of course all the bridges had been destroyed. But the autobahn skirts round the North side of all the big industrial towns of the Ruhr – Essen, Mülheim, Krefeld, Dusseldorf and so on, and finally one crosses the Rhine by the wonderful, but temporary, bridge "The Patton" with a marvellous view of the Cathedral and into battered, scarred and 'kaput' Cologne.

We went straight to the City stadium where we saw the end of a fine game of Handball between the F.R.S. Cologne team and a youth club – the Quakers winning 7-4.

Bunty Harman then took us through town again to see the Cathedral. It is obviously badly damaged and stands in a sea of ruins – in places quite flat. On stepping out of the car we were immediately besieged by a mass of young boys trying to sell us souvenirs – photos, crosses, Hitler Jugend daggers etc. It was both impressive and depressing to see this wonderful cathedral in the dying evening light. I should like to have spent longer there.

We went back and had supper with the team which includes John Pettigrew and *Pat Radley* who share a room. They were telling me how they had watched a Lesser spotted – barred – woodpecker on the branch outside their windows, and Pat had heard and seen a golden oriole. A friendly team in rather a grand house compared with ours – though they do sleep on camp beds and have no sheets. We were a very large crowd that sat down for supper.

As John had to go to a place in the Ruhr that evening we left together in the Dodge truck for Solingen where we looked in on the F.R.S. team and had a cup of tea with *Kjell Nahnfeldt,* a Swedish C.O., and *Alice* (*Eden*) who trained with us at Woodstock. It was wonderful to see them again. Alice seems quieter and nicer, and more ready to listen. Kjell was just the same. They both loved the work, but both looked extremely tired. Drove on along the Ruhr valley in the twilight and moonlight. Saw the extraordinary overhead hanging tramway over the Wupper river at Wuppertal – a massive steel structure, miles long.

We went through thick blankets of mist up and down the little valleys and finally back to Dortmund just after midnight.

Toni Althaus, former au pair, and self

Ruins of Münster

Ruins of Münster

Münster

With Magdalena Riemenschneider, Annemarie Grim and family, former au pair girls

Same, with Morna Smith

Morna Smith among the ruins of Dortmund

Ruins of Dortmund

Sunday 13th. Morna and I took a picnic lunch and went over to visit Magdalena[1] at Witten where she spends the week-ends with her parents. It was only 20 mins. away from Dortmund and we soon found the house as Morna had been there previously. It was wonderful to see Lena again after 13 years, and an even greater joy to see Annemarie and her little son Albrecht. The younger sister Gisele and the parents were also there. It was polling day and they had just been out to vote for C.D.U. – the Christian Democrats. Everyone else was out in their best clothes for the occasion.

Lena looked older of course and quite well and plump. Annemarie looked a lot prettier and happier. I remember as a boy of 13 I had not liked her very much since she had no sense of humour, was not very nice to look at and could not stand being teased. And she had, obviously because of my cruelty, not liked me very much. In those early days she was very pro-Nazi and I remember being able to reduce her to tears simply by jokingly saying "Hitler is a bad man". Since then she has changed a great deal – married – had 2 children and realised that Hitler was bad a long time ago. I asked her what party she supported now and she said: "Hugh, it's very difficult – one finds oneself in agreement with the things that the S.P.D. (the Social Democrats) write and say, and Dr Schumacher is a fine person, but one cannot agree with their methods." She and Lena anyway missed their votes because they were away from their own home towns.

After a lot of joyful happy talking and reminiscing about the old days we had lunch together. Lena was overjoyed at the things I had brought which besides a lot of tinned food cocoa and tea etc. included, soap, mending materials and so on, which are in such short supply. Albrecht went into raptures over the chocolate and the truck. He was content to scramble all over it and toot the horn for hours.

Though it was a rather dull and misty afternoon Morna wanted to show me some of the beautiful wooded hills and valleys round Witten, Iserlohn and Hagen, so we decided to take Lena, Annemarie, Gisele and Albrecht with us. He is a lovely natural little boy of 9, full of fun and humour and no shyness. He was just thrilled with sitting between us in front and flicking the indicator out when we went round a corner.

We came to one particularly lovely spot at the top of a hill, and went a wonderful walk in the woods, which were all colours, and with lovely views. It was a very happy occasion. We stopped to have a picnic tea before going back.

The Cellar Dwellers of Dortmund

Monday 14th. In the morning went out with Morna and Jean Low to see a bit of Dortmund. We went to some of the worst damaged and bombed parts, where the ruins are mostly flat. In this field of utter devastation where you would normally think no one could live, can be found, if you look carefully around you, tell-tale signs of human habitation. Smoke trickles up through the ruins out of an improvised cellar dwelling; a dog or cat dashes past into a ruined doorway; a smell drifts up from a dark looking hole. Then you can see you are among the cellar dwellers. In unspeakable conditions people are living in these ruins down underneath, in dark, damp and cold cellars without any glass in the slit of a window. Or one can see little home-made shacks about 15ft. x 10 ft. built out of salvaged bricks and wood – just anything – bits of cloth or cardboard. They may have a little garden by the side in the rubble also 15' x 10' with a few tobacco plants

---

[1] *Magdalena Riemenschneider and Annemarie Grimm – 2 sisters, also our pre-war au-pair girls.*

and cabbages. We went into one where an English girl was living. Her husband, a German, had built the little place himself and fitted it out beautifully inside. She had just had a baby – a very difficult confinement – a seven pound baby. It looked dreadful. Yet one was struck by the cheerful friendliness and determination of these people living from day to day and hand to mouth in impossible conditions. It was an experience I shall never forget.

We also saw one of the large bunkers now used to sleep 150 refugees and homeless people each night, run by the German Red-cross. One corner had had a direct hit during an air raid which had killed countless people.

Dortmund is a ghastly, depressing, damp, dirty, hopeless place. I should find it hard to work there. Berlin is different – not so industrial and dirty, and with wider, cleaner and tidier streets, and hasn't the coal mines and awful dust and smoke of Dortmund.

In vivid contrast during the afternoon Morna took me out to see the Schloss Bodelschwingh. It is a gem of a castle in the middle of a small lake set in lovely old surroundings and with a quaint old farm close by. I wandered round it quite spell-bound by its beautiful reflections, and the atmosphere of the whole place. There are now about 20 families living there – mostly refugees and relatives of the owners.

Reluctantly I started off again on the first stage of the journey home at 4.30 back up the autobahn and arrived at Vlotho just in time for supper. Had a talk with Eric Cleaver, then met *Winnie Wood* and *Alex Bryan* of the Cologne and Solingen teams on their way back from a conference at Bad Pyrmont. Also *Hilary Wright* on her way down to the Dortmund team. Fred Tritton was also there again. Slept at the F.R.S. Billet.

Return to Berlin

Tuesday 15th. Left Vlotho immediately after breakfast and got to the Hannover team's house at 10.30. I then had to pick up a couple of parcels and fill up with petrol. This took nearly 2 hours, and I arrived back just in time for lunch. *Morgan Johnson*, who was head boy at Sidcot when I was there, is a member of this team. It was good to see him again, also the 2 Americans whom I had met at Woodstock, and David Hughes the leader. Alice Scares brought *John Bourke* over from Goslar, and after lunch I took John on up to Berlin to join us[1]. He obviously did not want to leave Goslar one bit. It was nice to see old 'Liz' again unchanged, the truck, that is!

Got to the frontier by 5 to 5 and was caught up by a Salvation Army team truck. So we decided to go across the Russian zone together in case either of us should break down. No trouble, and got across the zone in the record time of 2 hrs 15 mins. It was dusk by the time we got to the British check point and were soon home to a hot supper and glad to be back after a round trip of about 900 miles. 'Liz' ran perfectly.

Wednesday 16th. A rather curious and interesting guest to lunch – *Dr. John Rickman* (Tavistock Clinic), who said he was a non-practising Quaker and had been a member of "Meeting for Sufferings" at the age of 23 (ex F.A.U.). He is a well-known psychiatrist and calls himself one of the "back-room" boys who had been working on the rehabilitation of P.O.W.s returning to England during and after the war, and had come

---

[1] *Though a non-Friend, he became our team leader in Berlin.*

out to Germany to do research for C.C.G. on the same problem, which is a much more serious one, of the rehabilitation and reorientation of German P.O.W.s – what he calls the science of "sociiatry". His theory, which he said adopts quite a new technique in dealing with these people, is to have them in camps, and instead of lecturing them and offering them expert advice he gets them to find the answers to their problems and questions from discussions amongst their own groups, and thus to foster mutual aid and community spirit. If this method is successful it could prove to be far more successful than the old way, and expert advice and help would be brought in only when the P.O.W.'s failed to get it from the group. He thought Quakers were just the people to take part in this work because their method of worship and way of life provided at least partial training in this form of group work. He talked till 4 o'clock, but it was by no means an afternoon wasted.

Ten Nazis were hanged at Nuremberg today.

Thursday 17th and Friday 18th. Mostly writing my report in an attempt to get it finished before going to London. Up till very late. At Nuremberg we heard that Goering had committed suicide by taking cyanide hours before his execution. I was unaware of any reactions amongst Berliners.

Lady Limerick's Visit

Saturday 19th. Lady Limerick, another Commissioner of the British Red Cross, Col. Gidley-Kitchen, and Admiral Sir Richard Bevan (the new B.R.C. Commissioner taking over from Col. G-K), came to pay us a visit, see our Red Cross store and talk about our work. In the afternoon there was another reception for them, similar to the one with Lady Falmouth, arranged by Miss Birkett up at the Red Cross Convalescent home. It was another perfect afternoon, with winter forgotten, and an unforgettable view over the lake. Part of the Berlin Broadcasting orchestra played us some really delightful chamber music. It was altogether a very restful occasion. Kathleen, who is having a week there (after a nervous breakdown) is looking a great deal better, and was much perturbed because she thought all the other members of the team looked as though they needed it far more than she did! I think we are all tired.

Margaret borrowed my photographs to show the Colonel during the dinner party in the evening. They were mostly of Lady Falmouth's visit. He liked them so much that he 'swiped' the lot as souvenirs. They had cost nearly a week's pocket money! We were on an allowance of 10/- per week. However, as Lady Falmouth and Lady Limerick had given Roger Wilson a lift to Austria they were forgiven!

First Free Elections in Berlin for 14 Years

Sunday 20th. The long awaited and discussed Election day in Berlin. After Quaker Meeting we went down into the centre of the city but it was all much quieter than we expected. The whole of Berlin is plastered with S.E.D. posters. The S.E.D. 'Socialist United Party' is Communist controlled. The "Unter den Linden" was just one mass of S.E.D. propaganda with loudspeakers blaring away. The S.E.D., supported by the Russians, has been given all the paper for propaganda. The Russians too have given large and handsome presents to Berlin as bribes for S.E.D. During the last month for example exercise books were distributed to schools by private individuals acting on behalf of the S.E.D., with the following delightfully disingenuous inscription on the title page:-

"Instead of using this paper for propaganda purposes the Berlin branch of the S.E.D. is giving it to you, dear Berlin Child. Work hard and please your parents by doing so."

The Kommandantura Education Committee was unable to agree that the distribution of such material was improper, the Russian member saying that as it was neither militarist nor Fascist he saw nothing against it. The matter has been submitted to the Commandants where agreement appears unlikely, but a repetition of the episode, even so, is improbable. (Education and Religious Affairs Department report Aug. '46).

I took some photographs in the Russian sector of the propaganda etc. (which was forbidden). About an hour later an American was seen taking photos and was stopped by the Russians and told to report to Russian H.Q. He was told to follow a car there in his own jeep but on the way tried to escape and was shot dead. The Russians later apologised.

It was the most wonderful sunny day. Went a walk in the woods behind our house. The colours of the trees were glorious as we picked some leaves for the house. Watched a greater spotted woodpecker from only a few yards away.

In the evening we had a lovely concert by Prof. Jakobi and his wife at the I.V.S.P. H.Q. to which we invited a lot of our friends. It was a memorable occasion for its friendly atmosphere through the arts, which breaks down all barriers, and one can share these great things in common and in unity.

Monday 21st. Brian and I went to *Hans Ulbrich's* birthday party in the evening, a friendly gathering of students, a lot of gossip, games and dancing but with a nice atmosphere. The Germans, denied these dancing parties for so long, certainly make up for it now!

Tuesday 22nd. A meeting of the 3 relief teams' Education and Youth Welfare Committee at which I had to outline to *Mr Creighton* at Mil. Gov. (Head of Education Dept.) what our work was and what we intended to do. He was in complete agreement with our plans and gave us every encouragement to go ahead. We felt it was a very satisfactory interview.

A discussion group in the evening at Dr. Quast's house in which she and I spoke to a group of pastors and teachers on the problem of delinquency and what we thought ought to be done about it. It was an extremely profitable and interesting evening, with a high level of discussion. Both pastors and teachers were very interested and willingly offered to co-operate.

Berlin Election Results

Wednesday 23rd. The results of the voting were extremely interesting – one felt that the eyes of the world were upon them.

1st. Social Democrats (S.P.D.) 948, 000 votes
2nd. Christian Democrats (C.D.U.) 431, 000

3rd. Socialist Unity (S.E.D.) 383, 000
4th. Liberal Democrats (L.P.D.) 182, 000

giving

S.P.D.	69 seats
C.D.U	29
S.E.D.	26
L.P.D.	12

on the Berlin city council.

It was generally expected that the S.E.D. would be defeated. "The Elections", says the "Manchester Guardian" in a remarkably accurate summing up of the situation and general feeling, "assumed almost international importance (which the Germans must have thoroughly enjoyed) as a test of opinion between East and West. One can regret that this should have been the case without necessarily regretting the result. If there had to be a test it is satisfactory that the S.P.D. have won a decisive victory and that the S.E.D., in spite of or because of Russian support only secured 3rd place. This is in marked contrast to the Russian zone where S.P.D. is forbidden and where in consequence the S.E.D. has won a majority over all its opponents. The same thing would certainly have happened in Berlin itself if the British French and American authorities had not intervened to prevent it. As it is the results confirm what most impartial observers have said – that left to themselves, the German people would choose Social Democracy rather than Communism. Conditions in Berlin of course are peculiar. It is probably true that a great many of those who voted for the S.P.D. or C.D.U. were first and foremost voting against the S.E.D., which the Germans naturally regard as the instrument of Russian power and of Communist dictatorship. Nor could all the resources of Russian propaganda remove the excesses, which were undoubtedly committed by the Red Army in the early days of the occupation. Yet the Berliners had many good material reasons for voting as the Russians wanted them to vote, and the fact that they did not do so is an encouraging proof of courage and independence."

It seems obvious that Berlin is not predominantly socialist, but that many who had loyalties to other parties threw in their vote with the S.P.D. to strengthen that party against the S.E.D.

When I went down into the city this morning and spoke with one or two people in the shops there was a great deal of wild excitement and indignation over the Russian deportations of 300 skilled technicians from Berlin, with their families and furniture, in the middle of the night. They were supposed to have signed their willingness but were probably ordered to go to Russia. Of course the Berliners put it down to reprisals for having lost the elections.

I spent most of the day rushing round from one Mil. Gov. dept. to another to get my Leave Pass for England stamped and signed. Everyone was delightfully vague and willingly stamped and signed all over the place. Finally I finished up with 2 Leave Passes and 2 different sets of stamps and signatures!

In the evening there was a lecture in our house by Monsieur *Fataud* (the Frenchman I had got hold of) on: "The Spiritual, cultural and intellectual life in France today". I had to miss it because I had to catch the night train back to England.

Though I didn't manage to get a sleeper I had the whole side of a first class carriage to myself, and slept soundly through the Russian zone.

First Home Leave

Thursday 24th. Reached Hannover at 5.30 a.m. It was still dark, and I was taken in a truck to the transit camp. Breakfast was waiting – 2 sausages stared up at me. 2 other officers joined me but unable to face sausages at that time in the morning, waved them away. One was a major, armed, and with a colossal sheep-skin coat, transporting 2 German generals back to London for interrogation. He gave me a lift back to the station. Saw dawn break, promising a perfect day. Left the devastation that surrounds the station at Hannover at 6.30 and finally got to the Dutch border soon after 11, where we all detrained for another "breakfast" at Bentheim. Once again, of course, the contrast between Germany and Holland was most striking – back to neat, clean, undamaged houses, rich fields and plenty of cattle.

I travelled most of the way with 2 men, one, whom I had already seen before on the C.C.G. Potsdam tour, and the other, *Mr Winterton,* publicity agent of the Church Army. The latter knew all about John Downing and so there were plenty of grounds for conversation.

We went through Holland via Utrecht and Rotterdam to the Hook of Holland. The part between Utrecht and the Hook is very lovely – flat and green with tiny canals and ditches dividing strips of pasture instead of hedges, and each little house on its own little island with a boat. You could see for miles, and little windmills dotted about.

We arrived at the Hook at about 5.0 o'clock and had another meal in the fine transit camp there. As there were several hours to wait I had a good wash and then went to the cinema. It was bitterly cold and we put on every stitch of clothing. The boat – 'The Duke of York' – a very comfortable Irish cross-channel boat, left soon after 9. We had very comfortable bunks. Turned in early. A smooth crossing.

Friday 25th. Woken at 5.0 a.m. and off the boat and through the customs without trouble by 7 a.m. Reached London by 10.0 and went straight to Friends House to report. Found that the conference was to be at Windsor and we were to leave at 4.0 p.m. So with one or two hours to spare dashed over to Cricklewood to see my Aunt Sylvia (Sylvia Brison) for lunch. Found she had turned vegetarian again.

Afterwards called next door to see Mrs Spreewitz to give her news of Mrs Friedrich – her mother – whom I am trying to get back to London from Berlin. The dear old lady hangs like a mill-stone round my neck, and dogs my footsteps. I cannot get rid of her.

Along with most of the other delegates I caught the 4.0 train to Windsor – a somewhat hilarious journey, with *Joe Brayshaw*, Lettice Jowitt (the administrative secretaries of F.R.S.), Eric Cleaver and *Magda Kelber* at their best and full of stories. A little more seriously we discussed the proposals that *Dr. John Rickman,* the distinguished psychiatrist, had put to us in Berlin and later to Lettice in London. They all thought it was a very good scheme.

It was wet and misty when we arrived at Windsor so the view of the castle was poor. Windsor looked very prosperous after Berlin. The conference was at the Y.W.C.A. hostel. We started straight away that evening.

It was reported on the wireless that the Russians are dismantling German arms factories and taking them to the USSR. This must account for the persistent rumours. Certainly, the Russian-controlled goods yard opposite my window is packed with mysterious objects.

F.R.S. Conference at Windsor

Saturday 26th. Conference continued all morning. Representatives from all the different countries where F.R.S. were working and all branches of F.R.S. We were free for a few hours in the afternoon. Rosamund Wallis lent me her car so I went in to Windsor to do some shopping, to get a few badly needed things for Berlin, and a little fresh fruit for myself. The shops were full and so bright and gay. Woolworths was crammed with things we so desperately needed in Berlin but can't get.

In the evening we were shown the New F.R.S. Film "While Germany Waits". It was very good – much better than the other "France, the hard road back". It was particularly interesting for me having seen most of the places in the film while touring on my 72 hr. leave – I saw again the cellar dwellers of Dortmund, and quite a number of those who trained with me at Woodstock were also in the film. Saw Cologne again and the D.P. camps at Brunswick and Goslar.

Sunday 27th. The conference finally finished at 12.30, and after lunch *Christopher Taylor* gave me a lift in his car up to Birmingham. The colour of the Beech woods in Berkshire and Oxfordshire were a sight to be seen at this time of the year.

Had supper with the Southall family in Kings Norton, and then went with Daphne, to whom I am engaged, down to Woodbrooke to see *Konrad Braun*, and to ask how his mother had fared on her journey to England from Berlin. She had stood it well. Called in to see Pastor Mensching whom I had met in my first few days in Germany, and also *Deborah Halfden-Nielsen*, a Danish Quaker and Woodbrooker, whom I had not seen for 7 years when Alan Maynard and I stayed with her family for a week in Copenhagen on our travel- scholarship. We had a wonderfully happy conversation. Poor Pastor M. was already very homesick and was very pleased that I could take his ration of chocolate to his family in Germany. The stuff stuck in his throat, he said, when he thought of his family, and he could not eat it. So he had to send it to them.

We also called on the Sturge sisters in Fox Hill, who have been sending me so many useful parcels, and the Butlers to see them. Rather hoping to find somewhere to spend my Christmas leave. Lovely to be home.

Back to Germany

Monday 28th. Caught the 9.0 train from Snow Hill. Daphne saw me off. M. met me at Paddington and we had lunch together and then I caught the boat-train back to Harwich. Travelled with one of the Aachen team. Very cold and miserable in the Harwich transit camp. On the boat by 7.0 and off by 9.0 p.m. All officers in a large dormitory on 3 tiered stretcher bunks. Not a very comfortable night.

Tuesday 29th. A good breakfast and wash at the Hook transit camp – straight onto the train.

Eric Cleaver and Lettice Jowitt
FRS Conference at Windsor

Arrived Bad Oeyenhausen (British Zone H.Q.) soon after 5 p.m. and taken by car to Vlotho and H.Q.5. In order to make myself tired in order to ensure sleep on the night train, I went a brisk walk. Had a good hour to wait at Bad Oeyenhausen for the night train. Could not get a sleeper. The conversation of the other officers on the platform was both illuminating and irritating. Really we might have been in India from the way they talked – as though we were trying to run the "Jerries" and their country like a colony of the British Empire. Another group kept up a conversation for the whole time about the shooting round Goslar – deer etc. rifle bores and what-not.

A violent political argument then took place in the compartment – Labour v. Conservative. I was too tired to take part – out of my depth anyway – but it was splittingly funny. Two of the worst type of R.A.F. officers forced their way in at Hannover at about 1 a.m. I'd noticed them on the boat. They swore at everyone and everything. They made themselves thoroughly unpleasant and were abominably rude. Each thought he was God-almighty, so conversation abruptly ceased, to prevent loss of temper and we tried to sleep.

Back to Work

Wednesday 30th. Back to Berlin in time for breakfast and very glad to be "home" again – but thoroughly tired out. Noticed a distinct difference outside my window – all the leaves had gone and the trees were quite bare. Mountains of letters waiting for answers.

Another lecture in the evening. This time by John Bourke on the "Meaning of Freedom" in his perfect German. A very good discussion followed.

Thursday 31st. Spent the day trying to get my report together. The evening with Dr Q. discussing it and getting final information and corrections done. We had to do it by candlelight as the electricity was cut off. This happens frequently as there is a serious shortage of the right type of hard coal nuts for the power stations, which come from British sector. Berliners of course blame it onto the Russian election result reprisals!

November 1946

Friday 1st. Was rung up by the Public Relations Dept. of Mil. Gov. (*Mr Trout*). Went along to see him, as he wanted to see my report. He wants it as the basis of an article he is writing for the British Zone Review. I was pleased of course, and he seemed enormously impressed by the first draft of the report, and so was *Major Denham.*

Visited another remand Home for girls at the request of *Father McEleney*, a Roman Catholic padré who was in France with Stafford[1] and knew him well!

Had supper at the I.V.S.P. to meet Brigadier Whales' wife who has expressed her desire to do relief work with the voluntary bodies. A nice woman and very willing but very huntin', shootin' and fishin' type, it will be a bit difficult to know what to do with her!

---

[1] *My brother Dr. Stafford Maw, in the Royal Army Medical Corps before he was wounded.*

3 hours at Ilse's, reading over and correcting my typed report – many mistakes. Still unable to catch up on sleep, as I promised to have the report in by the weekend. I was originally asked to produce it in 3 weeks, and it has taken over 3 months.

Saturday 2nd. Lunch with Mr Trout at a hotel mess in the Kurfürstendamm to discuss the British Zone Review article. Spent the entire afternoon and evening polishing up the report which is now over 40 pages of close typed information.

700 P.O.W.s Arrive

Sunday 3rd. When I woke this morning and looked out of the window onto the railway sidings I noticed a whole train-load of returning P.O.W.s. The P.O.W.s were walking all over the line. There seemed to be several hundred. The Cattle-trucks were decked with Russian flags and pictures of Stalin – all the usual. The chalking on the carriages indicated, that they were from Belgrade. There was also a considerable amount of S.E.D. propaganda. I went out to investigate and took Fritz and Gerhard with me. As I thought there might be some Russian guards about I sent Fritz and G. over to speak to them, as I was in uniform, and rushed back to collect up some cigarettes. Fritz returned and said there were no Russian guards and that I could go and speak to them. I only managed to collect about 600 cigarettes, not quite enough for all the 700 P.O.W.s. We sought out the leader and handed the cigarettes over to him to distribute. They were all extremely grateful. They were travelling in 12 cattle trucks (over 60 in each!) and had been already 6 days on the journey – without food for the last 4 days. Many looked tired and unshaven, and with a rather animal look in their eyes – but they all raised a tired and friendly smile, and assured me they would be getting something to eat at Falkensee – about half an hour's run. I did not have time to talk for long because the train pulled out, on its way down to the Rhineland where most of them lived. They would have to pass through a quarantine camp first. They waved goodbye. I confess to a lump in my throat. They had been captured in Greece a long time ago, I gathered.

'Stump Grubbing'

Brian and I spent the rest of the day "stump-grubbing" in the Grunewald with a few of the I.V.S.P. team and a gang of young boys and girls they had got together from Spandau. The idea was a co-operative effort to provide an old people's home with fuel for the winter. It is not permitted to cut trees down but Berliners are allowed to dig out the stumps of trees that had been previously cut.

It was a perfect day, and we had a picnic in the woods, and one boy played the lute and as usual the Germans broke into their lovely songs so easily. We provided them with hot cocoa, and soup for supper. They worked hard and cheerfully – much more so than the normal English school children on such a job.

Digging out the stumps is not such a difficult job as it sounds, because there are no stones but just pure sand. One digs and digs down and down all round the stump and chops through side roots and then waggles the stump till it finally breaks. Often this is the toughest part. Brian and I attached the tow-rope to the little 15 cwt. *Ford* truck and towed the unwilling stumps out of their unyielding sockets, and then loaded them into the 3 tonner. It was a skilful business driving through the trees over rough and sandy soil on which skidding was easy and the wheels soon inclined to bury themselves when a heavy load was on. By the time it was dark we had got well over a dozen stumps which were sent off to a saw mill. The I.V.S.P. had two trucks there also, but one would not start so we had to tow her free and then got both stuck in the sand. Finally after long and arduous work Brian managed to put all right and we got free. A grand hard day's work.

In the evening went to hear a most stimulating performance by the Berlin Philharmonic at the Städtische Oper. Afterwards worked till midnight dictating the last 2 pages of my report to Ilse.

My Report Delivered to Mil. Gov.

Monday 4th. Dashed up to Mil. Gov. first thing to present my completed report, and to have the whole thing retyped.

In the afternoon with Dr Quast I spoke to a large meeting of a section of the Women's Trade Unions and Welfare workers interested in the question of Delinquency. There were two other speakers, one from the Jugendgerichtshilfe, and the other from the Women's Criminal Police (which we found so bad in our survey). So it was very interesting, and the meeting has shown just how bad the Women's Criminal Police organisation (and its aims) was. They were clearly extremely interested in our survey and suggestions, and invited us to another special meeting to discuss the whole question again. As Dr Q. said afterwards: "I think we were clearly impressive. This sort of survey work is not well known in Germany."

Tuesday 5th. Went to visit two more remand homes with Dr Q. They both turned out to be homes for babies and younger children – with very few places for difficult children. The first was a Catholic home and there were many babies and tiny tots. All of them very sweet little mites, one's heart went out to them, as they so loved to be talked to, and to catch hold of your hand. 12 of the babies were half Russian, one English, one American, one French, one Dutch. Many little children were refugees and had lost or were separated from their parents. Many looked so pale in spite of the fact that they get extra Swiss food and extra Quaker food.

An Answer to Prayer

Wednesday 6th. Spent the morning getting supplies together of cottons, wool, needles, buttons and all sewing things, scrap material for making dolls, and a case of helmets to be unravelled and knitted up into gloves and socks, for two rather poor girls' remand homes. One was the Marienherberge, where I went at the request of Father McEleney, and the second a poor Protestant home in the American sector. The rapturous reception of all the things I had brought was something I shall never forget. When the Sisters saw just what I had brought immediately the head Sister called for silence and they offered up a prayer of thanks. It was really most moving to be "a direct answer to prayer", for they had got together, they told me, only on the previous night to pray for wool and warm clothes for the winter for the children. They were so pleased with every little thing – every scrap of material brought almost tears to their eyes. So many things ought to be made for Christmas.

700 returning POWs

Stump grubbing

Went to the Indian Mission to fix up a speaker for our Wed. evening series of lectures. As the Russian again failed to turn up I gave a lecture on what Quakers believe.

Thursday 7th. Consultation with Dr Q. She tells me that the results of our work are bearing good fruit already. The groups of pastors, teachers, welfare workers etc. that we have addressed have got busy with other groups and are taking our recommendations to the various district offices and putting them into practice. We have had floods of requests from pastors and teachers to attend our discussion groups and many invitations have come in for us to give talks and lectures on the subject – which is very encouraging.

In the afternoon went with Kathleen to Mil. Gov. to see Mary Bailey about my report, and broadcast. Went on to see *Colonel Harris* (Head of Legal) to ask for permission to go into Charlottenburg prison with occupational material to do some welfare work among the juveniles. He was a completely charming man and was much impressed by our offer and very pleased. We now have to write it down on paper and send the request through him to the Quadripartite committee on Prisons. All of this takes an agonisingly long time.

In the evening gave two talks at the new American Youth Club – one to *Dr Thiemke's* group, on Schools in England, and the second to *Sgt. Alvers* and Dr Thiemke's group on the present problem of delinquency and moral standards in Berlin. They seemed to enjoy it and thanked me profusely, begging me to come again as soon as possible and to fix a date. They asked good questions and discussed well in English. Some said "Well, why can't we be taught religion like that in schools?" 2½ hour session!

Friday 8th. With Dr Q. and a Fürsorgerin from Wilmersdorf (Frl. Podlesewski) we inspected a number of German army barrack huts with a view to making the place into a much needed remand home for girls after Christmas. It had been used for refugees and as a children's kindergarten. It was a suitable place and with a bit of help (as perhaps an I.V.S.P. scheme) could be cleaned up and got ready.

Went down to Nikolassee to see *Pastor Wenzel* head of the (Protestant) "Innere Mission" to put to him the problem Dr Q. and I have been studying and our suggestions in order to get his interest and his support for our ideas. He was sympathetic and interested and promised to help us. It was, I felt, a useful interview.

Dashed back home in time for a little supper, and then picked up Dr Q. again and drove down to Lichtenrade – about 20 miles, to give my lecture on Quakerism at the Ulrich von Huttenschule. There was an extremely enthusiastic and interested audience of over 100 people and after I had finished they plied me with questions for nearly 1½ hrs – much more intelligent and sensible questions than the last audience. I went away feeling I had made many new friends and interesting contacts, and was invited again. Dr Q.'s verdict was that the meeting was a great success and exactly what Germany needs. She is always very encouraging and helpful but her interpreting, I can tell, does not always get across the meaning behind the words.

Visit to Hamburg – An Accident on the Way

Saturday 9th. Cancelled all arrangements for the week-end and started off with Brian for Hamburg at 8.0 after an early breakfast. We took the 3-ton *Commer* and a *Ford* 15-cwt. It was pretty cold.

All went well till we were 15 miles from the British Zone – on a straight stretch of autobahn, when we suddenly saw the big French car that had overtaken us, down the bank, and a little further on an army lorry upside down. I was leading in the 3 tonner and thought we had better stop to render assistance, so I put on the brake, slowing down from 40 m.p.h. I began to skid broadside further and further round, and realising that I was in a nasty situation, I tried to get out of the skid before the truck turned completely round. I managed to get her out of that skid but went straight into another. The autobahn, I realised too late, was a sheet of black ice. I got out of the second skid only to go into a third, when fortunately the back of the truck hit the iron railings of a bridge and I stopped right on the edge of the autobahn. I got out to find Brian within an inch of the back of me having done the same thing exactly. If we had not been saved by the bridge rail at that particular point we would both have gone down the bank, a 15 ft. drop on that side. So we drove slowly onto the safety of the grass verge in the middle and went to see what assistance we could give, and got out our tow chains. A German lorry was pulling away in order to right the British lorry, and another had managed to stop to help the French car, which happened to be *General Koenig's*, (Commander French Zone). By a miracle no one had been hurt. Just then a 5 Ton American truck and trailer came hurtling along – tried to stop, began to skid in the same way – turned a complete circle – the trailer whizzing round and hitting a sand-bank and overturning. He finished up on the grass verge in the middle facing the way he had come. General Koenig's car had turned 1½ circles, going down the bank backwards on the second in trying to avoid a small German car. The French Colonel was pretty scared of having an accident and being stranded in the Russian zone and wanted to get out as quickly as possible. The American went to Helmstedt to fetch the recovery vehicle and left his trailer. Between us we pulled the General's car up and the Army truck was righted. We were just going to give the General's car a tow when the engine started and it was able to crawl on to Helmstedt at the zone frontier, and the recovery vehicle arrived, so we proceeded slowly on to the frontier ourselves.

The Colonel was profuse in his thanks – the General fortunately had gone by train.

Having filled up with petrol and oil, went in to Brunswick and had a quick lunch with the team. Then crossed the Autobahn and drove North 125 miles up to Hamburg. It was a lovely road through fields and woods with the last brilliant autumn leaves left. Meanwhile in Berlin they were having the first snow.

Soon after 5 it was dark and we had to do the last 30 miles in the dark since we could not make up time on the way owing to a rather damaged road in poor repair.

It was difficult finding our way through Hamburg in the dark to the H.Q. of the Salvation Army team, but at last we found our way to their palatial residence. They had booked for us to stay at the Reichshof Officers transit hotel. So we went back into the town, parked our vehicles, and tired and hungry were shown to our sumptuous room in this magnificent hotel.

We were served a fantastic meal in an elegant dining room and felt very guilty being there at all. Every sort of thing was done for you.

Afterwards I went out for a 30 min. walk to explore a bit. That part of Hamburg did not seem badly destroyed at that time of night.

We both turned in and had an early night being extremely weary after the long drive.

Observing the Ruins of Hamburg

Sunday 10th. Woke to a lovely day and longed to get out and explore. Breakfast was interesting – people's reactions on Sunday morning. Every type of uniform was there and many nationalities. Some never noticed the waiter waiting on them or looked at him – so they would not have recognised him again. The waiter's reaction was equally interesting. One wondered what was passing through their minds with not always impassive faces – knowing that their own rations were not always honoured outside and that there was a bread shortage owing to the American shipping strike. There was also a glut in the English fish market and Herring rotting in English ports, and here Brian and I were receiving this sumptuous hospitality as part of reparations and had to pay only 6d. a night! Heaven knows what that sixpence was for.

Went up to Red Cross H.Q. to report and get our instructions for loading and then had the rest of the day free to explore. We first made a tour of the worst damaged parts down by the docks and the industrial part. I had not seen anything like it even in the Ruhr or Berlin. It was fantastic and quite indescribable. Mile upon mile of rubble – broken and shattered homes and factories – hollow flats and buildings – side streets still full of rubble – weeds growing everywhere. It was terribly depressing and as usual makes one laugh at the idea of Germany ever being able to rise out of it again.

We passed on to the central part of the town by the railway stations and the two lakes. It is remarkable how this part is practically undamaged. One sees in Hamburg the two extremes indeed. The undamaged part is really very lovely and has an atmosphere which it has retained. In many ways it reminded me of Bristol, Stockholm and Copenhagen. We went up onto the hill from where on the one side there was a fine view of the docks shrouded in mist, and behind us towered the great statue of Bismarck.

During the afternoon we went to the Broadcasting Concert Hall of B.F.N. (British Forces Network) to hear a performance by the Hamburg Philharmonic. They played Bruckner's 9th Symphony, but though they were very good they were not quite up to the standard of the Berlin Philharmonic. During the evening I was fortunate enough to get a couple of tickets for the Hamburg Städtische Oper, and we saw and heard a wonderful performance of the "Marriage of Figaro". It was quite delightful and all the soloists had lovely voices. I have rarely enjoyed an opera so much.

Loading Up with Relief Supplies

Monday 11th. Up at 6.0 a.m. for an early breakfast and then up to the Red Cross Mess to pick up Mr Smith who took us down to the docks to the R.C. warehouse. When we arrived, found the service lift broken so thought at first we could not load up and would have to wait another day in Hamburg. However it was possible to roll the cases of Swedish Milk powder down 4 flights of stairs and load up. Took on just under 3 tons between us.

We saw in the warehouse also the bales of clothes that Brian and the others would have to come back for in the next few days. This then completes the link in the journey of the clothes which I have seen now right from the beginning. I have collected clothes, sent them to London, baled them at the Bedford Institute and taken them down to the warehouse at Tilbury to be despatched to Hamburg. Seen the stuff at Hamburg – taken it back to Berlin to our Red Cross store and then seen the clothes distributed to refugees and worn by P.O.W.s. It is a fascinating story.

As we had not needed the rations we had brought with us, we gave them to the dockers who had helped us load. It was a great day for them and they were so pleased. I was glad I had thought of it – for they were all such fine men – so cheerful and friendly, and uncomplaining.

Much to our relief we were loaded and away by 9.0 a.m. and it was not so cold. Out through the depressing ruins and back onto the Autobahn towards Hannover. Turned off down south to Brunswick and back through Lüneburg and the little villages and the lovely woods and fields.

The road all the way runs through a continual avenue of trees -typical of all country roads. I saw in one place a few deer dash across in front of me.

Without incident we arrived at the Russian frontier checkpoint at 2.0 p.m. and were through the Russian zone just as it got dark at about 5.0 p.m.

Then, as we entered Berlin, I was leading in the 3 tonner when suddenly we went slap into a dense pea-soup fog, which reduced visibility to 6 or 7 yds and our speed to a crawl. It took us well over an hour to get back the last few miles. Fortunately I knew every inch of the way perfectly – but every now and then one had to brake and swerve violently in order to miss a stationary vehicle which suddenly appeared in front. What with keeping a look out in front and keeping sight of the curb, by looking out of the side window it was pretty tricky – so we were profoundly thankful when finally we reached home exactly in time for supper and without incident or damage.

Tuesday 12th. *Pastor Georges Casalis* came to lunch. He is the French Army Chaplain and was formerly General Secretary of the French Student Christian movement, and worked in the French Underground Resistance movement. He is an extremely nice man and we all liked him at once[1].

In the afternoon went up to Frohnau again to Prof. Jakobi's house for another lovely evening of Bach and readings from Rilke.

Had to be back by 8.0 at Dr Q.'s for our discussion group, this time with teachers, pastors and welfare workers. Again a very profitable evening. We really feel we are getting our ideas across and getting support and action from different sections of responsible administrative departments of Berlin.

Ad Hoc Youth Committee Proposed

Wednesday 13th. A youth committee meeting at which we discussed the proposal to start an educational centre for youth problems and for people dealing with youth, as some concrete contribution we can make to Berlin, and also something we can leave behind when we pull out.

Went to Wilmersdorf to fetch a stove oven for Mrs Forrer from the factory and took it to her house in Schlachtensee. I carried the thing upstairs to a bedroom. It was so heavy it nearly killed me.

---

[1] *He visited Hess in Spandau prison and found him "a pitiable old man."*

Hamburg

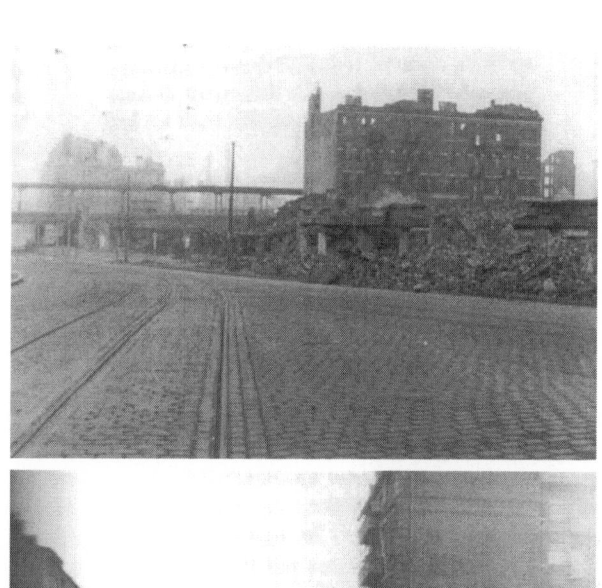

Hamburg

Called in at Mil. Gov. to see Trout and ask how his article was going. He had rung me up, and as he wanted to ask for a lot of facts and figures, asked me out to lunch again.

Final Report Presented

On the way back called in at Religious Affairs Dept. to give Mary Bailey a final corrected copy of my report. She seemed very pleased with it and said it was just what she wanted. She welcomed my co-operation and advice and encouraged me to go on with the work I was doing as she herself wanted to do it but could not get out of her office.

Friday 15th. Dr Q's and my first article on delinquency appeared in "Die Kirche", the Protestant Weekly newspaper.

Lectured to the Berufschule-Friedenau English Evening Class on Quakerism – a small but very keen little audience of 20.

Took a copy of my report to *Col. Percival*, Head of Education and Religious Affairs Dept. of C.C.G. and another to Maj. Boyce, Mil. Gov. Welfare Dept. 50 copies are being cyclostyled by Mil. Gov.

Saturday 16th. Took Brian to the Wilmersdorf Health office to have his lungs examined. I wanted to see how suspect T.B. cases were treated by the German Health service, and their equipment etc. Brian's health report showed there was some danger so I made him check up. They are fine people in the Wilmersdorf Health Office – so obliging, and will look up any facts in order to be helpful.

Visit to a V.D. Clinic

Mil. Gov. Public Safety had refused to give me permission to go on a Police raid when they bring in girls from cafes and bars etc., and give them tests for V.D. As I had wanted all the information for my report, the Health Office had asked me to attend and observe the whole process, but the Public Safety Dept. was afraid of sensational press publicity. So I did not go on the raid – which I could already picture, having been with the Public Health Fürsorgerinnen to the cafés normally raided, and seen the types and the environment. So instead I was at the receiving end in the clinic in a white coat and 'civvies' as a 'doctor'. The girls were brought in by the Military police from raids on cafes and bars in Grunewald and Fehrbeliner Platz – a rather high class – upper middle class district, and so a low percentage was expected.

The Problems of V.D.

One doctor told me, while we were waiting, the real facts of the V.D. problem in Berlin. He said the trouble started after the Polish Campaign. German soldiers returned infected and the first wave started. Then after the French campaign came the second wave. Towards the collapse there was rather an orgy by the German troops spending their last days in uniform. Then came the Russians, and many girls with V.D. and under treatment fled from the hospitals, so that the Russians themselves then became infected. He assured me that on arrival the Russians were practically free from it. He had treated many Russians and they were all first stage cases, having picked the V.D. up from infected German girls, or from Poland on the way through. The Russians were always most strict about V.D. and if a soldier is found with it he is immediately sent back to Russia, which he doesn't like! So sufferers pay German doctors high prices for private treatment, and enormous prices for Penicillin. He said V.D. infection was by far the worst in the Russian sector and then in the American. The British sector was not so bad. The Americans, he declared, did not treat their cases adequately – they more or less gave them some penicillin shots and left it at that, if they were suspect. There was a monthly examination but it was casual and insufficient and quite inconclusive. So that Americans had frequently been to him for cures having been only partially treated by the American authorities. He was pleased by the British efficiency of Sulphonamide and penicillin distribution. The chief V.D. Hospital where he was a specialist in the French sector got no penicillin, however. The Russians too got no penicillin in spite of having now a factory in their sector. It was all sent back to Russia or reserved for Majors and higher ranks.

I saw 45 girls mostly between the ages of 16-25, examined at the rate of one every 2 minutes. It was very well organised and very efficient, gently and considerately carried out by 3 doctors and 5 Fürsorgerinnen.

One doctor examined the girl, and made a slide – two smear samples from external and internal locations. The slide was then stained and examined microscopically by a second doctor for streptococci and gonococci. A third doctor took an intravenous blood sample into a test-tube. Fürsorgerinnen were cleaning and sterilising instruments, tabulating results, and seeing to the girls changing, keeping order etc.

I was shown everything and was allowed to do blood and microscope tests. The results were pleasing apparently. Out of the 45 girls I saw only 3 were suspect and one positive, all the rest were negative. Three had been previously treated and cured. 3 or 4 had been raped by Russians but without contracting V.D. The doctors seemed surprised at the large proportion of virgins. 7 out of 45! Only one girl, a virgin, made any fuss about being examined. She resisted and sobbed violently. Otherwise I saw little resentment. They were nervous and it was obviously not a pleasant experience for them. Altogether 160 were examined by 2.30 in the morning. Of these, 3 were suspect and 5 were proved to have Gonorrhoea by the blood test (3%), 19 were virgins i.e. 12%. I escaped under the nose of the military police at 12 p.m.

Sunday 17th. Took Brian and John down to the Russian Zone frontier on the Autobahn. They were going to hitch-hike down to Herford to pick up the new '*Volkswagen*' car that has been allotted to us. Spent the afternoon 'stump-grubbing' again in the Grunewald with the I.V.S.P., Salvation Army, and a Spandau youth group. We got a dozen large stumps for an old people's hostel.

Monday 18th. Called in at the Gesundheitsamt to find out final figures and results of the raid and tests for V.D.

Spent the rest of the morning watching a ballet rehearsal by the Städtische Oper ballet company of "Joseph's Legend", and took along 20 pairs of ballet shoes I had obtained from Mona Inglesby of the International Ballet Company I had danced with in London.

After lunch gave two English talks to English classes at the Berufsschule, one just talking about English houses, trams and tubes, and Christmas, and the second about schools in England and also the problems of delinquency and boy-girl relationships. Both were very interesting mixed classes, full of questions.

In the evening went to a lecture by Dr Wenzel. He referred to Dr Q.'s and my article in "Die Kirche" and spoke about the problem – which was a surprise to us.

With Dr Q. I then went on to speak to Dr Rengier's Catholic youth group. Prepared to speak again about Delinquency. I was, much to my surprise, announced as speaking about "Youth in England", which involved a bit of quick thinking! I spoke about the pre-occupation with material things and with the craving for a gay[1] life, and underneath it all a search for something deeper and for religion. I had time to think it all out in the intervals while Dr Rengier was translating but found I was not always being interpreted literally, and that the peculiarly un-Catholic things I said were being left out which might have caused offence. However they seemed deeply impressed and interested and were listening very intently and asked questions. I learned a lot myself.

Press Conference

Tuesday 19th. In the morning had a press conference with Dr. Q. when Berlin Newspapers interviewed us on our report, problems and possible solutions. It went well and all the reporters seemed genuinely interested and helpful.

In the afternoon had another discussion with an English class at the Berufschule.

Bishop Dr. Dibelius came to supper and stayed sometime afterwards. We had an interesting talk with him which went outside Germany to England – to Woodbrooke (where he had been a student 1927/28 with Ormerod Greenwood), to Scandinavia and Australia. It was refreshing to get away from Germany.

Collected Mary Bailey in the car and took her to Dr Q's house for the student discussion group, which I addressed this time and presented our report – a lively discussion followed.

A letter from my brother Stafford to say he was now stationed in Hannover at a military hospital there. He had been posted in September to the 106 (Antwerp) British Military Hospital as the venereologist.

Wednesday 20th. A national holiday for the Germans called "Busstag" or Repentance day.

During the afternoon I had been invited by *Pastor Helwig* to come and see his youth play in his church at Pankow in the Russian Sector and he asked me to speak to the congregation for about 20 minutes afterwards. I went with Dr Q., and Dr T. to interpret.

Arrived to find the church packed with about 500 people, and being prepared to give a Busstag sermon, I was again somewhat surprised when Pastor Helwig announced that I was going to speak about the "Problem of Youth in danger"!

After the play, which was very similar in idea and presentation to the one in Pastor Weckerling's church, I made my appeal which was very well received and I had many questions and thanks afterwards and invitations from the Youth group to come and talk to them again. I heard one girl say to a friend of hers in German:

"'He was our enemy but he talked to us as though we had always been his friends."

---

[1] *Primary meaning.*

Dr Q. told me also that several people had asked her if I was a pastor in England, which amused me. Many brought their problems to us afterwards.

When it was all over we had a cup of tea, a biscuit and a very friendly chat in Pastor Helwig's house with a few friends including *Pastor Jungklaus*, who has invited me to speak to another big church gathering in January on the V.D. problem.

Came back to the lecture that was going on in our house by *Herr Kuhne*, a German actor, reading poetry rather too loudly and too dramatically for the size of the room. Margaret Watts had also been giving her lecture at the Volkshochschule on 'Australia' which was well received. We are all kept busy this way in spare time. There is a tremendous demand.

Thursday 21st. Went to the Berufsschule in my new *Volkswagen* and joined in a game of basket ball with one of the classes.

When I had finished the other class came and asked me if I'd come and talk to them again, as they had a free period. They wanted to hear more and talk over the youth problems in Berlin. I looked at my watch and found it was 2 o'clock and that I was a little late for lunch! Brian and John and I were feeling a little "browned off", so we decided to drive out to the Officers' club at Gatow for tea to have an opportunity to sit in quietness in front of a log fire, relax and read an English newspaper. It was very pleasant and refreshing.

We read of the widespread flooding in the U.K. after eight successive days of continuous rain. In Jerusalem Jewish terrorists had killed a dozen British servicemen.

After supper went down to the American Youth Club again to talk to Dr Thiemke's English class and club members, this time on India, where the situation is very complex between Hindus and Moslems. The place was packed, and one or two Americans came as well including Sgt. Alvers who runs the place. Had a conversation with him afterwards and found that he was one of those Americans that instinctively I take to, and who talked from a Christian rather than a materialistic basis. He was really interested and keen on this youth club and the problem of endangered youth.

The wireless reported widespread flooding in England after 8 days of rain.

First Broadcast

Friday 22nd. Went with Dr Q. to the American Drahtfunk (Broadcasting station) as we had been invited to broadcast on the Youth Problem. Everyone in the broadcasting station was extremely young – very friendly and polite but refreshingly informal, and full of energy and interest in their work. We were taken to Studio one, where with the girl announcer (about 23 yrs. old) we made a recording on tape, of our discussion. We had to have several tries before it was satisfactory and it was difficult for me being entirely in German. The record was played over – and was extremely peculiar I thought, and sounded quite unlike us. I was quite shocked how awful and unattractive my voice sounded and at my German accent. However the others assured me that it was good.

I went straight on afterwards to give a talk at the Berufschule on Quakerism. After this yet another talk to a small discussion group of women teachers and welfare workers. Finally home for supper at 10.30 p.m.

London: the Government said food controls to be relaxed, but bread will still be rationed.

Saturday 23rd. A meeting in the afternoon with one of the heads of the Catholic Church to interest them in our problems and to seek their help. It seems that we shall have their co-operation for our work with delinquency. Our article in "Die Kirche" seems to have been widely read and discussed.

During the evening the whole team went to a performance of Brahms' Deutsches Requiem by the Choir of the Musikhochschule conducted by our friend Prof. Jakobi, at the Marienkirche in the Russian sector. We were among the few Allied invited guests.

It was a truly lovely performance and parts were very moving in that Church, but even so there was much that was not perfect. Afterwards we met Prof. Jakobi and the soloists in the ante-room.

Just arrived home in time to hear my recorded broadcast at 7.30 p.m. It had been given a very good listening time. The team section, the staff, and John's class gathered in the sitting room to hear it. It was a great occasion for me and I was very nervous, but the general verdict was that it was very good, and an important subject. 2 minutes after it was over the Keups kindly rang up to congratulate me. It was indeed an extraordinary sensation to hear oneself speaking in German out of the radio and hard to believe that it was myself at all.

Biro pens came on the market today!

Sunday 24th. In the evening went to the Städtische Oper with Margaret to hear "Cavalleria Rusticana" and "I Pagliacci", which were both very well done. It was a packed house.

The new *Volkswagen* car (Beetle) has now definitely been allotted to me for my work. I'm still running it in, but it is a joy to drive in this cold weather.

Monday 25th. Sat all day in committees from 9.30 a.m. to 6.30 p.m. and was worn out at the end. (1) Joint Team meeting, (2) Section Meeting (3) Youth Committee meeting.

As we were all feeling pretty 'browned off' by the end John, Brian and I went to see the play "On Approval" at the Jerboa.

The newspapers were saying that in London the government was relaxing food controls, but bread would still be rationed.

Tuesday 26th. Addressed a large class of social welfare students at the Pestalozzi Fröbel Haus for an hour on the problem and treatment of Youth in danger. A very interested group who promised help, and a good discussion followed. Invited again.

The usual discussion group at Dr Q's in the evening this time I spoke on our problems to a group of invited parents, with interesting results. They were a keen lot.

Wednesday 27th. The morning spent in catching up on letters, and preparing talks. In the evening talked to the Salvation Army's youth group in their house on Youth problems. They had collected a very nice group. Ended with a Service of the Salvation type led by Capt. Dale.

Thursday 28th. *Pater Matzka* and Dr Q. came to see me before lunch to talk over what the Pastor had been doing for our work in his Bezirk (Circuit) in Charlottenburg. He is a fine man and a great help to us, but is to be recalled to the Vatican soon, unfortunately, he said.

Went with Dr Q. again to the Pestalozzi Fröbel Haus and gave two 1½ hour classes on the subject of Delinquency, and our plans for helping 'youth in danger'. First was a class of 50, but unfortunately there was no time for discussion. The 2nd class of 40 was more brief and had an interesting discussion.

In the evening went to see *Ursula Fournier* in her home and had a long and interesting talk about Germany with her and her father. I pointed out the fact that it still seemed that each little group of Germans liked to have an energetic fiery speaking leader to tell them what they should do, and that the leaders themselves liked to have a leader over them to direct them. Each leader was proud of his importance and liked to be able to pull strings and exert his authority or show his importance.

It seemed to spring from an inferiority complex on the one hand and a desire to dominate on the other, and that they still think through the narrow channels of their own political party or their own brand of church. Mr Fournier agreed. He is interesting because he is one of the few pacifists I have met. But rather typically of some German pacifists, his pacifism consisted of avoiding war by getting out of the country in the 1st world war, and of keeping his mouth tightly closed in this. One cannot blame him.

Friday 29th. Mary Bailey was invited to our first Youth Committee meeting at which we put up (unofficially to her) our plan for an Education and Cultural Centre for Youth and those adults concerned with Youth problems. We had been encouraged to go ahead with this scheme because a hint had come from her that Mil. Gov. would probably look upon any such scheme with approval. She offered some useful suggestions and the final draft of the plan is now nearly ready to present to Mil. Gov.

During the afternoon I went round to the Education and Welfare Depts. of the American Mil. Gov. and to Col. Bevier, head of the Welfare Dept. of O.M.G.U.S. to give them copies of my report.

Talked to a class in the Berufschule on Youth problems, and then drove down to Lichtenrade to hear Margaret's lecture on Australia at the Volkshochschule, and brought her back.

Saturday 30th. Went with *Betty Dinwiddy,* now leader of the I.V.S.P. team since Douglas has gone, to see the possible house for the new educational centre. Saw two big houses next to each other at the back of Mil. Gov. house, previously occupied by the Guards and left in a frightful condition. It seems to be the only place available and has possibilities, though there will be many difficulties.

In the afternoon we had quite one of the nicest experiences since coming to Germany. *Pastor Kurz* had invited the team to come and hear some chamber music in a private house. It was a programme of Bach for 2 harpsichords, strings and flute. It was beautiful and just as Bach was meant to be played and heard. The harpsichord always thrills me.

John S. and I then went on to Hans Ulbrich's and Ilse's party which was quite International, with Joan, the daughter of the American Provost Marshal, Helen, a Portuguese girl, a French boy and girl, and ourselves.

December 1946

Sunday 1st. This being the first Sunday in Dec., and the first Sunday of Advent, it is a very special day for the Germans, and every house has its "Adventskranz" of fir twigs hanging from the ceiling by red or gold ribbons and with 4 candles – one being lit for each Sunday approaching Christmas. Other fir branches are placed in pots and vases in corners of the room and decked with gold or silver "angels' hair". The lights are put out and the candles burn. It is a very beautiful and purifying sight.

I did not go to Meeting because I had promised to go to a big Kinderfeier (Children's Festival) in Neukölln for about 600 young children. The children had a wonderful choir trained by a young music student and there was a dance group. They also had Lantern slides and pictures of their summer camp in Rüdesheim.

Met *Rose Kaschel* of the American Mil. Gov. Welfare Dept.

In the afternoon Dr Q. and I were invited to an "Adventsspiel" at the Marburgerstrasse Remand Home for girls. They did a beautiful Nativity play with very good singing. They also showed us an exhibition of the things they had made from the materials I had taken them. They had made 40 wonderful toys – animals and dolls – most beautifully done. Before the girls had received any wool to knit they had had to make a toy. They had also knitted some good warm socks and jumpers and gloves for themselves. I was so pleased, as it was so exactly what I had had in mind, and it was good to see some concrete results of one's ideas and work. We suggested to the girls that they took the toys themselves into a hospital at Christmas and sang some of their songs. They jumped at the idea.

In the evening the team was invited to Prof. Jakobi's house for an Advent gathering and music. Again it was another perfect evening, by candlelight and with the most beautiful music. Beginning with some Gregorian chants we passed on to Bach and Handel and then to Brahms lieder, and ended up with some English Christmas carols. Monsieur Fataud was there too, and it was a wonderful spiritual feast for us all in such a united atmosphere of friendship and sincerity in the midst of what often seems like a volcano.

Monday 2nd. Continued our discussion with the Trade Unions on Delinquency questions, hoping to include their representation on the Youth Committee.

In the evening started my new mixed group from the Berufsschule of the English class. Started with a general discussion about English Newspapers. Gave them a dictation, which also had a Quaker International message in it. They seemed to thoroughly enjoy this, and the warmth and cocoa. We finished up with a reading from the Bible in English and German – about which I commented a little, and then a prayer.

Tuesday 3rd. Had lunch at the Y.W.C.A. with *Mr Richard Law,* Conservative M.P. for Kensington, and *Mr Hogarth* and *Miss Roberts* of C.O.B.S.R.A. They were told about my work for delinquency and the proposed new education centre, and seemed very genuinely interested. In fact Hogarth and Mr Law decided to postpone a talk by the 3 teams on their work in order to see something practical being done, and as they had heard I was giving a lecture on this Youth problem they wanted to go and hear it and so went along with us to the Catholic Frauenbundhaus where, with Dr Q. I spoke on the

Youth Problem in Berlin to the Fürsorgerinnen from all over Berlin – these are the pastors' parish helpers, or women ministers.

In the evening gave another lecture to members of the Free Churches on the same theme, and to Dr Q.'s and my usual Tuesday evening discussion group.

Wednesday 4th. A long Youth Committee meeting with Miss Roberts to produce the final draft of our education centre plan before sending it in to Mil. Gov.

In the afternoon went to see *Pater Klinski's* new remand home which is being reconstructed in the British sector, with workshops etc. There is so much that he needs, such as beds, blankets, sheets etc. Many things, though, he himself admitted, he had had to get on the Black Market.

Thursday 5th. Supplied Herr Wittkowski (Head of Jugendausschuss Spandau) with wool and needles, cotton scrap material etc. for doll-making for his unemployed girls groups.

Went to Mil. Gov. to get permission to rescue 300 rotting wooden beds which are slowly disappearing for fire-wood in the deserted barracks behind us, for Pater Klinski's home.

In the evening went to Mr Eckhardt's birthday party at the International Red Cross. It was meant to be a surprise for him, as it was, it was a surprise for us all, because Mr Eckhardt had an engagement and was out!

Friday 6th. C.C.G. Education Dept. rang up to say that a *Mrs Champanow* had come to Berlin to advise them about the psychological aspects of the problem of educating British children now coming out to Germany. She was anxious to find out what influences there would be on the English children from the German side. So, she was 'wished' on to me so that I could give her an idea of the Youth problems in Berlin. She told me how British children were already mixing with German children and swopping cigarettes etc. and picking up all sorts of ideas about the Black Market.

I took her to see two of the Remand homes to see how they were getting on with the occupational material I had taken them, and we saw some of the wonderful things they had made out of scrap etc.

Lectured in the evening to the Wilmersdorf Frauenbund, a gathering of about 200 women. This is a very intellectual, exclusive and influential group. There was a large number of press reporters there, and *Miss Dunning* of the C.C.G. who asked if I would come to C.C.G. H.Q. to discuss my report which had reached them. We were also asked to broadcast again for the American Rundfunk.

Saturday 7th. Addressed a large meeting of Protestant Welfare workers concerned with criminal youth – Fürsorgerinnen, pastors etc. The meeting lasted till 1 o'clock and I was asked a lot of questions. Another big meeting in the afternoon on the same subject with the Protestant Gemeinde Hilferinnen. Felt pretty whacked by the end.

Went down to Dr Thiemke's house where he had collected some of his boys, and some of the I.V.S.P. for a musical evening. 4 boys had a very enjoyable recorder quartet, and there were also violin, viola and clarinet trios etc. and some equably enjoyable carols by candle-light in the usual German custom.

Sunday 8th. Felt as though I had a touch of 'flu. In the evening went to the Städtische Oper to hear Richard Strauss's opera "*Salome*". The story of the beheading of John was very moving.

Monday 9th. In the evening joined Prof. Jakobi's Musik Hochschule choir. He himself was absent but the practice was taken by a very competent student. Very few tenors. A difficult choir which included very old women and young girls, and an equally mixed bag of men – many novices and not a great deal of interest. Many of them were obviously tired, and inclined to sing flat. Supper with the Abshagens. Bitterly cold rehearsal room.

Visit to a Juvenile Prison

Tuesday 10th. In the morning went with Sofie Quast and *Michael Tarrant* to see the new American juvenile prison about which we have heard so much at Lichterfelde. We expected something very modern, but when we got to the 'Jugendhof,' as it is called, it looked for all the world like a P.O.W. camp – wooden barracks surrounded by double barbed-wire fences. We were at once struck however by the quality and personality of the leader *Herr Riese*, who had had long experience and training in this sort of work. Another of the teachers is a student of Sofie's. Two of the other teachers, one a woman, were not so good, being more of the Prussian Military kind. The place was obviously a beginning – primitive but modern and may turn into something fairly good. At present the leader is very worried by the numerous escapes, though guards walk up and down between the two fences in the cold weather, but without dogs.

The boys I found were most interesting and I longed to work among them. Most of them were open friendly types, easy to make contact with. One or two talked American. Two boys had been given 6 months for stealing 1 lb. of coffee from the store they worked in to take home to their mothers. There were also one or two "mascots" – boys picked up and adopted by the advancing Allied armies. One in particular I shall never forget. He was like some little dark furry wild animal crouching by the stove – mother French, father unknown, – had lost his mother and been picked up by the Americans. He only spoke English, but the other boys said he understood German. He would not speak to them nor they to him and he had a wild look of hate against all the world. He seemed utterly miserable, only wanted to go back to the G.I.s, he told me.

Then I was shown the dangerous cases – a much wilder looking lot. Spoke to one boy I recognised, whom I'd seen in Plötzensee prison. He told us that after my visit to that prison the food had got better and the guards had stopped bullying. The very young journalist who was also being shown round recognised an old school mate of his amongst this lot and spoke to him. Same trouble: broken homes and family life. A wonderful leader. He asked me to go again.

In the evening chaired the second meeting of our main Delinquency Committee. I felt extremely tired and didn't take much part – so Sofie took over for me.

It went very well, and we mapped out a basis of recommendations on which the committee was to work. I do like those hard working energetic, deeply concerned and interested specialists that we've got on this committee, and considering how different they all are it's surprising how much agreement was reached.

Wednesday 11th. A lecture in German by one of the Chinese Military Mission on life in China – for our International Group, which proved fascinating for all of us.

Thursday 12th. In the evening went to a wonderful performance of "*Madame Butterfly*" at the Staatsoper in the Russian sector. This is the first time I've been to this brilliant and magnificent theatre which has a wonderful atmosphere about it, and is much more patronised by French and Russian soldiers. The standard of opera too is much higher than in the Städtische Oper. One was immediately struck by the beautiful clothes most of the German audience were wearing. Ilse said they must be of Black Market origin! I've rarely heard such a moving performance.

Preparations for Christmas

Friday 13th. After a hard week of routine and winding up work before Leave, Margot 'phoned to tell me she had a seat for me at the Ballet – so I went, and after the Mozart they did a performance of 'Carnaval', but it was awful. Went on to tea afterwards with Margot and Puma and gave her a Christmas present of food and sewing materials etc. – she nearly broke down and wept, she needed the things so much. Ribbon for ballet shoes and thread for darning tights.

Saturday 14th. A quiet evening with Sofie and the 2 boys, Peter and Paul, in which I took them their Christmas presents and they gave me mine – books, pictures and a lovely piece of Dresden china. We had a German supper by candlelight because the power was cut, and it was rather cold – but we shared everything and there was a wonderful harmony of spirit and closeness.

Tuesday 17th. I took John and Brian with me to the formal Christmas party of *Lucie Klopsch's* English class at the Berufsschule – because they wanted to show us a little of what Christmas is like in Germany. They sang lovely Christmas carols and then Father Christmas came in – the German St Niklaus carries a bundle of twigs besides the sack of presents – it's rather like the end of a broom. Before he hands out a present the receiver has to recite a poem. When they have all got their presents they open them and then walk round and look at each other's. After more carols which of course they sing without copies of the words, there were recitations of poems and Christmas readings, while they eat (or used to eat) special things – now there were only flour and water biscuits – they were apologetic. Yet there was a lovely happy Christmas spirit there – with candles and simple home-made and artistic decorations and Cribs.

I went on afterwards to give a sermon at a small Protestant church in Wilmersdorf, after which the collection (80 R.M.) was given me for my work. I felt showered with gifts.

Finally finished up at *Joan Frank's* party down in the American sector and brought John and Brian and others back in the *Volkswagen*.

On Christmas Leave

Wednesday 18th. Just managed to get packed and ready in time to catch the night train back to England for my U.K. leave. What a journey! What a reception!

In the Midlands there was almost a shut-down of work because of the coal shortage, and a four day week.

January 1947

Wednesday 8th. Transport strike and shortage of basic foodstuffs and rationing in Britain. Servicemen being used to distribute supplies.

Back to Germany

Friday 10th. After my 16th Channel crossing, which was very rough, I arrived in Berlin 1½ hrs late, after my U.K. Leave. From the Dutch frontier on it got steadily colder. When I arrived in Berlin at 9 a.m. there was a snow storm and 20⁰ of frost.

On arrival at our mess I was told that my brother Stafford was spending a short leave at the officers' transit mess – so before breakfast got in touch with him, picked him up in my *Volkswagen* and brought him home to lunch.

I had to go and see Sofie at 3 o'clock as we were being interviewed by 2 members of the American Rundfunk to arrange a new series of broadcasts – we fixed up 3 for the end of Jan. and Feb. (1) With parents (2) about Employment problems for youth and (3) Health of Youth, to be in the form of discussions.

Cold getting intense – dropping to 30° of frost.

Some Effects of Winter

Heard that some of the transports of refugees and expellees coming through from Poland and Silesia were in a very bad state. 27 people had died of cold in one transport – it was found when they arrived, and over a hundred cases of frost bite. Negotiations are going on to stop further transports. We cannot protest because one of the British transports going to Schleswig-Holstein had similar though not so bad results. The papers are also reporting deaths from cold in Hamburg. The fuel position is, of course, desperately serious, though theatres and cinemas haven't closed down in Berlin as they have in Hamburg. But then Berlin is a favoured city. It is interesting to note that our own food and fuel position is not nearly as good as when I left.

Many children have got out their skis – though there are very few slopes, and there are many of the huge toboggans out and about.

Everyone wears little ear bags, which are very necessary – because in a few minutes without, the ears are soon painfully nipped. John Bourke says that very often people are just staying in bed fully clothed in order to try and keep warm, especially the elderly.

Had tea with Stafford at the Transit Mess, and after a 'flick' (film), supper with him also. There were only 5 officers in this large and luxurious mess – so well heated in contrast. One was a major in No.2 S.A.S. who knew my College friend *John Tonkin* of No.1 S.A.S. Unit, who won the M.C. and is now on an Antarctic expedition in the Falklands. There was the usual futile waste of time and life in the bar before supper while a German band played dance music that the others neither noticed, heard nor applauded – until the leader asked for a request. I shan't forget the look on those fellows' faces easily. There followed a fantastic supper.

Took Stafford down to Charlottenburg station to catch the night train back to Hannover. He was as wild as I was at not getting a sleeper.

Saturday 11th. Altogether an infuriating day. Astonished to find how easily I got annoyed, and how nearly I lost my temper once back in the old atmosphere – considering how cheerful I was when I arrived. I had no time in which to get unpacked and settled in, nor was I able to re-orientate myself or catch up with what had happened during my leave before I had to rush off and do silly little odd team jobs with our restricted transport. As a result it put all my own plans out, of things that had to be done for my own work with Sofie. Even more annoyed with myself for being annoyed, and resigned myself to doing the jobs – fetching labour forms from the Labour office, and rolls from the baker etc., etc.

A train-load of evacuee children returning from the old "Operation Stork" was supposed to be arriving at Grunewald station at 10 p.m. and it was arranged that we should give them hot drinks and food on arrival. Coincidence that my first relief job on arrival in Berlin (Sun. June 30th) was meeting the returning Austrian children. That day was one of the hottest, most airless days imaginable – this, one of the windiest and coldest – 30° below.

John Seed and I tossed up who was to go. I lost, so it was me. The station 'phoned – "train held up". Margaret waited up while I snatched an hour's sleep.

Meeting Evacuee Children

Sunday 12th. She woke me at 1.30 a.m. when I put on every stitch of clothing and loaded up the ambulance. Fortunately it was a good moonlight night and the ambulances started up without trouble. Collected Mary from 'Sally' Army and arrived at Grunewald station R.T.O. at 2 a.m. when a howling snow storm began. No sign of the train which had got as far as Charlottenburg, but then had to return to shunt onto a side line. Somehow it had got stuck – no one could find out why. One hour went past, two hours, 3 hours. 5 o'clock still no sign – definite news – engine had broken down and a new one had to be fetched – getting colder and sleepier. Had read all the papers and was wondering what to do next. 5.30 a.m. news that electrical points system had broken down and was being repaired. Russian goods trains and coal trains rumbled through, each one raising and dashing our hopes – the electric Stadtbahn trains started up for early workers.

At last, by 6.0 a.m. the train was shunted in. Howling blizzard – drove the ambulance along the Platform, and then we delivered the goods. It was worth it. The poor kids were tired and hungry and cold having last had coffee and bread at Hannover. At the sight of cocoa and chocolate, crisp white rolls and peanut butter, and biscuits they cheered up and there were wild exclamations of delight, and all were pathetically grateful. One carriage was without light, but they were heated and so not in a bad condition. The leader thanked us "with all his heart" for what we had done for the children, and so, feeling distinctly warmed and cheered ourselves, drove back home through a waking Berlin in the dawn and dropped into bed at 7 a.m.

Unfortunately woken at 9 a.m. for breakfast in bed in spite of barricading up my door. Soon fell off to sleep again and woke up again only in time for lunch.

In the evening Margaret K. and I went to an unforgettable performance by the Berlin Philharmonic of the Boccherini Cello concerto and Beethoven's 7th. I met there, in the interval *Brian Lloyd-Morris* who was at Leighton Park School with me (now a C.C.G. Transport officer) and his wife.

Monday 13th. Roads covered with ice – very dangerous for driving. Mail becomes irregular, having to come by sea and rail instead of by air and so many days late. Letters from Daphne and India delayed.

The team, with a large number of Youth volunteers, set to work to unpack bales of clothes in an effort to get them out quicker in this cold weather, and a general stock-taking so that we all know exactly what we have got in the store. Kathleen astonished to unpack from one of the bales – her own old dressing-gown!

Sofie and I went for an interview to the Nord-West-Deutscher Rundfunk who want us to give 2 broadcasts on Youth problems and delinquency.

In the evening went to Prof. Jakobi's choir to find it was cancelled because of lack of heating – so he, Ilse, Helena, *Eva Preuss* and *Rheinhold Krug* and I went to the Café Wien in Kurfürstendamm for a glass of hot "punch". It is a very large café and was packed because it was warm and had light. Many parts of Berlin now have no heating, and light does not come on till 9 or 10 at night. So from 4.0 p.m. till then, if they have no candles, they sit in the dark. Candles of course are scarce and are now the most sought after articles on the Black Market and when obtainable cost 8 R.M.(4/-) each. S.O.S. for more from England.

Tuesday 14th. Had to inform the Security Police Investigation Dept that our entire new stock of petrol – 28 Jerry cans (120 gallons) and 4 tyres had been stolen in the night. All the facts and circumstances pointed to the German driver of the Salvation Army team – a shady character who had pinched stuff from them before and owned a car workshop and garage. Police went off to investigate.

Setting Up the Formal "Free Joint Community Work Committee"

In the evening we had the third meeting of our newly formed central committee, or 'Freie Arbeitsgemeinschaft für Jugendhilfe' (F.A.J.H.) for dealing with delinquency problems.

A difficult meeting. *Frau Erna Maraun* the new head of the Jugendamt was present for the first time and threw a spanner in the works by saying that the city organisations (and therefore party political organisations) which she represents could not participate as committee members if the main emphasis and basis was labelled 'Christian'. The majority of us were for changing the words so as to include all, and so that we could do the work without worrying so much about the letter, but there were objections raised by the Catholics who cannot distinguish between a "Church" as distinct from Christian policy. Meeting adjourned while Catholics thought it over.

Wednesday 15th. Kathleen and I, along with Betty from I.V.S.P., *Vera Swift* and Mary from the Sally Army took the night train down to the Zone to the Leaders' Conference at VIotho. It was desperately cold outside.

Thursday 16th. Arrived in time for breakfast glad to find John Pettigrew there from Cologne, Bridgit from Brunswick and other old friends.

The whole day spent in listening to reports from the different sections. Berlin got a big look in. After 3 short reports in the morning I had about an hour's session in which to report on my delinquency work and answer questions. This was followed by *Miss Dodds* of C.C.G., who was a Home Office Inspector of Approved Schools, and has made a big survey of delinquency in the British Zone. Her account of conditions in German Approved schools was most interesting. So many of her remarks and impressions tallied with my own.

We all took the train back that night. The chilblains on my feet were irritating.

Sunday 19th. After 3 days of doing odd jobs, and catching up with correspondence and trying to write some articles, I went to see the ballet "Joseph's Legend" danced by the Städische Oper Ballet – a new production. It was magnificent with Richard Strauss's music.

Margaret is now on leave with Francis Bolling in Switzerland. We miss her.

Monday 20th. Found the house had been burgled. They broke in through the verandah and into the office. Stole food parcels and a typewriter and alas, my officer's trench coat with its lovely warm lining – my only really warm coat in this weather.

Committee Difficulties

In the afternoon went to see *Pastor Fritz*, head of a big Remand Home for girls in the Russian sector – but when we arrived we found that there was a meeting between the heads of the Churches (from our committee) discussing whether they would co-operate or stand out.

They invited us in, and with a shock we realized that the Catholics had consolidated their position. They say that the work must be based on Christian principles as such, but also that it must be directed and carried out only by 'The Church', and over this they had come together with the Protestants to make a firm stand. This was sudden news to us, as the Protestants had pledged their support for us. We put our point of view: that it was essential that all points of view were represented on the committee and that we should all co-operate for the benefit of the work for youth. The meeting was adjourned until Wed. Very difficult situation for Sofie and me. We wonder if it is the Communists who are resented.

An interview with the radio reporter from Nord-West Deutscher Rundfunk to arrange the script for our first broadcast from that station.

We too now are having the "strom-sperre" or electricity cuts-which makes things more awkward for us at Ruhleben.

Tuesday 21st. What a day! First I had to take my *Volkswagen* for its initial inspection which now has to be done monthly. All our vehicles have to have this monthly check done by C.C.G. car company from now on and we have to get petrol from them, which is a nuisance.

Fortunately the boss of the car unit is Brian Lloyd-Morris who was at L.P. with me and who's very helpful. But they are: (a) New to the job, (b) They've just changed the system, (c) We are an odd unit and so all sorts of exceptions which have to be made for us which adds to the complications. Brian and I managed to get the VW down there by 8.30 a.m. and then spent an hour going from one to the other of 3 offices and back to get all settled. Complete chaos!

We Give a Film Show

During the morning we showed the film "Children on Trial" to an audience selected (by Sofie and myself) of all those people we have worked with on delinquency problems, both in the survey, on our central committee and all teachers in Remand homes, welfare workers and pastors etc. – so we had many friends there, and we have made a great many friends on this work. It was an extremely good film showing the crimes of a boy and girl, their treatment in *Basil Henriques* court, and the treatment in the Approved schools. *Mr Simmonds,* whom I met in C.C.G. was also in the film. *Miss Dodds* the probation officer who spoke at the Vlotho leaders' conference was also there, and I got her to say a few words about conditions in the Zone, which was much appreciated. Finally got home to lunch at 2 o'clock.

Peggy Duff – Victor Gollancz's "Save Europe Now" secretary – rang up and invited me to tea with her at the Savoy. She was in Berlin to negotiate with the French and U.S. Mil.Govs. to accept the "Save Europe Now" parcels for their sectors. She talked a great deal about V.G.'s recent visit to the zone and of the good and bad effects it had had[1]. Apparently, formerly, he had been on very good terms with *John Hynd* who had invited him over to tour the zone on the pretext of the "Save Europe Now" Parcels scheme. No-one had calculated the effect of the present German "atmosphere" upon V.G. who had obviously been carried away. I myself believe that if you expect to see and want to see awful scandals in Germany you can always find them. He had, and made bad use of his discoveries. He also made bad use of a lot of secret or confidential documents and knowledge to which he had been given access. The shame of the whole thing is that the blame for all that is wrong in Germany did not fall on the Cabinet as it should have done but upon John Hynd who was violently attacked. V.G. had had a two-hour interview with *Atlee* which seems to have had not the slightest result – but only went to show how ignorant Atlee was of all that actually goes on in Germany. That is to some extent inevitable. No one person can know all the facts, not even Hynd himself, but he should be able to know how to get the facts immediately, which he does not seem able to do, according to Peggy Duff.

V.G.'s visit caused a lot of trouble in C.C.G. He was very unpopular and would not be allowed to come again. He is probably going to Austria next.

Grabbed a chance to go and see the film "Caesar and Cleopatra" and enjoyed it.

Cocktail Party

Finally finished the day with a cocktail party at Brian Lloyd-Morris' flat, an invitation I could not politely refuse. I went to their luxurious little flat. There were 2 or 3 men – a colonel and a couple of Mil. Gov. officers, and their wives. From my point of view, though it was sheer boredom and infuriating, it was interesting. The wives were fashionably dressed and beautifully made up. There were continuous rounds of drinks, and the room soon filled with smoke till my eyes hurt. The conversation from beginning

[1] *Published in "In Darkest Germany" 1947.*

to end amongst the men was 'shop': cars, and with their wives: discussion about each other's and everyone else's flat, the furniture and fittings, – what you could and could not get, where and how, the rations and the social life. It was one long stream of grumbles and discontent in spite of living in luxury, and having turned out Germans from their homes. I found it nauseating. Brian's wife Helena was the only one who did not grumble. She was content just to be with Brian. She was a model hostess. We discovered that everyone in the room, all 10 of us, had been in India, and for half an hour the torture continued-of Service life in India. I played my part so as not to appear too inhuman and the odd man out and tried to be a sheep rather than a goat – the IVth Advice was very much on my conscience[1]! Took my leave at the earliest possible moment politeness would allow at 11.50 p.m.

Had my supper when I got home just after midnight – pretty exhausted, for during the afternoon had gone through agonies of red tape – signing forms and going to and from office to office to get my *Volkswagen* back again. C.C.G. they say, stands for "complete chaos Germany" and never have I seen such chaos, disorganisation and inefficiency. Fortunately it was laughable and most of us only just managed to control frayed tempers.

An Ecumenical Committee?

Wednesday 22nd. A meeting with Miss Dodds and Sofie to arrange Miss D.'s programme while she is in Berlin.

In the evening we prepared our counter attacks for the meeting of the heads of the Catholic and Protestant Churches working with us on delinquency. It was a long battle but in the end we came to an agreement whereby we should continue with the central advisory committee made up of all the specialists, and representatives interested in the problem. It was to consist of personalities rather than organisations, and therefore of itself could do little practical work. The practical work was to be done by smaller district committees led and sponsored by the Churches (i.e. Catholics and Protestants combined). They were reluctant to bring in any other shades of opinion or to co-operate with other bodies, but we insisted. The Communists felt included.

Thursday 23rd. Spent the day taking Miss Dodds (helped by Sofie) round Approved schools and such institutions. In the evening went with John S., and Betty and Margaret (I.V.S.P.) to a dance at the Church of Scotland canteen. It was a small, homely and jolly affair where everyone is friendly, and the Church of Scotland padre and his helpers make everything go and are full of fun.

Food rations in Britain are cut again, I understand.

Friday 24th. I spoke to the Protestant pastors and their helpers of district Wilmersdorf with Sofie on the subject of delinquency and its treatment.

In the evening Miss Dodds gave a most interesting talk in Sofie's house on Probation work in England, to the heads of schools, welfare workers and pastors whom we collected. They were very interested and asked questions for hours, and

[1] *From the Quaker Advices & Queries.*

would have gone on all night. We were all extremely tired by the end. How Sofie manages to get these groups and people together so quickly I do not know.

Saturday 25th. Snowing again. Still freezing and plenty of skating. Interview with the Berlin Radio about our broadcast. A little misunderstanding with a Russian armed guard at the entrance. Still uncertain whether I shall be allowed to broadcast. The Kommandantura has to be asked because this station is Russian controlled. I had forgotten this.

Supplied the prisons with a large number of our old tins which can be used for plates – as they're so short of any utensils.

Took Miss D. to see the shocking Jugendhilfsstelle lock-up shelter at the back of the Kriminal Polizei. 14 girls in a tiny room with 10 beds among them and one blanket each. 120 boys in a foul room with 45 beds amongst them and 4 lavatories which stank. All types of boys, good and bad, mixed up together.

She was deeply shocked by the place.

Sunday 26th. Had a glorious morning skating with John and Brian up at the Olympic Sports club where they had flooded some tennis courts for the purpose. There was a German instructor and skates provided with a couple of men to fix your boots, for cigarettes – as usual.

In the afternoon took *Miss Simmonds* (the Red Cross Nutrition expert who has come to stay with us for a month to do another survey) to the Waldschule with Sofie to see the condition of the children and to take away little Peter who said he was unhappy. *Miss Cormack* the C.O.B.S.R.A. liaison officer was also with us.

Went on afterwards to give a lecture to *Dr. Hertzfeld'st*'s Protestant Academic women's group, again on delinquency. An earnest and interesting group – good discussion, many questions and offers of help. We stayed on for a short service held at the end of our meeting.

On the way back ran out of petrol and had to be rescued by John, which made me late for Ilse's birthday party.

The cold weather is relentless. It is getting everyone down. The Russians are blamed!

Monday 27th. Committee meetings all morning. The subject of the new Youth House came up again as we now have Mil.Gov's blessing to go ahead with this project.

Afternoon with Sofie and *Peter Thoran* went to the Studio of the Nord-West Deutscher Rundfunk to make a recording of our broadcast – which went fairly well. A beautiful studio and all the apparatus beautifully modern and efficient. Stayed to hear the play-back, an improvement on our first recording.

Electric light off from 6 – 10 p.m. now, but Brian has rigged up emergency lighting off the *Ford* 15 cwt., which runs outside. Temp still way below 0°C. Very difficult to get vehicles going. We all feel a bit tired, irritable and depressed.

Tuesday 28th. A long talk with *Phillip Gibbs* a Friend, and chief probation officer for Leicester, who rang me up as soon as he arrived in Berlin – brought him home to tea. Reuters rang up for an interview.

Wednesday 29th. A most glorious morning with bright sunshine on the snow. Took *Jean Dodds* , Phillip Gibbs and Sofie down to see the Tannenhof home for girl-delinquents in the American sector. The home has now changed its leader and there was a considerable improvement from when we saw it last time.

Lunched with Miss Dodds and Mr Gibbs at the Savoy Hotel.

During the afternoon was interviewed by *Mr Hampshire*, Berlin's Reuters correspondent, on my delinquency survey. He asked more questions about my life history and background than about the problem – which was disappointing. He leaves on Friday night for Venice to cover the Kesselring trial. He took my report with him.

Lord Beveridge was to have lectured here tonight but he couldn't come as he was feeling too ill and tired and had to cancel all engagements – a great disappointment to the 50 people we had invited to our house to hear him.

The wireless talks of chaos in the U.K. and power cuts spreading as temperature falls to minus 16 degrees F.

Thursday 30th. Another morning taking Jean Dodds and Phillip Gibbs to see a home for working girls in Alt Moabit, a private organisation set up by a very fine old woman.

In the evening went with Sofie to Pankow to talk to the combined church youth groups got together by *Pastor Helwig.* Spoke on Youth problems in the world and reconstruction on a Christian basis. There were about 70 young people there – a very interested group – a 2½ hour session!

Miss Simmonds told me that as a result of her visiting she had heard from 2 heads of Bezirksschulämter that V.D. was on the increase again because now that people know that Penicillin is available for treatment, as soon as they are cured they start sexual activities again. This seems to be a losing battle.

Cheerful letters arrived from Margaret on leave in Switzerland – Edith too went on leave tonight.

Friday 31st. An interesting morning with 3 wives of British officers. They had offered to help me correct the 80 reports of my survey which Mil. Gov. has just reprinted. We got through 30 copies. They were extremely nice, and very interested in the topic. *Mrs Brownjohn* was one – wife of Berlin's commander.

Went down to the travel bureau to see what had happened to *Mrs Friedrich's* papers and her visa to England – as she was in to see me again! It seems that she will at last get them within about a week and that she will be off to England soon, poor thing.

Unfortunate Incident

At supper a rather unfortunate incident occurred. Miss Simmonds proceeded to tell us of the awful conditions of a family she had been to visit. They were freezing to death, dying of hunger – husband shot by Russians, daughter raped etc. To us this was typical of hundreds of cases that we know of in these awful nightmare days. While giving us a list of the illnesses of the various members of the family she mentioned that the old mother "had a heart". Unfortunately I added the words "so have I". Miss Simmonds lost control. I could have bitten my tongue off. She had obviously been desperately moved by the awful scene and was very upset, wanting to help personally to do something to save this one case that had been flung directly to her notice. The others fortunately saved the tense situation by carrying on the conversation with interest. Naturally I felt despicable and remembered the time when the same thing happened to me, and the F.A.U. had made some harmless jest which had upset me, being new and deeply moved by some such case.

I believe though that one has had to get a hard core or shell around one. I did wonder if I had become de-sensitized to the awful conditions or whether I just took it all for granted or had got so used to it that I no longer saw it, or even whether I just cared less. It is not the first time this problem has cropped up. Margaret, in the fullness of her soft heart, had done the same at the beginning – wanted to help urgent individual cases where she found the need, and to bring all sorts of odd cases back to the house. We had decided, however, that the present suffering is a bottomless pit – we could all be engaged on it endlessly – spend all our energy on it and worry and care ceaselessly – but never get anywhere, never make any real impact in face of the need or leave anything behind, and therefore we could not do it all. It was a better policy to let the German relief agencies do this work and for us to help them get organised and put power and what small supplies we had into their hands.

I was relieved to find that the others of the team had felt as I had, after the meal.

As I was going to the American Jugendhof prison for boys John B. said in the car on the way, that one had to guard against this approach in our relief work – that in a sense we must have that hard shell around us that was able to maintain the necessary perspective and long term view, and not be swamped by such cases which blotted out everything else and hid the real purpose and aim of our work – it was hard but it has to be learnt. The 'stick' in my mind was whether I had learnt it purposely or whether it had 'crept up' on me naturally and unseen. If the latter it seems wrong. In any case with this cold weather our nerves are rather on edge and as a team we are reaching low water, but it was wise counsel, and for me a hard lesson..

We arrived at the grim Jugendhof and were let through the first layer of barbed wire – it was formerly a small concentration camp – "better barbed wire than walls" someone said – "you can at least see through barbed wire".

Herr Riese greeted us and led us through more barbed wire to the barrack huts. It was bitterly cold.

We left John to speak to one lot of boys while S. and I went off to talk with another lot. There were one or two lads that I recognised and had spoken to before including little Jimmy the mascot who speaks English. There was a marked change in him – he was cleaner and his little face had lost that scowling suspicious animal-look and he was more friendly and open. There was another little German orphan dressed as a G.I. adopted by his American "buddy", and speaking "perfect" American – a most attractive little fellow.

We had a friendly talk – I told them a little bit about Quakers and why we were there – about peace and war – life in England. Gradually we drifted back to employment – nearly all wanted to get out of Germany and find work. They were hungry – why did the Americans across at the Telefunken throw out enormous amounts of waste food, pour petrol over it and burn it in front of their eyes? Had I any cigarettes?

February 1947

Saturday 1st. A lecture to the Parochial-Gemeinde at the invitation of *Dr Schrott* – one of the members on my committee. There were about 70 people from all over Berlin and with questions and discussion afterwards the whole thing was a 2½ hour session. *Max Worner* my sculptor friend was there – brought him back in the car.

Sunday 2nd. Bitterly cold weather starts another week, still well below freezing. The first real day of rest for some time.

In the evening finished up with a Schubert concert at the Funkturm. The last of a series in the Schubert festival week. They played the Great C major. Sergiu Celibidache, the conductor of the Berlin Philharmonic, looked worn out.

A Children's Village?

Tuesday 4th. Miss Simmonds had invited 2 lady doctors, Dr Muller and *Dr Hamann* to tea in order to tell "us" about the latter's ideas. I was the only one able to be present. Dr Hamann told me of her idea to form a village for children in Mecklenburg (Russian Zone). Homeless and orphaned children from the ages 4 – 14 were to be taken there, live in small families under a house mother – grow up and eventually marry – and so form the village. She wants the very best doctors, nurses and educators to work on the project. The community would be as self-supporting as possible, and workshops and apprenticeships set up in manual trades – handwork, arts and crafts etc. Artisans would help to do this and their wives encouraged to adopt children and add to their own families building up small groups again. Money to be raised by public appeal and subscriptions, and donations from particular people for certain children – controlled by a board of really interested people.

All this sounds ideal of course. I asked her what was the basis and foundation of the whole thing. What the aim and purpose was and what would be the driving force. She did not answer at once, and her answer was vague – humanistic – a community helping each other.

I felt bound to say that I felt that a vaguely communist ideal was not enough, and that unless it had a Christian basis with moral Christian teaching and was started on this foundation in the long run it would not be a success, and would ultimately fail. Had she heard of Pestalozzi?

Frankly she had not given all this much thought and did not seem to like the idea. I was disappointed because she is a most striking and fine looking woman and at first sight it looked as though this was her faith.

I persisted and said I thought this was the most important point that had to be considered first – the children one day would be bound to ask, or at least wonder, and as most of them would probably be 'problem' children anyway, unless they had a secure foundation and sound religious moral guidance the community would not grow into the new world idea she hoped. So I asked if she wanted it to have a political bias. Again she said no, she did not want a Church or party political bias.

Again the old problem – the Germans seem unable to distinguish between the narrow Church angle and the broad Christian approach; the party bias and just plain disinterested service and devotion. Every big undertaking is suspected of having some

Church or Party motive or significance. Always these things and the theory are more important than disinterestedness and dedication to the practical work to be done, and the personality of the individual. In England we value a person for his practical work or service. That comes first and we often do not know whether he is Labour Party or devout Catholic. In Germany he is primarily a Party member or member of a particular Church organisation, and consideration for Party or Church comes first – there lies his devotion and loyalty. The Party is as much his religion as the Church.

People say that the English are very like the Germans and therefore it is easy to get on with them. Outwardly we are very alike – in culture too perhaps – but inwardly, Oh how very different! With the French however it is perhaps the opposite. Outwardly we are very different but inwardly much more alike.

I tried to explain to Dr Hamann that by "Christian" I did not mean the narrowness of the Church in its worst sense. But it seems impossible to get understanding of this idea in Germany. It is hard to get it across. I've come across the same difficulty in dealing with the delinquency problem. She promised to think it over and seemed genuinely pleased to have had the opportunity of telling us about the idea and talking it over openly.

Sofie told me later she was a staunch Communist and member of the S.E.D. This was a little disconcerting because I had said that modern communism has never been seen at its best and what we had seen was not near Christianity which, basically, was truly communist, in its best sense. Obviously she wants to get back to the early simple Christianity for her communist village. I believe her idea has the support of the Russians.

The Delinquency Advisory Committee Meets

Went on to the Delinquency Committee when we had to present to the rest of the members the decision we had reached at the meeting with the heads of the Churches – namely that the central committee was advisory – to be made up of individuals (rather than representatives) – for pooling experiences, free to all, to express opinions, receive new ideas and hear outside accounts. The active work to be led in the Bezirks by the Churches. It was well received and we reached complete agreement – much to my relief, though S. was not really satisfied as she wants the work to be directed by the main committee representing all views. That would be ideal but would be impossible to achieve all at once. That the Churches have combined and want to lead the work is a good beginning though it may remain rather narrow.

Wednesday 5th. Addressed a meeting of Protestant pastors and their helpers in district Kreuzberg which was very successful – 2 hr session. We received enthusiastic support.

Later in the evening went down to the American Youth Club to talk to Thiemke's Youth Group on Quakerism. Sgt. Alvers told me of his attempt to start religious education and how he had to start with the very simplest Bible stories because of the complete lack of any religious knowledge among children.

Arrived back feeling extremely tired and done in, and felt as though I was about to have 'flu. It continues to be very cold.

Thursday 6th. *Lothar Hoffman* came to see me. He is a nice lad. Told me his experiences and travels in Hitler Youth as a "flak" helper and how much it had ruined his chances of a good education and his dream of being a teacher. He wanted, like so many, to emigrate to relatives in America. His parents were Catholic – but his father was difficult – R.C. in name – went to Church on Sunday but treated his mother abominably immediately afterwards. He himself was Catholic he thought, though he didn't really know what to believe.

My talks at his school had deeply impressed him and given him hope and some ideas to live by. A deeply sincere and thoughtful boy – we understood each other and talked the same language. I expect much from him.

In the evening I really felt ill but had to go and talk to a Youth group of an apprentices hostel in Neukölln. Not very successful – the most difficult group I have yet had to deal with. Talked about Youth in other lands and England and on peace and war – answered questions on Quakerism and talked about family relationships. Met one definite little Nazi there. Deep snow outside. I had got it wrong this time, and I did not sleep well.

Friday 7th. A bitterly cold morning but such a lovely sunny day I could not resist going out and having a skate. It was wonderful – beautiful ice – plenty of room – few people. I needed a break.

In the afternoon attended the Arbeits-gemeinschaft representing "open" and "free" Welfare organisations – leader *Frau von der Decken* and supervised by *Miss Chaskeln* and *Miss Bickland* of the American Mil. Gov. Welfare Dept. The meeting was held in a beautiful panelled conference room of what was once a conference centre for Nazi guests, and now the H.Q. U.S. Berlin Mil. Gov. I do not take to Ruth Chaskeln. She was German – a Jew emigrated – got an American degree and obviously dislikes the Germans from her "I'm now an American" attitude and definitely behaves as conqueror and top dog. Miss B. on the other hand – the head, is charming. At the meeting representatives from the Sozialamt and Jugendamt from each of the 6 U.S. Bezirks were present and from the Caritas Verband and Evangelisches Hilfswerk – including one or two people of my Arbeitsgemeinschaft. Herr *Müller* of the Jugendamt Neukölln is obviously one of the outstanding men, young and active, and the others, apart from the Church representatives, rather old and sleepy. Frau von der D. is a very fine woman – inspiring.

Support From Lady Violet Bonham Carter

Saturday 8th. A really bitter morning down to 32° of frost again. Had an interesting talk with *Lady Violet Bonham Carter* at the I.V.S.P. mess. She wanted to talk to representatives of the relief teams because they "really knew what was going on" and often "knew so much better than people in Govt. Depts, who can hardly see out of the windows of their offices for paper". Mr Creighton of Educ. Dept. Mil. Gov. had recommended her to ask for a copy of my report – which she did and I gave her one. She asked a lot of questions, and was most interested in all questions, and asked where and how she could best help. I was very impressed by her and liked her very much. She had travelled up in the same train as Kathleen who, however, was not impressed.

I received a wonderful parcel of 150 candles today from High March School, Beaconsfield, as the result of one of my Bristol talks which one of their mistresses heard. She had organised an appeal and this was the result. Somehow it put new life into me and I felt light hearted.

The glow of a large fire in Spandau as I went to bed.

Tragic Fire Disaster

Sunday 9th. Altogether a bad day. On the previous evening the boys told me that the back window of my car had been mysteriously broken while in the car park – they had borrowed it to go to the theatre. First thing this morning I went to have a look. As I feared my beautiful pair of skates only just sent from England had been stolen – but a blanket left untouched. That's the third time in as many weeks I have been robbed. A run of bad luck.

We were told at breakfast by the kitchen staff that the fire in Spandau had been one of the most frightful disasters it was possible to imagine. The largest and best dance hall left in Berlin, the Loebel Café, had gone up in flames in the middle of the first fancy dress and masked ball that they had since the end of the war. 50 people were feared dead and many – over 100 – badly burned. Some had died of cold outside. The tragedy was that there was only one exit and with the panic when the roof fell in women had been trampled to death at the exit. It was so cold the fire hoses had frozen up. I was surprised that we had not been called up to help. It was only about 4 miles away. John had been to a ball there 2 nights previously when the Kant Gymnasium had their annual festival. Margaret had also been there once to the Butchers' Ball.

At Meeting we met *Eva Lee* a young American working in U.S. Mil. Gov. She is a Jew emigrated from Germany and educated at the Quaker School of West Town. We brought her home to lunch.

As the fire was still on at the dance hall we decided to take the ambulance along to see if we could help, as apparently they were still getting people out.

We arrived at the place in the woods but only a gutted shell was left. I offered our services to a medical officer who had just arrived but he didn't think there was any need now for an ambulance. They wanted trucks to carry the dead bodies away. They were to be shifted at 2 o'clock. We approached nearer the building on which the tired German firemen were still pouring water. One English soldier near us said that one of their fellows got out with his girl and then went back to fetch her sister and never came out alive. Apparently at least 9 soldiers died. About 200 had helped with rescue work. Survivors said that the windows were barred and the exits blocked.

The death roll was something like 80. It was an appalling sight!

We found ourselves staring into the gutted and smouldering charred remains. Suddenly with a ghastly shock I realised we were standing in front of the main exit and that the sea of red, yellow, black, charred smouldering remains were the last signs of unidentifiable human bodies. The horror and the smell before us I shall never forget. I suddenly felt ill and strange as I've never felt before – probably just plain shock.

"God!" said the Captain quietly, "they'll never identify any of those." We walked silently back to the ambulance and drove home.

During the lunch hour a personal intense and depressing talk with Kathleen about team difficulties. We are at a low ebb.

Afterwards Eva invited us out to come with her to the American sector to the "Titania Palace" to see a film and to have tea, and cheer us up generally.

It was interesting but the film, the Americans, the lavishness of everything and the awful waste made us feel sick, which hardly had the desired effect.

A *Mr White* – a friend of *Philip Zealey's* came to supper. He is here to lecture to Forces education groups on "The film". We took him with us to hear the Berlin Philharmonic. Seats for all of us are free at all entertainments.

Monday 10th. The frost has continued. Often as much as 30° of frost, and now we are without water as the mains pipes have frozen up, and some have burst underground. Icy winds from the East, blamed on to the Russians!

Tuesday 11th. Spoke to *Ulli Abshagen's* Student group on delinquency and had a very interesting discussion which rather drifted off onto the Russians as so often happens.

Wednesday 12th. Went to Sofie's birthday party at her flat. Just a few guests. We clustered round the stove for warmth and ate cake and drank tea, and had wonderful conversation, and fellowship from this sharing. Sacramental.

Thursday 13th. Eileen Groves arrived on leave and came to lunch. She is very fed up with being in C.C.G. at Minden with the Economics, Textiles and Light Industries branch and goes back to England in a week. In the evening I took her to a dance at the Church of Scotland Canteen.

Headlines in the papers: Frozen Britain works by candlelight. Heavy snow storms and sub-zero temperatures, power cuts. Chaos!

Friday 14th. Went to make recordings at the Berlin Radio – but Youth Dept. leader was ill and so we had to postpone. Took Eileen Groves to the Officers Country Club for tea where there was a glorious log fire.

In the evening we went to the Staatsoper for a concert by the Staatskappele.

Saturday 15th. Interview with Bishop Dibelius at his house, arranging to speak to Berlin pastors.

Watched the Glockenturm being blown up at the Olympic games stadium, as it was considered unsafe. The massive bell landed on top of a pile of rubble still unbroken but with a shell hole in it. I got the photographs.

Youth House

Sunday 16th. A few of us spent the morning with some of the I.V.S.P. and their youth group cleaning out the new Youth House at Reichskanzler-Platz (renamed Karolinger Platz), and re-arranging the remaining furniture. It will still have to have a great deal of repairs done. Brian and I attacked one attic and removed an enormous lot of old junk. It was bitterly cold work without heating.

In the afternoon went, with John B. *Miss Lyons* the Chaplain's Assistant and *Franz Gayl* a returned P.O.W. from England, to the Weltbund Gebetstag of the Evangelische Studentengemeinde in Neukölln. Short accounts were given by an American, Miss

Lyons and Georges Casalis on the Student Christian Movement in U.S., England and France.

Monday 17th. With Sofie went to see *Hans Koebner* director of the Gara film studio to talk to him about the influence of German films of the future and to see what his ideas were. We hoped to get a word in edgeways for the making of good social films. We found him very sympathetic and keen to make short films on social questions and with a particular awareness for the problems of youth.

More Broadcast Recordings

Tuesday 18th. During the afternoon made a 6 minute recording with Sofie at the American Radio – which I think was quite successful. It seems to improve each time. They want us to do a lot more.

Had supper with S. and stayed on for the Arbeitsgemeinschaft at which Herr Beuster gave a Report on Juvenile Delinquency and Youth in danger in Stuttgart – S. Germany. *Frau Rengier* also gave suggestions for the Rehabilitation of the family.

Youth Problems in the U.S. Sector

Wednesday 19th. The Jugendamt Neukölln (American Sector) had asked S. and me to come to try and help and advise them about some of their Youth problems. They told us of the 30-40 new cases they are getting each day of Youth in danger; of the shortage of homes to keep them in, of educators, food and so on. Conditions really do seem bad in this the most working class district of the U.S. sector. U.S. Mil. Gov. (Miss Chaskeln) had refused to help, throwing it back on the Germans. They were really at their wits' end, having tried everything. As we talked a young boy came in to ask for help about his brother who was just selling all the furniture in order to buy food and cigarettes. Furniture now is universally being bartered for food or put into the stove for warmth. There is an enormous craving for tobacco, as great as for food amongst young and old. Children too are forced to barter their own clothes and shoes for food. What are we coming to?

On the way home inspected a school in Wilmersdorf to see that the school feeding was being carried out efficiently and that the children were really getting it.

Children, mothers and teachers seemed pleased with it – though the soup could be thicker (as ever). Some doubt as to whether they really are getting full quantities.

John B. had lunch today with the father of the threatened suicide case Klaus Egilen, whom I caught stealing from my bedroom cupboard. John had been to see the boy who had flatly denied it. The father today had said that they had read in the boy's diary that he had stolen the stuff and that J.B. had asked him about it and promised not to take police action, which was not true. The father said the boy had smoked the cigarettes he had stolen himself.

Thursday 20th. Herr Wittkowski brought some samples of the things that his sewing classes for unemployed girls have made out of the helmets, wool and cloth scraps I supplied – they had made really beautiful pullovers, socks, gloves and dolls out of them.

During the afternoon went to look up *Juna Passuth* for a friend of *Marion Cadbury,* only to find she had died a few days previously. Apparently she had been chopping down a tree for fuel when a chip of wood flew off and hit her breast causing an abscess. She had had to have an operation, had begun to recover and then through lack of resistance had a relapse and died. I spoke for some time to a dear old lady *Mrs Lorenz* – a cripple with whom she lived and is now alone, who pathetically asked me to enquire whether her son was a P.O.W. in England as she had had no news and thought he might be still alive. I gave her a little food, and she was pathetically grateful – not having seen anything like it for so long.

Went on to look up the parents of *Karen* and *Heinz von Tucher*[1]. Found 4 sweet old people gathered in the dining room – the only room they could keep warm, making dolls for a living. *Herr Magnus* an old Naval commander was out of work and unpensioned. They were extremely nice and quite cheerful in spite of all and a room full of smoke.

Lord Mountbatten the new Viceroy of India.

Friday 21st. Inspected the school feeding at 2 schools in Wilmersdorf. All seemed to be running well and everyone seemed very pleased, with few complaints. My word! The teachers do have to battle under unspeakable conditions. I just do not know how they survive.

Had an interview with *Herr Erdmann* chief of the Berlin Criminal Police. Though we found him obviously an uneducated man, we found him extremely interested and a very human person with understanding, and a sense of humour. We pressed for better co-operation between police and the Jugendamt, and the Welfare organisations. He was also very ready and eager that we should give some lectures to each police training course, and to co-operate and help. We also offered him our services with the youth problem.

All the team went to the theatre this evening and had one of the best laughs for a long time. Saw the farce "See How They Run".

Eileen sent me a wonderful pair of fleece-lined flying boots. If only I had had them earlier! My feet have been very swollen with the cold.

My last Tuesday's recording was broadcast tonight, and came across well at a time when electric light was not blocked.

Richard Law M.P. reports to the Commons

Saturday 22nd. I was interested to read the following extracts from a speech by Richard Law M.P., (who visited us recently) opening the debate on "Conditions in Germany" in the House of Commons 5th February.

"I do not believe anyone in this House or in this country, has any conception of the value of the work which is being done in the British Zone today by members of the British voluntary societies such as the Red Cross, the Quakers, the Salvation Army the Catholic Committee for relief, and so on. I think it would be difficult to over-value that work. They are there in teams of ten, or a dozen, isolated and grappling with these hideous problems of administration, helping the Germans, cutting through red tape, and doing it all without any kind of sentimentality, but with pure devotion, disinterestedness, and very great efficiency. What is being done there should be more widely known than it is."

[1] *Former Friends Service Council workers in India.*

Demolition of the Bell Tower (destroyed below)

Self with Margaret Watts

John Seed, Fritz and Brian Burtt

Karolinger Youth House – 1947 ...*and 1998*

First members of the Youth House

The Hellwig family at Tegel

This was cheering news.

He also quoted word for word from the lecture I gave which he attended:

"In Berlin", said Mr Law "the little toddler is sent out to pick up cigarette ends to trade in the Black Market, the child of 10 or 11 is sent out to play with the troops to get cigarettes for the Black Market, and the girl of 14 or 16 is sent out to solicit to get cigarettes to trade in the Black Market. That is not uncharacteristic of the whole range of classes in Berlin at the moment. All that means that there is a vacuum and a nothingness in Germany. I don't believe that with all our good intentions we are filling that vacuum but it is being filled. It may be with Communism – I don't know. I rather doubt it, – but it is being filled by something that is going to prove in 10 or 15 or 20 yrs time – perhaps even before – something very terrible for us all."

Was invited with I.V.S.P. to go up into the French sector to meet socially some French people at the Cercle Féminin. They have a charming house and entertained us to tea, most of them speaking good English. It is curious that when I started to try and speak German a year ago only French words would come. Now when I tried to get any French out only German words will come. The only name I remember amongst this very interesting lot of people was that of *Nicole de Fourchier.*

Sunday 23rd. *Friedel Bialke* turned up unexpectedly to see me. I knew something dreadful had happened as soon as I saw her face. She could only just hold in her tears until she got to my room, when she blurted out that her grandmother had died the previous night. Friedel had been here Saturday night and on returning found her grandmother alright. The grandmother had asked for some food and Friedel had given it. She had complained of being cold but that was nothing unusual, but Friedel had put her in her own bed, which was warmer and more comfortable. During the night she died suddenly. Friedel is now left without parents at all. She has an older sister who has "gone to the dogs" and recently ran away, she doesn't know where, because she could not get on with the grandmother. She also has a younger sister of 16 to look after and now has to deal with the corpse, and the flat. She was full of terror at the thought of going back to the house, and especially to the room where her grandmother lay. She felt she could never sleep in her own bed again. The 2 sisters had between them forced themselves to wash the tiny little shrunken body. Friedel said she looked just like a little helpless child. There was little I could do to help – as in any case they live right on the other side of Berlin. However she borrowed 100 Rm.'s, and I was able to give her some food, soap and candles etc. She regained her composure once she got warm again, and said she could manage. "This time next week it will all be over," she said as she went out, "Now I must try and find a black dress from somewhere. Think of it – me in a black dress! I think my grandmother is in the best place." Friedel is now looking for another job. Poor girl. She very nearly committed suicide recently when she discovered she had the beginnings of T.B. She had to go when we cut the staff.

Monday 24th. Sofie and I had a long consultation with N.W.D. Radio about the script of our future broadcast.

In the evening I gave a lecture on "Christian Reconciliation" to the 1st meeting of the newly formed Charlottenburg branch of F.O.R. at which about 30 people were present in a bitterly cold room.

Tuesday 25th. Kathleen, after her nervous breakdown, is still away at the Convalescent Home, and John Seed in bed. Still bitter frost, and snow, and no water in the house. It all has to be hauled from the camp.

More Red Tape

Charlotte Friedrich came to see me this morning, in great distress because she had received a letter from the passport controller to say that her case had been reconsidered and the visa refused. She burst into tears on producing the document. I had planned to try and see about it today and so took her with me down to York House to see the Travel bureau and the passport control officer. *Mr Sturdy*, a fortnight previously had told me that I could tell Mrs Friedrich that her visa would be at the Red Cross office by last Monday. He promised she could collect it then and as she would be off to England in a few days it would be safe to give up her job and make arrangements for leaving the flat, which she did before this letter came. This was the end of everything.

So I started my distasteful and difficult task of trying to find out what had gone wrong, where and why, while Mrs F. remained in the car. I finally got to *Mr Cove* (in place of *Mr Couldrey* who had gone to South America) who was next in seniority to the Major – the passport control officer. He told me that Mrs F. was the least deserving case he had seen, that she had too many relatives in Europe -that she didn't really come under the distressed persons scheme – that she ought to have been told "No" right from the start.

Cove said he could not understand how the case had ever got as far as it had – somebody had slipped up somewhere or allowed their heart to get the better of them. I did not tell him it had got so far because I had pushed it from one office to another and that Couldrey had got over the initial difficulties and allowed it to go through. But now it was a cruel shame to be told that there wasn't a hope of her ever getting across to her daughter. There was nothing more I could do. I just didn't know how to face going out to the car to tell Mrs F. as I knew it would almost if not entirely break her, judging by the effect it had had when I had to tell her, that her first lot of papers had been mislaid, and that she would have to start again from the beginning, a delay that would mean months. I truly thought that this was one of the most agonising things I had ever had to do. I told her at once, but she had guessed and had already begun to weep. The emotion was awful and her whole body writhed with anguish, and her breath came in deep gasps. She went white and trembled all over. I expected her to faint at any moment. Her last hope had gone – there was no future – nothing! I could not leave her in that state and so drove her to our house. On the way I tried to explain why and give all the reasons. I felt thoroughly inadequate to deal with such a situation. She was desperate and more or less had to be carried into the house. I hoped Margaret would be about to help calm her down but she was out, so I had to see the thing through myself. *Frau Appel* (our housekeeper) made her a cup of coffee. Gradually she began to calm down and proceeded to tell me her tragic life history again – about her husband, a writer, from whom she had to separate, because of cruelty, her half-son – by her husband, the other son a P.O.W. and so on, periodically breaking down into floods of tears of self-pity and saying she could not go on. She suggested suicide as I expected but I managed to stop this idea by bringing in her daughter. Finally by lunch time she felt strong enough to go, and to try and start again. As the door closed on the pathetic figure I felt utterly drained. Never have I seen so much sadness and suffering in a person's eyes and utter despair, or felt so inadequate.

In the evening I went along to one of the Spandau Jugendheime at Wittkowski's request to talk to the English speaking group in English. I found a very nice group of about 30 boys and girls between 16 and 22 yrs old. We talked intimately about the delinquency problem and its relation to moral and health problems and building a home under present conditions.

Again in the mind of this group one can see the frustration and bitterness growing, and the seeds of future Nazism and future wars being sown again. I hope to try and work with this group fairly regularly, there are so many of these opportunities being wasted. This cold winter does not help. They write from England that domestic fuel rationing seems likely there too.

Wednesday 26th. Went to the American Radio to make a 30 minute discussion recording with Sofie and 3 parents including Alfred Thoran on youth in danger. The whole thing took 2¼ hours to complete, and even then it was not too good, and will need a lot of cutting. It was extremely difficult for the parents, it was their first time and so they were not used to the radio technique.

Another Prison Visit

Thursday 27th. Rang up Legal-Prisons Dept. of Mil. Gov. to ask for permission to take some old unmended clothes, and games, cotton etc. to Plötzensee Prison. An extremely nice man answered the phone, and told me how pleased he was for anything we could take, and how pleased they had been that the girls were now employed at Charlottenburg prison. He had had contact with the Quaker teams elsewhere and so he knew and appreciated our help and we certainly couldn't have done anything better than the help we had given the prisons. What a different tone from the first contact I had with their department! It is always the same and it makes one glad to be a Quaker. For wherever some one has had a contact with our teams or our people – it smoothes the way for further work and a quicker understanding. The slow, patient, persistent, personal work of the Quaker method does seem to work in the end and produce results.

I took the stuff along to the prison. It looked the coldest most dismal place on earth in the snow, and badly bombed area.

Friday 28th. a.m. – spoke to a group of pastors – as result of the interview with Bishop Dibelius. Found they were a very old and sleepy lot. Did my best to wake them up, and got a better response than I expected, but it was freezing in the room with a stone floor.

Heard the sad news that Direktor Franke – the leading Juvenile court Judge had died. He was old and tired, but a fine man, and much respected.

March 1947

Saturday 1st. Got up early to go and meet *Joe Brayshaw* and *Margaret Backhouse* (christened "the Bagshaws") at Charlottenburg off the night train. There was a snow storm going on. Still no let-up in this awful weather.

In the afternoon went back to American Radio with Sofie and Alfred to make a re-recording as the last one was not satisfactory. This one went really well without a hitch.

Sunday 2nd. More snow. We all went down to Meeting, and on the way back called in to show Joe and M.B. the new Youth House.

We had invited all the Berlin Friends to a tea party at the Y.W.C.A. to meet Joe and M.B. A happy friendly affair – with lots of talking which could have gone on indefinitely, as usual and took about ½ hour to break up, also as usual.

Our Mercedes Stolen

Monday 3rd. News that someone – probably an Englishman – had calmly walked into C.C.G. Workshops and demanded our Mercedes and gone off with it! We never saw the car again. Hasso was distraught.

Joe and M.B. attended Inter-section and Section meetings. It seems that our feeding scheme of 4000 technical university students is going well, and that we have between us clothed 12000 in this cold weather and the stores are now nearly empty. Margaret R. is doing wonderful work getting every conceivable type of salvage turned into something useful and practical.

Bob, Margaret, Sofie and I went round to look at some of the 300 "Warming Halls" where cold Berliners can go. Of the 7 we visited 2 were closed and 3 were not warm. The air was pretty foul in each – mostly stone floors – cold for feet. Crowded with old and rather hopeless and helpless people pathetically mostly just sitting. No warm drinks – bad light in many – a few bored children – little to do – altogether a depressing experience, but there is so little we can do about it. We must at least get hot drinks to them.

Tuesday 4th. An interview with Frau Erna Maraun (Socialist) at the Magistrat (City Council). She asked for my help in obtaining paper supplies in order to start an independent non-political social welfare periodical.

Her second request was that I should put in a good word with the Allies to help them accept the large increased Youth budget for the City of Berlin.

She also expressed great interest in the German translation of my report and asked for more copies and leave to use the material for articles and speeches.

She also outlined the policy she hoped to work out when she took over the Hauptjugendamt. I was impressed at its non-political aim. She is full of good active practical ideas and suggestions, and asked for our co-operation in reforming and helping the state homes for delinquents, better trained teachers, and more psychotherapy. Also a big kindergarten programme – better paid workers etc. I will try.

Went on to give a talk to the Gemeindehelferinnen in Pankow. Supper at the I.V.S.P. to meet *Mrs Henschel*, out here, as Mrs Champanow was, as psychological adviser for the education of British children – but also extremely interested in the German problem and German Youth. *Mr Simmonds* in C.C.G. had asked her to see me and read my report – she was very kind about it. With the I.V.S.P. youth group she led a discussion on what we can do to build on the peace process.

Afterwards they stayed on to listen to our broadcast which went well, caused discussion and interest.

Brian went on leave and I took over as transport officer for the team.

Today has been a glorious day of clear blue skies and most wonderful life-giving warm sun – so that at last the temperature rose for a short while above freezing and a little thaw began. But the appalling weather in Britain continues, with towns cut off by deep snow drifts. 300 roads blocked.

Wednesday 5th. Freezing again and more snow. Started the complicated transport duties – taking vehicles down for inspection to that shambles of inefficiency – the C.C.G. workshop.

Tea and discussion with *Pater Matzka* and *Pater Odilo Braun* (Jesuits) and *Pastor Poelchau* – the 2 latter are prison pastors. Also *Fr.Dr. Runkel* at Sofie's flat.

Went to call on Alfred Thoran with S. as it was his birthday, and had another tea. Great discussion about our broadcast last night.

Members of Norwegian Mil. Mission to dinner – as one of them was giving a lecture for our International evening, on the effects of the German occupation of Norway.

Thursday 6th. The whole team took the night train down to the Zone. In my compartment there was a very nice young Norwegian officer from Bad Salzuflen by the name of *Horsberg* (Ålsund in Norway) who promised to look me up next time he was in Berlin. Spoke perfect Oxford English.

The Bethel F.R.S. Conference

Friday 7th. After an uncomfortable night we arrived at Bad Oeynhausen an hour late – 8.30 a.m. Met by Tom in the Humber and taken to Vlotho for breakfast. The Weser was frozen over so that you could walk across it. This is remarkable as it is supposed to be one of the swiftest rivers in Europe.

After lunch a number of us were taken to Bielefeld along the Autobahn in the Red X bus. The roads were a menace and covered with several inches of ice. Finally arrived at Bethel at 5 o'clock and were shown to our billets – mostly in private houses in this community.

From then on the other members of the other teams began to roll up in all manner of ambulances and other assorted vehicles. It had been a frightful journey for most of them and was bitterly cold. Bethel is fairly high up in the hills and valleys of the edge of the Teutoburger Wald.

It was good to see all one's old friends who trained with us, and others, and to make new friends. About 120 of the 150 F.R.S. workers gathered here together from all over Germany including A.F.S.C. workers from U.S. and French Zones, and some of the German workers working with other teams.

We started that evening with a meeting for worship in the Studentenheim. John Pettigrew and I shared a billet with the Schwedes family. The whole conference had their meals in the theological students' refectory.

Bethel Bielefeld

John Seed, ???, Rupert Ford? and John Pettigrew

Edith Snelgrove, Eleanor Monkley, Joe Brayshaw, Bill Huntingdon, Liz, Roy Jarvis, Nell Lunnon, Margaret Watts, Alan Blake and Kjell Nahnfeldt

Saturday 8th. After Meeting for Worship there was a session on internal policy and domestic affairs, where too many and diverse points were raised and the conference wallowed in introspection.

It was a most glorious sunny day. We were shown round just a little of Bethel. Bethel is the largest religious welfare establishment of its kind within the German Protestant Church where many thousand mentally and physically incapacitated men, women and children are cared for. Its special interest is in epileptics. It is a more or less self-supporting colony of 10 thousand people – 6000 of whom are patients I believe, and was founded just over 70 years ago by *Pastor Friedrich von Bodelschwingh* – whose beautiful Schloss (castle) I saw just outside Dortmund on my first short leave.

The small town in a wooded valley is clustered loosely round the church. Besides the homes and hospitals for the patients are the theological college, schools, workshops, brick factory, bakery, power station, and the salvage workshop where all "waste" is gathered up and the useful stuff used by and for patients and the community. We saw a school for epileptics and a children's epileptic home – an unforgettable sight, which deeply impressed us all. Here were many children more like little wild beasts than human beings – cruelly misshapen – hideously ugly and stunted – unreal – some jabbering, some wailing and crying out – others hitting themselves mercilessly on their thighs or boxing their own ears, laughing insanely, leering, clutching at you with misshapen arms and claw-like hands with the mentality of babes -helpless, horrible! One could hardly refrain from staring aghast. And yet what left the deepest impression was the devotion of the nurses who treated each one with infinite tender affection, never questioning its right to an individual personality, treating them all naturally and calmly as though there was nothing very extraordinary about them. Every 2 mins. on average, we were told, there is a fit at Bethel. In normal life a fit is something extraordinary, and alarming, and causes a great deal of anxiety and fuss – here very little notice or exception is taken and all are treated quite normally and naturally. What a nervous strain on the nurses! – one found oneself thinking – and what service! to give one's life to these "useless" creatures. One thought of the case for euthanasia. One wondered why they had not all been exterminated by Hitler, as was thought. We were told that Nazism had been closing round them and that they had all been in great danger and were expecting to have their patients exterminated when an English bomb was dropped and fell on a ward killing 15 helpless little hopeless epileptic children. Pastor Bodelschwingh's sermon preached at their burial service spread all over Germany and to other parts of the world outside in 1940, and saved the place, for after that it was not touched.

We heard a most inspiring lecture in perfect English by one of the Pastors, telling us about the wonderful spirit of this place, and its amazingly peaceful Christian, and loving atmosphere and devoted service.

During the afternoon some of us who had been at the Woodstock training course together went for a beautiful walk through the snow and the woods.

For the evening I had to prepare an entertainment, and managed to get quite a good show together which was much appreciated. *Kjell Nahnfeldt* played on his violin and sang with his lute, William Hughes the flute – others recited and told jokes or sang. I produced some mimes, and the 'milk jokes' which brought forth roars of laughter.[1]

Sunday 9th. A very good morning meeting for worship followed by a session relating to the future of F.R.S. work in Germany. Magda Kelber asked Kjell and me to entertain *Admiral Bevan* to lunch, after which he made a short speech. There was also a moving speech by the young Pastor Bodelschwingh – nephew of the founder.

Before the evening session we went another glorious walk with John P. and David Hughes and John S. through the valleys.

After supper we were given an unforgettable concert by part of the famous Bethel brass band. Never have I heard Bach Chorales more beautifully played. As a rule I hate brass bands – but here the sounds and harmony produced were really heavenly – quite exquisitely perfect of its kind – something I have never heard before and probably never shall again.

John Bubb took me down to the station by car. We had to crawl along as the roads were still covered with ice and it was extremely dangerous.

Took the night train to Berlin and was lucky enough to have a side to myself all the way.

Monday 10th. The Big Four are meeting in Moscow today to discuss the future of Germany.

The train arrived quite punctually at 7.00. Got home to find the house upside down and spring cleaning in full swing. In spite of this they got a wonderful breakfast for me of bacon and eggs. It was welcome after a more or less sleepless night.

What a day! I spent it rushing around trying as best I could to cope with everyone else's job but my own. First there was the transport to see to – taking vehicles to C.C.G., lending out others to the I.V.S.P. for their work – and fixing up the work of the drivers, getting stores, coal, water – petrol etc. *Miss Jowett* rang up for 200 red cross parcels which had to be loaded onto the wagon and unloaded the other end – and the post to fetch.

Mrs Morris arrived wanting materials to mend unmended clothes for her German sewing circle and so on – not a minute to breathe! By the end I was quite whacked and went to a 'flick' (film) because there was no light in the house.

News from India that in the Punjab violence had left 293 dead at Amritsar.[2]

Tuesday 11th. Sent Erich down to meet the others off the night train – but train 2 hrs. late because of a howling snow storm and blizzard – it was awful – struggling with vehicles again. Eventually they arrived.

During the afternoon made an interesting recording at the American Radio with Sofie, Herr Müller of the Jugendamt Neukölln, and Herr Roil the master Baker at the Johannesstift Apprentice Bakery, on "Juvenile Employment".

---

[1] *Wartime letters to various Ministries in England.*

[2] *I learned that my mother and other Friends in India responded to the call from Gandhi, through Horace Alexander, to assist with the relief work among those who were killed and injured.*

Thursday 13th. *Rosemary Linke* rang up and came to see me all the way from Lichtenrade. She had just left school having passed her Arbitur (School Cert.) and now wanted a job in the British sector – mother more or less an invalid – father divorced.

After the heavy snow, thaw and then sudden freeze up the roads were frightfully dangerous – accidents everywhere.

Sofie and I went to the Staats Oper together to hear *Erna Berger* in "La Traviata". It was a most wonderful performance.

Friday 14th. Thaw at last! And a bit warmer.

Spent the entire morning at the Nord-West Deutscher Rundfunk making a 15 minute broadcast recording.

Went to Mil. Gov. on behalf of *Pastor Wenzel* of the Innere Mission to see *Mr Hall* of Property Control to appeal for some property now derequisitioned and needed for kindergarten, nurseries, youth clubs and other church purposes.

Also called on Dr Melvin, head of Public Health to appeal on be-half of *Prof. Dr. Hermanndorf* who, for no apparent reason, had been dismissed from his post at a hospital even though he was cleared at his Denazification court.

Saturday 15th. Moscow announced today that the USSR says it holds 890,532 German prisoners of war. Sofie wondered if her husband was one of them.

Perhaps the first day of spring. Made a few welfare visits. *Bill Huntingdon* of A.F.S.C. arrived from Paris by jeep.

A letter from *Mr Basil Henriques*[1] to whom I sent a copy of my report. He offered to have it given publicity in various periodicals.

From a request in London went to deliver a parcel to *Kathrine Vassiljera.* She is a large and elderly Russian opera singer – formerly a well-known opera singer in the Moscow and St. Petersburg State Opera. I found her in her extremely bare, untidy, bitterly cold single bed-sitting room, in a large black fur coat which made her look like a massive great bear.

She told me all about her present employment with the Russians in Karlshort teaching opera in the Russian theatre. "Ah these young Russians they have 'fantastische Stimmen' (voices) and only 22, 23! I was trained in Italy – there they have fantastische Stimmen too – only the Russians and Italians have such fantastische Stimmen! – their language is so beautiful for it – English not! I sang many times before the Czar and Empress of Russia – I married the tenor – fantastische Stimme! -Du lieber Gott! fantastische Stimme! – and we left Russia – the Communists no good – but I like the English – great respect – gentlemen from their bottoms to their tops, No? But they cannot sing!"

Sunday 16th. A hard day working off letters that have accumulated during the week. Finished up in the evening at the Städtische Oper to hear a lovely performance of Verdi's "Aida", which I have always wanted to see. It was a most spectacular performance and the ballet was particularly good.

---

[1] *London Juvenile Court Judge along with John Watson J.P.*

Monday 17th. At the request of Victor Gollancz went to see a family in the Russian sector who had appealed to him to save his children suffering from T.B. I found a fine young mother with two lovely little children – who had safely got through the winter thanks to the school-feeding. The youngest obviously had serious T.B. and I was able to leave milk and food for him.

Lothar H. came in the evening with many questions about Quakerism.

Went down to the station to see that Sofie got safely onto the military train for the Red X conference in Vlotho.

Tuesday 18th. On my way down to the Russian sector again called on *Colonel Alan Andrews* of Education and Youth Welfare in C.C.G. to hear of the proposed visit of *E. St. John Catchpool*[1]. Delivered some pamphlets on nursery schools sent by *Corder Catchpool* to Willi Wohlrabe in charge of Education in the Russian Zone. Went on to deliver a packing case of bandages, swabs and dressings at the Charité Hospital University Clinic as they had completely run out and were unable to operate, and could get none from the Russians. (I think it must have been here that I met a young Russian woman doctor – Mamusleva – later Prof. Dr. of the Leningrad Peace Committee 1988).

In the evening Sofie's and my 5th broadcast came over the air for 25 minutes – there was much interference from other stations.

Wednesday 19th. At 9.45 a.m. spoke to the pastors of Tiergarten Kirchenkreis on delinquency problems and found them a very active group from what looked like a lot of sleepy old men. They hope to start a home for endangered youth in Tiergarten district.

Jack Catchpool to lunch. He is over here to see about Youth Hostels and exchange visits of young Germans.

Went with him into the Russian sector to the Schlesischer Bahnhof (station) to see the work of the Catholic and Protestant combined Bahnhofs Mission which looks after stranded travellers and the numerous lost and homeless young people who turn up at the station. We went to see the air-raid bunker that is used for these people. We went in civilian clothes so as not to attract the attention of the Russians. The horrid smelly dimly lit, low-ceilinged rooms of the bunker were packed with a dirty black mass of people and families of all ages seeking warmth, somewhere to sit, or spend the night, a lavatory, and so on. Black market deals were in full progress. I saw one young boy of 13 or 14 counting 100 mark notes in his wallet which was bulging.

Went on to a tea-dance at the Technische Hochschule given in our honour as a 'thank you' for the Student feeding scheme.

Thursday 20th. A small meeting at the I.V.S.P. to discuss with *Gunthar Sondberg* of the Swedish team in Hamburg, the contribution Sweden could make in the way of materials needed here for Youth work of a practical kind.

In the evening gave a lecture at the Quaker meeting house to the Berlin F.O.R. on Christian reconciliation. An enthusiastic audience of 50-60 people had gathered, in spite of the cold.

---

[1] *Founder Secretary of the Youth Hostel Movement; author of 'Candles in the Darkness'; 1st World War Quaker Relief Work. Corder Catchpool's brother.*

Friday 21st. Spent the whole day devouring an extremely interesting German report on the conditions of family life in Berlin made from the critical examination and study of a cross-section of 200 families.

In the evening gave a lecture to the Gemeinde-helferinen of Charlottenburg on delinquency.

Saturday 22nd. Went out to Lichtenrade School again to talk to the 3 upper classes on their responsibilities in the delinquency problem.

Had a most interesting talk with *Hildegard Dericksweiler* – the Head mistress about the difficulties and struggle of education under present conditions – the school feeding problem – the problems of delinquency in the school itself, the problem of party politics mixed up with the giving out of coupons for shoes, and the problem of how to give the young people new ideas and ideals to replace the old Nazi ideology. There is no doubt that they enjoyed the Hitler Jugend and the B.D.M[1] and that nothing has been given them to replace them except badly run clubs which only do harm to democracy.

In the evening a few of us went up to Prof. Jakobi's in Hermsdorf to a Spring concert in his house. It was a beautiful evening, and quite unforgettable as always in this lovely house.

Monday 24th. An entertainment in the evening arranged by Wittkowski of the Jugendausschuss Spandau for the youth, in which we took part. For the first time I tried out some of my mime sketches on a German audience. It is an international language, and they went down better than I expected. We enjoyed the evening as it was a good show.

Tuesday 25th. At my Arbeitsgemeinschaft in the evening. Frau Maraun spoke on the idea of a Children's village which I brought to the committee. The idea was taken up most enthusiastically and well discussed. So something may one day emerge, and it would be interesting. We might get the architectural students interested through Franz.

We now have to get this committee recognised by the Kommandantura. It may be difficult for I believe it is the first of its kind.

Wednesday 26th. At the youth committee meeting in the morning we heard Bob's ideas and plans for an International work camp which may make use of the empty barracks behind us for a housing scheme.

The lowest food ration card (5) has been abolished in Berlin at last.

Gangs of women workers are again working on the ruins. *Col. Nuttall* – head of housing said at the present rate of 'coal output' it will take 170 years to rebuild Berlin!

I daily see the same small child, and railway officials raiding the trains for coal and turnips etc., outside my window. One trainload of reparations going East has been standing there for well over a week now.

---

[1] *Bund Deutsche Mädchen.*

Concern for V.D.

This afternoon I was invited to attend a very important meeting of the Landesgesundheitsamt (Public Health office) chaired by the Burgomeister *Frau Schröder*. I was the only Allied person there and was invited as co-founder of the F.A.J.H. with Sofie. The Public Health office had appealed to all persons and organisations willing to help in the city's fight against V.D. to come together to co-operate and form a working committee. We heard talks on the problem and recommendations. In the worst areas of Berlin 1 in 10 of the girls of 18-20 has V.D., and 50% of the children have T.B. The fact that the V.D. curve has fallen sharply in the last few months is not due – as is popularly supposed – to the increase of penicillin, but to the cold period and therefore lack of activity on part of "Razzias" (police raids) and the Gesundheitsämter, and will rise again sharply. The ratio of Gonorrhoea to Syphilis, which used to be 8:1 is now much more equal due to the increasing number of homosexuals. At this meeting representatives were present from Jugendamte, Trade unions (F.D.G.B.), welfare organisations – churches, teachers, doctors, press, radio and film, and they gave their views on what could be done. The meeting was broadcast. It was an inspiring meeting. The importance of biology teachers and sex education was much stressed and I was able to give some account of what was being done in England, and one or two other points which hadn't seemed to occur to them.

In Britain it was reported that the Marriage Guidance Council is to get government aid in a bid to stem the flood of divorces running at a record 50,000 a year.

Friday 28th. Went with S. to see the Trade School for unemployed youths in Tiergarten – a good attempt but sadly handicapped, as everywhere else, by lack of materials to work with.

Spoke to *Dr Klein* in charge of youth welfare of 800 youth in Plötzensee prison – who pleaded also for materials and for more visits from us and educational work for the prisons. It is frustrating as we are not allowed to do this. Shall make further approaches to C.C.G.

In the evening S. and I went to a most wonderful performance of Verdi's "Rigoletto" at the Staats Oper, and then I went back and had supper and a long talk about our future work in her flat.

Serious flooding in England in the thaw after the big freeze.

Saturday 29th. The radio reports quite serious food strikes and some riots down in the Ruhr area.

George McNiellage dropped in on his way back by plane from Warsaw. He is marrying Hetty Tinkler of the Dortmund team and they are going to settle down in S. Africa in a job with *Maurice Webb*.

Finished an article for "Relief News".

Sunday 30th. Went to a most wonderful concert in the morning with *Ursula Müldner* a philosophy student and newspaper reporter. Brahms' Festival. His "Song of Destiny", 1st symphony, and the violin and 'cello concerto which I had not previously heard.

Richard Law M.P. Article "Good Samaritans"

Prepared material for youth reports. Richard Law *M.P.* writing in the Times of March 29th wrote in an article on the work of the British Relief Societies in Germany: "There was an afternoon in Berlin when I listened to a young Englishman speaking, as one having authority, to an audience of German clergy and elderly social workers, analysing the current problems of juvenile delinquency and showing how they could be solved. Afterwards his hearers set to work to solve them .....". See December 3rd.

April 1947

Tuesday 1st. Thankfully we forgot about April Fool's Day! Lectured in the afternoon in the Russian sector to a group of Protestant Church workers on Youth problems and V.D. control etc. – 2 hrs, very exhausting. Disturbances and riots reported in Brunswick. Apparently both Mabel and Douglas found themselves in the middle of it all – M. was quite frightened and waited in Mil. Gov. till it was all over. Mostly throwing stones, and demonstration marching. Some British vehicles overturned.

Anti British feeling is even worse in Palestine. In India the death toll in the riots there has reached over 1000.

On Leave to Goslar

Thursday 3rd. With a week's leave John and I started off in the *Volkswagen* for Goslar at 9.30 a.m. It was a lovely day and we were in holiday mood. But we did not get out of Berlin before an alarming crack from the engine and a flashing red dashboard light indicated a broken fan belt. I got out to put in the spare and found Brian had forgotten to include the very large spanner needed when he checked the tool kit – so I sent John back along the autobahn to phone for it, while I tried to stop vehicles. Eventually a German lorry stopped, and they insisted on doing the whole thing for me. I gave them some cigarettes, but they were more pleased with the chocolate for the children, as a surprise present for Easter. Just as everything was fixed John turned up with Brian in a 15 cwt., with the spanner. So off we went, delayed by an hour.

Crossed the Russian Zone in 2 hrs. 5 mins., a new record for the team, and arrived at the Brunswick team exactly according to schedule but an hour late.

Mabel told us of her experiences in the middle of the riot and demonstration when stones were thrown and cars overturned. She had felt pretty frightened.

After lunch went on down to Goslar – it began to get cold and cloudy – obstructing all good views. We passed through a lovely little town called Wolfenbüttel, with old timbered houses, and a very attractive church.

Arrived at Goslar among the Harz mountains, round about tea time. One enters the town through a very old and narrow archway. We both fell in love with the town at first sight the moment we entered. As we drove up the main narrow little street – we could only exclaim "Incredible!" and "fantastic!", the contrast after Berlin was so extreme.

We found our way to the team, left the car and walked back into the town as fast as we could to explore as much as possible before the light failed. Goslar is without doubt one of the most beautiful little places I have ever been to in all my travels, and will always be vivid and unforgettable. "Fancy living and working in such a place!"

John said, and I could not but agree. One is taken right back to the 16th century when this little town was surrounded by a wall and a moat. The streets are narrow and winding and full of vivid colours. The timbered top-heavy houses lean towards each other – in one little street they actually touch. They are beautifully decorated and the colours so warm and friendly. The tiled roofs are pointed and angular, and there are so many irresistible and quaint shapes and architecture. The Rathaus and market place are really old gems and the churches are old, mellow and lovely. By moonlight it was like being in a land of Walt Disney. John and I wandered round in a spell, entranced with all we saw.

On each side of some of the front doors of certain houses were placed 2 fir trees and upon enquiry it turned out that these are the houses where there is a child for confirmation. The custom is that sand is spread from each of these houses to the next, and the child at the end of the village starts the procession – follows the track to the next, calls for the next child and so the procession grows on its way to the church.

We sat down to supper with the D.P. section of the Goslar team – Anne Hodgkin, Alice Scares, Timmy, Ian, Douglas, Peter, Johnny Bubb, Rosemary, Miriam – a jovial and friendly lot who gave one the impression of being firmly welded together as a happy and co-operating team.

John and I then went down to the Young Friends' conference assembly at the school – met *Wolfgang Müller* and *Horst Legatis*, the two leading members, and had a Meeting with the group, after which plans were discussed. Almost immediately I started to develop a heavy cold, which was disappointing.

We were blissfully unaware that in the U.K. the flooding had killed 2 million sheep (a week's meat ration) and damaged 500,000 acres of wheat (a month's bread ration).

Friday 4th. Woke to April showers and very English weather. There is a lovely view from the windows at the back of the house. There are gently sloping fields for about 200 yds, which then rise steeply and give place to the beautiful fir-wooded Rammelsberg, a mountain of 2 or 3 thousand feet. I was itching to get my camera out and on the job – but the weather was poor and I did not get much satisfaction. Spent the whole morning wandering about the town, which is quite enchanting in any weather.

In contrast to Berlin one notices that the people and the children look less pale, better fed and altogether healthier. The place is crowded with refugees and D.P.s besides the local population. There are a lot of shops all with glass windows – for the town was quite untouched by the war. What is more there is a lot more in the shops than in Berlin. I feel that I have already had more exercise here than all the time I have been in Berlin.

In the afternoon Anne took a few of us to a little village outside Goslar where we walked through the fields to some low wooded hills to look for spring flowers. Besides the fir and birch there were typically English beech woods, and one almost expected to find wood anemones. Instead one found wild blue Hepaticas – bright and delicate, appearing everywhere among the beech leaves or here and there the large wild "snow flakes" and the larger snowdrop. We each picked a bunch to take back, and a few to press. We climbed the hill and saw the glorious view across the fields towards Goslar and the dark blue rolling Harz mountains. It was breathtakingly lovely.

There was a meeting in the evening more or less in the form of a service given by Köln Young Friends, after which we listened to Bach's lovely St Matthew Passion on the radio.

Saturday 5th. Liz, Alice Scares and I set off for the whole day in the "*Volks*" – and made for the American Zone. First we climbed and crossed the Harz. There had been snow in the night and everything was lightly sprinkled with white, making the road, the trees and valleys breathtakingly beautiful. Passed through bright little timbered villages, and then across awful "pot-holey" roads and finally down to Göttingen. This too seemed undamaged but a far less attractive place than we had expected.

Once more back onto the Autobahn and sped South. In one place across the Werra river the bridge was blown and so we had to make a very wide detour round about Münden. As usual when one leaves the autobahn the country becomes much more attractive and exciting, much more interesting, and real Germany. Münden was so lovely that we had to stop and wander round. Another old and timbered town in a lovely wooded valley. Climbing out again there was a most wonderful clear view down to the river – so we stopped and had our picnic lunch.

Back onto the autobahn we crossed into the American Zone and into Kassel without anyone taking any notice, stopping us or looking at our papers, much to our surprise. The barriers have now gone.

Kassel again was fearfully depressing, just a mass of ruins, red rubble, bricks and dust with trams threading through and a motley crowd of chewing Americans lounging about. Having found that we were still some 20 miles from the place we wanted to get to we did not penetrate into the ruins any deeper but left.

Again across glorious country with brilliant colours, almost autumnal but not yet spring-like, to Witzenhausen.

Then suddenly, rounding a bend of the Werra river we saw the enchanting old castle, the Schloss Ludwigstein on the top of a steep hill rising out of the river, right on the edge of the Russian Zone. Across the valley behind was another ruined castle on top of another hill in the R. zone. It was unforgettably beautiful. We climbed the steep hill spirally up a rutted cart track and finally arrived before the Schloss – where we met the I.V.S.P. team. Another wonderful view all the way round from the top.

When you go in at the Schloss gate you enter another world – of the 14th century. Inside there is a fascinating little courtyard round which the Schloss is built. It was all quite dream-like. The team consisted of an American Quaker, *Grace Rhodes*, British, Swiss, French and Germans, all working together to rebuild the place for a Youth Hostel – and to help refugees living there. I met there 2 of the boys from a Catholic Youth group who help the I.V.S.P. team in Berlin, and also, another boy who knew Corder Catchpool.

We could not stay long as it was getting late, and I had not got a great deal of petrol left – we did not want to get stranded. A good run back – arrived tired to a good supper, after a wonderful day and a run of over 200 miles all round.

The Harz Mountains

Monday 7th. Went with the Goslar team up into the Harz Mountains for a picnic. With 3 vehicles we went through Bad Harzburg, passed the Brocken to Braunlage and on to Hohe Geiss – the highest village in the Harz, on the Russian border. We left the cars and went for a long and glorious walk through the fir woods onto the hill-top. It was very windy but the views were wonderful. The woods were quite deserted but every now and then there were a few grim reminders of war – a rusting tank, a bullet, strips of silver paper dropped from British and American planes to obstruct Radar, or a German soldier's helmet half hidden under the low sweeping bough of a fir.

We had a fine picnic with hard-boiled eggs[1]. The party then split up – half going home and the other half going on with 2 cars to another place, and then another glorious walk through beech woods and valleys to Neuer Teich – a small still frozen lake and down a lovely stream with waterfalls to Zorge, a beautiful timbered village.

Just as we got back to the cars a storm started. We went back via Altenau – a leave centre for skiing, and stopped to have a cup of hot chocolate at a café. Met several of the Brunswick team there. Finally down a great rocky valley and back to Goslar.

Tuesday 8th. I decided to have a shot at getting right across to Hameln[2] today, and so set off in the Volks at about 10 o'clock towards the West. Passed through Bad Gandersheim, another enchanting little town. After this through the country the little villages and farms were lovely – the roads steadily deteriorated and slowed the pace down. So I did not get to Hameln and reluctantly had to turn back, for lack of time.

In the afternoon went with Douglas to see 2 D.P. camps, the first for Estonians in a hotel, and the second for Poles in a dreary camp of barracks on a bleak airfield. The first place was lovely and most artistically kept, the second was depressing, but it gave me an insight into their lives.

In the evening there was a dance down at the D.P. club – to which 6 of us went. It was a gay happy affair, and everyone was most friendly, and one family invited us into their rooms for delicious coffee and cakes. Heaven knows where they got it from. To bed well after 2 a.m. tho' others did not come back till 4 a.m.

Wednesday 9th. As my cold was better I decided to stay on for an extra day and not go back today, but it was miserably wet and cold all day and snowed with a howling gale.

Went to see another Estonian camp – a very good one, in a hotel, and went a walk up the mountain behind, getting soaked.

In the evening went down to the D.P. club again with *Ian Abbott* and *Doug Lazenbury* to play table tennis.

Back to Berlin

Thursday 10th. At last a glorious sunny morning. Spent until 11.30 trying to get some of the photographs I wanted, and then loaded up the *Volks* and started off back to Berlin via Brunswick. Glorious day with the wind behind and the *Volks* sped along beautifully. Saw more of the ruins of the centre of Brunswick than I had seen before. It must have been a most beautiful place. Malcolm Sadler came up with me.

Crossed the Russian Zone in 1 hr. 45 mins. – establishing a new record, and an average speed of 60 m.p.h.! thanks to the wind behind. All day it was beautifully clear, and the dark greens and blues, and the vivid greens and orange browns were lovely.

---

[1] *In London the Food Ministry says that retailers must replace bad eggs issued in rations.*

[2] *Of Pied Piper legend.*

On leave in untouched Goslar

Goslar

Goslar

Goslar

Goslar

Just before reaching the British check point in Berlin, some Russian soldiers tried to stop me with red flags. This was unusual. I was going well over 60 and decided not to stop. I saw they were armed. When I arrived at the check point the corporal asked if I had been stopped by the Russians. I said I had seen them but had not stopped. "Well", he said, "that was a Russian patrol authorised to stop you – you were lucky they didn't shoot you!" "Well, how was I to know?" I replied. "I must say they looked a bit surprised to see us flash by." The other corporal chirped up "Ooh there would have been trouble if they'd have shot at the Quakers, the Quakers aren't allowed to carry arms are they? Cor! that would have caused some trouble!"

We were stopped again in Berlin by British C.I.D. police and German Police to have all our papers and inter-zonal passes examined but I had been warned about this – that there were big raids and check-ups in Berlin, to round up deserters and suspicious people suspected of the many crimes being committed. Home again safely by 3.30 p.m. to find a heap of letters and parcels, and at once the phone started ringing.

Friday 11th. A lovely day for mother's birthday. Spent the day vigorously trying to catch up with all that had happened during the week I was away. Sofie had arranged for us to see the ballet at the Staats Oper. The classical dancing of this company is distinctly better than at the Städtische Oper. The first ballet "The Arrow" was virile and impressive. The second, to music by Hindemith was called "Nobilissime Visione" – a good idea but primitively and naively done. It was disappointing with great opportunities missed.

Finally they did "Petrushka". This was the first time I had seen this great ballet – though it was, I thought, well done I was disappointed. The costumes throughout were poor compared with the other company.

S. and I returned to have supper at her flat and talked far into the night about our work and plans for the future.

Saturday 12th. Meeting with a publisher bringing out a series of booklets on Youth. Sofie and I were asked to contribute the Sociological aspects and a lot of other material for the second of the series on "Youth in Danger".

This was followed by an interview with *Dr Mamlock* head of the small German committee on Penicillin questions. He mentioned his difficulties and those of the Landesgesundheitsamt (Public Health Office) to limit the use of penicillin to 10 hospitals and a small group of specialists – so that results may be more easily ascertained and that certain doctors might become specialists in the use of the drug. All other hospitals and doctors were angry. It was the obvious thing to do though, to limit the number of centres or "banks", and in these hospitals there were proper research facilities. Also it was easier to collect fresh urine from these few hospitals for the "chloroform process" for penicillin recovery. On the average 20% can be recovered, though up to 50% is possible. It is costly work but necessary owing to the shortage of penicillin. It <u>is</u> proving successful and reducing the number of gonorrhoea cases. He also spoke of the fact that medical research is practically impossible. He gave as an example: the work of one professor on Influenza who needed 25 fresh eggs. These were impossible to get even after hours of filling up forms and getting permits, and going from one office to another, and then a bribe or something similar being needed to persuade the farmer.

In the afternoon gave a party for the relatives of P.O.W.s whom Edith and Bob had met in England. The men in England knew of it and were thinking of them because a telegram arrived from them helped by the "Elders" of one of the Friends' Meetings which the men attended. It was extremely successful and obviously meant a great deal to the relatives. One could not help but wish we could do it for the many other thousands. The mental suffering that is caused by keeping these men apart from their families is appalling, and the problems of their rehabilitation are equally alarming. This is why Dr Rickman came.

Went to meet *Rudi Walton* at the airport on her way back to England from the F.R.S. team in Poland.

Sunday 13th. A lot of old people seem to be dying in this warmer weather – their hearts just giving out, e.g. Franz's grandmother and 2 mothers of people in Sofie's office. People have been really frightened by the arrests and disappearances from Berlin University of prominent C.D.U. students. There is a more general feeling of fear as to the failure of the Moscow conference, of war, or at least that the Americans and British and French will evacuate from Berlin leaving it to the Russians. In Moscow on the 9th, Secretary of State Marshall had proposed the revision of Poland's borders.

Brought back *Richard Harland* and *Francis Bolling* to lunch, and Claude Shotts came too and talked solidly till about 4 o'clock without anyone getting in a word edgeways – but he was entertaining.

It was the first really warm day and everyone was out enjoying the sunshine. The Tiergarten and Unter den Linden were crowded and the fair at the end by the Dom was full of drab life.

I went down to the R. sector to call on Ursula to see how she and her family had survived the winter.

Parcels sent through the ordinary post are at last coming through to individuals, and the first load of undesignated and designated parcels from "Save Europe Now" have arrived after months of waiting, as a result of Victor Gollancz's efforts.

Buds have miraculously opened and the strange birds are back again.

Monday 14th. Gave a lecture during the afternoon to a group of very active and interested Church Youth leaders on delinquency problems. Here were some of the first representatives of the missing "Middle Group", and I found them full of energy, enthusiasm and idealism.

I go to many of these lectures now, perhaps a little tired or lacking in enthusiasm but I go on because always I am encouraged by the eager response and reaction it awakens.

The Fears of German Youth

Tuesday 15th. Conference at the American radio with *Frau Englebrecht*, *Dr* Hötzendorfer, Sofie and a man from Landesgesundheitsamt about the form of our next broadcast on "Youth and Health". It certainly is a difficult subject to offer helpful suggestions about health when there is so little food, and mental and physical exhaustion is everywhere.

In the evening spoke to a small group at the Spandau Youth Club, and sounded them on the general feelings of youth. I came away feeling most depressed by the atmosphere of complete hopelessness and fear of the future, and bitterness. It was not against me personally but the "ordinary soldier" who is just not interested either in youth or the future of Germany, or what is happening before his own eyes: and that is of course "Russia and her wish to dominate the world". "Does not the world realise the danger?" "Still no freedom – deportations, spying, grabbing, political intrigue and dictatorship." They did not know about concentration camps and what went on in them during the Hitler time, nor do they know now what was going on with the Russians, or they did know but the rest of the world seemed blind.

In Moscow George Marshall is accusing the Russians of trying to bleed Germany dry by excessive reparations demands.

No one had expected any good results from the Moscow conference, and now they were afraid of what might happen. One boy told me of an American soldier who had said to him that as the Moscow conference was a failure the Americans would withdraw from Berlin, perhaps from Germany. Indeed one can sense this atmosphere all over Berlin of the fear that the Western Allies will withdraw from Berlin leaving it to the Russians – some Germans have already left Berlin for the British Zone for safety – some are thinking and preparing to go such is the fear, but there would be no room for them – the zone is packed out. Did the failure of the conference mean war? That was the only solution -for the Western Allies and Germany to fight Russia and end the menace, Russia meant to conquer the world. Germans in the zone were fools to riot and demonstrate, and complain of the British. Didn't they know when they were well off? It would be much worse under the Russians – deportations, disappearings, secret police etc.

The Allies can't agree, democracy was an awful failure. During the war they were told a lot of lies (so they have since been told) about England. The bad things such as the slums were emphasised. Then, disillusioned by Nazism they expected liberation and a new way. It never came – it brought only much, much worse conditions – moreover those conditions after nearly 2 years have not improved, only grown worse – there was no silver lining, no hope for the future, no signs of improvement. It was better in fact under the Nazis and yes, they had enjoyed the Nazi time – slowly they were being turned back – "perhaps Hitler *was* right after all ..." and so on.

One had expected the end of the winter and the warm spring weather to bring relief and thankfulness – instead it has brought, as it coincides with the Moscow conference even greater depression, and with the memories and experiences of last winter still close and fresh upon their minds the fear and horror of next winter stares them daily in the face.

At the present rate of production there is the prospect of one overcoat each in 48 years, one suit in 26 and one pair of shoes in 18 years!

I find myself in profound sympathy with these young people – powerless against the mistakes we British have and are making, and what is more, increasingly in sympathy about their attitude towards the Russians. They do seem to block and thwart everything. Bad things do happen, and one is powerless to make any friendly contact or to try and come to any understanding. We ourselves are continually thwarted in this desire.

The New 'Youth House'

Wednesday 16th. First meeting of the Youth Committee up at our new "Youth House" at Karolinger Platz. It is a really pleasant place in the summer and the garden is already showing great improvement. It was a glorious warm sunny day.

I went for a walk in the woods behind the barracks before lunch. Whereas formerly they were so deserted now they were full of bird song. I heard the first chiff-chaff, and the woodpeckers busy, and the chaffinch was loud and sprightly. I saw four different butterflies Tortoiseshells – a little bedraggled but having somehow survived the winter – a tattered Peacock – several bright and lazy Brimstones, and a Blue. I also saw a dragonfly and several Bumble bees – Mayflies and so on. Yet deep below the ground remains frozen and we still have no water. This is trying on everyone's tempers.

In the evening saw Lucie Mannheim and Marius Goring in "The Third Man", with Ursula. These two are doing the same play in German for the Germans for the rest of the week.

In London the Budget puts a packet of 20 cigarettes up one shilling from 2/4d to 3/4d.

Thursday 17th. On my way home gave a lift to *Mary Lehrs*, found she was on the way to buy a tennis racket from N.A.A.F.I. It turned out she was P.T. mistress for the English Secondary School here, and had been to the same Summer School courses at Loughborough as I have, and so we knew a lot of people in common such as Joan Goodrich and 'Mac'. We decided to have some tennis. It is a good thing as I seem to get so little exercise now.

Prison Visit

Friday 18th. Went along to the Legal Prisons Dept. of Mil. Gov. at *Mr Cager's* request for sports material and games for the Girls' prison, and went with him on an inspection to the Kant Strasse prison. When we arrived a few of the girls were at "exercise" in a small courtyard not more than 15 metres by 15 – round and round in a circle looking the picture of misery and hopelessness. They were so pale! It was a glorious day outside but the walls and the surrounding buildings were so high that only a little sun got into the courtyard in one corner where a few girls were clustered. As they walked round there was the sound of the wooden "shoes" on their feet – "clopping" on the stones. Pathetic!

The gratefulness with which they greeted the balls, skipping ropes and other things I brought was rapturous!

The "inspection" consisted of a visit to a room where there were 4 mothers of small babies. The women looked pale and dirty and the babies were being fed from emaciated breasts and a little "milk" food was being prepared. It was a pathetic sight! Then we went downstairs and spent 2 minutes in the kitchen seeing the food. In one boiler potatoes were being steamed in their skins, and each girl's ration had been weighed and put in a string bag, so that it would be fair and they could not quarrel.

The Fürsorgerinnen showed me with great pride, the blouses, dresses, pullovers, gloves, socks, etc., beautifully made out of the stuff I had collected and taken along. Those girls, who have nothing when they go out, can draw on their store now being built up. Mr Cager again said how pleased he was with our help and that as a result it was one of the best prisons in the zone as the girls were occupied.

During the afternoon I took another large load of unmended clothing, cottons, wools and mending scraps collected, to keep them going, and a small parcel of babies' clothes and nappies for each baby and smuggled some milk in on the quiet, though this was against all regulations.

When I went back to deliver this load, coming from the courtyard I heard for the first time sounds of the girls actually laughing! When the massive door was opened – I saw they were playing with some of the balls.

The place had improved, I thought, since the last time – it was cleaner and did not smell so nauseating, and each girl had on a pair of stockings knitted out of our wool.

In the afternoon recorded another broadcast discussion at the American radio on Youth and Health questions.

In Moscow the four-power talks on Germany are reported to be in disarray.

Saturday 19th. Went to help in the garden of the new Youth house, and cleaned out a large shrubbery at the back. The place really is beginning to look lovely, and the Forsythia and blossom of the fruit trees are coming on.

For lunch we had *Reg. Sorensenn*, M.P. (Labour) who has had 2 sons in the F.A.U. He was a very charming and a very interesting and interested man, and asked a lot of questions. I was so pleased that he is so particularly concerned about the moral side of affairs in Germany. Kathleen took him round in the p.m. and they visited amongst other things the Fichtebunker, where young prisoners are kept, and were very shocked by it. He stayed on to supper and a long talk afterwards.

Had a very nice letter from *Vera Brittain* acknowledging my report on delinquency and account of conditions in Berlin. She and her husband she said were expecting to visit the Zone and Berlin perhaps in August for lectures. She invited me to come and see her in London to talk things over.

During the afternoon went to an extremely interesting lecture by *Dr Citrön,* head of a big nerve hospital, on "Psychological problems of today". He himself is a Jew and an ex-Concentration camp victim, and having a difficult time.

It was held at the house of *Fr.Professor Thornwald* whose report I read recently on "Family life in Berlin". She and her husband asked me if they might use information out of my report, and asked me to collect material for them in America, when I go in August with the British Young Friends.

Sunday 20th. Spent a wonderful afternoon with the *Hellwigs* in Tegel in the French zone, a family that *Norah Douglas* (an Irish Friend) had asked me to look up. He is one of the chief engineers in the city in charge of city transport, and underground trains and works for Siemens. They have 3 really lovely and most attractive boys of 8, 13 and 15. Christoph, Klaus and Peter. Klaus the middle one speaks excellent English for a boy of his age. We all went out in the car in the evening – a great thrill for the boys, to the lake, and had a walk beside it – it was very lovely. We sat for some time and watched the children sailing little boats and catching crawfish along the edges, in large quantities to supplement the evening meal.

Monday 21st. After the usual day of committee meetings spent a pleasant evening with Roger Thorpe. We had dinner first at the massive "Truman Hall" where most Americans eat in lavish style, and then went in the car to a glorious old German Inn overlooking part of the Wannsee (lake) looking towards Potsdam. It was a wonderful time of the evening and the sun on the fresh spring colours, and the stillness and distinctness of every sound was unforgettable. After seeing a film we went to Roger's flat and had a long talk over glasses of delicious fruit juice

Tuesday 22nd. In the morning took *Rupert Ford* and *Miss Lewis* (Red Cross Publicity people) to see the new Youth House then out to see "Grünes Haus" Remand Home in Tegel. It was really pathetic in spite of the sun. 97 boys from the ages of 10-20 with shorn heads, poor clothes and dreadful shoes. The youngest with nothing to do; a few in class learning, singing, or choral speaking by heart – no exercise books or pencils. Shortage of every possible needed thing. 25% are bed wetters, which shows how unsuitable the treatment and environment must be, and the problems it produces for the "educators".

The kids were so pleased with the sports material I took them and it brought many friendly smiles to their faces, and they presented Miss Lewis with a bunch of Forsythia, which was very touching. Both she and Ford were deeply moved and shocked by this place.

During the afternoon I snatched an hour's tennis before going to address a very large parents' meeting of 3 to 4 hundred parents – a church gathering. It was difficult to control such a big audience and to get the right sympathetic personal contact with them, and such a big audience easily becomes emotional and excited, over such questions as children. Quite exhausted after 2 hr. session!

Wednesday 23rd. A very heavy and exhausting day. Started at 10 with a talk to the pastors of Spandau district on delinquency problems. They were a live and active sympathetic group. But how they can talk! The session lasted 2½ hours, by which time I felt I could nearly burst they talked so fast!

After lunch went with Sofie out to a hospital in Neukölln to *Professor Dr Lange's* house where there was a meeting with him, *Professor Gottschalk,* Herr Beuster of the Jugendamt, an Oberstaatsanwalt, and the editor of "Horizont", and a publisher, to discuss the new book we have been asked to bring out on "Youth in danger", following the first book by Dr Lange on Youth and V.D. It was a good discussion and we found we were all in good agreement and that politics and Church for once did not enter, and the problem itself remained the most important thing. Afterwards Dr Lange showed us his V.D. Clinic and hospital.

We went straight on afterwards down to Lichtenrade to *Dr Feigel's* house where we drank a cup of tea before I had to speak to the parents' meeting at the Ulrich von Hutten Schule. This was a smaller group and included some of the students, and so was a little more personal, and the discussion afterwards was more positive and helpful than on the previous evening. Finished thoroughly exhausted again after another 2½ hr. session!

Almost daily one meets the deep searching question of whether it is right in cases of absolute necessity to steal or get things dishonestly; and if this is permissible or not. It is a hard question for me to answer. It is the same fundamental question every C.O.

tribunal puts to the young pacifists. If England was invaded and your sister or wife would be molested, would you defend her or stand by and let it happen. There is an answer, but ...

Thursday 24th. Gave a talk to the English speaking Youth Group at Spandau. Also read them a beautiful Tolstoy story. Some seemed surprised that something so beautiful could come out of Russia.

After 42 days the Allies in Moscow agree to disagree as the conference ends, and a commission to examine their disagreements on the post-war settlement. Molotov and the French opposed the administration of Germany as a single economic unit under a central German government.

In London the government banned the use of coal and gas fires until September.

Friday 25th. As it was such a lovely day I took a morning off and played tennis at the Blue and White club.

In the evening went to see a very beautiful Russian Film in Technicolor called "The Snow Flower". A simple sincere fairy story about the quest for beauty.

Saturday 26th. Spoke in the morning to a group of Kindergarten teachers on their particular responsibilities in child education with a special emphasis on the needs of difficult children, and delinquency problems. This was at Bethanian Protestant Hospital, where as a Quaker I was given a very royal reception.

Went on to see *Frau Dr.Kuhr*, the leader of the committee for V.D. questions, to discuss how we could work together in the forthcoming education week, and other points on delinquency work. I was given one of the first copies of Dr Lange's and Dr Brandt's book on "Youth and V.D.". Here is a circle of really interested, enthusiastic specialists keen on the youth problem from a non-political or sectarian basis.

Sunday 27th. A glorious sunny day. Took Lothar to Meeting and afterwards we went a walk in the woods behind the house. During the afternoon played more tennis at the 'Blue and White' – a little stiff from complete lack of any exercise. Finished up at the Opera to see a lovely performance of "The Bartered Bride".

Monday 26th. The morning in committee as usual. Spoke in the afternoon to a meeting of Gemeinde Frauenhelferinnen at Lichterfelde – but as the average age was over 60 made it short and concise. There was however, more interest and life than I expected.

In the evening Margaret invited the *Bollings*, the Duchess of Mecklenburg and ourselves to see the Australian film "The Overlanders", a lovely natural and unusual film which we all enjoyed.

Tuesday 29th. Went down to Lichtenrade to talk to one of the senior classes of the Ulrich von Hutten Schule. They wanted a small discussion group and to ask me questions about their everyday problems. A very sincere desire arose out of the class to do some social work to help – they suggested prison visiting, and then gripped more onto the idea of helping the girls' Approved School in their own area.

We got onto religious questions and I got the story I get everywhere from Young Germans. They are all deeply concerned about religious questions but they do not want the "Old", "dogmatic", "credal", "narrow", Church – but want it modernised, in their own way. They also want to see more co-operation between the churches. This lack, and the strife between the Churches, political parties, and organisations for them is hard to understand.

We discussed deeply from 10 o'clock to 1 o'clock. It seemed like 5 mins. There was a short break in the middle when I had to see a mother who had come to appeal to me for help with her son who was beyond control. A typical case and getting more frequent. I was able to refer her to the right place and people to see who could help her.

In the evening S. and I had our Arbeitsgemeinschaft which was this time to report on the work that was being done by individuals and organisations represented on the committee for Juvenile Delinquency. It seems that there is a lot of interested keen work, and slowly things are moving.

Wednesday 30th. Youth committee all morning at the Youth House. P.m. went with Sofie to give a lecture to Protestant workers in Köpenick – the far Eastern corner of the Russian sector. A very keen and active group.

In the evening we had to speak again to a group of parents in a church at Spandau, for their education week. Not such a responsive group because they are led by a poor pastor. We talked to some of the youth afterwards who were very keen and had many complaints about their pastor who never understood them or their problems. (They later left the church).

May 1947

Thursday 1st. *Leslie Harris* dropped out of the skies on his way back from Poland, and so I took him round Berlin before breakfast. We went down into the Russian sector to see what was happening on May Day. One could not go through the Brandenburger Tor and down the Unter den Linden which was a mass of red flags, so we went round. Already there was a large number of processions with red banners, and slogans: – "workers of the world unite", "Work for a united Germany" and so on. And pretty miserable processions they looked, and largely composed of older women and men: and saw one starting, of students, and a large procession of policemen of the S.E.D. brand.

We finished up at Hitler's Chancellery and then came home.

In the late afternoon went for a glorious walk by the lake at Wannsee and then went to a German Cabaret show of which I understood about half. The first half was thoroughly boring but it warmed up towards the end – practically all the jokes were about food, hunger, black market – shortages, the ruins and so on.

Friday 2nd. *Robert Gibbs* came to lunch and afterwards I was able to have a good long talk with him about delinquency problems in Berlin and what Mil. Gov. and C.C.G. have not done. He is responsible for this question in the Zone.

He will see *Mr Robert Birley*[1] about the appointment of a Youth Welfare or Youth Activities officer for Berlin for which I feel there is great need. The different departments have no co-ordination about Youth problems here at all. I am going soon and then there will be no one left to make any attempts to help with this problem here. He spoke of a Home Office delegation and specialists coming out to work on the problem in the Zone – it is a pity I shall miss them – but he admitted there were no plans for Berlin at all – because of the quadri-partite difficulties, but that when he had got things organised and working in the Zone he hoped to come up here to work on the problem. I was interested that his conclusions about the problem in the Zone and his methods were very similar to mine, and it is encouraging to feel I have been working in the right direction.

In the evening spoke in the parents' education week at Rudolf Weckerling's church in Spandau (where the Downings were married) to about 300 parents. At Rudolf's suggestion I tried a new technique of having questions and discussions as we went along which was quite successful. Afterwards we had tea in his flat and saw their baby *Ruth* (8 wks) for the first time. *Helga* breast fed the child as we discussed the evening. Rudolf feels we must stress far more the point that the Germans are too full of self pity and that there is not enough self help, and helping each other. He had asked in the church for two practical things – a money collection for the work and offers of help to put their names on a list. The collection was large. There were 2 offers of help – and those from P.G.s – (or ex Nazis) who begged to be allowed to help – but were not allowed to because of their party membership.

We discussed the whole question of <u>the German character</u>. So many of the deep characteristics seem to have been changed by the war or the Nazi time. There is the same willingness for and submission to leadership. People are unable to get on with things under their own initiative. Give them an order and they will do it – blind obedience. Rudolf says he is still tempted to use this method in the Church. They are dependent on orders, and naturally turn like sheep to a leader. There is the apathetic state of mind that says such problems have nothing to do with me personally – we have an organisation or a law to deal with the particular problem. Organisation must have been one of the crowning features of Germany. There was a law or an organisation to deal with everything. The main thing which followed from this was that one worked for one's organisation be it State, City administration, Church, party, or smaller organisation rather than on the problem itself. What happened to the organisation was more important than the problem being handled by the organisation. At the head must be a supreme leader with his title directing operations – a dictator. He holds all the strings. Then leaders below him with their titles who are themselves smaller dictators of groups of smaller groups, or suborganisations. Then the leaders of the organisations with their titles, and their deputies, and sub-deputies in charge of departments, and then the common people to obey the orders and instructions to the letter and the theory, rather than to the practical side of the job. Each leader was jealous of his title, and each leader of an organisation jealous of his organisation – its good name and so on. One worked for division rather than co-operation. One worked in a narrow divided way for one's party or organisation – so that co-operation on a particular problem, say between the churches or parties becomes impossible. In England I feel we are more practical and

[1] *The new Head of Education for the British Zone. Formerly Headmaster of Eton.*

attack a problem for the problem's sake: we may have specialists to deal with it but people work together on the problem – what church or party they belong to may never come up, may never be known – it just isn't important. In Germany it is the most important thing, and they are still inclined to work on a problem as a secondary concern with ulterior political party or Church party motives. So there is little trust or reliable co-operation – in fact no tradition of freedom and democracy. They may be willing to talk together but rarely to act together.

There is still a struggle for position and power. I believe it arises from an inferiority complex, for this insistence upon retaining and frequent use of a title gives them a confidence they do not really feel within. If one can dominate even over a few others it gives one confidence. There still is the wrong use of position and power to dominate over others. A leader still must be a leader, rather than the servant of the group.

Partly due to the times there is very little help-thy-neighbour spirit. There is much dishonesty and corruption amongst individuals and organisations for private or party gain. Because of this I believe that half the efforts of the Allies are wasted. Both organisations and individuals could help each other far more – but there still is the callous indifference to the suffering and feelings of others – that sensitivity has been blunted. Some individuals for example who still have a lot of clothes or books or furniture could help others in dire need, but all these things have a high barter value, and anyway formerly it was the job of organisations to help.

The German standard of living before the war must have been very high. They always point out they had no (or few) slums, and point with horror at ours. But they expect to keep up to that superiority of living standard, and will go to any lengths to prevent it being lowered. Others, and other countries with a lower standard of living are "inferior".

Then undoubtedly one must admit their morbid self pity and the clever organisation (so often unconscious) of sympathy, which together with lack of self-help costs the Allies so much. Frequently I hear that "nothing the Germans could ever have done has been as bad as what the Russians have done and are doing." It almost amounts to an expectation of relief and help as a right, and then a dependency.

Again in these times there is the complete submission to military occupation. Military Government is the God – people run to it as unto a god expecting it to work a miracle in any direction at any time, and so often over completely German matters and concerns, and if Mil. Gov. does not work the miracle (whatever it may be) Mil. Gov. is to blame, and not the German organisation which is really in charge of the problem. It is easy to blame Mil. Gov. and easy to get sympathy.

Perhaps I am hard – perhaps this is too black a picture – or purely negative – there is much that could be said on the other side of the good and fine things one has seen and met. But all that I have written is important for the future and are the things which will ultimately shape Germany's future. And one of the things I foresee is the tragedy of the German church which because of its narrowness – its dogmatism, its old-fashioned ways, and elderly pastors is losing its hold over German youth, deeply religious though they are. The German church means less and less in their everyday lives. How is the change to be brought about?

Saturday 3rd. Went to see Dr Melvin head of Mil. Gov. Public Health about penicillin supplies, in answer to Peggy Duff's letter from "Save Europe Now". I got the whole complicated story from him: that there was enough; that the German doctors were in complete ignorance as to the use and abuse of the drug and its administration, that it has to be strictly controlled and organised, and that in spite of the tight hold some is trickling in from other countries and even through C.A.R.E. packages. I enquired about a permit to get Hildegard Dericksweiler to Bad Pyrmont so that the dreadful psoriasis all over her body may be cured by a specialist there, *Dr Buchinger,* a Friend.

Then went to see Mr Creighton Head of Education Dept. about the setting up of new Remand homes in the British Sector. He is a very over-worked man (and a very good one) and had had a frightfully busy morning and this was Saturday – so he looked tired out and 'dopey', so I got little sense out of him which was disappointing. However he promised to see *Mr Edney* head of Property Control and speak to the Burgomeister of Spandau to set free Pionier Strasse Barracks for the Innere Mission to set up a home for Youth in danger. I came out of Mil. Gov. to meet Mary Bailey head of Religious Affairs Dept. and Creighton's co-worker to find she was doing exactly the same thing, which shows how little co-ordination there is over youth welfare and how little they know of what the other departments are doing.

I dread to think what Edney will say when they both see him, as he has already written to me to say that it's no longer anything to do with him but purely a matter for the Burgomeister of Spandau. The Innere Mission had been to see the B. of Spandau who said he had to await orders from Mil. Gov. before he could do anything else than make flats out of the Barracks, which was the last order he had had: this all shows how clear the British are of the power they have handed over to Germans, and the Germans of what power they have got from the British! I came away a little disheartened by the futility and waste of time, and beaurocracy.

So, played tennis in the afternoon and had tea at the 'Blue and White'. On the way back tyre burst and had to get Brian to tow me home.

Sunday 4th. Was notable for a wonderful performance of Beethoven's opera "Fidelio" at the Städtische Oper. Not only lovely singing but well designed costumes and decor, and of course the music.

News of *Lindhorst's* release (Head of teachers' organisation) who was thought to have been taken by the Russians the other day. His wife had been nearly frantic. Apparently however it was not the Russians at all but the German police using such kidnappings for their own purposes, using the Russian G.P.U. threat and under the pretence of their orders. There were no Russians about and when he asked to see the Russian commander he was not allowed to do so. He feels sure that it had nothing to do with the Russians. He told us that many people from British and U.S. zones had been taken this way. One cannot help wondering how general this is, and how much such a practice is used to ferment feeling against the Russians – it is so easy to blame them. Such a thing is easy for just anyone to get away with and because of the Russians people will keep their mouths shut.

Monday 5th. After a day trying to get little Willi Stockman into a suitable Remand home and attack my letters, I finished up with Sofie at a beautiful performance of Gluck's "Orpheus and Eurydice" sung by Margarete Klose and Tiana Leuwitz, both outstanding voices.

Tuesday 6th. Attended Mil. Gov. Education Committee, and was pleased to hear that I had at last won my point of trying to get a Youth Officer appointed for Berlin – one has been applied for – but with regard to setting up Remand homes etc. Creighton said "We can't do anything more than deplore the conditions until the Youth Officer is appointed and can get to work." However plans are going ahead for the formation of a new home in Spandau by the Innere Mission.

Talked to a small youth group in Spandau – about belief in God. Some had no belief and could get on without – others believed in God but not in Jesus Christ, others in God and Jesus Christ. Few went to Church now except at Xmas and Easter, they said.

Wednesday 7th. Really the first warm day and summer, perhaps at last.

Had a delightful evening and talk with Roger Thorpe – dinner at Truman Hall – a flick, Harnack House – quite sumptuous and finally a walk, and games of chess till midnight.

Thursday 8th. Took repair materials, old shoes, exercise books and pencils etc. to Grünes Haus Remand home. The kids gave me a royal welcome and swamped the car. All smiled and said how they enjoyed the footballs – helped to carry things in – and gave me flowers. The Staff were most pathetically grateful. The complete poverty of this place is staggering – boys going wild over pencils.

In the evening talked to the group of Religious Instruction teachers of Tiergarten district. I felt very humble when the leader thanked me afterwards and said how much he agreed with me and how much he wanted to help and do things – but: "Es fehlt uns die Kraft" – "our strength fails us".

Friday 9th. Spent almost the entire day preparing my lectures for next week – especially the one at the Cathedral in place of *Kathleen Bliss*[1] – which must be especially good to make up for her not speaking.

Glorious hot summer weather – the white pear and cherry blossom of which there is so much in Berlin has given way to the glorious lilac blossom and its thick heavy scent. The horse-chestnut trees too are a sight.

In Hamburg 150,000 people are reported to have marched through the city to protest at food shortages.

Saturday 10th. In the evening went with Kathleen to a concert given by the boys of the approved school Ulmenhof. It was very good, singing, sketches, block flute and so on. I was most struck by the quality of the boys and the spirit behind the whole thing – also by the aliveness of the staff who were young and active. The boys were neatly dressed in shirts and shorts of a pattern, and with scrubbed hands and knees.

Sunday 11th. We are having a spell of glorious continental weather. Today was lovely. We went to Meeting to which we introduced George (Polish), and Helga, for the first time. It was a good one. Came back with the Kellers and called at the Youth House where Eberhardt's youth group were hard at work cleaning and scrubbing.

---

[1] *Editor 'Christian News Letter'.*

In the afternoon I went for a walk through the woods behind, and hearing great cheers coming from the direction of the Olympic Stadium walked over in that direction to find that there was a crowd of 24 thousand in the open-air Dietrich Eckhardt Bühne watching some boxing matches. Of all the sports I loath most, boxing ranks high with fox hunting for futility, even though for both I find a certain fascination. I stayed to watch and enjoyed it – there is something fascinating about crowds and the experience of crowd psychology.

Worked until 2 a.m. to get my lecture prepared.

Monday 12th. Meetings all morning. Sofie rang up in the afternoon to ask if I would spend the evening with her – talk over lectures, and then to see the film "The keys of the Kingdom". It was one of the finest and most moving films I have ever seen – the life and struggle of a Missionary in China. I came out feeling very inspired and very humble, and feeling how very far from such a life and example I was myself, and what a lot there was still to learn. Would that my service in Germany had come up to it just a little.

The priest showed in reality the words of William Brien arriving in Pemba: "My great longing is so to live that even though I am unable to speak their language, they shall see by the life that Christ is a reality". One remark I shall not forget and that was "We are nearer to heaven on this earth than you realise". My mind has been very full of these feelings which we have, as a family, been exchanging with our parents in India.

Tuesday 13th. Gave the last of my series of lectures at Lichtenrade – at the Volkshochschule – on Christian Reconciliation and Human Progress. Again a big and interested audience amongst which I feel I now have many good friends. The Class 7a with which I have concentrated presented me with beautiful bunches of Lilies of the Valley, a book of paintings and a poem in German which translated means:

"*We cannot yet realise*
That Mr Maw will leave us
To go to America
In order to observe
And also to try and to bring to others
Faith, Joy and comfort.
It grieves us greatly that you go
But still we express our really heartfelt thanks,
For all the hours you found here for us,
And with good word and deed
Have constantly helped us, that
We shall also ever afterwards strive
To live in your spirit.
We like to listen to you so much
But still as you go into distant lands
So we ask you no more than this:
Dear Mr Maw come back to us."

I was very touched by the friendship shown me by these sincere, thinking and active boys and girls. Their trust and their interest, and the action it produced has given me great inspiration and is ample reward for coming here at all. They have adopted the Tannenhof Remand home, are collecting books, helping difficult children in the school, welding together as a community and seeking to be of service.

Afterwards *Arne Kollwitz*[1] and another boy came up to me and asked me about a sex question that was worrying them. They did not know to whom to turn for answers. Teachers and parents were evasive. "It says in the Bible that the great sin and the greatest temptation is the lust for women. Jesus Christ never had a woman himself. Is it right therefore to follow his example and never have a woman, or is it right to follow one's instincts, and to have what you want homosexually or with any woman, as most people seem to do." I answered as best I could. It was not easy in a few minutes, but my heart went out to them in the difficulties they have to face. We needed more time, and I said so, promising to return.

A woman brought me her daughter of 16. Never have I seen such a pale thin child, and so beautiful. She had chronic anaemia and haemorrhage. The mother had tried everything to save her only child who was slowly dying before her eyes. I longed in that moment to be more worthy of the complete faith and trust these people have in me - to have more healing understanding and wisdom, for there was a psychological trouble there somewhere as well. I felt totally inadequate.

I arrived home late to hear the news that Robert Gibbs had just suddenly died. He was quite gay and happy and alive when we had a long talk together in my room just over a week ago (see May 2). It was a great shock, and an even greater loss for youth work in Germany.

My room is full of the glorious scent of lilies of the Valley. This time last year we had them at the Mount Waltham mechanics course, picked from the garden.

Wednesday 14th. A very full day. In the morning attended Dr Kuhr's special V.D. committee – to report with other members of the work we were doing, and to hear plans for the "Action Campaign Week" starting June 1st.

Went on to talk to the pastors of all denominations at Schöneberg. This is a really fine active group in spite of the fact that so many are old and long past retirement age.

In the afternoon my lecture on Pacifism to students at the Cathedral. Kathleen Bliss of the Christian News letter was expected but could not turn up so *Pastor Bethge*[2] asked me if I would take her place. Only about 100 turned up – it was a glorious sunny day. It was up hill work to deal with this audience which had come expecting another person and talk. It was held in the huge underground church below the ruins of the cathedral which is quite destroyed – but deathly cold down there. Miss Bailey turned up to hear with *Mr Stevens*. There were some tricky questions afterwards. I met afterwards *Pastor*

---

[1] *Grandson of the renowned German artist Käthe Kollwitz who died in 1945. When her own grandson was killed on the Russian front she wrote: "Everything could be so beautiful if it were not for the insanity of war". She lost her son Peter in the First World War. She found beauty in the grimmest poverty. Guardian 8/5/95.*

[2] *Eberhard Bethge, friend of Dietrich Bonhoeffer.*

Harald Poelchau[1] one of the chief members of the Kreisau resistance group and Lutheran pastor of the Tegel prison, where Dietrich Bonhoeffer was a prisoner and where *Helmuth Graf von Moltke*[2] – leader of the group was imprisoned after his trial. This is a fascinating story, and Moltke's letters from Tegel prison have been published in England under the title "A German of the Resistance"[3].

Went straight on to the new Youth House where the first lecture was being held by *Mehne* the violin maker (a returned P.O.W.) who told us about his craft. The House was looking very nice and full of people.

Took Prof. Jakobi and his wife home in the car as he was looking so pale, tired and ill after his recent operation.

Gave a lift to a charming French soldier on the way home, and we carried on a long conversation about life in France in German!

Thursday 15th. Himmelfahrts Tag (Ascension Day) in Germany and a public holiday. A very hot day with thunderstorms. Went with Sofie down to Lichtenrade to hear a performance of Haydn's "Creation" by the choir of the Volkshochschule and the local church with part of the Opera orchestra. The soloists were particularly good, and it was one of the loveliest performances I have ever heard. The choir really looked and sang as though inspired. "The Heavens are telling" chorus was most moving. The whole performance was recorded, and I heard part of the recording as well.

Afterwards we went to a Market gardener's living on the outskirts of Berlin in order to get tomato plants for Sofie's garden – as they are practically impossible to get in Berlin.

In the evening I went for a glorious walk with Helga through the woods in the region of Kaiser Wilhelm Tor and Karls Berg to the lake, where frogs were croaking loudly and birds singing. The nightingales are really lovely.

In London Bevin announced that Britain and the U.S. have agreed to merge their German occupation zones.

Friday 16th. Attended, with Sofie, as guests the Gründungsversammlung (Foundation Gathering) of Municipal and voluntary Welfare Workers of district Charlottenburg presided over by a Bezirksrat and *Frau Ziesler*. We represented our Arbeitsgemeinschaft für Jugendhilfe, and other representatives were from the Freiwilige Hilfsdienst und Sanitätsdienst (old Red Cross) Arbeiterwohlfahrt, Caritas, Innere Mission, Heimkehrer Ausschuss etc.

This was an attempt to co-ordinate and get the co-operation of municipal and voluntary organisations along the lines of the Arbeits-gemeinschaft in the U.S. sector (referred to previously). It is hoped to get this good scheme going in each Bezirk – to link up with that which exists for the whole of the U.S. Sector and gradually to include the whole of Berlin. Dominant note was action rather than discussion. This was a big step forward.

---

[1] *Associated with the July 20th 1944 conspiracy against Hitler – See Vera Brittain's 'The Rebel Passion' p136. F.O.R.*

[2] *Executed in Plötzensee prison Jan 23rd 1945 – See 'Conscience in Revolt', Andor Lebe, p231.*

[3] *O.U.P 1946.*

Saturday 17th. Felt pretty mentally and physically exhausted by the end of this week – so went right away into the woods along the lake and lay in the sun overlooking the lake and watched the sailing boats – there was a lovely fresh breeze. Helga proved to be a delightful companion.

In the evening went down to Dr Thiemke's house in Zehlendorf where we had a musical evening, singing May songs and listening to trios. We could hear the cuckoo quite plainly outside.

Sunday 18th. Again a good morning Meeting. Afterwards *Marie Horstmeier* took up my point about religious education and we fixed a date on which to speak together to a group of boys and girls on "The reality of God". Many Friends and friends of Friends expressed an interest and will probably join.

I went for lunch to the Hellwigs in Tegel where I was given a royal welcome. The rabbits which were born when I visited the family on 20th of last month have grown rapidly and are very sweet. Their little bantam hen is sitting on half a dozen minute little eggs and two big ones. They are so fond of these pets. Peter is so good with them – yet they are so preciously guarded as extra food too – and how they hate to think of them having to go into the pot!

I took the family for a long ride in the car all round the Havel up in Tegel and through the woods. It is very countrified and away from the atmosphere of the City.

When we arrived back found I had a puncture – so spent the next 1½ hours getting that put right, so missing my next appointment.

F.R.S. Team 'At Home'

Monday 19th. Today one of my long wished dreams came true, and was, I feel, a great success. I proposed to the team a long time ago that we should have an "At Home" for Mil. Gov. officials and prominent Germans with similar interests from the City administration. Recently the team took up the idea and it was arranged for tonight that we should invite first the Public Health Dept. of Mil. Gov.(our sponsors), Dr Melvin, *Miss Thomson, Dr Cathcart* and *Mrs Darling,* and *Mr Watkins*, head of Welfare for Germany from the C.C.G. The Germans we invited were *Dr Halms* – head of the Landesgesundheitsamt (Public Health) Dr Mamlock also Public Health and specialist in penicillin questions, *Dr Franzmeyer* from Spandau Public Health, and Dr Kuhr head of V.D. committee, and *Sofie* and *Frau Ziesler.*

The idea was that there seems to be very little informal contact between such Germans and Mil. Gov. They only see each other in Mil. Gov. offices when Mil. Gov. is formal, in uniform and busy, the German official harassed, embarrassed, somewhat fearful and in a hurry. We wanted to bring them together so that there would be some possibility for them to get to know each other a bit better, and to talk over various problems informally in the neutral atmosphere of our house.

The Germans, in spite of traffic difficulties and living a long way off, arrived punctually at 7.30., Mil. Gov. with their cars at 8. Coffee was served – a few cakes and sandwiches. First tactlessness was committed by Mil. Gov., which shows their insensitiveness, when they refused sandwiches, saying aloud:- "we've just had a big dinner and couldn't possibly eat another thing". However with everyone out of uniform they all got down to it remarkably quickly. It was quite fascinating to watch it all work out just as we had hoped. I steered Miss Thompson onto Dr Kuhr and her V.D. committee and the 'Action Week', starting next week. Miss T. knew nothing and was very interested. I steered her over to Frau Ziesler and got her onto child welfare, delinquency and the Gründungsversammlung – which corresponds to the Arbeitsgemeinschaft under Frau von der Decken in the American sector run by *Miss Bickland*, Miss T's opposite number. Miss T. knew nothing about the effort started by Frau Z. in Charlottenburg, and it was just what she wanted to know.

Drs Melvin and Cathcart got going on Dr Mamlock about Penicillin problems and V.D. It was fascinating to watch Dr Melvin, of his own accord, give all the information and answer all the questions that Mamlock told me he was puzzled about and too scared to ask about; and similarly having talked to Dr Melvin previously, to see Mamlock clearing up the questions which Melvin was not clear about. They found a lot in common and talked away without trouble – quite absorbed. Miss T. told me what a good idea such a meeting was – she had learnt more in this one evening than she had in weeks in the office – and that she would like to start such a meeting herself regularly. Dr. Mamlock was so grateful that everything went well. Dr. Halms made a speech at the end thanking the Quakers. It all went so successfully, I was very relieved and pleased, feeling something lasting had been accomplished making it easier for both sides when they next meet in office or street.

Tuesday 20th. The 'phone went early as Dr Melvin and others rang up to say how much they had enjoyed last evening. I feel it was a very fitting climax to a year's work that we are now on such good relations with Dr Melvin and Mil. Gov. generally, when this time last year they were fed up with the old F.A.U. and John Downing and trying to get rid of us too.

Went down to the Travel Bureau, Lancaster House with a Red X rubber stamp to stamp Margaret's travel papers as the stamp had been forgotten. As I went in to Lancaster House fat little *Air Chief Marshal Sir Sholto Douglas* rolled into Lancaster House in an enormous 5 starred Rolls Royce with R.A.F. jeep escort and much noise.

The clerk in the travel bureau said "You don't mean to say you have had to come in all the way from Spandau with a rubber stamp just to stamp those two papers. Well I never!" I said I would be appearing again in a few weeks with my own papers as I was going to America.

"Coo, you lucky thing", said the C.C.G. girl secretary. "Think of we poor starving C.C.G. when you are eating all that lovely food on the Queen Elizabeth".

Called with the car at Brigadier Whales' residence to pick up *Mrs Whales* for coffee with the welfare committee at our mess. She recognised me to my surprise as one of the people at her first meeting with the I.V.S.P. "After that meeting", she said, "I came home and told my family I'd been in a den of conchies and had been actually sitting next to one, which was you, and there was a most terrific row and argument!" We went on to talk about the "conchie" point of view, which frankly she didn't understand, but was nevertheless very interested in. She had read and thoroughly agreed with Victor Gollancz' book "Our Threatened Values" much to the annoyance of her friends and relations who frown on and disapprove of V.G. as "being – well – not exactly against the old country".

I like Mrs W. very much: she tries hard to see the other point of view and to do a good job – she has too a very sensible attitude about the Germans against her former ideas, and now helps all she can without going against the grain of disapproval of "the others".

She was tired. She had just got off the night train – it was 2 hours late – "those blasted Russians inspecting the Germans' papers – the Germans ought to have a separate train if it holds things up." She had been choosing porcelain down at Holzminden, and her son was hunting.

After her meeting with Margaret and the welfare committee in which it was decided that she should help distribute the "Save Europe Now" parcels, I took her back. We at once got onto pacifism again at her suggestion – she was so interested because I reminded her I was one of the conchies her husband had had to try and deal with in the early days of the war in Brecon, at Tyn-y-Cae when looking after Austrian Jewish refugees.

When we arrived at the residence she said: "You must come in and meet my niece and have a drink, I've got to rush off." In the hall I was presented to a slim lovely girl I'd often seen in the royal box at the opera.

"Darling, you remember that frightful argument we had after I had been to the I.V.S.P. about conscientious objectors: well this was one of them", she said triumphantly pointing a finger at me, and expecting to have dropped a bomb-shell. Mrs Whales was a little astonished that she provided no reaction whatsoever in the rather lovely blue eyes of the slim girl, who chatted away quite naturally and led me into the sitting room. What beautiful luxurious rooms, full of great bowls of flowers – all so artistically arranged – long windows looking on to a sunlit garden.

"Do you smoke?" "No – Nor do I – mix yourself a drink and one for me – what would you like?" She curled up on the sofa and a spaniel loped across the room and by two stages settled comfortably into her lap. We talked about Brecon, about Germany, India, Opera, ballet, riding, and books.

"Well", she said smiling, as I got up to go, "We've very successfully managed to keep off the controversial subject of pacifism."

"Yes", I teased, "I'm glad you see, even though I am a conchie, I can talk about other things fairly normally." She laughed at that. "But of course I simply can't begin to understand your attitude as a pacifist. What did you do with yourself all the war? I should have thought you had to do something for the country".

"Don't let's begin now", I said, "as I can't begin to defend myself in 5 mins. and as I'm going, but I'd love to try and explain my attitude some time, even though it's not easy to talk about." "Well I hope you will come back and see us again, in fact you'll have to get Pam's address in London that Auntie promised you." I got into the car. "At least my brothers were in the army", I said as I waved goodbye. She laughed.

I called in at the Youth House on the way back at Mariane Braum's request, to find the place reeking and full of smoke. There had nearly been a fire. Some of the emergency lighting system her brother had put up had not been insulated properly and had got red hot. *John Bourke* – Team Leader – and Edith were there too. John had found a 'strange man' in the premises and asked him: "And what, may I ask, are you doing here?" The man replied he was from the Siemens factory. They had been so grateful for the black overalls we had given them (made out of black-out material by one of our sewing groups) that he had been sent by the factory to see if they could do anything for us. He offered to send an electrician to overhaul the electrical system and offered us an electric cooker. You never know!

In the evening I had my last Arbeitsgemeinschaft meeting. There was a very large attendance. Mary Bailey (Mil. Gov.) spoke on Christian Education, and said some very strong things.

Sofie made a little speech thanking me for the work I had done, and on their departure it was most touching how many of the members said how much they hoped I would return to continue, including Frau Maraun the head of Youth Welfare in the Berlin Magistrat with whom I am often in friendly disagreement and opposition because of her strictly Party political motives.

Margaret Watts left for England.

Wednesday 21st. Spoke in the evening to one of John's groups of boys about the practical part they can play in the field of delinquency. A most keen and enthusiastic group from which something is bound to emerge.

Thursday 22nd. Tried as an experiment to speak, at her request, to *Lucie Klopsch's* group of trade school boys and girls on "The reality of God". These are mostly difficult young people, learning English to get a job with the Allies and who have normally left school. Mostly working class and with elementary education only, they have never thought very deeply about such things, and this was really to see how interested they would be. It was up-hill going at first and I thought it was not being too successful, but afterwards they showed great interest and asked a lot of questions. I showed them over the new house and garden, and at the end they sang me a song before leaving.

Friday 23rd. Had a long talk with Fred Tritton of F.S.C. down at the Savoy where he is staying as a 'Brigadier'! We talked about the work of Friends in Berlin and the future of F.S.C. work, and the International situation as it affected us here.

A formal dinner in the evening with the Lloyd-Morris's in their sumptuous new flat in the Grunewald.

Went on afterwards to talk to *Pater Matzka's* group of Catholic Youth Leaders in Charlottenburg – about delinquency problems. Found another enthusiastic group ready to start work.

In London today the Cabinet took the historic step of agreeing to Lord Louis Mountbatten's proposal for the partition of India into two states, one Moslem and the other Hindu.

Saturday 24th. A great day for us because the water came on. Every one went mad with joy and laughed and cheered to see and hear water actually coming through the taps for the first time for about 4 months. Never was it more appreciated!

Heard by telegram that the *Downings* had been blessed with twin boys – for us this was a great joke!

In the evening there was a sing-song up at the Youth House organised by Edith. About 120 Young people turned up in their groups and each group performed one or two little songs. There was a small group of French children who went down very well. The whole evening was a great success and much enjoyed by all. It was fine to have the place full of young people, even though there were not so many boys. Still troubled in this house with no water or light yet.

Sunday 25th. A very good and well-attended Whitsun Q. Meeting. It was a most glorious day. We had visitors. *Madeleine Yaudé, James Patrick* from Solingen team, and Bill Huntingdon A.F.S.C., on his way back from Poland.

Spent a very pleasant afternoon by the lake, sunbathing. Some people were swimming but it was very cold.

A few of us went to see the first Berlin performance of Benjamin Britten's opera "*Peter Grimes*" in German at the Städtische Oper. It was a fine and moving performance. I liked the opera much more than I expected and found it a most interesting and dramatic, as well as a pleasing work to listen to.

Monday 26th. A holiday for us all. Spent the morning writing in the garden, and tennis in the afternoon with my friends the English school teachers. It was very hot perfect weather.

Tuesday 27th. A meeting with *Frau Dr. and Dr Kuhr*, and *Dr and Frau Brandt* psychotherapists and doctors of the V.D. committee about the Youth Problem in Berlin. Fine interested people – the Kuhrs are C.D.U. party and staunch Catholics, and Dr Kuhr looks at the problem from the educational side. They have a sweet little adopted son.

Dr Thiemke came to dinner and told me of his journey ('hamstering' – calling on rural farms for food – potatoes etc.) into the Russian Zone. Stories of corruption of police -rumours of war and fear – most depressing.

Sofie and I broadcast again tonight on Youth and Health questions. It went off better than I expected.

Thursday 29th. Memorable because Roger took me to hear Furtwängler conduct the Berlin Philharmonic orchestra including in the Beethoven programme the Egmont Overture, and 5th and 6th Symphonies. The Egmont was done well, the 6th I nearly fell asleep over, but the 5th was beautiful. I found it difficult to follow his beat, and I was much less moved than I expected – in fact disappointed. Roger was also, perhaps we expected too much – we both had been more moved by the conducting of Celibidache. Anyway the applause at the end was memorable from the Germans who called him back at least 10 times. I felt it was perhaps not so much the music as his presence again and old memories of what he must have been – perhaps I was unreceptive, it was so emotional.

We had a fantastic dinner at Harnack House and then moved to another table to talk with *Lois Wells* and *Judy Glaisyer*, about German Friends, Germans, the Neighbourhood centre, *Elmore McKee's* very successful interview with *General Clay*. The General apparently has taken a personal interest in the centre and given his warm support. He was apparently immensely impressed and humbled that American Quakers actually lived with German families.

Roger and I finished the evening with a moonlight walk in air laden with scent of the acacias.

Today the wives of top Nazis were arrested, including Frau Goering.

Friday 30th. Sofie and I have mentioned on more than one occasion to German officials concerned, and in public, the unsatisfactory state of affairs in the U.S. sector whereby young girls are brought into the Public Health office after Razzias (raids) and kept all night in a locked cellar until they can be examined the next day, which may not be till 4 in the afternoon. Meanwhile no one knows where they are.

Dr Pfable of the Landesgesundheitsamt invited Sofie and me therefore, to a conference with the doctors and nurses responsible and to see the place again in order that we suggest ideas on what might be done to make some improvements.

We first went to the "Wald Krankenhaus" to see *Dr Fussels'* V.D. clinic and the V.D. wards. They were much younger and prettier girls compared with those in the wards of *Dr Lange* in Neukölln. There was a large number in a ward converted from a large gymnasium. Since they had nothing to do all day, and there were no books except what they brought, it is obvious that the subjects of greatest interest were food and sex, and obviously a great deal of harm results from the 8 wk. treatment for Syphilis. This was otherwise a clean and well run hospital.

We then went on to the Bezirksgesundheitsamt und Pflegestelle where the doctors, nurses and welfare workers were ready for us, at a round table conference to answer our questions. We made the suggestion that a central clinic be set up at some central hospital where girls from 'Razzias' would be taken and examined at once during the night so that they could get home. This was enthusiastically taken up by the doctors and the Public Health office – who will now set it up.

We were also shown the daily routine and methods which differed little from those I saw at the Wilmersdorf clinic during a raid. Here they examine 150-200 girls a day, 10% of whom are infected. We saw several girls – some quite ordinary, some voluntary – some compulsory (from raids) and some prostitutes, (who had been through a dozen times), go right through the whole process of examination, Wasserman Test and Blood test etc. The trouble is the shortage of doctors.

It had been arranged – mostly by Marie Horstmeier (German Friend), that she and I should speak to a group at the Youth House on 'The Reality of God'. This arose out of what I said one morning at Meeting that Friends should take a more active interest in helping Berlin with the religious problems and interests which were not being satisfied (see for example April 30th). 2 girls who said publicly at a lecture I gave in Pastor Herzberg's Church, that they were not getting understanding or co-operation or help with their questions and seekings. These two were afterwards severely ticked off and caused a split in their Church Youth group.

The Church was to my mind missing a great opportunity, and instead of winning the youth is turning them slowly against the Church. We should therefore try and help – for they are earnestly seeking God and trying to believe in Him.

M.H. took this up and arranged it, but unfortunately announced it in Meeting and invited Friends along. So tonight there was a difficult audience. A large number of girls turned up (for as yet we have few boys interested in the Youth House) quite a lot of the German Quakers, *Kathleen Brookhouse* and Fred Tritton, Kathleen and Edith – English Quakers, and Fred had asked if he might bring *Lady Ravensdale* who (as usual) wanted to "see something of the work". I tried to explain that this was an experimental evening: that we did not know how many or what youth would come and so on. To add to the difficulties I was very badly translated by Sofie for once. She was nervous. Marie H. tried to force a discussion too soon and went on at once to try and form an organisation – for a regular group. In short the evening was not a success but a rather dismal failure which was a great pity. Lady R. did not seem pleased, but on the whole people thought it was a worthwhile experiment. It made me wise to the fact that my German is not yet fluent enough. However we must try again.

Saturday 31st. *Gertrude Jaffa* the new member of the team arrived to take Margaret's place.

Kathleen Brookhouse came to tell us about her trip to Meissen and Dresden. It was incredibly interesting, but oh how depressing! After a long struggle she had got her permit and was escorted in a car to Meissen at 8 o'clock in the evening. Only once or twice was she able to give the escort the slip and get away. Most of the time she was watched. There were, she found, spies everywhere in the Russian Zone. First there is the G.P.U. the Russian secret police and then the Germans in the pay of G.P.U. forced into the business.

Undoubtedly the Russians were getting things going in their Zone – factories working – little unemployment – all that was produced went to Russia – but still people were working – were made to work – no regard for individuals – the work was hard – terribly hard – if they collapse too bad. Only good S.E.D. party members got the jobs – if they made mistakes – they went. It didn't matter what your past record was – Nazi or otherwise if you were a good S.E.D. member all was forgiven. Everywhere fear and insecurity and the threat of disappearance, except for work and if you worked you got a better ration card.

As for the Freie Deutsche Jugend it was nothing more than Hitler Jugend in disguise with cleverer slogans and without military training, otherwise all was the same. In fact the whole impression given was that all that the Russians did and stood for, and their methods are so similar to the Nazis, and often worse. They are communising their Zone alright – propaganda against the West is rife. The whole set-up sounded quite fantastic and the Youth had every facility – lashings of paper for publicity, microphones, flood-lighting, processions, singing, sport, and incredibly efficient organisation. Education too is as much a farce as it was under the Nazis. Former Nazi youth are easily attracted to F.D.J.; it is more what they are used to. We in the West are accused and accuse ourselves of not filling the vacuum left in the minds and thoughts of Germans. In the R. Zone they are being offered something – the same sort of thing as before – and all they want now is a uniform.

K. had managed to slip away in order to see some Friends in Dresden who had welcomed her with open arms even though it endangered their lives, and heard much of their difficulties. They so longed for someone in the West to tell their troubles to. They had had to join the S.E.D. party. So people are still in the same dilemma. Force – Compulsion – no respect of the individual, spying, party intrigue. All very depressing.

June 1947

Sunday 1st. Started off to Neukölln but got a puncture in the car, had to ring up as I was without spare tyre or pump. Another vehicle came and mine towed away. So was an hour late to Dr Kuhr's V.D. clinic.

Matinee at the Stern Kino – the opening of "Actions Woche" against V.D. There was a newspaper photographer still waiting for Sofie's and my photograph for the Magazine "Heute".

The programme consisted of a rather odd collection: Music by Mozart (young string orchestra). A speech by *Hilde Korbe* an actress and member of the city parliament, and a frightful P.T. display which I just could not look at, a speech by the local Burgomeister, lectures from Dr Brandt and Dr Lange, a short and rather amateur film about V.D. – more music, to an audience of about 6 or 7 hundred. At the end I felt I had to say a few words to balance up things that had been left out, and as I was the only Allied person present. I spoke of the necessity of all organisations and churches, press, radio film etc. working together on this problem from all sides but in a spirit that was above Church and party politics. I admitted also the Allied share in the responsibility and that basically we must get rid of war. I also pointed out the necessity for preventive education on this problem – the responsibility of parents, teachers, pastors and doctors, emphasising this rather than the giving of information only about V.D. Afterwards there was a buzz of general conversation, hand-shaking and congratulating amongst all the important people assembled.

I returned to a big gathering of Berlin Quakers in our house, to meet Fred Tritton and Kathleen Brookhouse. They stayed until 3.30.

Monday 2nd. I was greeted at 12.30 a.m. while I was still working, by Bob who came into my room – looking like death warmed up in his pants to wish me a happy birthday!

It turned out another perfect day during the heat wave when temperatures were up around the hundreds.

A delightful morning spent in committee meetings till 1.30.

I took the opportunity during the afternoon of having a swim in the Olympic pool – it was perfect.

Spent the evening with Sofie and Alfred at a little party arranged for me by my two original and greatest German friends – presents, candles and cake.

The staff at home also gave me a delicious cake, flowers, and a beautiful card with all their names, and the Berlin crest.

Tuesday 3rd. Very hot again, took the morning off instead of my birthday and went out for a row on the lake with H. It was perfect, and the water very warm for a swim. She gave me a book bound by herself.

In the evening went with Sofie to see Rimsky-Korsakov's opera "Sadko", a most impressive production, put on by the Russians in the last few months – stage effects of sea and sky, and an underwater scene were quite incredibly wonderful and realistic, and the under-water ballet too was fantastic.

Wednesday 4th. A meeting with two of John Bourke's boys to advise them as to what to do to help in a practical way with the delinquency question. They will try now to go and help in the Protestant house of Ulmenhof.

Afterwards there was a special farewell tea-party with a few of my best German friends amongst doctors, teachers, pastors etc., which I did enjoy – they were all so very kind.

During the morning, I took a whole lot of sewing materials, occupational material etc. to the Hauptpflegeamt Remand home in the Russian sector that had appealed for some more stuff to keep the girls going. It was made up from parcels people had sent from England. Also supplied prisons with more cotton and old clothes shoes etc. It is pathetic what they need. Gave some delightful little urchins that gathered round the car, a lift to the end of the street – it was such a great treat for them.

Visit to the New A.F.S.C. Quaker Neighbourhood Centre 'Mittelhof'

Thursday 5th. Spent the morning at the new Quaker Neighbourhood Centre the Mittelhof in Nikolassee. It is the most wonderful and suitable building with a glorious garden – a drive of birch trees – fir trees, and sand for a children's play centre. A lovely shaded bank, ideal for resting tired mothers and social workers – a quiet shady spot in one corner, ideal for meetings. The building was formerly part of the German Kultur Ministerium, and so it is very artistic inside.

Thatcher Clark and *Elaine Simon* showed me round. They were so full of vision and enthusiasm, and showed me just where everything is going to be. It was all being tidied up and cleaned – the beautiful parquet floor scraped etc.

The centre is to be divided into 2 parts. A Conference centre and Neighbourhood Centre. It is ideal for both. In the latter there will be a children's play centre, mothers' and social workers' rest centre, a trained social worker for case work, a kindergarten teacher, and feeding. There will also be weaving and shoe-repair work-shops. Judy Glaisyer who has done so much to get the place going was there, full of enthusiasm which was so infectious, also *Erma Schwerewski*, the German Warden. There will be a library, music room, games room, studies and staff quarters etc.

We had lunch together with *Elmore McKee* who is battling with *Col. Howley*, Miss Bickland and other American Mil. Gov. officials to get the place started, and I was primed with details, difficulties and enthusiasm to take to America. Hans Albrecht is causing considerable difficulty.

Spent the evening with Prof. Jakobi and his family in Hermsdorf.

Friday 6th. The whole morning spent rushing from one office to another, getting travel papers signed, and fixing things up before leaving.

Went to see *Mrs Wagstaff* head of Women's affairs and now in Public Health and Welfare C.C.G. H.Q. (who was formerly a Fry and of Quaker stock) to fix up for Vera Brittain to visit Berlin, and her talks and broadcasts here.

Mr Robert Birley the new Head of Education for the British Zone of Germany came to lunch. He is a great tall impressive man. When he left we all felt no one better could have been appointed. He has great knowledge, interest and insight into German problems. His mind is big and impartial enough and open to see and hear all points of view, and also prepared to learn from the Germans. He is an excellent person and filled us too with hope and enthusiasm for the future. He is working on many things so desperately needed in education and youth problems. (Years later I was to meet him again when he became the President of the Selly Oak Colleges in Birmingham).

The Hoffman Family

After the party for the Berlin Quakers, the F.A.U. boys related to us the story of this remarkable Quaker family, the Hoffmans, during the Battle of Berlin before the end of the War. The Russians were the first to enter Berlin. Gunfire, looting and rape were widespread in the chaos. Terror, abject fear and mistrust were everywhere in the air. People hid in their cellars, watched and waited. Girls cut off their hair.

As the gunfire and screaming got ever closer to their house the Hoffmans decided to carry on as normally as possible. Lotte Hoffman sat and played the piano and the family sang together in the living room, undamaged by the bombing. Simple food was left on the table.

When the Russian soldiers burst into the house with guns at the ready, the family were at peace and relaxed, and showed no fear – they just continued singing together in harmony. The Russian soldiers were amazed. They had encountered nothing like it before, and soon saw that there was no intention of any armed or violent resistance or danger. They put down their guns and listened. They were then welcomed with smiles and offered the simple fare – all that they had. The officer in charge shook hands with them with tears in his eyes, and ordered some of his men to stand guard outside and round the house so that the family should not be further molested by any drunk or rampaging troops.

On Leave to America

From June 25th to August 21st I visited America with 5 other young Friends from England. A full account of this can be found in my American Journal.

I gave much time over there to speaking about conditions in Europe, and the world outlook as regards future prospects of peace and war. Everywhere I was given a sympathetic and interested hearing. I also visited the A.F.S.C. office in Philadelphia.

During the few weeks I had in England before my return to Germany several important personal events happened. The most important of these was the formal announcement of my engagement to Daphne Southall.

Then also, much to my disappointment Magda Kelber in spite of previous assurances, decided that I could not return to work in Berlin but must move to Cologne. Friends House informed me that the reason was that all teams in Germany had had to be cut to 6 people. Also there was a great shortage of men. The Berlin team had already 7 or 8 people, 4 of whom were men, and that as Cologne was particularly short of people I should be wanted there. This naturally was a very great blow to me. My original intention was to serve one year in Germany but I felt that my concern to carry on with the work in Berlin was such that I offered another 3-6 months' service there. Berlin is where my real concern lies. I had made plans accordingly and had informed Friends House of the fact and they had agreed.

I therefore had no choice in the matter, and as my equipment and all my personal belongings had been left in Berlin, there was no alternative but to return, pack up my things and move to Cologne to start up again, without further fuss or protest, though I felt I might have been consulted earlier. I discovered later that this was not the only reason for my removal and I feel there was an unfortunate lack of frank honest discussion on several people's part which was not in the spirit of Friends. Often I felt bitter in my disappointment and ready to start disputes, justifications and complaints at what I feel is not altogether fair treatment. I felt however that there was no alternative but to keep quiet and accept the course of events humbly, and make the best of it, for my life at the time of this great blow was so happy that I did not want to spoil the peace by outward disharmony and unpleasantness.

Certain events during this time are worth recording.

One was a talk I was asked to give to the packers and balers of Davies Turner & Co and who now bale all our clothes for overseas relief.

This was one of the toughest assignments I have had for some time, and meant talking to these working class men and women – Cockneys and others – about what happened to the stuff they baled, over the other side and why we sent it, and then to answer the questions which they fired at me, such as why we should send all this good stuff to the "blinking enemy" when our own wives had to queue for it; and if we did this sort of thing for our enemies did we do anything like it for our own people in need, of whom there were many in England, and so on. It was hard work but they gave me a courteous hearing. I would like to have had longer time to answer and argue with them, but I think some ground was definitely gained, though by no means all were nearly convinced. It must not be forgotten that there were considerable hardships and rationing etc. in Britain during this period.

Then over tea at Friends House with Vera Brittain, I had a long and interesting talk with her about her recent trip to Germany, and her visit to Berlin in particular, and she asked me about certain aspects of my trip to America. I had been impressed by her balanced commentary in Peace News and this had been violently attacked by cynical anarchist *Ethel Manin*, wife of Reg Reynolds, and to which I felt I must reply. My letter was published in Peace News of September 26th.

V.B. felt that of all the cities she had visited in Germany she thought Cologne needed the most help, for it was the most depressed. This helped me to re-focus my attention to the future.

I was also interested that neither the Berlin nor the Cologne authorities were impressed with her visit. I was struck by how very much older and frailer she looked, but still full of spirit and interest. She was shortly going to Switzerland to take her son to recover from T.B., and is finishing another book, 'Born 1925', which I reviewed for 'The Friend' in 1949.

One good piece of news was that the *Catchpools* have now got back to Germany for a considerable time and are wardens of the rest centre at Bad Pyrmont.

Three days before I left for America on June 22nd in Moscow it was reported that the USSR had agreed to attend talks with Britain and France on the Marshall Plan for European aid. The talks actually started on June 27th.

The day before I left the Government announced that the milk allowance was to be cut to two and a half pints a week. We had used powdered milk all the time I was in Germany and I was naturally disappointed. However I knew this was in great part due to the disastrous winter we had all been through.

I have kept some of the menus of the meals we received on the 5 day crossing in the 'Queen Elizabeth' which followed. I had never seen anything like it in my life before. In addition, everywhere I went in America with Friends I was presented with quart bottles of full cream milk.

One more date and event I wish to include in part one of this journal, to set it against the historical background, is June 15th, for on this day the headlines in the press, in large letters, proclaimed that India's Moslem and Hindu leaders Jinnah and Nehru had accepted the British plan for the partition of India and Pakistan.

PART 2

COLOGNE WITH F.R.S. 125

SEPTEMBER 23RD 1947 – MARCH 16TH 1948

It's up to you again to make things happen and hope for the best.
Anon

Contents

Following a Star: Introduction to Part 2

In Part 1, I quoted from Roger Wilson's 'Quaker Relief' p247. I must include at this point the second half about our team's work with the young people of Cologne, culled from official reports.

"While team members were looking for some means of interesting these [post war] youths and girls, a gift arrived from the A.F.S.C. of a 72-foot Swedish wooden barrack, which was erected on a drab site under a railway embankment in an unlovely part of city. A motley group drifted up to watch these uniformed foreigners digging: a gypsy or two from the neighbouring encampment, a small boy named Willi in very ragged clothes. Before long they had borrowed spades and joined in, and the others too; and by the time the hut was complete, it had been well and truly adopted by the 'unorganisierte Jugend' of the neighbourhood. The name became a kind of cachet for the ever increasing swarm of boys and girls who gravitated thither every evening and often throughout the day; young toughs who would have scorned the respectably instituted youth clubs under church leadership which marched to rallies carrying banners. The history of the 'unorganised youth' of Cologne would fill a book in itself; their unshakeable loyalty to the Centre they had built, resisting all efforts to interest them in other more established clubs which were crying out for membership; their attempt at self government and the epic part played by the volunteer opposition (an element of British democracy which seemed to wear a special aura of romance for their eyes) – all carried along on a tide of voluble Kölner exuberance and bonhomie quite emphatically 'unorganised'. The Centre grew and extended its premises; a day time play and feeding centre for the little children was established, and a cobbler and a sewing room installed, and it was one of the projects which the Friends Service Council took over, with A.F.S.C. financial support, when F.R.S. closed in 1948." [And developed into a Nachbarschaftsheim or Neighbourhood or Community Centre]

"In consequence of activities of this sort, all the German welfare teams found themselves collecting little knots of personal acquaintances, eager to talk and to re-establish contact with an outside world. This was not limited to youth, but a great many of the team's friends were young, perhaps because young people felt even more at a loss than their elders when the ideas on which they had been brought up fell suddenly into disrepute. In Berlin and in Aachen these groups grew to such an extent that both teams found premises which they turned into a special kind of community centre – in Berlin a 'Youth House', in Aachen a centre where groups of all ages met for discussion, music, study, social service, art and handicrafts, modelling and sewing. Groups in touch with almost every team were fired with altruistic zeal and launched out into all kinds of public work, from rubble clearing to collecting firewood for the aged, or making toys for the children of refugees. The summer of 1947 brought a spate of work camp schemes, some of them international, in which F.R.S. had the help of the German I.V.S.P. and other bodies."

September 1947

Return to Germany

Tuesday 23rd. Set sail again for Germany, my call forward at last having come through. Every time one crosses the Channel the system seems to change, which all adds to the muddle and general confusion. It was a smooth comfortable crossing.

On the way over I met *John Goodland* who was at Leighton Park in my time, and now in Political Control branch of C.C.G. Intelligence at Dusseldorf, who does quite a bit of youth work in his spare time. Also met *Roger Stanger*, a Friend of New Barnet meeting, and ex F.A.U. member and now in one of the Red Cross teams in the Rhur. So this provided good company on the way over.

Wednesday 24th. Up on deck by 5.30 to see that we were already at the Hook of Holland, and a lovely sunrise gradually brought soft colours to the flat Dutch landscape. Instead of going to the transit camp for breakfast, as on previous occasions we got straight onto a C.C.G. train and had breakfast almost immediately. Travelling by this route one crosses the Dutch frontier into Germany at Nymegen, and down to Krefeld. It was just 15 months ago that I first came into Germany at Krefeld and proceeded up through the Rhurgebiet, Duisberg, Mülheim, Essen, Bochum, Dortmund and Hamm. So that it was interesting to compare the conditions with that journey.

Firstly one noticed that there were no children begging and crying along the line, or at the stations. There were more rust and weeds everywhere, the crops looked dried up after a hot and barren season. But there were more signs of life and hope in these sheltered Rhur towns. More factory chimneys were smoking and coal mines working. More houses had been patched up, and made habitable, though there was precious little new building going on. There was more livestock in the fields, more cows, goats, and single sheep tethered and being used as goats. The stations were still crowded with pale drably dressed Germans who stared at us, not with hostility but with expressionless faces. I particularly looked at their shoes, which were not as bad as I expected. After the luxury of New York it is still a ghastly and a moving sight to go through all that rubble and ruin, dust and poverty, and one still feels uncomfortable eating in the train in full sight of waiting Germans. But somehow I felt more at home amongst all this than I did in New York.

The train arrived at Bad Oeynhausen at 7.00 and I was met. Back at H.Q.5 at Vlotho supper was ready and many familiar faces gave me a cheery welcome, and were interested to hear about America. But there wasn't much time for much more than a wash afterwards and a rush to get my papers ready to travel on to Berlin by the night train.

I felt I was lucky not only to get on the night train, but to get a sleeper and a good night's sleep on the train.

Back to Berlin

Thursday 25th. Arrived in Berlin once more soon after 7 a.m. No one to meet me, but got a taxi, and was back in the billet just as Fritz was ringing the 'getting up' gong. The staff gave me a wonderful welcome.

Visit to the Jugendhaus

In the evening I went to see the Youth House – now called 'Jugendhaus' quite simply. It has progressed. It looks a great deal better and work is in full swing. It was recently opened by *Brigadier Hinde*, with *Colonel Alan Andrews* and all buttons were pressed to get repairs under way. So it now also has water and light. This evening there was a lecture by a Greek journalist on Greece, in the International series, and chaired for the first time by a German girl and boy members of the Jugendheim, and very successfully. The policy now is for us to withdraw as much as possible and leave it to them. So each group sent a representative to a House meeting and democratically, (though they did not realise it) a House Committee was elected to serve with the joint relief teams' Youth Committee in running the place – deciding on programmes etc.

Three F.A.U. Post war service (P.W.S.) lads are also living in the place, ready to do odd jobs in the house and mix in with activities. One of these is *Christopher Alexander*, son of my Housemaster at Leighton Park, also *John Gray* son of the late headmaster of Bootham. They are a very fine addition. *Marianne Braum* still looks after the place with her brother. Many groups and activities are now in full swing.

Visit to the Mittelhof (A.F.S.C.)

Friday 26th. Went down to the Mittelhof Neighbourhood centre in Nikolassee to see *Elmore McKee* and the others to report to the American Friends on my visit to the States and to the A.F.S.C. office in Philadelphia, and to deliver letters. This place has also greatly improved and is now a flourishing concern. While I was away it was also officially opened and is now in full swing with the help of German Quakers and *Naomi Jackson* A.F.S.C. (formerly working in Finland), and later *Mary Jewell* from our team will also help.

During the afternoon I had a long talk with Sofie Quast, to bring me up to date with the progress made in our work, and conditions and events during my absence. She still has not been able to get glass for her windows. She could at 600 RM. per pane! We went along to see her garden, which considering the dry season and the sand has done remarkably well. The English seeds I had had sent over, had done particularly well, and the tomatoes we had fetched from Lichtenrade – but Paul had spent hours of his free time watering. It had been poor for fruit, but Sofie had managed to bottle enough beans and fresh vegetables and fruit for about one good meal per week. The boys too have got a little Chinchilla rabbit, to which they are devoted.

Sofie told me that all Germans are dreading the winter, *John Bourke* too was terribly pessimistic. It is interesting that Black Market prices are falling simply because of the shortage of money, all except for fuel, which goes up. Rumours are still flying and refugees coming from the East, and people thinking and planning to move West.

Saturday 27th. The Germans cutting my hair in the barber's shop after giving me a warm welcome, went on to say that conditions had not improved, and thought a war with Russia as soon as possible to get it over with was the best thing! I groaned.

I finished up the day with a visit to the Staats Oper with Sofie to see Wagner's "The Flying Dutchman", an impressive and lovely performance. We had supper together afterwards and long talks about the future work in Berlin.

Britain decides to quit Palestine.

Though I felt I should have gone to Meeting I could not resist *Roger Thorpe's* invitation to hear *Furtwängler* conduct the Berlin Philharmonic in a Beethoven programme with *Yehudi Menuhin*[1] playing the Violin Concerto. This was a very great musical event for Berlin and it was certainly a superb concert. I have never heard anything like the applause that the Germans gave.

We were expecting *Douglas and Dorothy Steere* (A.F.S.C.) to lunch. They kept us waiting a considerable time and then rang up to say they would be later still. Some of the team who had other engagements had to go, and the rest of us did not wait. Casually with *Bob Byrd* they turned up at 2.45, as Americans do. We were rather put out but otherwise it was extremely nice to see them for they are fine people. I had met Dorothy a few weeks previously at Pendle Hill, Philadelphia.

Klaus Hellwig called in the afternoon to bring me a large basket of tomatoes and fruit and a small book of German garden birds, as a farewell present from the family.

I spent the evening at the Youth House talking with the F.A.U. boys and playing chess.

Monday 29th. *Mr Monro* came to see me from the S.A. team. He's interested in taking on my work in co-operation with Sofie.

Farewells

John Seed – now a British Red Cross officer insisted on taking Brian Burtt and me out to dinner and the theatre as my farewell "binge". He is a member of the officers' club. It certainly was a fantastic meal for Berlin and I felt rather guilty. We enjoyed seeing "Arsenic and Old Lace" afterwards. Meanwhile at all odd moments I am collecting up my things from here, there and everywhere and packing them into crates.

In a Ministerial reshuffle Sir Stafford Cripps was promoted to Minister for Economic Affairs.

His post as President of the Board of Trade goes to Harold Wilson who now joins the Cabinet as its youngest member at the age of 31. Atlee regards him as a possible high-flyer. The Government asks women to avoid the trend for longer skirts and save cloth in the national interest.

Tuesday 30th. I went with Sofie and Paul to *Dr Feigel's* school at Lichtenrade. I had promised them when I went to America to give a lecture on my return, and they got in touch with me at once. I expected, as before, to just enter quietly and speak to one or two forms, but found on my arrival a programme arranged and about 200 boys and girls waiting in the large Hall. There was a song, speeches, a violin solo, and then I gave my talk about my experiences in the U.S.A. Afterwards I was presented with a wooden bowl full of grapes, pears and apples and flowers. It was a most touching farewell and I was most moved by their appreciation and thanks for the little help I had been able to give. All the staff said how the children loved to have me and were sad to see me go. There is a most lovely atmosphere in this school. Afterwards I had coffee with Dr Feigel and a few of the staff for whom I have a very high regard, particularly *Hildegard Dericksweiler.*

---

[1] *First performance by any 'foreign' soloist since the end of the War.*

In the evening for the last time I was able to take Roger to the Staats Oper to see Tchaikovsky's "Eugene Onegin" with Fiona Lemnitze. It was a very fine performance. Afterwards we had dinner together at Harnack House – the American officers' luxury club, which, (so *Vera Brittain* told me,) was redecorated with German priority materials, and which, if it was so, is a scandal. Certainly inside it was like being back in America.

October 1947

Wednesday 1st. Took some parcels and things to the Hellwigs in Tegel and spent a lovely afternoon with them – such a happy, loving and friendly family. Their garden, and the rabbits and chickens are always interesting. Klaus had made a raft with the 6 oil drums I had given him, from the design in the Penguin holiday book. With this raft they had had great fun and it was their only excitement for the summer holidays.

John Watson J.P.'s Visit

Jean Dodds of Penal Branch C.C.G. and now in charge of Juvenile prisons for the whole of the Zone 'phoned me up to say she was in Berlin and that *John Watson J.P.* the London Juvenile Court Judge wanted to see me and Sofie to ask questions. Could I have dinner with him at the Savoy? I don't like the Savoy but I couldn't miss the chance of a talk with J.W. who has been so kind about my survey. I had a long interesting talk with Jean Dodds first while J.W. was out visiting prisons, and *Major Sabo* the U.S. juvenile court judge. She gave me her report on Approved Schools in the Zone.

Over dinner had a long talk with J.W. who was simply horrified by conditions in Berlin for delinquents, had already done an amazing lot, and was determined to return to Berlin, and announced that his schedule must be rearranged so that he could see me again in Cologne. Considering he is deformed from paralysis, he is a man of amazing energy, vitality and enthusiasm. It is wonderful that he was invited out and given a free hand. He was tickled that he had been given the equivalent rank of General and therefore a very, very V.I.P.! We went on talking until it was almost time for his train to leave, so that by that time it was too late to go on to Mittelhof as I had intended.

Thursday 2nd. Spent the whole day getting myself and the vehicle prepared for tomorrow's journey.

Last Farewells

Before I knew that the staff had made a farewell cake for me, I had already promised to spend the last evening with Sofie, and left all final arrangements to her. We also went along to see *Alfred Thoran*, back 'Schwarz'[1] from the Zone, where he had gone to make a few enquiries about the future, work and living and so on. He looked tired. R.A.H.[2] is attempting to get *Peter Thoran* to Sidcot, and he and his brother and sister are in correspondence with the Sidcot people, in whom they take a great interest. We had a really lovely evening together. Sofie gave me a beautiful cushion cover as a leaving present.

---

[1] *Illegally*
[2] *Dick Harman*

I Leave Berlin

Friday 3rd. Up at 6 a.m. when there was still bright moonlight. A hasty breakfast at 6.30 with Bob and then loaded up the Fordson truck with rations and last things, picked up *Ingela Keup* and by 7 a.m. started down the autobahn.

The journey was without mishap, and though it was bitterly cold and in some places foggy, we were across the Russian Zone and through both barriers by 10 a.m. and freezing, but we warmed up with tea and buns at the N.A.A.F.I. at Helmstedt. I filled up with petrol and we were off again past Brunswick and Hannover. It turned into a most glorious hot sunny day with wonderful views.

Arrived at Vlotho by 1.30 and ate our lunch on the bridge in the sun. There was a bit of unloading to do and certain 2nd year equipment replacements to obtain before we could set off down the autobahn again for Detmold, which was about another hour's run. Finally arrived at 4.15 in time for tea – a run of about 265 miles.

FRS Conference

The actual conference was held in the Berkenhof Hotel – Pivitsheide – about 7 km out of Detmold, and we were all in separate billets in Detmold. These had to be found – so after tea I set off with a load of about 8 people to deliver to their billets which I had to find and then collect them up and take them back to the hotel for supper. This was a long process and I was already dog tired after the long drive and it was beginning to get dark after a glorious, unforgettable sunset.

After supper there was a Meeting for Worship, but most people were very tired. The exhaust fumes from the Ford had made my eyes very sore.

Finally I had to take all 8 back to their billets, which I managed to find without trouble in the dark, much to the surprise of us all, and explain to them how to get to a central point where I could pick them up next morning. Then I had to park the truck in the military car park and walk back to my billet. Like a foolish virgin I had not brought any oil with me, and the truck was almost empty. However I managed to scrounge some from a wise one in another team.

I had a sofa in the dining room of Frau Lange's – a charming middle-aged lovely woman, whose son had been killed in the war, and her daughter married. I was ready to drop into bed – as it was midnight but she wanted naturally to talk and know a little bit about us.

Saturday 4th. Collected up the others safely by 8.30, and drove to the hotel for breakfast at 9.00 a.m. This was followed by a Meeting for Worship, and there followed a discussion on the future of F.R.S., closing the work down in May '48 and the handing-over to the Friends Service Council (F.S.C.). This was led by *Kenneth Lee* of F.S.C. and *David Jenkins. Jean Hughes* (a cousin of mine) was also there.

Further discussions followed in the afternoon and in the evening we entertained the Municipal officials and their wives. Following a speech by the Regierungspräsident, the Burgomeister, whom *Bunty Harman* and I had to entertain, also spoke. We only had tea to offer and I thought it was rather a sticky evening and was relieved when a local trio energetically played a Haydn and then a Beethoven trio.

Copy of the hand-made card expressing thanks and gratitude to the staff

Edith Snelgrove, Magda Kelba, Morna Smith, Neville Bailey and Liz at the Detmold Conference, 1947

The Open Door Youth Club Conference, Cologne

Sunday 5th. German Friends attended today's morning Meeting and discussions, which were on the needs of German Friends, and in the afternoon the East-West question was discussed.

In the evening *Ron See* had arranged an entertainment in which he, *William Hughes* with limericks, *Geoffrey Wareing* and I took part with mimes and sketches.

In Washington, Truman appeals for a meatless Tuesday and a Thursday without poultry and eggs, to aid Europe.

Journey to Cologne

Sunday 5th. After Meeting the conference broke up. I packed all my belongings into the Cologne ambulance, and with Bunty Harman and *Roger Craven* (A.F.S.C.) we set off again another 150 miles down the autobahn.

On the way we picked up a small fair-haired, dirty little girl, and later a man going in our direction, and we stopped at the N.A.A.F.I. and Y.M.C.A. canteens on the way to get cakes and rolls for lunch. The small girl ate hers ravenously, and Roger pumped her with bread, peanut butter and sweets.

I took over driving half way and at about 3.30 the great black cathedral loomed up across the Rhine, and we were in Cologne.

One's first impression of this city is that there is more general destruction over a much wider area than anywhere else, and many of the streets, though one can walk through, still remain uncleared, and the rubble covered with weeds. There seems to be more dust and dirt, more shabby people and more traffic than in Berlin, and the trams which have glass are far more overcrowded. This area too is occupied by Belgian troops.

Arrival in Cologne[1]

I found several letters waiting for me, including one from *Basil Henriques* enclosing the "Probationer" and the "Magistrate" in which my report had been summarised. Also a letter from the Howard League for Penal Reform.

Went to see the Swedish barrack presented by A.F.S.C.[2] and used in the day time as a convalescent home for up to 15 undernourished children, and in the evening as a Youth Centre – two nights a week for "unattached" youth.

Roger Craven is erecting a Nissen hut close by to be used as work rooms. The Swiss Red Cross have Barracks near by, and the Arbeiter Wolfahrt are building their offices next door. The aim is to form a Neighbourhood Centre.

One's heart went out to the little children being fed there, for they were so thin and pale, but surprisingly full of energy and noise, and obviously so pleased to see Bunty and Roger back again.

George Hogle is another A.F.S.C. worker who lives in the billet, but he is loaned to work with the F.O.R. and *Pastor Mensching.*

Our billet here is larger than the one in Berlin and more convenient, though the bedrooms are barely furnished. There are however better washing arrangements, and

---

[1] *See also Auden's friend, Stephen Spender's poetic description of Cologne, 'European Witness '46,* The Thirties and After, *Fontana, 1978, p.133.*

[2] *Bunty Biggs says it was not AFSC but Swedish Quakers.*

central heating if we get the coke. But there are no sheets for the beds, as we had in Berlin.

First Jobs

Tuesday 7th. Took my vehicle – a Ford 5 cwt. truck with a new engine, a few miles down the Rhine to a small village called Sürth, where I picked up a load of washing for some refugees living in a large school in another village about 5 miles the other side of Cologne called Frechen. On the way stopped at the main station to pick up a crate of apples which had been broken into and only half were left. Took the load out to Frechen and dumped it there.

This F.R.S. 125 section has its team meeting after supper on Tuesdays following an "at home", when Allied and German guests can drop in and chat together socially.

Wednesday 8th. Went out to Bergische-Gladbach, a small town about 10 miles east of Cologne across the Rhine, to pick up a load of Glass Wool from the Glass factory there to be used as insulation for the Nissen hut. While loading I got covered from head to foot with the stuff and, without gloves, my hands got full of tiny pricks, as did my arms and neck. Took it all back and stored it by the barrack.

On the way I picked up a painful piece of rubble in my eye, or it may have been a small piece of glass which flew up off my clothes. The engine of the Ford gets so hot that I had to open the windscreen and there was so much dust about.

Thursday 9th. Went along to the M.I. room for my annual inoculations. Had three shots in the same arm; Tetanus, Typhoid and Diptheria. They could not remove the piece from my eye.

During the afternoon had a very interesting interview with *Oberinspector Peter Schmidt* governor of the Siegburg juvenile prison which holds about 800 boys. I read an interesting report of his that the conditions there are much the same as I had found in Berlin, and also the causes of delinquency. I was most struck by the fine spirit of this young man – devoted to the welfare of these boys, and promised to go and visit the prison after I had obtained formal permission from Miss Dodds. He is shortly to visit England for 3 weeks with *Mr Malone* to study the Borstal system in England.

By the evening I was seriously beginning to feel aware of the effects of the 3 inoculations and in considerable pain went to bed early.

In London the government cuts the bacon ration to one ounce a week.

Friday 10th. Though I got up for a breakfast I felt so ill and thoroughly depressed and useless that I decided to spend the whole day in bed, and slept for most of it.

In the afternoon received the great news by post that my sister Gill had given birth to a small son Ian on Oct. 2nd. I was an uncle. By the evening I was feeling considerably better and got up for supper.

Saturday 11th. Felt very well again. Got my truck going again, after having to have a tow, and changed the water in the tank for "anti-freeze". Found some petrol had been stolen while it was in the car park.

In the morning went out again to Bergische-Gladbach to pick up the last load of 14 bales of glass wool from the glass factory there – gave a Belgian soldier a lift out there. This area is occupied by Belgian troops.

On Saturday afternoons at this house *Winnie Wood*, in conjunction with a German Friend, gives a series of talks on different aspects of Quakerism, and these people are available to answer questions and supply literature to those who want it. I attended the one today which was on 'The Friends' attitude to the sacraments'. There were only very few people there, but they were very interested and young people. Generally there are a lot more but today there was at this same time a special F.O.R. meeting. The F.O.R. is strong in this area.

Roger Craven is at present sharing my room. We have already had some interesting discussions together on the question of pacifism and alternative forms of service. He talks about the 3rd World War as inevitable, and the position he is going to take in it. We also talked about the question of disciplining ourselves with regard to the company we kept and the entertainment we accept, e.g. how far one should accept hospitality from people who live luxuriously, or drink alcohol at meals or who black marketeer, who nevertheless may be specialists at their jobs etc. and 'good' people, and the risk involved in refusing their company at least in their environment and often as a result their friendship or regard. I know John Woolman's answer to this question – but in modern life these occasions come upon one so quickly, and normally one all too easily becomes unaware of them or lets them slip by unthought about, or one fails to make a decision and acts quickly on it and in time. I do not always feel a strong enough spirit to make that refusal. It is part of the question, shall one stand away from the main stream of life, or shall one take part and be in on it? It is hard to know where the line comes.

Sunday 12th. The morning Meeting for Worship was held at the team's house. It was small – only about 10 people altogether.

In the afternoon went to an interesting 'Versöhnungsbund (F.O.R.) and Friedens-gesellschaft' joint meeting in the Martin Luther hall at which one of the visiting 4 Dutch pastors *(Pf. Striet)* spoke on the guilt question, freedom and German relations. There followed an interesting and heated discussion – all talking and arguing at once.

One of the other Dutch pastors *(Pf. Hugenholz)* has been staying with us. He too is a very fine man.

Monday 13th. Spent practically the whole day scraping the rust off the corrugated iron pieces that cover the Nissen hut and painting them.

In the evening joined the youth in the barracks. It was a dancing and games evening. They are a difficult but interesting lot, certainly hard to control and rather too many. Some things were stolen from my Ford 15 cwt. outside – probably by some of the gypsy children living in some of the caravans which have just settled nearby. Who can blame them?

Today for the first time a U.S. plane broke the sound barrier over California with a noise like a clap of thunder at over 600 m.p.h.

Wednesday 15th. Another day spent at the barracks painting and scraping metal sheets for the Nissen hut. Shared a mid-day bowl of soup with the children and a vitamin tablet. They are a most touching lot and will be leaving on Friday, so this afternoon there is an "Abschiedsfeier" or party given to the parents. I stayed to watch the little play they gave which was very sweet, and the songs they sang.

In the evening I went to the Toc H club where *Mr Greenwood* of Education (Mil.Gov.) runs an English discussion group for German and English people. The topic was supposed to be what it will be like in the year 2047, but actually it developed into a political and economic discussion on the probable events of the next few years – East versus West , World War 3 – causes of war and so on – which was nevertheless interesting.

Thursday 16th. From 9.30 – 3.30 I drove *Frl. Hilda Vogel* the Kreis-Jugendpflegerin – a Youth Welfare Officer – round to Wesseling and Brühl, two small towns near Cologne, to interview boys who had been charged with some offence and had been summoned for a court hearing. Her job was to provide a comprehensive report for the court on each case. It was very interesting to go into the lives and families of these boys and their places of employment, and talk to their bosses. Some of the refugee families were living in the most filthy conditions. In most of the families there were about 8 children and all were hungry, and the crime was stealing food or coals. I saw one filthy room where two small children were being fed, and the place was crawling with flies.

I visited *Frl. Prenzel's* group of English teachers at a nearby school who were being addressed by *Dr Beckhoff* (the Mil.Gov. officer in charge of Köln university) on his recent 5 week visit to America. It was interesting to compare his impressions with those of my recent visit.

Friday 17th. Went to the offices of the Kreis Jugendamt and met *Herr Preuss* the leader, and *Peter Moll* the Catholic youth leader. We collected up various things from here, there and everywhere in Cologne and then went out via Bergische-Gladbach to a Youth Hostel at Kürthen – east of Cologne, and on again through glorious wooded country in the best autumn colours to Marienfelds about 30 miles away. Having picked up a load of food left over from the summer youth camps we started back and finally arrived home at 8.0 p.m. after a long and tiring day.

Saturday 18th. Met *Heinz Stuckmann*, a Catholic Youth Leader, in the Stadt Jugendamt and arranged with him to see various institutions dealing with delinquency.

In the afternoon went to Bonn in the Volkswagen. It was a glorious clear sunny day and the Rhine looked very blue, and the Siebengebirge behind Bonn, very inviting. *Frl. Cunnie*, our 'Hausmutter', came with me. We went to inspect the Catholic home for wandering and homeless youth started by *Kaplan Hieronymi*, a fine young youth leader whom all the boys obviously liked. There was a very nice spirit in the place and a collection of about 50 boys from all over Germany, including one from Berlin.

The place was a renovated bombed building and some windows were still without glass, so it was bitterly cold. There were no electric light bulbs and the place was in darkness by 6 o'clock until 7.30 a.m. The boys slept in double or treble tiered bunks with no sheets, on straw sacks and with only one blanket each. It was pathetic.

Sunday 19th. Quaker Monthly and morning Meeting held at the team's house. About 30 people were present. *Fred Tritton's* letter to German Friends was discussed which included the suggestion that German Friends should form their own Church Discipline and get better organisation into their business meetings.

Also the handing over of the Youth Barracks with German Friends as trustees was discussed.

Prison Visit

In the afternoon I went to Siegburg to spend the afternoon with *Oberinspector Peter Schmidt* and his wife at their house by the prison. This was a very pleasant friendly time. He is a fine man and we came to a close understanding.

Juvenile Court

Tuesday 21st. Spent the morning at the Juvenile Court. It is tragic that there is so little idea of what a juvenile court should be like. Fortunately though, the judge was a fairly good one – one of the best I had seen, and the main thing was that he was deeply interested and understanding, and co-operated well with the Jugendamt Fursorgerinnen.

During the morning I saw 7 or 8 cases of serious theft, mostly second offenders. Nearly all of them were for stealing coal, clothes or potatoes, and a pathetic story behind each one, so often involving parents in the guilt. At one time the judge said "We are all hungry, we all need coal and clothes – we stand all of us in bitter need, but what if we all stole just what we needed all the time – there would be no sense, no order, and fair distribution, and rationing would be impossible, even fewer people would get anything – so that the need would if possible become even greater." Clearly many families are desperate.

In the afternoon I took *Hilda Vogel* round in the car again to visit some of her cases in Brühl who were due to appear in court in a few days' time.

Martin Niemöller's Visit[1]

Wednesday 22nd. The great event today *was Pastor Martin Niemöller's* speech to the Evangelisches Kirchengemeinde Landkreis Köln – an audience of several thousand, quiet, deeply interested and slow to respond. Niemöller spoke for 1½ hours. For me it was doubly interesting because he spoke about his six months' visit to the U.S. and on the state of the church there, as he saw it. To my mind he gave a very rosy and exaggerated picture, though I agreed with his conclusions. He said it was the congregation in America that was the church and who did the social work. He said there was a strong unity and working together of the churches in the ecumenical movement. This does not tally with my experience or Dr Ivan Gould's statement that religion is the most divisive force in American community life today. He also stated that 50% of American people go to church – the churches are full. Again I did not find this, though it was no doubt true to say that 50% were "book" members or registered on the books of the churches.

Out of 60 sermons that he had heard, however, from only one had he come out of the church feeling a different person. The majority were recipes for pious and happy living, and that the Cross of Christ and the Sermon on the Mount were not the central theme to be found. The American church was a young Church and therefore needed all our united prayer to lead it in the right way so that it might and must develop into the only real hope for the future. All through the Hitler period the American Church had prayed for the German church, now they need all our prayers.

It was my privilege to be introduced to him afterwards and to have some conversation with him at tea at the Toc H club, when other Mil.Gov. officials were there.

Colonel White, the commander of Stadt Köln, was telling him that it was getting increasingly difficult to control the people of Köln, and instanced the tram strike, where citizens had rushed a tram as usual to get on, started fighting and a conductor was seriously wounded. So all the trams went on strike. McMillan pointed out that the

---

[1] *'Martin Niemöller (1892). A Lutheran pastor, who was ordained after serving as a U boat commander in the First World War. At first a supporter of National Socialism he later actively opposed it. He led a campaign against the Nazification of the German Church, was dismissed in 1934, arrested in 1937 & later went through gaol & concentration camp, remaining a prisoner throughout the Second World War. In 1946 he proclaimed Germany's war guilt at the International Missionary Council in Geneva, & in 1947 was elected first Bishop of the newly formed Evangelical Church of Hesse-Nassau. In 1961 he became a president of the World Council of Churches. Joined F.O.R. in 1954 as a convinced pacifist. He died in March 1984. Alec Lea in a letter to The Friend of March 16th 1984 paid a tribute to Martin Niemöller & his message at the conclusion of the 1957 Aldermaston March. Niemöller quoted from Deuteronomy 30:19 & exhorted the marchers to "choose life". I was unable to take part in that first Aldermaston March but joined the second in 1958 with other staff & pupils from Sibford, but on the same rostrum as Niemöller was a Sibford parent, Harold Steele, a Quaker from Malvern & the father of Hugh Steele, who also made an impassioned speech. He had just previously been at his own expense to Japan in a vain attempt to join a group of people who wanted to sail a ship into the area of the Pacific in which the first British H-bomb was going to be tested. I was acting in loco-parentis for Hugh while he was away.*

people had got to the same state as in England during the height of the difficulties when little things easily irritated the nerves, and that a combination of such little things might easily set something off. "Yes", said Niemöller, "but it also depends upon whether the nerves are embedded in fat".

At tea Niemöller was pessimistic about the future and talked of the 3rd World War as almost a certainty. He saw Europe as a black hole with a vacuum that has to be filled. It will be filled with something, if not democracy by communism or something as evil. He would like, as *Pastor Mensching* and the leaders of the F.O.R. and the German Quakers would like, Germany's destiny to be that of a mediator, and the reconciling power between the East and the West. He thought people had realised that a war over Europe was too expensive, and it would be cheaper for America to have the next one with Russia over the North Pole. Unfortunately he had to go on to give another lecture at the university.

In the evening went to the Toc H discussion group to hear *Miss Dawson* of the Summer Lane Settlement talking on social work.

Film star Ronald Reagan appeared before a Congressional Committee investigating Communism in America today, and warned of the dangers of a witchhunt in Hollywood.

Friday 24th. An expedition with my truck, at the request of *Professor Konig's* son, to visit his farm for a load of vegetables. The village was about 15 miles to the West of Cologne where he had a very large farm. We loaded up with 10 cwt. of cabbages, 1 cwt. of carrots, and a sack of sugar beet. Most of this supply was for himself and his family – but for the transport he allowed us 2½ cwt. of cabbages and ½ cwt. of carrots for our feeding scheme at the barracks.

Saturday 25th. Today Roger and I were to have gone to Brussels, but this was impossible owing to the fact that the Commer has broken down and was beyond local repair.

Visit to Bonn

So instead I took on a load of blankets and mattresses from our bunker to take to the Catholic home for wandering and homeless youth in Bonn. It was a glorious afternoon and after I had delivered the goods, with which they were more than pleased, I spent some time exploring this beautiful little old town, which, though it is very heavily damaged round the region of the Rhine bridge, has not received much destruction elsewhere.

I first went to see Beethoven's birthplace at 20 Bonngasse – a simple little street which includes this humble building. It has been restored to its original condition and is now fitted up as a Beethoven museum. Here in a tiny little garret in the back of the building Beethoven was born. The measurements of the little place were no more than 9 ft. by 12 ft., and I could just, only just, stand upright in the room, which had one tiny little window.

The contents of the museum include numerous busts and portraits of Beethoven, his family and his contemporaries, his quaint pianos, quartet instruments, ear trumpets, scores and letters etc. Many of the scores were illegible and had wild crossings out.

The little house is covered with vines and creepers and in the tiny garden stands a large bronze bust of Beethoven by Aronson, a pupil of Rodin. There were also in the house portraits of his father, a tenor singer, and his grandfather, band-master to the Elector in 1770.

I also went to see the picturesque Münster, a cruciform church with two choirs, four small towers and a tall octagonal principal tower, all beautifully lit and coloured by a dying sun. The west part of the crypt and the part of the church above it date back to the 11th century.

Monday 27th. Spent the evening at the Youth Barrack. I'm beginning to get to know these youngsters, though it is still very difficult to understand Köln Platt Deutsche[1]. Each of them is a little individualist with his own special little problems, jealousies and so on, which are for him or her the most important things. This evening, on Mondays, is the time for the younger group, and mostly we had country dancing. Most of them came to the Barrack because they had nothing better to do.

Some belonged to the "Internationale Strassen Ecke Stehe" – "The International Street Corner Standers", a self-named lot of street corner loafers who were rather tired of loafing about and so came to see what the Quakers were doing. Others were just bored at home and wanted somewhere to go – others were seeking friendship with their own or the opposite sex. Their greatest difficulty at the moment is to learn to get on with each other. For example, the "better educated" boy despises the hut dweller or the gypsy lads and so on.

Tuesday 28th. Another round with *Hilda Vogel* round Brühl district making reports of boys due for the court hearings. During the afternoon an "at home" for German and English guests. During the afternoon *Ron Greenwood* 'phoned up and asked me to take the discussion group at the Toc H club – so I spoke on delinquency problems here in Cologne and Berlin, and a very good discussion followed and many people wanted to see my report.

Wednesday 29th. Picked up *Heinz Stuckmann* and Hilda and went to see the "Kloster zum Guten Hirten", a Catholic Remand home for 280 girls, similar to the one in Berlin. It was well-equipped and doing wonderful work. There was also a warm atmosphere of love and caring.

The Oberschwester again was a beautiful character in her very elegant robes – but one can't help being sorry for the girls in such an institution. Every minute of their lives here they are under supervision, and really it is a very different world, quite divorced from reality outside.

We then went on to see two large orphanages, the Evangelisches Waisenhaus Kupperstift and the Städtischeswaisenhaus. Both of these were for boys and girls up to 14 years of age. The latter had been an enormous organisation for 1,000 people. But both had suffered severely from the bombing and were left in the most primitive state. The little orphans were really pathetic. So thin and pale and with skin diseases – longing for affection, and their beds with only 1 or 2 blankets.

---

[1] *Cologne Dialect – so different from the Berliners*

After lunch at Heinz's house went to see another very badly bombed Catholic orphanage in the centre of the town.

Finally spent the evening coaching the Youth Barrack drama group in a Fairy story play.

We had as our guest *Homer Coppock* of the A.F.S.C. This was of particular pleasure for me because I had met Homer at Quaker Haven (U.S.A.) where I got to know him, and like him greatly. His wife kindly did my laundry for me over there, and so I was able to return a little of their kindness.

Thursday 30th. *Elmore McKee* for breakfast from the Neighbourhood Centre Berlin.

Went over to Metman in the morning to fetch a load of Red Cross supplies from the sub-store there with Erhardt, our mechanic.

In the evening started to coach the beginnings of a ping-pong team at the Barrack. The evening went a little better.

November 1947

Saturday 1st. During the afternoon took over *John Pettigrew's* VIth form schools discussion group. Gerd was giving an account of his visit to England. It was interesting to hear of the things that struck him most. Many of these things were first impressions that had struck me in a similar way when I was in America, i.e. differences in transport and housing – honesty – such as a pile of newspapers being left unattended on the pavement and people putting their pennies into a tray and helping themselves. He also noticed the courtesy and kindness of people to each other in comparison with here in Germany, and of people's general feeling of freedom, and of being treated as a human being. Many of these were impressions also gained by Gisela after her visit.

This group, following Gerd's experience in England, were keen to try an English debate, and to try and make the group into more of a real discussion group rather than a lecture and question group, as so many of these groups are.

Monday 3rd. Another morning with *Hilda Vogel* interviewing boys prior to court proceedings in Brühl and Frechen.

During the afternoon I went to see *Dr Beckhoff*, Mil.Gov. education officer in charge of Köln University about Bristol University's report on Cologne, and my own report which he had asked for to circulate through the university, and to discuss my giving a series of lectures and taking a discussion group in the English faculty.

He gave me a very interesting confidential fortnightly education report which included a talk by *Mr Simmonds* on Juvenile Delinquency in Berlin. Amongst his remarks were the following: "The term 'Juvenile Delinquency' is a misnomer in the unsettled society such as is found in Germany today. There are two moralities – the official one of the planners and the unofficial one of the Black Market. This engenders a new attitude to society, as a result of which the only distinction between the delinquent and the non-delinquent is that between the caught and the un-caught."

Some account was also given of *Jean Dodds'* report on approved schools in the British Zone – rather damping I thought, and also a very interesting supplement on education in the Russian Zone, too long to summarise here.

The Nobel Peace Prize

Today the news was confirmed in the newspapers that the British and American Quakers, that is to say the A.F.S.C. and F.S.C. had won the Nobel Peace prize. There was much rejoicing about this, and it acted as an encouragement to all of us.

Went to a symphony concert at the university, conductor *Gunther Wand.*

Tuesday 4th. News from *Sofie* that *Staatsanwalt Pöratek* is to set up an institute in Berlin for juvenile welfare with a special interest in the problems of endangered and delinquent youth.

Dr Kate Mende the aged welfare worker, who until recently, was welfare adviser to O.M.G.U.S., will be librarian. She is an excellent person for this.

Sofie was also invited by *Mary Bailey* to meet the Home Office Delegation which proved to be very valuable. She had also had an afternoon with *John Watson J.P.* and had been invited by him to attend his juvenile court in London, during her visit to England in a few weeks' time. This visit is to be sponsored by the German Reconstruction Group.

The 2 C.A.R.E. packages I sent her from America had just arrived, taking exactly 3 months.

She had also had an interesting afternoon with *Mrs Bell*, the Bishop of Chichester's wife.

An interesting letter also from my parents telling me of their visit to Delhi, of how they had met *Ranjit Chetsingh* back from America (where I had met him) and England, to appeal for help with the desperate situation in India. They had been helping, for a day or two, with *Horace Alexander* and the F.S.U.[1] with the refugee problem in a huge camp just outside Delhi in an old ruined fort for 60,000 Muslims waiting to get into Pakistan. My mother said that there were no sanitary arrangements and practically no water. Conditions were altogether appalling and comparable to Buchenwald. The F.S.U. had set up an Enquiry Bureau and Post Office in the camp, two greatly needed things. They saw the most pitiful sights and heard terrible stories of atrocities.

They had also attended with H.A. a meeting between him and *Gandhi* who had paced up and down the room talking together for half an hour.

The letter took only a week to reach me.

This was an interesting day for me. I picked up *Herr Herbrand* from the Lindenburg hospital (the 2nd largest in Germany, I was informed, the biggest being Charitée in Berlin). With the truck drove about 70 miles N.W. through Neuss, Krefeld and Geldern to a little village called Twisteden about a mile from the Dutch frontier near Nijmegen. We were given a wonderful lunch at the largest farm in the village – where they were very well off, but simple sincere Catholic folk. Everyone was most kind.

Afterwards we went round to various little farms loading up with vegetables. The type of land and farming with greenhouses is very similar to the Dutch across the border and there are windmills about as well, and the land is flat. The autumn colours in the woods were beautiful, though not so vivid as in previous years – too yellow, probably because of the very dry season.

---

[1] *Friends' Service Unit*

Finally we loaded on a little pig, which made us all laugh with its comical grunts and squeaks, and started off for home. At the hospital everyone was most kind and grateful, and workmen at once descended on us to unload and get the vegetables stored.

The nuns insisted on giving me some tea, and that I should take a box of fresh vegetables with me because they knew that the Quakers too didn't often have fresh vegetables.

In the evening there was an interesting discussion group at the Toc H led by *Ron Greenwood* on the Level of Industrial Plant, and the question of dismantling factories and reparations[1]. A very heated discussion followed. I am entirely in sympathy with the Germans over this question, but the way they squealed and complained, and the self pity so embarrassed and infuriated me that I found myself arguing in favour of the plan and supporting it! So much Nazi propaganda came out – that the plan was hopeless, leaving Germany crippled and open to Communism – and then the danger to the West and war!! Complete and unfounded pessimism and panic. They take themselves far too seriously, and are just not conscious at all of what the Nazis have done to the world and the motives behind this plan which is far more generous than we all expected.

Wednesday 5th. The games group on Wednesday evenings at the Barrack is beginning to show signs of wanting to form a table tennis team.

Thursday 6th. Spent all the morning going round ironmongers' shops in Köln to find screws and hinges for the doors of the Nissen hut. Everywhere it was the same: an 'Eisenschein'[2] was needed, but all the same we were lucky, and especially when the shopkeepers heard it was for the Quaker Jugendheim they were kind, and either let us have what they had got without the 'Eisenschein' or gave us a little extra to help. I was much impressed by this willingness to bend the rules.

Invited to tea with Bunty by *Leslie Barnes* to meet *Vera Swift* the new assistant youth officer. Vera was in the Salvation Army team in Berlin and worked with us on the Youth committee for which she did a lot of good work – so it is really nice to have her down here. She has come to take charge of more of the girls' side of youth work than that of the boys.

First Drama Production

In the evening the Drama Group of the Youth Centre presented "Prinz Rosenrot and Prinzessin Lilienweiss" – a fairy story. There was great excitement at the club with this first production. At the last moment the Prinz went to hospital with Diphtheria and his place was bravely taken by "Big Willi". The older boys had rigged up a wonderful stage at one end of the Barrack with stretchers and a curtain of blankets, and improvised lighting which was really staggering for its ingenuity.

The costumes too, that were also improvised were really amazing, and they had great fun putting on primitive make up.

---

[1] *I have the feeling that this discussion was influenced by Victor Gollancz's visit to Cologne last November & his book 'In Darkest Germany' that produced the row in Parliament.*

[2] *Iron Certificate or ticket*

The Dress rehearsal before the actual performance was an absolute shambles, it was killingly funny (though unintentionally) and the poor prince could hardly remember a single line, though he had been up all night learning it.

The performance for the rest of the club members which followed was absolutely marvellous, an experience none of us shall ever forget. The prince improvised most of his part and the others responded nobly, at the end the prompter was in a state of collapse; the moon went up and down on string and the curtain jolted, and stuck and the cast enjoyed themselves enormously. It certainly welded them together.

Friday 7th. Another morning spent going round from one ironmonger to the next for odd things for the construction of the Nissen hut. Finally got some assorted nails. Nails and screws of all sizes are practically unobtainable.

The whole afternoon, with a few boys, we tried to remove an enormous tree stump from the back of the barrack. It was loose in its huge socket but even with the 15 cwt. truck pulling, straining and tugging in all directions we could not pull the thing out.

Unlawful Tree Felling for Refugees

Saturday 8th. In the afternoon I took John's German I.V.S.P. group out by truck to a refugee camp at Bergische Gladbach. We then proceeded into the wood near by and, rather to my astonishment, they at once started picking out immature trees and felling them. Down they came, it seemed in a matter of seconds, with a splintering crash, and the sound of the axe and saw resounded and echoed through the wood. The logs were loaded into the back of the 15 cwt. and off we went back to the camp. It crossed my mind at the time that this was rather unusual. We ourselves could not get permission from the Förstmeister to fell any trees. In Berlin we were only allowed to dig out the stumps, so I asked if they had had permission, as the Germans really are so proud of their forests and look after them. They replied that they hadn't the permission but they had it last year and it was alright. They asked the refugees whether the Förstmeister was about, and they said no. So we went ahead felling the second lot.

Just as we began cutting them up along came the Förster on his bicycle. He was a tall handsome lad of 19, in a green uniform with green cocked hat and plume, and a pair of field glasses hanging around his neck. He was furious. A long argument ensued, everyone talking, the young forester shaking with indignation at the destruction all round him, and also by the fact that we had not got permission or even asked him. It was stealing. He was perfectly right, of course. They had tried to get permission 10 times and to do it legally. What alternative had they? Refugees were supposed to get an allocation of brickettes – they hadn't had any. They had to work, they had to keep from freezing during the winter – what could they do but go out and cut some. The Förster understood, but he had his orders, and there were the laws of the Forests – he understood their situation and plight completely.

Actually he was very decent about the whole thing considering the seriousness of the offence, and let us carry away what we had cut – about 4 cubic metres. He took particulars and promised not to report us, but if he caught us again we should get into serious trouble. That put an end to the work. I felt acutely uncomfortable

There were about 50 or 60 refugees, mostly women and children, crowded into this village hall and living there in indescribable conditions. Double bunks, and blankets stretched between were their only privacy. The place, naturally, was dirty and the smell nauseating, and conditions for working unbearable. They were pathetically grateful for the wood we had cut and the fact that someone at last was interested in their welfare. They were loveable people, making the best of appalling situations.

On the way home we called in at an Old People's Hostel which the I.V.S.P. were also caring for, and they too needed wood. By this time it was dark and we finished up for ¾ of an hour in a Tanz-local which was just "warming up".

These are a grand crowd of young lads and girls, very enthusiastic about helping other people in this way and largely inspired by John Pettigrew. They thought the world of him, and always talked about him. They all speak English well.

In the U.K. potatoes are now rationed to 3 lbs. per person per week.

Sun 9th. Went to tea with *Prof. Rothmann* head of the Biology Dept. of Köln University. He is a friend of John Pettigrew's and has been exchanging books with *Penelope Jenkin* my Biol. lecturer at Bristol University. We had a long and very interesting talk about Germany and the East West question. One of those evenings where good conversation is one of the greatest delights in life.

To Brussells for Relief Supplies for Catholic Churches

Monday 10th. Set off with *Mr Topham* and his C.C.G. 3 tonner for Brussels. It was a rainy windy day and leaves were flying – the last of the autumn colours were very beautiful.

The first town we had to go through was Julich. This is quite the worst damaged town I have yet seen in Germany. One has grown used to the ruins in various other towns, but this small place impelled one to look again. It was literally flat, and riding in the 3 tonner one could look over the ruins for miles around with hardly a building left standing. Yet still thousands of people live here. Most of the destruction was caused by the very heavy fighting and artillery bombardment which raged round this little town for days. The farms round the outskirts are all shattered, and the fields still littered with rusty old tanks.

The next town was Aachen, or Aix la Chapelle where we have a F.R.S. team also. This place seemed deader, more characterless and as badly damaged as Cologne. We did not stop but went straight to the frontier a few miles beyond the town. There was no difficulty about getting through either the British or German frontier posts, no visas being required.

After Aachen the road mounts up to a plateau of about 900 ft. from which there is a fine view of Belgium and away on the south across to the Ardennes.

Suddenly the road quickly descends to the industrial town of Liége with its large black slag heaps. Though many of the bridges are down, round the river Maas it is a picturesque and attractive town.

In Belgium one at once notices that the shops, even the village shops, are full of everything one needs to buy, and at this time especially full of fruit, apples, oranges, bananas, grapes and pears. I was also astonished at the number of huge American export 1947 cars, and the little English cars.

The next place of any importance one passes through on the way to Brussels is the attractive old university town of Louvain. Finally we arrived in Brussels at about 3.30 – a drive of about 150 miles, and soon got to *Herr Müller's* house in the Rue Frédéric

Pelletier. Frau Müller at once made us very welcome and prepared a hot cup of coffee and some cream cakes.

Herr Müller at once took me off into the city before the shops closed – because tomorrow, being Armistice Day, they would all be closed, and as it was my first stay in Brussels he was anxious that I should see something of the place.

We took a taxi from the Palais de Cinquantenaire into the city. This Palais, erected for the exhibition of 1880 to commemorate the 50th anniversary of the Revolution, is now a museum. A huge triumphal arch, rather like the Brandenburger Tor in Berlin, joins the two wings of this palace, and the broad Rue de la Loi runs on into the city.

We stopped first to see the enormous church, misnamed a cathedral, of St Gudule founded in the 11th century, burnt down in 1072; but reconstruction began again in 1225. So it is very old and certainly very fine, and quite different from others. It is one of the most impressive Cathedrals 1 have ever been in.

Not far away is the show piece of Brussels – the Grand Place. This wonderful old mediaeval square is the centre of old Brussels. On one side is the pride of Brussels, the old Hotel de Ville and Maison du Roi. All round the rest of the cobbled Square are the lovely old Guild houses in the Renaissance style or of the Spanish dominion. In the soft evening light the buildings were lovely pastel shades of pink and gray and gold.

Gradually all the lights came on and the main Boulevard Anspac became a blaze of colour. We wandered down looking at the shops full of everything at huge prices. It was really lavish. Shops full of jewellery and watches. Windows crammed with toys for Christmas. The streets were filled with excited happy crowds – there seemed to be such a light-hearted atmosphere in the air so noticeable after the heavy numbed and dulled atmosphere in Germany.

We went into photographic shops to buy films – there were plenty, and then into the huge Bon Marché – the main stores in Brussels. It was magnificent and reminded me of course very much of New York. We bought a few things and I strolled about quite amazed at this world's goods and tempted not a little. Everyone was most kind and helpful, and so many people spoke English, whereas I could hardly get out a word of French. All this prosperity, I was told, was due to the rich rewards from the Belgian Congo. An understatement![1]

Finally we went home to a delicious supper and a long talk in the evening until midnight, over a delicious bottle of port wine.

Topham and I shared a bed and I can't say that I slept much.

Remembrance Day in Brussels

Tuesday 11th. It was raining again. We had decided to load up the truck just before lunch and to start home afterwards. So I went down into the town again to try and get near the tomb of the unknown soldier for the Armistice Day service.

Silent crowds lined the pavements of the Rue Royale waiting patiently, in black, with umbrellas up. There were smart police with white helmets – the armed forces, the old veterans with their war medals, many different Allied uniforms, and military bands. A fanfare of trumpets was being played. Suddenly a whistle blew – the police jumped to duty, the soldiers presented arms and saluted – the band played and everyone took

---

[1] *The history of the Belgian colony and King Leopold's reign, and the rape of the Congo, needs to be understood as well as the involvement of H. Roger Casement.*

off hats, as a motor bike escort brought the huge car of the Prince Regent Charles down the road with Mr Mackenzie King[1]. It was all beautifully timed. They stepped out, placed a wreath at the tomb, and the guns went off for the 2 mins. silence. The guns continued to resound as the crowd waited for the huge car to drive back, and the processions began. I took a tram back to Herr Müller's house.

We soon loaded up the truck and after lunch set off home again, Herr Müller riding in the back, amongst the relief supplies and bags of clothing.

Just as it was getting dark we stopped off at Liége for a cup of coffee and some hard boiled eggs and rolls, and to buy some fruit and a little coffee for the team.

My Truck is Impounded at the Belgian Border

We got to the Belgian border at 6 p.m. and the Customs ordered us to back the truck to the office. The customs officials then ordered us to remove the sacks of clothing and shoes from the back so that they could make a passage through to examine the contents at the back. Right at the back, of course under everything they found the parcels of food sent by the Bishops and Catholics in Belgium to their opposite numbers in Cologne and to the Seminary in Bonn.

Müller's export licence contained no permit for food, and so there was naturally great excitement, and they ordered us to unload the whole truck. All the parcels had to be torn open and examined. Everyone spoke heatedly in a kind of Flemish French, and I couldn't understand a single word of what was going on except from their faces that things were serious. After a great deal of argument it was decided to dump the food and let the rest go on. Then suddenly they changed their minds and decided to impound the whole lot, truck and all. There was nothing we could do. The name and address of each parcel – the sender and receiver had to be taken, and then the parcels reloaded onto the truck. We had to leave the whole thing sealed up and backed up against the wall. Apart from all this, just to make things a little more difficult, there was a howling gale going on outside.

We then were allowed, rather than ordered to walk with our personal belongings across the frontier and across the 500 metres of no man's land to the British control post in Germany. This was the longest half mile I can ever remember, battling with the wind, and with Müller's huge battered and heavy suitcase full of food for his sister. Müller and I carried this together till our arms nearly broke. For the first time I realized a little more fully what it must be like to be a refugee these days.

About half way across Müller, who is an old man, and was a hunted fugitive by the Nazis from '36, and a really sick man, could carry the case no longer, and I took it alone the rest of the way. It was pitch black and the tantalising lights of the frontier seemed to approach agonisingly slowly. At last we got there. I was sweating like a pig and ready to drop.

We had decided that all 3 of us would spend the night with the Aachen team and to try and arrange to free the wagon by 'phone from there.

Müller realized too late that it was a mistake for him to cross into Germany and it would have been better for him to stay in Belgium and arrange things from there, as he only had a pass to make the one journey into Germany. However by this time we were too tired to care. Müller looked like death and blood was trickling out of one of his ears.

---

[1] *Canadian Prime Minister*

I asked if it was serious and he replied it was an old war wound and all this excitement had been too much for him. Topham was fed up but patient. The Aachen team at once rose to the occasion and came and fetched us in a truck. We finally got there by 10 p.m., and they provided a meal and beds, but though we were ready to drop straight into bed we had to start 'phoning Brussels and Cologne to tell them what had happened, a laborious process which meant hanging round the 'phone till after midnight. Müller's head dropped onto his chest once or twice as he went off to sleep and the 'phone bell would wake us with a start.

Finally to bed dog tired, dissatisfied with our bad luck, and rather disheartened. It was an anxious time.

In London the Government says that vegetarians will not receive extra potato rations. Reports reached the West indicating that Russia has exploded her first atomic bomb at a secret site in Siberia. The Russians say the 12 lb. device functioned perfectly.

Wednesday 12th. A morning of waiting by the 'phone to hear from Brussels. In the afternoon we decided to go back to the frontier to ask for the wagon's release and to dump the stuff so that Topham could go home with the borrowed C.C.G. truck. But they refused to let us do this at the frontier and so Müller decided that the best thing for him to do was to go back to Brussels and see to things himself. He was confident that everything could be arranged quite easily and that we should be away tomorrow.

Thursday 13th and Friday 14th. Spent these two days waiting by the 'phone impatiently for news. There was only negative information. So filled in the time reading and doing odd jobs for the Aachen team who were most kind, helpful and hospitable to us. The team themselves were going to and fro into Belgium almost daily with 2 Catholic brothers from a neighbouring Cloister, to fetch apples. They had already brought over 180 tons, enough to make ¼ of jam for every inhabitant of Aachen for Christmas.

One evening we saw a charming and artistic marionette show led by *Betty Bowen*, one of the Americans. I also went round with *Leonora M. Bishop* to visit some of her "old ladies", living in awful conditions. Aachen has been left almost characterless and dead, and the bad weather kept it up. The team which also consists of *Vernon Thomas, Olive Goodykoontz* the leader, another American, and *Nell Lunnen*, were a fine lot and there was a very happy atmosphere.

Saturday 15th. Still no news, so that we decided to ring up for a car from Cologne and go back after lunch. The Volkswagen didn't finally find us till nearly 5 p.m. and we were back home to our intense relief in time for supper, where the team had a good laugh about the whole affair.

Sunday 16th. Monthly meeting. The Aachen, Sollingen and Oberhausen teams brought Friends down with them to Meeting. *Magda Kelber* spoke on the future of our work after F.R.S. draws out in May '48.

In Palestine the first British troops leave.

Monday 17th. Today we had snow for the first time this winter.

In the evening I went to the club, but instead of joining in with the folk dancing went to the home of Felix at his invitation. He is one of the older boys at our club and one of the most difficult. He had been running after all the girls in the club and caused considerable difficulties.

Rather to my surprise I found *Felix Eckhardt* had two extremely nice elderly parents. I soon came to the conclusion however that Felix's difficulties were due to the fact that he was an only child and had been very spoilt.

Two English soldiers had been billeted on the family after the last war, his parents told me, and they had been very fond of them. I was given a warm welcome, and they insisted that I should share their meal.

Both Felix and his father are ardent stamp collectors and as I had brought some stamps along for Felix it followed that I must see their collections. They have an enormous collection, one of the biggest and most well arranged I have ever seen. We spent 1½ hrs looking at German stamps alone, so that there was little time or opportunity to speak to Felix alone about his problems. However we managed it on the way back to the Barrack and I discovered how relieved he was and how pleased to find a man who not only understood but was willing to talk things over with him freely and to help him. His parents were too old he told me, and no one else understood.

There seems to be a great need of this kind amongst so many German young people, not only over sex problems, a major part though these play, but other problems too.

Tuesday 18th. Received a request from *Dora Humphries* in Bournville for the names of 40 boys and girls between 5 and 10 to whom the juniors of her Sunday school class could each send a Christmas present.

A Christmas Story[1]

I went along at once to the Kuperstift Protestant orphanage to speak to *Schwester Kathe*. She greeted me with a smile and said: "Ah, good, the Quakers haven't forgotten us." I broached the subject.

"Ah yes", she sighed, "Christmas. The other day I went into Cologne to see what I could buy for the children to brighten their Christmas, a few little presents, some coloured paper or things for the tree. There was absolutely nothing, and the trash that was on sale was much too expensive for us. When I got back the children gathered round and asked me:

"And did you see the Christ Child to-day, Schwester?" "Yes", she replied, looking down at their upturned expectant faces.

Their bright beady eyes searching her face. "Yes, I saw the Christ Child".

"And did he have anything for us for Christmas?" they asked.

For a moment she did not know how to reply. The little faces so pinched and pale longed for her answer.

"Well", she said slowly after a long pause, "the Christ Child is very poor this year, poorer even than we are, and though he loves each one of you he's finding it very difficult, but he's trying to do his best. But", she added lamely, "he is so poor this year."

---

[1] *Published in* Peace News *by Vera Brittain. See postcard sent to Daphne by Sister Kathe.*

"Never mind", one child replied, putting out his hand to reassure Schwester Kathe, "we'll try and make it a happier Christmas for the Christ Child."

Schwester Kathe put her hand on the boy's head, but had to turn away to hide the tears in her eyes.

The Recovery of our Confiscated Truck

Wednesday 19th. Word had got through from Müller in Brussells that our truck was cleared. I was up early ready to meet Mr Topham who was calling for me at 6.45 with a Volkswagen. It was still dark as I waited outside in the road, and bitterly cold, the snow was falling heavily.

The V.W. came half an hour late by which time I was already frozen. We were supposed to be meeting Herr Müller at the Belgian frontier at 8.30 a.m. The driver asked if he might take his wife with us to Aachen – they lived only 5 mins. away. I could not see why not so we went to fetch her. It turned out that she lived 5 km. on the north side of Cologne, which by the time we got going and left Cologne made us a further half hour late. The roads too were really dangerous, and we were fighting to make up for lost time, but the snow slowed us down considerably.

Soon after 9 a.m. we reached the Aachen team where a warm breakfast was waiting for us. We just had time to thaw out before going on to the British Border control post where the driver left us.

We walked across the mile of no-man's-land and met Müller and his friend at 10 a.m.

Then followed a long argument with the Customs again. We had expected to be away in half an hour and back in Cologne for lunch, but no such thing. They weren't going to be hurried, the papers still weren't right – they'd probably have to keep the wagon. Finally it was decided to unload the truck at 1 p.m. when the men arrived to do it. We ourselves, though prepared, were not allowed to unload. There was nothing to do but to wait. So we decided to walk over into Belgium to a little village near the frontier and have lunch. And a very good lunch we had – the one bright spot in the miserable day. Fortunately there was no snow in Belgium.

We were back promptly by one o'clock but the men did not arrive till 1.30 to start work. More arguments followed in violent French whether or not we could have the truck. Finally, at long last it was agreed that everything that was not on the export licence, i.e. all but the used clothes must be confiscated. This meant that every single parcel and sack had to be minutely examined. We knew we were stuck there now for hours. It started. Even then we had to do the unloading, while everything was mercilessly ripped open and examined. The tins of milk and Quaker oats! The coffee, cocoa, chocolate, soap and tobacco was put on one side and weighed and listed down. Every garment was searched and stuff was found in the pockets and in the toes of the shoes. They haggled and argued over practically every garment to see if it was used or not.

The hours slowly ticked by and not half had been done. When the stuff had been examined we had to collect up the remains as best we could pack it and place it on a separate pile outside ready for reloading. In order to speed the process up, while the customs were not looking, we quietly slipped a sack on to the 'examined' pile. It was not discovered. Several small parcels found their way mysteriously onto this pile also. Some of the officers were trying to be helpful but there was one man who was taking a positive delight in ripping everything open down to the smallest parcel and confiscating everything he could, and if the others did not follow his example he ticked them off. He was being openly called a bastard by everyone – the kind of person who if the others let anyone off he would report them straight away to the government, and though there was apparently no proof against him he was known to have reported "erring" Belgian peasants to the German occupation authorities. Nobody could do anything about him and all his senior officers were afraid of him.

Finally by 6.0 p.m. they had finished and we had reloaded the truck. They had confiscated 4 large tea chests of food and new clothes etc. It was tragic to see all that good stuff so desperately needed in Germany going we knew not where. As it was, I saw one of the customs officers helping himself to 100 cigarettes. He saw that I saw him. But by this time we were beyond caring and about dead beat. How the goods were to be sorted the other end none of us knew – they were all mixed up, and had lost their addresses. Finally got back to base at 9 p.m. and ready to go straight to bed.

Thursday 20th. Princess Elizabeth was married today to Prince Philip the Duke of Edinburgh at Westminster Abbey in a glittering ceremony such as the nation has not seen for a decade. I listened to the wireless commentary and took a day off.

Saturday 22nd. Spoke to the World Federation of United Youth Groups discussion group on methods of dealing with Germany's youth problem today. An interesting discussion followed and a lot of keenness. The whole session lasted 2½ hours.

In the evening a few of us in the team went to the residents hostel for the university D.P. students – mostly Poles, Jugoslavs, Balts etc. who had invited us and the Belgians and other Mil.Gov. people to a dance. It started at 9.30 and by midnight was warming up with some schnapps which smelt like the "Absolute Alcohol" in the Biology lab. By this time the dancing got wilder and more "national" and there was considerable merriment.

Sunday 23rd. Went out with a few of the I.V.S.P. group in my truck in the morning to cut wood again for the refugees, who had now got permission from the Förstamt to cut 20 cubic metres of wood. When we arrived at the refugee hostel the Förster was ready to show us the trees we could fell, and he watched us do it. Altogether we cut only about 5 cub. metres, and the rest has to be cut by 5th Dec. which doesn't give us long. This amount of wood will probably only see the refugees through till about the end of January, when the problem will arise again.

Monday 24th. Spent the morning first going round Köln looking for paper cement sacks, and having found some at last at 4.50 RM. each I took them back to the station where 2 truck loads of cement were being unloaded, of which we took 17 cwt. One of the labourers – covered with cement dust suddenly started to speak perfect English much to my surprise. He turned out to be a Philosophy student at the university, and had to do this work to earn money for his studies.

Took the cement to a factory 10 miles north of Köln to be made into posts, in order to put up a fence round the Youth Barrack.

Spent the evening at the club doing country dancing with the younger group.

Tuesday 25th. Started my first English conversation class with about 20 students at the university at the invitation of *Professor Papajewski* head of the English Dept. This was also to help Winnie out whose class had grown too big. I outlined the programme I had planned for them, and afterwards this was discussed. It looks a keen and interested group, and as it is the first class of the day for them at 8.30 they are all wide awake.

I had a talk afterwards with the Prof. who knew *Hans Buchinger* whom I had met in America. He had also studied at Woodbrooke and so we knew a lot of people in common.

Spent the rest of the morning at the Juvenile Court hearing *Dr Bäcker* judging about 5 or 6 cases. The invitation was from his wife who had come to one of the Quaker Meetings and heard I was interested. Dr Bäcker was elderly and having difficulties. It was bitterly cold all over the court building, and no heating I wondered how I could help.

Thursday 27th. Snow again. Went to a large factory at Euskirchen, about 25 miles south of Köln, where we heard it was possible to get wash basins and lavatory bowls etc. which we needed for the Nissen hut, but we were unfortunate and could not get any. They were very willing to help us if they had had the stuff, but that part of the factory making these fittings had been badly damaged and was not yet repaired sufficiently to start production again. They had simply run out of these things. They were practically impossible to get now anywhere.

Euskirchen is another small town which has been frightfully badly bombed. It is a lovely drive there and back from Köln, through a small range of wooded hills, and past the vast great surface brown coal mines.

In the evening there was a crisis at the Barrack with the Drama group. Everyone shouted at everyone else in Cologne dialect which was impossible for me to understand. Gradually it emerged that there was dissatisfaction with Anelise's play, and that they wanted to do a 'proper' Nativity play. Anelise, who runs the group and comes from the official Jugend Ring organisation, to help the 'unorganised' youth, said that unless she could run the group in her own way without dictation from the Quakers she wouldn't have anything at all to do with them, and refused to do another play. She also said if they didn't like her play, she wouldn't do that either. Then there was panic because a play is to be produced for the Parents' evening on Dec. 20th which is not far off. So after a lot of quarrelling, even though half the members had not turned up they decided to go on with Anelise's play provided a more Christmassy ending could be made. Everyone got everything they wanted off their chests, and temperament was flying. Anelise was highly satisfied with her victory and everyone for the moment seemed content, so I took them all home in my truck, which they all love, and we go through the Cologne streets making a terrific noise of singing and shouting cat calls and so on. It will be interesting to see what happens next week.

Another Wedding

Friday 28th. A relief worker may be called upon to do absolutely anything, and this morning I was called upon to be the driver of a wedding coach. At 7.15 a.m. I set out with *Doris Roper* in Bunty's Volkswagen to the North Cologne suburb of Riehl to pick the pair up, and take them to the Registry Office for their wedding at 8.0 a.m. The couple were interesting. He had been a P.O.W. in England and got engaged to an English girl in London. She was now pregnant and had been more or less turned out of her home, and had come over here to settle down and marry. He was now working as an interpreter for court cases in one of the Cologne prisons and had a good job and a flat.

She could not speak a word of German. They seemed a very happy couple, and with 2 C.C.G. officers as witnesses, friends of the groom and Doris as interpreter for the girl, they were formally married, with a nice little registry ceremony. It was one of the first occasions in Germany, certainly in Cologne of an English girl marrying a German, so there was quite a lot of publicity, and that evening they were to speak on the radio.

Later on I had the interesting task of moving a whole lot of gypsies and their caravans off the plot of ground next to ours at the Youth Barrack, so that the Salvation Army could start building their youth centre. Bunty had prepared the way by talking with the gypsies and explaining the situation, and they were certainly very helpful and most friendly and jolly. We had a great time, and I towed one lot right to the station – they were moving down to Bavaria anyway. No problems.

The Food Ministry promises more meat, sugar and sweets this Christmas in Britain.

Saturday 29th. In the VIth form discussion group, acting on Gerd's idea, we had a formal debate on the Motion: "This House considers that the theatre should not be a place of instruction, but rather chiefly for recreation and amusement". The speeches on the whole, by the proposers and seconders were good, but very little actual debate followed and the motion, to my surprise, was defeated by 8 votes to 7.

Sunday 30th. Roger back from his holiday in Switzerland, much to my relief, as I have had a great deal of his work to do as well, and was really beginning to feel it this week-end. He had visited the Pestalozzi children's village at Trogen, where I hope to go one day, so I was anxious to hear all about it.

Went out with the I.V.S.P. again to cut wood. It was raining and everything was soaking wet and miserable. However we stuck at it and got a lot cut, and came home pretty worn out for the first free afternoon and evening for a long time.

December 1947

Monday 1st. The more time I spend with the young people at the Barrack, the more I realise how different they are from the well-educated youth at the Youth Centre in Berlin. It was remarkable there how little they had been affected by Nazism, and how friendly were the relations with the British, and their opinion of the British as a Nation.

With these unorganised youth in Cologne one can say that they are at the opposite end of the pendulum. They still have much of the disease left, successfully sown by the Nazis, and they are very bitter against the British and in fact all the Allies. To my mind the clue again lies in the family. In the Berlin Centre most of the youth came from good 'normal' families with intact standards and values, which had managed to retain their good influence on the children. Here in Cologne it is not the case, and they have no longer got that influence and control from their parents, for they are mostly 'problem' children from socially deprived or fragmented families. Their attitude against the British is one of savage bitterness – but – when I say that I am English and part of the British nation they reply:- "Oh no, you're different, you're a Quaker!" One cannot help wondering if we are getting anywhere at all with any of these young people – their appalling difficulties and problems, and giving them what they all so desperately need.

Starved of friendship, affection, interest, and unbiased knowledge, they are all mixed up.

Tuesday 2nd. Went to interview the director of the Opera House, with Werner Bochamp to ask for the loan of scenery and costumes for performances of fairy story plays by the "Heinzelmänchen" group of volunteer students, and Dieter's Junge Laien Spiele (junior amateur dramatic group) for hospitals and refugees this Christmas time. Partial success probably increased because I, as a representative of the Quakers, was "used" i.e. the Quakers were supporting the venture, though in fact we have nothing to do with it.

Wednesday 3rd. An extremely interesting conversation class with my university group. I had intended to hear more life histories – but the first student told us about his experiences in a local public library. This was so interesting that after asking certain questions we got onto a conversation which lasted a full hour and led gradually on from good literature to bad, the influence of American 'trash', the place of fairy stories in children's lives, to bad fairy stories i.e. some of Grimm's which show brutality, and then the effect on children of suppressing brutal instincts, and on to the good and bad in man, his animal instincts, will, conscience, inherited characteristics, the difference between good and evil, crime and punishment and so on. It was not a good discussion but it was good conversation – one thing led on to another and nearly everyone took part, and was thoroughly interested in the subject itself and not in the art of talking as so many seek. So many are already fluent.

Thursday 4th. Tea with Prof. Papajewski at his flat. We talked about our mutual friends in England at Woodbrooke and in America, also about nationalism among the students, youth problems, and the state of the Church. He is a good conversationalist but a hard man to get to know on any terms of intimacy, quite different from *Prof. Rothmann.*

The Drama group in the evening went much better. Everyone turned up and they had decided to go through with it.

Friday 5th. Went to Dusseldorf for the first time with Marty.

This is the H.Q. of Mil.Gov. for Nord Rhine Westfalen. This great city about 25 miles further down the Rhine from Köln, is not as badly damaged as I expected, and the people are noticeably better dressed than in Köln, and it seems a more active place. I took to it much more readily than Cologne or Aachen.

Parents' Meeting

I got back in time for the first parents' meeting at the Youth centre. About 25 mothers turned up and 2 fathers. Hildegard Janca explained briefly the history of the Barrack and what we hoped to do there, and then gave the mothers the chance of airing their problems or grievances or of making suggestions. It was very interesting and they discussed heartily, and readily fell in with the suggestion that there should be a regular monthly meeting for parents when some definite subject is discussed or lecture given. It was interesting for us to meet the mothers of some of our young people and to hear their problems.

Sunday 7th. At morning Meeting met for the first time *Prof. Friedrich Siegmund-Schulze*[1]. He gave a little message in Meeting about love. We knew that God loved us and that we loved God. But that led on to something else. He referred to Jesus' question to Simon Peter: "Lovest thou me?" Peter's reply and how Jesus went on to say: "Feed my lambs". From our love of the Lord must follow our responsibility for looking after others.

Unfortunately I did not have time to talk to him afterwards, but we heard of some of his extraordinary history during Nazi times, and how he was saved by the head of the Gestapo, from the S.A.[2] and allowed to go to Switzerland. He is now returning to Münster university. He formerly started a famous Settlement in the East end of Berlin (Now Russian sector.)

Tuesday 9th. Received today a new Volkswagen car, similar to the one I had in Berlin only Navy blue. It was straight from the factory and a few things were wrong with it which had to be attended to, but that is not unusual.

Wednesday 10th. At my university discussion group this morning I got those who were returned P.O.W.s from England to give us their impressions and their thoughts during captivity and on return home, and the difficulties they have experienced here. I felt that the other students had no real appreciation of the difficulties these men have been through, and for me it was incredibly interesting to see the reactions of the others, some of whom were obviously bored and uninterested, whereas the P.O.W.s themselves were passionately sincere and anxious to get it out. The Nobel Peace Prize was officially awarded today to F.R.S. and A.F.S.C. relief workers in Europe.

Taking Children into Care

Thursday 11th. Picked up *Hilda Vogel and Heinz Stuckmann* in my "*Volks*" at the Jugendamt. Then went out to the Police Station at Bickendorf, and picked up 3 large policemen and proceeded to a small house to pick up some children. On knocking at the door there was no response and the door was locked. They banged on the windows and saw inside two frightened children who began to cry, and who were too terrified to open the windows or door. The louder the policemen shouted the louder the children inside began to wail till all the neighbourhood was looking on.

Eventually one of the neighbours arrived and managed to persuade the little girls to open the window – one was 15 and the other 13. The children were then told they were being removed to a Home. The parents were absent at the wedding of the oldest daughter. The children were inconsolable and almost in a panic having to go away just before Christmas and cried for the mother.

They were finally removed from the house and put into the car. We proceeded to fetch the younger brother from school, a little mite of 11, and took them out to the Catholic Home at Dormayer. I was told that all 3 children had V.D. and were being separated from their parents by the Jugendamt as they were considered incapable of looking after them properly.

---

[1] *German Pastor & Secretary of the International Fellowship of Reconciliation*
[2] *Storm-troopers*

There was however a lovely atmosphere in this Home, Raphaelshaus, which is one of the best of its kind I have so far seen in Germany, taking children of all ages from 0 – 18. It is a receiving and distributing centre for orphans, homeless and endangered youth, and it has modern buildings built during the war, and good equipment, a large amount of good farming land and greenhouses – so there was good food.

During the afternoon the F.O.R. had arranged a meeting at *Asta Brugelmann's* house – the Oberlander Ufer, which some of us attended, including *Mary Hartley* who was passing through Cologne.

The large room was packed with people. *Douglas Steere* (A.F.S.C. and Prof. of Philosophy at Harvard) spoke first on his experiences of International Work Camps in Lapland, and the work in Poland pointing out that there were many people in these places who were far worse off than the Germans and who yet had spirit and energy and hope, in fact "Ewige Baumaterial" or "living building material".

F.O.R. Piano Recital

This was followed by a piano recital by *Elli Ney*. I understand that Elli Ney who is a vegetarian and a non-smoker, was attracted to Hitler for the same reasons and therefore joined the Nazi Party fairly early, under which she gave many concerts and did well. Before the war she was regarded as the greatest pianist in Germany. Since the end of the war she has not been de-Nazified and so is unable to give public concerts.

Recently she put her house at the disposal of the F.O.R. for a meeting and had afterwards played to them. Taking an interest in the movement she was now helping them and had volunteered to give a recital

She is a large powerful woman with white hair and a face that strangely resembles Beethoven. She is in fact renowned for her Beethoven playing.

Unfortunately today she had a poor piano and I was sitting too close fully to enjoy the music, but as it was I had a magnificent view of her face which alone was a fascinating study. Her programme consisted of Bach, including a beautiful little quiet chorale, followed by Beethoven's 'Apassionata' sonata, magnificently played. To see all the changing moods pass vividly through her face was really absorbing, and she finished with two delightful Schubert Lieder. The audience was obviously considerably moved by her playing.

At the end *Cato Fritze* (an elderly little local Quaker lady, very active in the F.O.R.) rose to thank her, but before she could break up the meeting up jumped an oldish and untidy man and announced he had something to say. Whereupon much to our amazement he pronounced Elli Ney as the mother of Germany and compared her with Beethoven, Brahms and Schubert, and announced that as a token of his appreciation he was now going to sing. Everyone was considerably embarrassed, because he is known to be a crank, a street-corner preacher, making loud exhortations to conversion on trams etc. wherever he is, but otherwise harmless.

Cato Fritz rose and said she thought the meeting should end there and people go quietly home. Whereupon people began to rise, to leave the room, to greet each other and chatter as is usual when a meeting is concluded.

Undisturbed and undismayed the man went on and began to sing in a tuneless hideous voice about Germany – the finest land.

While all this was happening, I was standing close to Elli Ney who was, I noticed, the only person who knew exactly what to do. She was standing, and in desperation looking round at the noisy departing audience she said "Let him sing. Oh why don't they keep quiet! He needs to get this out." Whereupon she sat down, as did *Douglas and Dorothy Steere*, and listened to him in all seriousness. At the end she was the only person who clapped her hands and cried "Bravo!" as the poor man with the disarranged mind rushed forward and kissed her hand. Here was one of the most gracious and spontaneously sincere and sensitive actions I have ever seen, and again the impression left upon me of a truly great artist was a deep one. The man was pacified and quietly proclaimed his theories to a bewildered Douglas Steere who saw himself a captive for hours and pleaded with me to get him out of it. I managed to rescue him, and they came up to our house where he addressed the Quaker group and then stayed on to supper. Meanwhile I had to go down to the Barrack for the Drama group which was a failure. The chief character failed to appear.

Saturday 13th. A handicrafts exhibition at our Youth Barrack, with contributions from all the Youth organisations in Cologne, and to which our lot also contributed. The standard was very high and much of it was of very high artistic merit, by far the best contribution coming from the Catholic youth. Considering the lack of materials the ingenuity was amazing. I have scarcely ever seen such beautiful carving and delicate woodwork done by young people before.

Sunday 14th. I wrote and sent off a message which I felt drawn to write to the Indiana (U.S.A.) Young Friends who are meeting round about Christmas time for a "mid-year" conference, and which this time was to be a follow up of the Richmond conference held in July. Also I wrote a Christmas message to the German people which may be broadcast from Berlin.

The following extract taken from 'The Friend' of Dec. 12th, quoted from the "Christian Science Monitor" is worth inserting into this diary (on the occasion of the award of the Nobel Peace Prize):-

The Red and Black Star and the Nobel Peace Prize

"The old Chinese saying 'If not I – who? If not now – when?' might well be the slogan of the workers under the red and black (Quaker Relief) star. For anyone who has joined in this work has found himself swept into the habit of doing first and talking – but not much – afterwards. Quaker or not, he or she is apt to have become convinced that an evil is more quickly cured by providing a better way than by condemnation. And that no matter how vast the problem may be, each human being has done his bit when he has done his individual best".

Rufus M. Jones, Honorary Chairman of the A.F.S.C. once wrote:

"The three Wise men of yore followed a star and it led them to the manger where love had come to birth. It is the birth of love in human hearts that has carried the red and black star, not through the sky, but across seas and lands to places where agony and suffering have invaded life and made it almost impossible to go on without a hand of help ... The bearers of this star are not easily defeated by obstacles. They do not give up in face of hindrances. When they hear "No" they go on whispering "Yes" – for there is an inside push which in the end wearies opposition and conquers obstacles."

A German writing to a Friend in England also wrote of

"the universal joy here in Germany that the Nobel Peace Prize was awarded to the Society of Friends on December 10th. Not only in the papers everywhere you hear the satisfaction. You were the first, and after the first great war the only ones that acted as Christians. Now also the Christian Churches prove that there is a brotherhood among them."

These two extracts are not inserted for any reason of smug self-satisfaction but purely because to the relief worker, who, after a considerable time of such work tends to become tired, and lose his freshness and sometimes inspiration, and sometimes even wonders if there is any sense in going on – a drop of fresh water to the salty ocean of need and suffering, such writings are an encouragement and a source of renewed strength.

Monday 15th. Went to the Gymnasium school down the road to give a talk to Frl. Pretzell's English class about Christmas in England which they especially wanted to hear about. Their standard is very high and they were a most bright and attentive lot.

Went to visit *Frau Münden* of the Bahnhof's Mission on Deutz station. She is sister of our 'hausmutter' in Berlin. The Bahnhof's Mission helps to look after and provide some sort of meal for P.O.W.s, refugees and wandering youth who are passing through from one town to the next.

Tuesday 16th. Went over to Lüdenscheid by car to see *Lena Riemenschneider*. Heard the good news that her husband was to be released from P.O.W. camp in England in 3 days' time, and though he wouldn't be back for Christmas he would probably be back for the New year. After 3 years and 8 months of separation, she was naturally so excited she could not sleep at night. It was much colder in Lüdenscheid which is higher up, and in fact it was snowing all the time.

On the way back standing in the centre or market place of each little town was a large Christmas tree which was lit up with electric light bulbs and looked very pretty.

Wednesday 17th. Gave the third of my English classes about Christmas in England at the Gymnasium down the road.

Went to see *Dr. Beckhoff* at the university to give him a present of cigarettes for each of the professors and their assistants and also 4 cwt. of potatoes from Holland for those students working on the Studentheim.

In the evening at the club there were great rehearsals for the Saturday party, and at this stage it all looks hopeless.

My university class had asked for a reading from Dickens' 'Christmas Carol' which I gave them, and readings from the English Bible, and some English Carols with German tunes such as 'Silent Night'.

Thursday 18th. Was the day of the children's party at the Barrack. They gave a sweet little fairy story shadow play. Each child has made a Christmas present for its mother and the children all received a little present, and a bag of biscuits, sweets and apple rings. They sang songs – any number, which they know by heart and had a Christmas story read to them, and the mothers and children all received a cup of cocoa and the children something to eat.

In the evening final dress rehearsals of the play, dances and songs which looked even more hopeless – the kids making no real effort – so that Bunty, Roger, Hildegard and I were all a bit fed up and cross with them.

An Unexpected Adventure

Friday 19th. I decided to go over to München-Gladbach at the request of Australian Friends to enquire into the Welfare of the wife and child of a P.O.W. ill with T.B in Australia who had not received news for a long time.

This was a drive of about 35 miles through flat farming country with little villages every few miles. The roads are all tree-lined, and so it is like motoring down the aisle of some endless cathedral. A snow blizzard made it bitter cold and the snow froze on the wind-screen and made the roads very dangerous.

Always when driving alone like this one has plenty of time to think or meditate. I was thinking of the effect we can have on completely strange people's lives by some completely unexpected contact with them, or they on us. I was also thinking of Harry Emerson Fosdick's words: "It is not what a man finds in life that matters most – he may find a valley of weeping – it is what he makes of it that counts."

I had just passed through a small village and, quite deliberately, I passed a woman with a rucksack on her back who, though she didn't signal for a lift could obviously have done with one and would have welcomed it in such weather.

As I proceeded on my way I reasoned with myself thus:- "You know that you are in a hurry; you know that it would have been dangerous with this ice to have stopped suddenly, but you have deliberately chosen to miss an opportunity, if you like, or an adventure, which there is certainly no justification for you to burden yourself with, but which nevertheless is an experience you have the power to make or pass by on the other side. Now go back and see what might have happened if you were in the next car that had stopped to pick her up."

Whereupon, taking this good advice to experiment, I turned back. The woman was overjoyed at being offered a lift. She was wet and bitterly cold, her fingers and feet were numb.

"Could you take me to the next village?" she asked.

"Yes of course, I'm going through it. Where have you come from, Cologne?"

"Yes"

"Hamstering?"

"Yes, I have to", she sighed.

"Any luck?"

"Very little", she said, and showed me half a loaf, a rather wet cabbage and a large turnip. She turned her head away so that I should not see that she was crying.

"How many in the family?" I asked.

"Seven. The youngest is 5, the 11-year-old died 3 weeks ago, just before Christmas – he had T.B."

"And your husband, is he a P.O.W.?"

"Yes, in Russia, but I've never heard if he's alive or dead. It's 4 years now."

"So what are you going to do now, try the next village?"

"Yes, I still have 2 bars of chocolate." She showed me them guiltily.

"Where did you get those?"

"Mil.Gov. gave all school children a bar for Christmas, but the children gave them up so that I could barter with the farmers for potatoes or oats."

I remembered the time in Berlin last year when I discovered that Black Marketeers were waiting outside the schools to take the chocolate off the kiddies in exchange for something more filling and temporarily more satisfying, after which Mil.Gov. had ordered the chocolate to be broken up and the teachers to see that it was eaten on the spot.

I had nothing I could give the woman except a few cigarettes with which she could barter. For a moment I pondered again the old perpetual and insoluble dilemma of how far one is justified in assisting in the vicious circle of a cigarette economy. But I wanted her to keep the chocolate for the children's Christmas.

By this time we had arrived at the next village. She promised to send me her address. The look of gratefulness in her eyes as she got out of the car almost unable to speak, it seemed to me, reflected the tears in the eyes of God as he looks down on how much suffering in this world was caused only by 'man's inhumanity to man', and because again we have wandered away from Him like sheep from the shepherd. I saw again the truth of *Vera Brittain's* words: 'there is no such thing as the sum of human suffering or joy since each person reaches, with the maximum of individual emotion the utmost pain or enjoyment that the universe can hold.'

This woman was typical of hundreds from the big cities this winter who daily bitterly struggle in the same way to keep the spark of life alive in themselves and in their children.

How easy it would have been to miss this little experience in a hundred different ways. But are we not called to build our lives on the bricks of such experiences? We cannot give strength or help to such people unless we can sympathise with them, but how can we begin to sympathise with them unless we have learned to suffer with them? Was it by chance that my eye saw this particular woman?

I picked up one or two others with much the same story – completed my mission to enquire into the welfare of the wife of a T.B. P.O.W. in Australia, and about an hour later returned, hoping that I should be able to give some of the same women a lift back to Cologne, if they had been successful, but they must have been still foraging for they were nowhere to be seen on the road. I thought of the line:- "Opportunity passes by those who are not prepared to avail themselves of it."

In the evening by the light of a big fire and a few candles we listened to a piano recital by *Herr Manstedt's* sister, which we had arranged for the team's friends.

Christmas Party

Saturday 20th. The whole afternoon was devoted to the Christmas party at the Youth Barrack where a programme was put on for the parents, which included country dancing, a Christmas fairy story play (got up at the last moment) and carols with the singing group etc. Afterwards the parents withdrew, and things began to warm up a bit. For each of the 50 young people gathered there, there was a plate of biscuits and a cup of cocoa. The Barrack was decorated with fir, silver stars and tinsel, many candles, and two large and lovely Christmas trees. Then came the presents. Each of the club members had written their name on a slip of paper. Then each person dipped in a hat, drew out a name and prepared a small Christmas present for that person – so everyone had a present.

Then Bunty, Roger and I were thanked for our services at the Barrack, Bunty was presented with a beautiful lamp, and Roger and I told that our presents were still being made. We all then had to make speeches. After all this followed games, and some speeches by Felix, Hans and Willi – the older ones calling for a better community spirit in the Barrack which will produce something better next year.

Sunday 21st. Monthly Meeting of Friends -followed by a carol concert with readings, which was very good. After dinner we had a meeting with Friends to explain to them the work of the team and what will happen when we withdraw, and plans for the Neighbourhood Centre.

In the afternoon I took all the sweets and toys and etceteras I had collected as the result of my little article in the Dec. 5th 'The Friend' to Schwester Kathe and the Orphanage. There were at least 2 things for each child. Schwester Kathe was overjoyed, and as excited as any child, and really they were lovely and answered so many of the children's "wish letters" to the Christ Child and which otherwise they hadn't a hope of getting. Then all the other sisters were invited to see and they also were as excited and joking as children. Some letters will be sent from the children to those people who sent parcels. For me it was a great moment and I was only sorry not to see the children as they received the gifts and opened the parcels.

Monday 22nd. Went up by night train to Berlin.

Tuesday 23rd. Arrived in Berlin for breakfast. The weather was very mild compared with last year, though the remains of 7 ins. of snow were still about. Went straight to see Sofie Quast.

At 1 p.m. the Nord West Deutsche Rundfunk broadcasting station rang up to ask if I was aware that I was recording at 2 p.m., which I wasn't, since the letter had never reached me. However I went along to the Studio and made the recording in German of my Christmas message to the German people which ran as follows:-

"Über alle Grenzen"

"At this Christmas time I would like to take the opportunity of sending you a message of friendship and hope in these dark times.

Since the end of the war the Quakers have worked among you, with you and for you as guests in your land. Fully conscious of your troubles and problems they will try to continue in a small way to help in the physical, mental and spiritual reconstruction of Germany and other war torn lands in a spirit of love and reconciliation in order that Christ may truly be reborn in the hearts of all men.

Conditions do not seem to have improved greatly in the past 2 years, and this Christmas may seem the blackest you have ever known: Yet Christmas should be a time of rejoicing and of hope; a time when men should forget their differences and come together in the realization of their common unity as the sons of the one true Father.

I am sharing this Christmas with you this time and so are men and women from other lands East and West. Your, Christmas which is perhaps more beautifully and sincerely celebrated than in any other land. May its quality and spirit be such that it will help to heal the differences between East and West.

I can do no better than to give you again the message that the Quakers issued in 1919 after the First World War and again in 1939.

We appeal to all men to recognize the great spiritual force of love, which is found in all, and which makes us all one common brother-hood. In spite of sacrifice and devotion there is dissatisfaction and unrest in all lands. Consciously or unconsciously, men are seeking for a new way of life. They cry for a bond that shall unite the world in freedom, righteousness and love, that shall liberate it from its suffering, its hatred, its disunion. They cry for a religion of life, for an active spirit of peace on earth, of goodwill to men.

Through the dark clouds of selfishness and materialism, shines the Eternal Light of Christ in man. It can never perish. This light of Christ in the heart of every man is the ground of our hope, the basis of our faith in the spiritual unity of all races and all nations. Because we have been blind to this essential fact of life we have failed in social and international relations, and are now in confusion. The profound need of our time is to realize the everlasting truth of the common Fatherhood of God – the Spirit of Love, and the oneness of the human race.

There is a Power within the world able to set men free from fear and anxiety, from hatred and from dread: a Power able to bring peace within society and to establish it among the nations. And because we know of this power we call all men to turn towards it.

The Spirit and power of God enter into our lives through love – through tender pity and patient yet undaunted opposition to all wrong.

God is love – love that suffers yet is strong; love that triumphs and gives us joy. So we stretch out our hands in fellowship, sympathy and love across frontiers, lands and seas. To men and women of all nations we dare to say: "Turn from the way of strife; unite in the service of healing the broken world; bear one another's burdens; admit the power of God into your lives, nor be dismayed at all."

This message was broadcast all over Germany at 6.50 p.m. and again on Christmas Eve.

Most of my week in Berlin was spent in going round to the families of my various friends to spend a little bit of Christmas with them.

The Hellwigs, Dr Quast, Dr Thoran, Abshagens, Keups, Weckerlings, and so on, with visits to the Youth House and the 5 F.A.U. boys, Doug Simmonds, John Gray and Christopher Alexander, Ben and Bob from Hildesheim.

Christmas Day

Thursday 25th. There was a magnificent and quite traditional Christmas dinner with Turkey and Plum Pudding, prepared by *John Seed* and Frau Appel, which left us torpid.

In the evening Sofie and I went to hear Erna Berger in a superb performance of "La Traviata" at the Staatsoper. And then finished up with supper at her house when she told me all about her amazing trip to England. She had certainly made good use of it.

Friday 26th. Saw more friends, Lothar and Arne. Main event of the day however was the chamber concert at Prof. Jakobi's house, when we heard the first performance of *Rheinhold Krug's* Christmas music. Both he and Prof. J. have grown their hair rather too distastefully long.

Sunday 28th. Went to Meeting for the last time and to say goodbye to many Friends.

In the evening went with *Ursula Müldner* to a fine performance of "Der Freischutz" by Wiler at the Stadtische Oper.

Was unable to get into the night Duty train.

Monday 29th. Travelled down to Herford on the Day train – night at transit hotel.

The Berlin team it seemed to me was even more unhappy and disunited than 3 months ago. This seems to me a tragic shame. The atmosphere of bickering and pettiness had a demoralising effect. It is even more a collection of difficult individualists, each pulling his or her own way. All admitted the team had outlived its usefulness in its present state and that it was a good thing it was breaking up in March. Many Germans were really sorry things had turned out as they had and some told me quite frankly, especially the staff, that it was not a good advertisement for Quakerism.

I was glad to get back to the atmosphere of the Cologne team.

Tuesday 30th. An enormous pile of mail waiting for me, partly my Christmas mail, partly response to my recent articles in American and British 'Friend'.

There were also a number of food parcels from America from friends I made there.

My *Volkswagen* had had a tyre stolen and the side bashed in, in my absence.

I received the following letter from Toronto:

Dear Friend,

I saw your letter re a Protestant Orphanage near Cologne a few days ago in 'The American Friend'. I realise of course that it is too late for me to do anything in the way of Christmas cheer for the children but I feel sure that a little extra food will help even if late in arriving. I may say that I thought I had done all that I possibly could in the way of sending food parcels before Christmas, but then I saw your letter, then received $10 from one of our Meetings for a parcel, a dear old lady of 90, a member of our Meeting handed me 3 dollars to help send a parcel to some one, so I added 6.50 myself to make up enough for a double parcel which our University Tours offers and which is supposed to be sent from stock piles in Germany which come from Finland, so I think it should not be too long in arriving. It is very hard to think of little children without any little gifts to symbolise the coming of God's great gift to us, still harder to think of them as lacking food and warmth this winter as so many, what one can do is so very little, but we must just do what we can.

I must ask you to excuse all sorts of errors in my letter. I am just an old lady of past 81, who finding her hand growing shaky with much letter writing, has resurrected an old typewriter and is trying to get used to using it.

I wish I could say 'Happy Christmas' to the children at the Orphanage and send something that would help to make it happy, one feels so helpless in the face of the great need everywhere. I have been in touch with a good many people on the continent who need help, Friends and others, during the past 2 years.

With all good wishes
Your friend
Ella Firth

I thought this was a very beautiful, humbling and inspiring letter.

My VIth form discussion group led by Gerd had their Christmas party. The programme consisted of a serious first half with Bible readings, carols, Christmas music on gramophone records, poem and stories, followed by a funny half, of comic acts and games.

Wednesday 31st. Back to the Youth Barrack. Helped to decide the programme of lectures for the parents of the Youth, with Hildegard, Roger and Frl. Wesener.

Games evening at the club, and discussion group on the 'Meaning of Discipline'. Went home afterwards to *Felix Eckhardt's* family to spend the New Year's Eve with them in the traditional way. We played the old game of Spilikins and had supper. Finally to bed at 2 a.m. in the New Year.

January 1948

Thursday 1st. A public holiday for the Germans. I spent the entire day catching up with my mail. In the UK the railways were nationalised today.

Friday 2nd. In 2 ambulances went on the Children's transport taking 30 children from the Gesundheitsamt to the Children's Convalescent home at Asbach in the French zone about 40 miles away.

The Rhine is beginning to flood into the city streets.

Today I was invited to coffee with *Asta Brüglemann* head of the F.O.R. in Köln who lives down by the Rhine. She showed me her cellars, in which a family lived, which at one time were 5 or 6 ft. deep in water, but it was just beginning to recede.

I met here *Herr Kunstler*, adviser to Mil.Gov. University officer – a very active little man, full of life and an ardent Socialist and a Catholic. We had an absorbing conversation over the East West question, Socialism, Capitalism and Communism, and work for peace.

We Visit a Dangerous Man

Saturday 3rd. Went to see *Fritz Topp* living with his old mother (British Born) both of whom speak fluent English. Fritz Topp is perhaps the most bitter man I have ever met in my life. Winnie suggested I might use him to do a translation for me as he is too ill to do other steady work, as the result of his experiences. He was originally denounced as a war criminal, as being responsible for the shooting of a thousand French men. He spent a long time in French jails without trial, and as he says, because he refused to be a spy, was finally released but then spent 6 months in the British internment camp at Recklinghausen for dangerous Nazis, where *William Hughes* contacted him, and also Cologne jail. So he is a nihilist without faith or trust in anybody or anything, very sick in mind and body, and a difficult person to spend time with. He returned home to find, after being married for 16 years and with 2 children of 15 and 8, that his wife had run off with a labourer and wanted a divorce. He got the divorce and she married the other man. The whole is a tragic story.

Sunday 4th. Drove over to Weidenau, a suburb of Siegen, about 80 miles away, to see *Annemarie Grimm* and her family. It is a glorious drive through lovely country up the Sieg Valleys – lovely hills, woods and later mountains with wonderful views. The children, Albrecht 9 and little Renate, were terribly excited to see Onkel Hugh as they call me and showed me with pride the 6 hens, the rabbit and the goat. We all had an egg for lunch and then I saw all their Christmas presents and photographs, gave them a ride in the car, and returned getting back to Cologne just as darkness fell.

The Formation of Youth Committees

Tuesday 6th. One or two of the boys at the Barrack called Roger, Hildegard and me together because they wanted to make the suggestion that they should form committees with us to run the Barrack activities. This was what we had been hoping for a long time and had dropped many a hint about it. A colossal row had to be overcome first because one or two others wanted to attend this committee to which we personally saw no objection. Felix swallowed his pride and eventually joined in but not Hans, who remained outside. I felt it was a most productive evening. Though we still refer to the Quaker Youth Barrack, it is now known as the 'Open Door', a drop-in Youth club, non-political, non-sectarian and used only by the young people in the evenings. They once threatened to burn it down. Things have changed!

Wednesday 7th. This meeting was continued today when we collected together all those who were regular workers with a real interest in the Barrack, and elected 3 committees, one to look after the games and dancing etc., one for entertainments – play producing, parents' evenings, concerts etc., and a third for the work that has to be done, i.e. building, digging, electrical installations, furniture and curtain making etc. It is hoped eventually to form a central committee for the general affairs, the running and discipline of the barrack, but that must come slowly.

Willi, who is emerging as the leader with the most responsibility and best ideas, could not be present. His is rather a tragic case. He was himself a leader in the Hitler Youth. His mother has forbidden him to come to the Quaker Barrack any more. His parents were the old ideological type of Nazis. The father was killed by British bombs. His mother is therefore alone and poor. She expects Willi's help in the house and expects him to go out and make a living on the Black Market, or by stealing etc., instead of spending his entire evenings with the hated English. The boy has had to fight to go straight, to learn a trade – and does not want to go to the B.M. and steal coal etc. He wants to give his time to something better and to do something more constructive with the youth at the Barrack. He says he has his own future to think about, naturally, and not be entirely dependant on his mother. He is quite a remarkable person. Later Hildegard visited his mother, told her about the Barrack and what we were trying to do, and set things to rights.

I also attended a meeting at Mil.Gov. organised by *Vera Swift and Les Barnes* of the Education Dept. with the Legal Dept. and members of German Welfare organisations and the Juvenile Court Judges etc., on the delinquency question. It was stated that because of the growing seriousness of the situation the Germans must get together to start a campaign against delinquency. Juvenile delinquency in this area has increased 2500% compared with general delinquency which had risen only 50%. The basic problems of the German authorities – judges and welfare workers were discussed, and it was suggested to them that they should form a special committee along the lines of the one Sofie and I started in Berlin and based on our proposals. This was agreed to and copies of my plans will be duplicated and sent out.

Thursday 8th. Marshall tells the Senate in Washington that U.S. failure to help rebuild Europe will put it into the hands of police states.

Friday 9th. Went on a children's transport of 3 ambulances to a children's convalescent home in Adenau in the French Zone. This is a glorious spot in lovely steep wooded valleys and mountains with little towns. The southern slopes of some of the hills are terraced with vines. The children were very excited, and the Nuns at the convent received us warmly and with a good meal.

Saturday 10th. Spent the whole day down at the Barrack with the young people. In the morning about 12 came to help, and we dug holes 1 metre deep to receive the posts which will make the fence to go round the property. They worked well and we had a good lunch all together. In the afternoon there were about 20 altogether, which was really remarkable, and it was a pleasant time for all, ending with hot cocoa.

Sunday 11th. Visited Siegberg Prison again to spend the afternoon with Oberinspector *Peter Schmidt* and his wife. Peter was back from his trip to England, arranged by Penal Branch, to visit Prisons in England and see the Borstal system and Probation Service etc. He was full of enthusiasm for the ideas, and also for the kindness and understanding he had received. He is 50 lb. under normal weight and during his trip to England had gained 8 lb. He had managed to save from his 19/- a week pocket money and buy presents for his wife and child, including 4 lb. of coffee. 1 lb. he immediately bartered for 2 pairs of stockings because his wife literally had none left. He also brought some cooking fat because Cologne has not had any fat at all on the ration cards for 6 weeks.

Monday 12th. Took some food to a very old couple recommended to me by one of the garage mechanics, both of 70, husband in hospital with hunger oedema and earning a pension of RM 40 a month (10/- a week).

Tuesday 13th. Went to see *Frau Nickels* (see 19th December) the woman 'hamstering', to whom I gave a lift. She sent me her address, so I was able to take along the contents of a food package sent to me from America. They were sharing a filthy little suburban house with 3 other families. The two youngest children Heleni and Willia, both sweet kids, were at home, and the eldest married daughter who was pregnant and filthy. The stench was awful, but I warmed to the family. Frau Nickels told me she would never laugh at a belief in prayer again! Their joy, excitement, and gratitude was unbelievable. "And now 'mutti' you won't have to go 'hamstering' any more", the youngest said. She had sold my few cigarettes and bought a few things and the children had had the chocolate for Xmas.

A letter came from a Friend in Ireland in response to my article re the incident on 18th November asking if a Protestant orphanage with which she was connected could adopt Schwester Kathe's orphanage and help a little materially, and by corresponding with the children. When I suggested this to Schwester K. she was very enthusiastic, so it looks a good thing. The Irish orphanage is well off, the children are well looked after and get everything. The job is to make them look outwards. This is a chance.

Friday 16th. Spoke to the Parents' meeting (parents of youth at Barrack) about some of the problems of their youth outside and inside their homes, and how we could best solve them. A good discussion followed.

Saturday 17th. Took the VIth form discussion group. Most of the afternoon spent in discussing what we were going to discuss. Tiring.

In the evening went to the Nord West Deutsche Rundfunk to take part in an English play for the Schulefunk[1] entitled "London Traffic". Vera Swift and 2 others also took part – the whole thing taking us until midnight to record satisfactorily. Everything had to be said painfully slowly and simply, causing us much amusement.

Sunday 18th. Went over to Solingen Wald with Hildegard to see our proposed Youth leader at work with his own group. There were 15 boys gathered round a table in the parsonage listening to a dried up old woman delivering a lecture on the "All-powerful God", reminiscing about her missionary parents, and evil spirits, and the power of prayer, in a most dangerous way, and all but about 2 boys thoroughly bored. This lasted an hour after which our man put the boys through some hymns and songs and then gave them a solid hour of "Bibel Arbeit" in which they read a passage from the Bible taking parts, and then asked questions, and explanations followed, about evil spirits. The whole thing was tragic to my mind and doing more harm than good. The result was we could not engage Herr Grau for our work with the youth at the Barrack, which has now been officially named the "Open Door", and is the first of its kind in Germany.

The Russians are reported to hold art worth £42m from Dresden.

Saturday 24th. Taught at the Kreuzgasse Schule in the morning with advanced English pupils, and talked about America – relief work and pacifism to answer their questions.

In the afternoon the I.V.S.P party at the Frick's house at Biesse. Collected up 18 members of the I.V.S.P. in an ambulance and just as we got there a 'big end' went, and we had to push the last 100 yds. Liz came out with another ambulance to tow us back again.

Sunday 25th. Drove up to Mulheim-Rhur to see *Karl-Heinz Keller* whom I had met in London. Called in at the Oberhausen team, and then had lunch with *Ilse and Rheinhardt Schmidt* after which Anneliese joined us. Later visited the Y.M.C.A. in Mulheim, spoke to the warden and learned all about their work, which is much the same as our work in Cologne with youth but without the help of the Allies.

The Coal Mines

Went on to meet *Herr Wellhöner* a Communist T.U. leader of a Coal mine, to ask for permission to visit his mine next day. This was all fixed up, and we had a long and interesting talk with him about Rhur mining, the life, and grievances of the Rhur miners.

---

[1] *Schools Radio*

Wellhöner told us that the miners' major grievance is over food. Yes, they get enough but not the right type for good production and to keep their health, and then what can a miner do when he comes home to find his family hungry and his children waiting on the door-step asking for bread? Is it not natural to bring home one of the two large sandwiches they get with butter and sausage, for the children? Fat, Fat, Fat is the cry you will hear everywhere, and bacon.

Then there was the C.A.R.E. package bribe. Miners were told of the C.A.R.E. package bonus scheme. If they reached a certain target they would receive a C.A.R.E. package. The first lot had arrived but not all those entitled had received them. The miners were disgusted with the 'Care' packages when they opened them because they contained not one drop of fat – all sweet and starchy things and with little vitamin content. Moreover they were mostly packed in 1943 and 44, as army supplies. These were surplus stocks, and had gone stale. The cigarettes were so stale the normal consumer in America would not touch them. Everyone had a craving for tobacco, but it had to go to the farmers to be bartered for fat, or to be sold on the black market.

Then they were smarting under the fact that during the time they had produced the extra coal by a huge effort, and had received 10 million dollars for this extra production, they had not got what they had asked for – more fat and bacon. Instead they could buy only peas, dried fruits, coffee, tea and such things which had only a barter value.

True, the miners (underground) got the 2 sandwiches and all got a hot meal at the end of the Shift, above the heavy workers' ration card, but it was not the right type for good mining work. They admitted that on the whole, they could have enough for themselves – "but ask my wife and children if they get enough", he said, "and then see what a miner, has to live on". It was also unfair that the miners' fat ration, low as it was, should be kept up to its present level at the expense of the normal consumer who had been without for weeks.

True, there was the export question and the price of coal. Under Hitler, I was informed:

440 million tons was produced, of which 30 million tons was exported – about 8%.

Now only 30% remains in Germany and 70 % exported. "We realise we are guilty for the war"' said this Communist, "and that we should pay reparations, but let us keep more coal to get our production going and then pay reparations with our produce and for the food we must buy."

The price Americans were paying for the coal today – as reparations value was 15 gold Reichmarks (3 dollars). (A gold RM is worth 1/- or 5 to a dollar). On the world market the Americans were then selling this coal at 16 dollars per ton, i.e. 5 times more than they paid for it. Someone was getting a profit of 13 dollars a ton – not the miners. The mines could not afford to pay higher wages to the miners as this money had to be raised by direct taxation of the people. The highest wages for a miner working an 8-hour shift was RM 12 per day. The lowest wage for adults was 6.94 RM. Youths got less (round about RM 4 a day i.e. between 2 – 4/-, and for 8 hours work). "Those youths who did the same work should get the same pay," he said.

The job nowadays was to find good miners. The old ones were dying out. Hundreds of people came to the mines now as a last chance of obtaining a livelihood, and so they come from all sorts of trades and professions, refugees, expellees and wandering homeless youth. Their attitude was that this was not their job for life but simply one to keep body and soul together. Altogether 30,000 new miners had been equipped, with clothes from the miners points system, received the extra rations and benefits, and 20,000 of these men had then left almost immediately. As a result Mil.Gov. had said: "Stop, that's enough – no more equipment" – *so* now there was nothing to equip people with.

Two other interesting facts I learned were that the average number of children per family of miners was 5.8 before the war and now 3.2. Also, the German P.O.W.s returning from Britain, having seen Scottish mines, thought the German ones were more modern and up-to-date.

Went back to Karl-Heinz's house, parked the car and met all his family. His father is very rich, a self-made man in the wholesale tobacco business and very anti-British. Karl-H. too has had a fascinating history for a boy of his age.

Visit to the Mine – Zeche Humbolt

Monday 26th. Up at 6.0 a.m. and took the car out of the garage and was at the mine promptly at 7.0 a.m., as the miners were cycling in for the day shift. Still dark. Considerable interest shown in my car as I drove in and much staring at me. I sensed immediately a rather hostile look. Announced myself and asked for Herr Wellhöner. The Gate Porter glowered at me, showing by looks and sounds his dislike, quite openly. Herr Wellhöner and the Youth Welfare officer turned up – both greeted me warmly and were very friendly. The Porter could contain himself no longer "Just look at these figures", he said – "Absenteeism from sickness. Here's December – the month when people worked like slaves to get the bonus Care packages. Some got the first lot but not all, when's the second lot coming? Now look at the January figures – look at all the illness entries. No fat, not enough fat. It's bacon we want, my man, not charity. Either you Allies clear out and let us do the job properly on our own, or help us. We want to nationalise these mines – why are you stopping us?" Herr Wellhöner and Herr Füssing interrupted and pointed out that the gentleman was a Quaker. "Oh well, that is not so bad". "But about this nationalisation?" I said. "We've nationalised our own mines, so what makes you think we don't want the German ones nationalised? It's dollars," I said to him "- don't forget we are short of dollars too, and this is now a joint controlled area – American and British, and where we can't agree with the Americans is about Socialism, but we happen to be penniless and so it's the little dollar that rules us too." He became more friendly and we began to find points of agreement. He was somewhat surprised, and we left good friends when he agreed to give me all the information I wanted. But I could sense this feeling of bitterness all around me, and hostility. "You Allies," I heard said again, "during the Hitler time you broadcast about giving us freedom and delivering us from the Hitler tyranny. We weren't fooled by Hitler and we believed you – then what did you do after the war was over?"

"Gluck auf" is the greeting you hear everywhere in a mine between miners. I was introduced to the head of the Day Continuation School for young miners who was about to make intelligence tests on a batch of new young miners who had just come in. He explained to me the system of training. Boys come out of the mine for 1 day a week schooling. There are some 300 boys in the mine and so with shortage of teachers, specialist classes may be as many as 50 boys. They receive this extra training for 3 Years. The first year is spent in the Apprentices' workshop. 2nd and 3rd years are put into groups according to aptitude and ability, and then begin the real underground work. I was shown a large number of working and sectional models on which they can learn mining – the mistakes and dangers, and where they can see and test all the different types of apparatus. Soon there is likely to be a uniform plan for all such mining schools.

I was then introduced to the Director of the mine and given final permission to go down, in spite of it being against rules and regulations. They thought it could be done on the quiet, and they were anxious that I should see the working conditions and problems of the youth. I was also able to ask questions of the foreman in charge of underground work. Always came the question: "Can't we have more fat? When are the C.A.R.E. packages arriving?" I asked questions about compensation and insurance which they thought was adequate, and about accidents. There is an increase in accidents especially towards the end of the 8 hours shift, due to the fact that the miners so easily get worn out, and accidents which normally would never have happened do now occur simply from fatigue, and the carelessness and laxity produced from over-strain.

Quite an amazing sight was to go into the miners' changing room, a drab and dingy place, and see all the limp, drab colourless clothes hanging lifelessly from the roof and held up by their long chains on pulleys and locked at the bottom.

I was given a completely clean set of miner's kit by the attendant and boots, which I put on. I was presented with a miner's stick, helmet and lamp, and then with the teacher and welfare officer set off, with the two large miner's sandwiches in our pockets.

The sights and sounds at the top of the mine shafts were new and exciting, deep rumblings, load clangs and thumpings, musical squeaks and rattlings, hissing steam and more rattlings, grating noises and sudden metallic bumps. We talked to the boys working on the moving belt onto which the coal was tipped for sorting and grading, as they picked out the stones. They all crowded over to speak to 'the foreigner'. Was I American?

Then we entered the cage and shot down the shaft to a depth of about 1500 feet, and out into the first gallery. Here it was dark and draughty, but quiet. The trucks were being pulled along by little electrically automated trains, pushed into the shaft with a crash and up out of sight. We walked along this gallery for about 300 yards and then came to the second shaft down which we descended another 1000 feet to the second gallery. Here it was quieter still and this time quite hot and no light except for our lamps. We must have walked about 100 yds. along this shaft when we suddenly came to a little hole in the wall through which we crawled. This appeared to be a low shaft sloping downwards at an angle of about 30°, in which it was not possible to sit up comfortably. We slid down this shaft on our bottoms and sides, from one pit prop to the next. All sounds were muffled, and we could hear in the distance the drills working somewhere below us on the coal face, and various rumblings and muffled shouts. We must have crawled about 100 yds. and all was quiet when suddenly we came upon a solitary boy lying in the middle of the shaft. It was a pause for lunch. The boy had been hurt in the leg by a falling rock and was made to rest by the others who had taken his tools away, about which he was annoyed. He was a little Berliner, 16 years old. Had wandered down here with his father in search of work which they had been unable to find in Berlin. We talked about Berlin – he was a nice kid. We passed on and came to a group of 16-19 year olds also having a pause. They were without shirts, just in ragged trousers and old boots, which were mostly the only pair they each possessed. Black from head to foot, their white teeth and eyes flashed in the darkness. The atmosphere was hot and full of coal dust. It was hard to breathe and I was already sweating.

I found out that some were local boys whose fathers had been miners, others were from Cologne, others were refugees, expellees from the East occupied by Poland, Ober Silesia and so on. Most of them said they would never do mining in normal times; one said he wanted to study medicine, another music; some did not know what they wanted; some had come here as a last resort when there was nothing and no alternative left – they wanted a bed and food and were tired of just wandering. One had just found his mother that week. Most of them had arrived very poor and now earned RM 4 a day which was barely enough. They were all fairly satisfied with conditions in the hostel and the food was enough even though it was sometimes badly cooked and all the same. When were the Care packages going to arrive? Is it possible to have more fat? I asked what they did with their free time. They said it was hard. They thought about food and how to get cigarettes to 'organise' things, how to get clothes and so on. They didn't play games – no football, a ping-pong table but no balls – what was the use! They went to the films – they liked the English pictures. One boy spoke English, he was an Interpreter for a time at a British camp, well-educated. They liked to go dancing but were ashamed of their clothes, and it wasn't easy to get new ones. The points system helped, but for 32 points you only get a shirt. There was politics mixed up in it somewhere. They were not forced to produce as much as possible but to learn as much as possible. Some liked the school, others felt too tired for it; others were interested only in work, some didn't like either, and what would it lead to anyway – there was no future. But one said: "A pound of flesh makes good soup. We take what we can while we can." They would like some sport as a relaxation, it wasn't possible though. Many didn't know what they were working for and they weren't interested in politics – they felt tired easily.

"Gluck auf!" we passed on; the drills started, everything shook and rattled and rumbled, and the coal shovelled onto the chute shot away down one side into the darkness. "They're fine boys," I shouted to the welfare officer. "Yes", he replied, "but its difficult to use them. A miner must do his job by profession – he must have a love of the job and a sense of purpose which these haven't got – the older ones are dying out."

We came to another group who stopped work to talk to us. "Gluck auf!" they greeted us, rather surprised to see a grimy English Quaker in such an undignified position. The two men had come to see this corner where the boys were working because it is supposed to be particularly dangerous. The seam had slipped ages ago a few feet to the left and down. The welfare officer, who had an immediate rapport with the boys and was intimate with each one, always got a pleasant reaction from them and he always had a joke or some pleasant remark to make. He pointed out they were putting in much too thin pit props and cross pieces. Indeed they were bulging dangerously. More would have to be put in, as there was a lot of falling and cracking rock. We crawled down through a hole only just big enough to get through, and wormed underneath a ledge and round into the continuation of the shaft and on another 50 yds down. Then suddenly it got steeper, so that one could look down through a maze of pit props to black gaping holes beneath. I was not sure that I could cope. We descended the pit props like a ladder. I dreaded to think what would happen if one gave way, not being tight enough, or if I should slip. Then the man disappeared through a hole and I heard him drop through into the main gallery below. I had to follow. We were able to stand again, and watch the coal hustle down the shoot into the trucks. More boys came up to talk to us.

By this time I was pretty hungry. We had been below ground for 3 hours and so I gladly ate one of my sandwiches. We then walked back along the third gallery. The men were eager to know my impressions. All I could think of at the time was: "My God, how tragic! God never meant young people to go through all this – Coal, what is coal? What do we do for it? What of the coal shortage in England?"

Whenever I use coal for a fire I shall see a picture of those 16-21 year old boys in that dangerous corner, unable to sit up properly, hacking and shovelling, and drinking cold ersatz coffee (made out of acorns) for 8 hours a day and probably finishing up with dust disease of the lungs.

At last we shot up the shaft and out into the cold fresh air – a glorious sunny spring day. There was a piping hot bath waiting for me and a hunk of miner's soap and a scrubbing brush. I was black. So was the bath water at the end! Then I had to sample the miners' hot meal – in a drab and depressing dining room. This was a large bowl of sweet noodle soup. I could not eat it all. There was little fat in it, or the right stuff for a good job of work. I longed for some paints to brighten up the place, like the great Newton and Chambers mine I had visited once near Sheffield in 1944. I offered the men a cigarette – the boys looked hungrily towards them. "A lot of this juvenile delinquency and stealing could be stopped if the boys could get cigarettes", someone said. I went to see the boys' hostel, a modern enough building, but with the very barest equipment. Tables, chairs, no books, few pictures. Double decker bunks with straw mattresses, and only one double blanket each. In the beginning there had been a lot of wilful damage to tables and chairs – they had little responsibility, and what books they had were used as toilet paper. It was depressing to find another huge problem.

I thanked the men for giving me so much of their time, but they were the ones, they said, who were grateful – grateful and surprised that any English person should be interested in the conditions of the youth at all. They hoped I would tell people. They did not ask for help.

I drove back to Cologne feeling as though I had been beaten. I felt stiff all over. It was a glorious sunny spring day. I was reminded of the words of John Woolman in his journal (p.138 Everyman), "But how lamentable is the present corruption of the world! How impure are the channels though which trade hath a conveyance? How great is that danger to which poor lads are now exposed when placed on shipboard to learn the art of sailing." How easily the words "mine" and "mining" can be substituted for the words "shipboard" and "sailing". The cigarette economy really worries me.

News of Mahatma Gandhi's assassination on Jan. 30th has only just percolated through to us. The news was staggering and I wondered how my parents must have been feeling. We knew that he was fasting again for Hindu-Moslem unity, so now riots are bound to break out again in India.

February 1948

Sunday 1st. Went over to Lüdenscheid again by car, this time to see *Heinz Riemenschneider* back from being a P.O.W. in England. He was looking fat and healthy in comparison with other Germans, and seemed very happy and content with his time in prison camp, about which I got a great deal of information for my book. He had painted a beautiful picture of German wild flowers for me in oils.

Monday 2nd. Broadcast in the Schulfunk Programme in 'English for Beginners' from the Nord West Deutsche Rundfunk, much to the amusement of the others who listened in. Gave an English lesson at the Kreuzgasse school, and immediately left for England.

Called for Interview

Tuesday 3rd to Saturday 7th. In England, for interview at Birmingham University Education Dept., and called in at Bristol University.

Carnival Time in Cologne

Monday 9th. Carnival is still in full swing in Cologne. Children are in fancy dress in the streets all the time, and much singing. Parties and Balls in the evening. Rosenmontag and a public holiday today with processions, 'sitzungs' at the theatre etc. Went to see "Der Kaiser's Braut" at the theatre, a Musical show – story a traditional one of an English Princess who came to marry a German Prince and on her way stops in Cologne and incognito goes into the streets to get to know the Cologne people and 'Kölsch' – the local dialect. Her double takes her place – meanwhile an actor takes the part of the Kaiser and is received and introduced to the Princess's double as the Princess – they fall in love. Finally the real Kaiser comes to claim his bride, the deception is discovered and forgiven and everything ends happily. The music too is a very clever mixture of classical, light and jazz and it is an all male cast with a male ballet.

I later saw a performance of *Carl Zuckmeyer's* play "The Devil's General" with quite first class acting. It is itself also a most interesting play, and has caused much discussion here in Köln amongst everyone. The action takes place during the war shortly before America's entry, and tells of the conflicts of a General in the Luftwaffe who is purely a flier, and the Nazis for whom he has no respect; of realizing that the war is wrong and will not be won, and of the underground movement.

I used the theme during my discussion class at the university and it produced many different views.

Wednesday 11th. I have tried to help one of my students, who lives in very bad conditions and is unwell. *Klaus Blum* is a music student and an ex P.O.W. from America and England, a serious and bitter young man – but full, of goodness. He refuses to deal on the Black Market and is having a great struggle – he now lives in the cellar of a bombed house which is without doors and is bitterly cold and damp.

Broadcast again on the Schulfunk programme with Liz.

Friday 13th. *Eric Savage* paid a pastoral visit to the team. It was good to have him – he deepened our morning devotionals, and we were able to talk of the deeper things in spare moments while washing up. He was full of humour and life – enjoying himself and learning with the eagerness of a schoolboy – friendly with everyone.

I took him to see Schwester Kathe's Orphanage when I took them a whole lot of parcels from America and England sent to me in response to my articles. It was pathetic again beyond words.

Had my discussion group with boys from the Kreuzgasse Schule who wanted to know more about Quakerism. They are a fine set of seeking young fellows.

Cologne Cathedral

Cologne Cathedral

Ruins of Cologne, taken from Cathedral Spire

Monday 16th. There is trouble brewing in the Falkland Islands. A Royal Navy cruiser has been sent to the area. Argentina is trying to enforce its claims to sovereignty. The Government wants the International Court to decide.

Thursday 19th. It got colder again, with snow storms.. Took *Herr Röseler* to Dusseldorf. Visited a wonderful old Schloss, once the abode of a Princess and now with many refugee landed Barons and Dukes reduced to very low means. These people had nobility and good breeding stamped indelibly on their personalities, and their poverty was pathetic.

Sunday 22nd. A glorious drive through Sieg country to Weidenau to visit Annemarie and the children for the last time. It was a very happy visit, and they gave me a lovely Furstenberg Porcelain bowl for a wedding present.

Tuesday 24th. *Peggy Duff*, secretary of Save Europe Now turned up for a couple of days. I always enjoy meeting her, as she always has interesting and authoritative information.

Sorted a large number of books for university and schools sent out from England.

Wednesday 25th. Took the books and a large number of parcels from Bristol University to Cologne University and had a meeting with the students to discuss this adoption and exchange scheme.

Thursday 26th. Broadcast again on the Schulfunk. Turned up late because the headlamp bulbs on my car had been stolen.

Friday 27th. Discussion group again. These groups bring out constantly the theme that Mil.Gov. is deliberately working against the Germans; that production is not allowed go ahead because we fear competition on the world market; that the bridges over the Rhine are so slow in being completed to hold up the Russian advance, which is feared; that war or/and communism is bound to come, and so on. One not only gets depressed by all this but very tired of it.

Ilse Abshagen came to pay me a visit.

Saturday 28th. Ilse, Gene and I went over Cologne Cathedral, damaged in the great Bomber Harris raid on my birthday, June 2nd 1942. It is much more damaged inside than appears from outside, and it will take many more years to repair. From the top of the tower, about 350 feet up, there is a most incredible view. One cannot get any idea of the awful destruction of Cologne until one sees it from this aerial view. It is simply staggering, and fascinating at the same time. The Cathedral itself is very beautiful. It was hard to know how to pay the tired old chaplain who showed us around. Cigarettes seemed out of place – money worthless. He needed a pair of shoes more than anything else. We also visited the wonderful Roman mosaic nearby, discovered when they were constructing the deep air-raid shelter. The whole experience was quite unforgettable and only showed up more clearly the awful tragedy and futility of war and its aftermath.

On one of the spires the star of Bethlehem remains. The most precious relics in the Cathedral are said to be the bones of the three Kings or Magi, bearing gifts for the Christ child who followed the star. The bones were said to have been discovered by Queen Helena, and are preserved in a shroud.

The last British troops left India today.

Sunday 29th. During the morning Ilse and I went to see a former school-friend of hers in Cologne. She had been married to a former SS officer. They had one child before he was killed in the war. She then applied for a job with the British and filled up her "fragebogen"[1] to the effect that her husband was in the SS. The British Control Commission officer who read her form tore it up and sent another telling her to omit any reference to her husband. The girl filled up her form as before, not wishing to hide anything. The C.C.G. official was so impressed he went to visit her to advise her, and then fell in love with her, and has been living with her since. The girl's father, who was a prominent German historian and propaganda writer for the Nazis apparently, seemed to get on with the man well, in spite of the relations with his daughter. Furthermore, I was also told that the C.C.G. Official had declared himself a Quaker, which was interesting. He did not mention it to me on seeing my uniform and in fact I did not take to the man who continually grumbled at everything about the C.C.G. policy in Germany and the fact that he was not allowed to be the boss of his job – something to do with the coal control board.

In the afternoon we motored out to the other side of Bonn, took the ferry across the Rhine to the "Siebengebirge" and climbed one of them – the "Drachenfelds", on the top of which there is a rather "kitschish" ruined castle with a glorious view overlooking the Rhine, and where groups of young Germans were singing romantic songs with a lute around the war memorials. However it was a glorious day, the view was very impressive, and on the way up through the woods we saw some wild deer. Ilse told me of her visits throughout the zone to her old school friends, most of whom were now married and had babies, and described the lives and new beginnings of these courageous young couples, making the best of things in tragic times, building not only something essential of a home life, but of a life of service in the community. It had given her great hope for the future of Germany.

Ilse, much to Roger's joy, was able to give him lessons on his accordion, which she plays well. He also played duets with her. She liked the atmosphere in our team here much more than in Berlin.

Most of this week was spent in going round collecting my things, doing last minute jobs, making arrangements for going home, seeing to travel papers – rushing off to Düsseldorf, visiting and saying farewell to my friends, families, and institutions, and coping with engine trouble in my car.

The situation in Palestine continues to deteriorate.

March 1948

Friday 5th. *Toni Althaus* came to see me from Münster about something urgent; from the tone of her letter it sounded as though she was desperate and about to take her life. I

[1] *Questionnaire*

spent much of the morning and afternoon waiting at both Deutz and the Hauptbahnhof meeting every train that came from that direction. It was hot and dusty. Saw some of the Black Market that goes on continuously in the shady places and around the baggage and waiting rooms of the station. Eventually gave it up.

Toni finally arrived at the house after a ghastly train journey, and dead beat. I could see her nerves were stretched to breaking point. After supper she poured out the whole story, which concerned her love for British Major B. with whom she had been in love and living with for the past two years, and who had always promised to divorce his wife, get Toni back to England and then to marry her. He had now been demobbed and she could get no sensible replies to her letters. She begged me to seek him out on my return to London and to get from him at least the truth or some explanation. This I promised to do, but it was sometime before I was able to carry it out. I followed the man all over London one day, chasing him from one address to the other and never being able quite to catch up with him.

But at least I learned that he was living with his wife again in hotels. I later learned from Toni that this was not his wife at all but another woman, and that he hadn't lived with his wife for many years. It seems that he was a complete rotter and scoundrel.

Anyway it caused Toni so much distress and excitement to let all this story out to someone for the first time that all this suppressed and bottled up neurotic energy thoroughly upset her and she was practically in a state of collapse. Her heart was almost giving out and I expected hysterics at any moment. Not realizing beforehand that she had made herself as ill as she had, I had made up a bed for her in my room to sleep with *Ruth Oechslin*, who was also our guest at that time, and I was to change to the little room or 'slot'. However I saw that it would be impossible for Toni in her state to sleep with Ruth, who is a loud and unsettling person herself, and so I put Toni by herself with a hot cup of tea and aspirins into the 'slot' for the night.

As Hannah was sleeping on the sofa in the quiet room, and Gene had 'flu in the only other big bedroom there was no bed left for me, but I slept soundly and comfortably on a mattress under the grand piano in the sitting room without anyone knowing.. But what a night!

The Governor of the Falkland Islands protests to the Argentine Navy for its presence at Deception Island.

Saturday 6th. Toni fortunately was feeling better by the morning, but I gave her breakfast in bed as she did not feel like facing anybody. I was not able to see very much of her because I had to give two talks in the morning to the Kreuzgasse schule, and then I took her to see *Klaus Blum* in his cellar. I finally packed up a large parcel of food for Toni and we saw her off at the station.

In the afternoon I talked on America to the VIth form English discussion group, and answered a great number of questions. This was the last time, and I managed to get away without too much speechifying. However the group presented me with a very handsome brass paper-knife with a Cologne coat of arms as a farewell present.

A delegation of boys from the Kreuzgasse school also presented me with some fine reproductions of German art as a token of their appreciation.

Sunday 7th. During the afternoon went over to Siegburg to have tea with Oberin-spector Peter Schmidt of the Juvenile Prison, and he took me out to an old disused gravel pit where they are setting up Nissen huts in preparation for a new Borstal. It is an ideal spot as there is plenty of farm work for them all around, and also a large lake for excellent bathing, and places for sport etc. Peter was tremendously keen about the whole thing, and is keen to make use of his experience in England, and is full of vision.

In London all political marches in the city were banned for three months to thwart a Mosleyite march on May 1st.

Tuesday 9th. Roger and I had decided to go down to Frankfurt, capital of 'Bizonia'. He had to get his passport and military entry permit renewed, and I wanted to see the A.F.S.C. Neighbourhood Centre there.

We got to the Hauptbahnhof to find that the train was already an hour late, then 2 hrs. Finally heard it had broken down and that a relief was being put on. We had expected to get down there for lunch, but instead we did not start until after 1 p.m.

This was one of the most glorious train journeys I have ever been. After Bonn we were following the Rhine all the way through the French Zone. The sun came out and shone on the beautifully neat and miraculously terraced famous vineyards clinging to the steep sides of the mountains. Every mile or so one would pass a gem of a ruined castle or Schloss standing on some peak, or other advantageous place. They were all fascinating, but the best was that famous one which stands like a great stone ship in the middle of the Rhine at a rather narrow part.

Roger and I stayed at a small Hotel on our arrival, and went out immediately to see some of his personal friends who were in the U.S. Mil.Gov., and then on to see something of the work of the A F.S.C. in their centre, similar in many ways to our work at Cologne and at the Neighbourhood centre in Berlin. There was that same friendly informality – an atmosphere into which one could fit immediately.

One chiefly remembers Frankfurt for its complete Americanisation – the police and traffic controls were along American lines, and everywhere were large and prosperous American cars, Coca-Cola trucks and adverts everywhere.

Also the palatial buildings occupied by the American military authorities for their offices (I.C.Farben?) and the sumptuous food and meals in their canteens. In contrast the Quaker group were living in real simplicity – mostly on C.A.R.E. packages etc., but were well equipped, for transport etc.

We had the same breathtaking scenery on the way back that compels one to stand in the corridors looking out of the windows all the time – this time the train returned on the other bank and gave us a glorious view of all the castles on the other side. I could not resist photographing each one.

At last we rumbled across the ruined bridge with as yet its single track onto the dismal Cologne station under the shadow of the Cathedral. Bunty picked us up from the youth centre.

The End of My Service

Sunday 14th to Tuesday 16th. The final few days of my service abroad were spent in winding up my own affairs and work, a final round of visits and farewells, and packing. A sad and miserable time this, and so no more entries appear in this diary. One never likes parting with trusted colleagues and firm friends made. Bunty had welded us into a happy and close family and team. But one felt that the work would be carried on and was being left in capable hands.

The farewell parties, little presentations and speeches, were personal and deeply moving, and words in a diary cannot express them. I had come to love Germany and Germans very deeply. One inevitably leaves part of oneself behind, but I took with me very much more than I could ever hope to give. Wonderful memories and happy experiences become a part of one's make up. They may become dim but they remain woven into the very fabric of one's soul. You cannot live with such people for eighteen months without becoming changed, enriched, and I hope ennobled.

I did not know when I should come back, if in fact I should ever come back, and so it was with a lump in my throat that I looked across the fields, already showing signs of spring and rebirth, as the little Volkswagen sped along the autobahn on my last journey to join the train. Then came the inevitable slow train journey, passport control, embarkation at the Hook of Holland and another channel crossing in comparative comfort.

I received the following note from Bunty Harman, the leader of F.R.S. 125 just before I left:-

'I'm heartbroken that you've gone and I can't take a touching farewell of you. I have to go and meet Herr Lading and I fear you will be gone before I get back.

It has been nice having you here with us. I feel somehow you are one of the oldest members even though you have been here a comparatively short time – I couldn't pay you a greater compliment!

I shall miss you, along with the others who are going, and shall always be glad that we have had you here.

As far as I am concerned it has been a very happy transfer from Berlin to Cologne!

Many thanks for what you have brought to the team and for all you have done to help us. I think perhaps I have appreciated this more than the others because I have known more about the difficulties and disappointments that preceded your arrival here.

With all good wishes,
Bunty"

As always one ended up in the peace and quiet and orderliness of Friends' House in London. As the Friends' Relief Service winds up, another relief worker hands in his equipment and uniform – things which also meant a lot to him. There were interviews, papers to sign, final leave allowances and rehabilitation grants to collect and, of course, testimonials.

In civilian clothes once more it was back to ordinary life again, home and a spot of Leave. One took up the threads again, not quite where one left off, and not ever quite the same person again. One kept up one's contacts, looked eagerly for news and reports from that part of the world, and gave talks and lectures.

I had to get used to rationing again. On March 27th, for example, the Government announced a cut in the cheese ration from two to one and a half ounces a week.

It was not as difficult to settle as I expected, and there followed for me a wonderful summer term at Ackworth – back to teaching – before taking up the Diploma in Child Psychology course at Birmingham University for which I had been accepted.

The Friends Relief Service was finally wound up and handed over to the Friends Service Council in May 1948. Some workers stayed on. *Doris Roper*, for example at the Neighbourhood Centre in Cologne.

On 31st March, in Germany, the Russians began to control Western military trains travelling to Berlin, and on April 1st the Cold War took a turn for the worse as the Russians began imposing rigid checks on all road and rail traffic between Berlin and the Western Zones. I could just imagine it all, and the fear that this could trigger off a full scale blockade in an effort to squeeze out the West or at least protest at the way Marshall Aid is affecting Soviet influence throughout the country. Britain said it would resist any attempts to stop its trains to Berlin, but today cars on the road to Berlin were all being delayed by Soviet checks.

Tension was heightened by a mid-air crash on the 5th between a BEA airliner and a Soviet fighter and 15 people lost their lives.

I had to take a driving test and get a driving licence. The Southalls kindly lent me a car. I felt guilty when it was announced by the Fuel Minister Hugh Gaitskell that motorists were to be rationed to 90 miles a month from June.

However, by the end of the month the weekly milk ration was put up by a pint to 3½ pints. This was a relief after all the tinned milk.

In schools, at the end of the spring term, a new General Certificate of Education was unveiled, to replace the School and Higher School Certificates that I was used to. Ah well!

In May a huge boom in babies was announced by the Registrar General. The birth rate last year was apparently 21% greater than the year before – attributed to the fact that many couples were "catching up" on the lost war years. At the age of 28 I felt I had some "catching up" to do and had already brought home from Germany and Belgium some small items towards our wedding day trousseau and bottom drawer.

I was amused to read in the press that on June 26th, shortly after my 28th Birthday, while I was at Ackworth School, that the Soviet Army Chief in Germany was arrested for speeding in the U.S. sector of Berlin. Was it a coincidence that immediately after this the Western Allies started a round-the-clock airlift to beat the Russian blockade of Berlin? 200 Dakota aircraft were landing daily at RAF Gatow in the British sector of the city to take in supplies to stop the population starving as the Russians put on the squeeze. There was enough food to last a month, and it was estimated that 2500 tons of food a day would have to be airlifted to meet the requirements of the Western sectors. The shuttle service between Hannover and Berlin is already so fast that an aircraft lands every 4 minutes, operated by Carter Patterson.

Bevin says that Britain will use all possible resources to keep the city alive, and George Marshall, the U.S. Secretary of State, says: "We are in Berlin to stay". The Russians have banned all movement of food from the Soviet Zone into Berlin and all surface transport is blocked. Are they blundering us into the 3rd World War? I was often asked.

At home the Government was taking draconian action to deal with the dock strike. Mr Atlee was broadcasting: "We must see that the people are fed". Last week the ration of meat was reduced to 6d worth of fresh meat and 6d worth of canned meat. The school cook is finding it tough going!

It was a glorious summer term for weather at Ackworth and I was able to keep fit while teaching swimming, P.E., cricket and tennis. The Bursar was having great difficulty in calculating my salary and pension payments. Though the Government did not recognise F.R.S. service years for compensation purposes, the governors were generous towards me and in filling up the numerous forms for the Ministry of Education and my Pension book record, which they recovered.

The school raised large amounts of money for charities and overseas aid. I was put in charge of this for the term.

There was much talk in the Staff rooms at Ackworth (for we were not yet fully co-educational) about the National Health Service. So we were all delighted when on July 5th the NHS – regarded as the most sweeping reform so far introduced by the Government – actually came into existence: (we had had mock elections during the term and this was a popular plank). And in addition a National Insurance scheme and other welfare systems for the unemployed and old people were introduced. The Health Service was offering us free medical treatment for everyone, with free prescriptions. Dental care was included, free glasses and even wigs, under prescription! This was indeed a personal triumph for Aneurin Bevan, the Health Minister, who had to face powerful opposition from the BMA, though Dr. Kenneth Southall, my future Father-in-Law, was all in favour, and during that summer term was giving Health Education and Sex Education sessions in the school.

Having been reprimanded by the Russians in Berlin for attempting to teach young Germans how to play cricket – classed by them as 'military activity' – I was naturally glad to get back to serious cricket again – especially as I was now in Yorkshire, the Australians were touring in England and the Test Matches were on. Once again England was being humiliated by Australia's domination under Bradman's captaincy.

On August 14th, after I had left Ackworth and was taking some welcome holiday with Daphne and the Southall family caravanning in Wales. I was following the final Test Match at the Oval on the radio. Donald Bradman was my school days hero, having given me a signed cricket bat (much too big for me) after I had scored a half-century at my Prep School, "The Downs".

After I left Leighton Park I was given a trial at Edgbaston for Warwickshire schoolboys and accepted, though I never played in a county match. Wyatt was another hero – the Captain of Warwickshire, and the county bowler Eric Hollies was playing for England.

The great surprise in this Test Match was that Bradman, coming in to bat in his last Test Match to a standing ovation, and as the press described it: "with England at his mercy, was bowled second ball for a duck by a crafty googly from Eric Hollies". A mere 4 runs would have given Bradman – the most prolific batsman the world has seen – a Test Match average of over 100 per innings. However he had the satisfaction of ending his career with yet another triumph over the old enemy, who collapsed to 52 all out to the fast bowling of Ray Lindwall.

By now the French Zone in Germany had been economically merged with the Anglo-U.S. Zone. In Moscow, British, U.S. and French envoys were having talks with Molotov to try and end the Berlin crisis. In Berlin itself Soviet troops opened fire on Germans demonstrating against Soviet occupation of the city. I was anxious for the safety of my friends and trying to keep up communication and sympathy with them, and encouraging those I knew who were preaching the gospel of non-violence and ecumenical work.

Twelve years and two abandoned Olympic Games after Hitler's 1936 propaganda spectacular in Berlin, the London Olympics was opened amid all the strictures of post-war austerity, despite the absence of three major sporting powers – Germany, of course, the Soviet Union and Japan. Once again, Emil Zatopek, the Czechoslovakian athlete I had watched in the Allied games in the old Berlin Stadium, won the 10,000 metres by almost a full lap, setting a new record, and came within a whisker of taking the 5,000 metres as well.

By September Donald Bradman had wound up his first class cricket career with centuries in his last 3 matches.

The Allies were flying 895 planes a day into Berlin in defiance of the 3 months old Russian Blockade, with food and fuel including coal.

In Karachi the first Governor General of Pakistan, Jinnah, died.

Another shock was provided by the death of Swedish Count Folke Bernadotte, the UN mediator, in a gun attack on his car by Jewish terrorists in Jerusalem. All British troops had been withdrawn last month.

It was also announced that contamination from the Bikini Atom bomb tests was far more difficult to eradicate than anyone had anticipated, according to a new book published by a scientist, David Bradman, who had taken part in the tests. It was the July test apparently, the 2nd underwater test in July '46, that had caused the most trouble.

I had now, more or less, settled back into civilian life, and with great eagerness took up my place at Birmingham University on the first postgraduate Diploma course run by Prof. Schonell, in Child Psychology at the Remedial Education Dept. It was tough going amongst other mature students getting down to academic studies again. But it was what I most wanted to do and it was a year that was to change my life. I was now amongst a most congenial group known as the "Dip Chips". But that too is another chapter.

Postscript

Janet Kreysa reports in 'The Friend' of 15th December 1995:

> *"Cologne Friends meet every Sunday in the Senior Citizens' Day Centre which was renamed 'Doris Roper Haus' on Dec. 2nd 1995 to commemorate the life and work of Doris Roper."*

Doris, originally from Wigton, Cumbria, came to war-devastated Cologne in 1945 with an international team of Friends to start relief work. They established a neighbourhood centre, providing shelter and occupation for children living in bunkers. Mothers were given the opportunity to form a 'helper group' (Nothelferinnen), making and repairing clothes for needy families: and one of Germany's first non-political, non-sectarian youth clubs in the premises in the evenings.

The Quäkernachbarschaftsheim (Neighbourhood Centre) eventually moved into more spacious premises and the city of Cologne became responsible for its operation, although Friends are still represented on the Board. As Cologne prospered, the work changed, the emphasis being on providing a place of welcome for all age groups and all nationalities in an area with many immigrants. This sense of welcome is now even more important in times of increasing poverty and unemployment. The original team of Friends left, but Doris Roper stayed on until she died in 1988. Her life was dedicated to the work of the Nachbarschaftsheim and to the well-being of Cologne Meeting (which has always met in the day-care centre). Doris kept in touch with me every year until she died, sending us news of the centre. She was so proud that one of our boys, Norbert Burger, rose to the position of Mayor of Cologne. I visited her at the new Centre twice in intervening years.

Tony Benn, in his Diaries, writes:

> "5th Nov 1957. The trouble about a personal diary is that it is entirely subjective. It is not a history, nor has it any value except such as it gets from the personal slant it shows on events. But of course these events are the framework on which the personal story is woven. Every now and again one has to step back a little and assess the changes that are taking place outside."[1]

In this journal I have tried to do both.

---

[1] The Benn Diaries, *selected and introduced by Ruth Winstone (Arrow Books, 1996).*

Appendix I
How a Group Trains for Service
by Betty Baker

Near Primrose Hill stands Woodstock the house where most of the workers in Friends' Relief Service train for relief work overseas.

It is Sunday evening – all our courses begin on a Sunday evening, and twenty unknown people are arriving; we cannot tell what we shall make of them or they of us. But they are hungry and weary, and soon we are seated at table, where tongues are loosened. We find that our neighbour has done all kinds of interesting things and the atmosphere grows warm and friendly.

After supper, dish washing, and rumours of floors to clean and endless potatoes to peel on the morrow, for the housework is shared by all. But novices need not fear; the confusion of the first few days soon emerges in harmony, both in the work and in the strains of song which float up the stairs.

Rising bell at 7, breakfast, a reading – anything from the Gospels to T. S. Eliot – and chores. Then follows a short period for quiet of mind and body.

Many come fresh to the way of Quaker worship, and some leave us still having found no satisfaction in our silent approach. Even so we can value the more the spiritual unity which can and does exist in such a heterogeneous group.

Next on the programme is the language hour; little groups of people disperse over the house to learn a foreign tongue. As they become more proficient, or perhaps more confident, daily intercourse takes on a somewhat international flavour, as odd phrases learned and remembered find their way into conversation.

Then tea – and that oft-despised standby of F.R.S. – peanut butter. A hasty clearing away of cups. Then for the morning lecture – perhaps on the history and significance of Quakerism, or the place of F.R.S. against the larger field of relief; perhaps on medical relief or child feeding; perhaps on the problems of displaced persons, or the general background of European history. All these lectures are given by people well informed on the subject concerned, and they are followed by a stimulating half-hour of questions and discussions. Physical training and a late afternoon lecture conclude the organized activities of the day. One or two evenings each week are kept for discussion and questions on Quakerism with older Friends, or visits from workers returning from the field, but the afternoons and most evenings are free for reading and study, or for relaxation – a very important factor in the life of a relief worker, or indeed of any integrated human being. So much for the daily programme. There are in addition the gathering together of "clobber" and the inoculations; the various practical exercises, for example the week at camp when we cook in field kitchens. But these activities are but the framework; the fabric, which we can only build piece by piece, consists in the learning to live and work together.

Most likely we shall never need to build field kitchens, a few may never have to cope with medical problems, and some may well have learned German assiduously, only to find themselves in Greece or Poland. But this is not to say that our time has been wasted, if we have learned to put up with the comparative discomfort of a bedroom shared with six or seven other people, some of whom may snore; or to do physical training, when- we would much rather sneak off into a corner and do a little serious reading; and, hardest of all, to recognise and accept our own limitations, which show up so very clearly in a community.

When we have come so far, we can the more easily enjoy life in its unity and entirety. Frivolousness and fun bubble on the surface, and a quietist Friend might wonder how far this is compatible with our serious purpose; yet, beneath, are the deep undercurrents of genuine search after the Spirit of Truth and the united effort to do what we believe to be God's will in the field upon which we are entering. We seek in Him the strength to achieve His work, and we say with Thomas Kelly, " We sing, yet not we, but the Eternal sings in us".

Glossary of Abbreviations

A.F.S.C.	American Friends Service Committee
A.P.O.	Army Post Office
B.A.0.R.	British Army of the Rhine
B.M.	Black Market
B.R.C.C	British Red Cross Commission
B.R.C.C.R.	British Red Cross Civilian Relief
C.A.R.E.	Cooperative for American Remittances to Europe
C.C.G.	Control Commission Germany (British)
C.D.U.	Christian Democrats
C.O.	Conscientious Objector
C.O.B.S.R.A.	Council of British Societies for Relief Abroad
C.R.A.L.O.G.	American – unknown
D.P.	Displaced Person, Foreign Workers Organisation
E.N.S.A.	Forces Entertainment Organisation
F.A.U.	Friends Ambulance Unit
F.A.J.H.	Free Working Party for Youth Help
F.D.G.B.	Free Germans in Great Britain
F.D.J.	Frei Deutsche Jugend (Free German Youth)
F.O.R.	Fellowship of Reconciliation
F.P.O.	Forces Post Office
F.R.S.	Friends Relief Service
F.S.C.	Friends Service Council
G.I.	American Soldier ('General Issue')
G.P.U.	Russian Secret Police
G.R.C.	Unknown
I.R.C.	International Red Cross
I.V.S.P.	International Voluntary Service for Peace
L.P.	Leighton Park School
M.M.	Monthly Meeting of Friends
N.A.A.F.I.	Navy, Army and Air Force Institution
O.G.P.U.	Russian Secret Police
N.K.V.D.	Russian Secret Police
O.M.G.U.S.	Office of Military Government of United States
O.S.	Old Scholar
P.E.	Physical Education
P.O.L.	Petrol, Oil and Lubricants
P.O.W.	Prisoner of War
P.S.C.	Pacifist Service Corps (U.S.)
P.T.	Physical Training
P.T.I.	Physical Training Instructor
P.W.X.	Prisoner of War Exchange

R.A.M.C.	Royal Army Medical Corps
R.I.	Royal Infirmary (Bristol Hospital)
R.T.O.	Railway Transport Officer
S.A.	Salvation Army
S.C.F.	Save the Children Fund
S.E.D.	United Party (Communist)
U.N.R.R.A.	United Nations Relief and Rehabilitation Administration
V.D.	Venereal Disease
V.E.	Victory in Europe
Y.M.C.A.	Young Men's Christian Association

Index